Secrecy and Esoteric Writing in Kabbalistic Literature

JEWISH CULTURE AND CONTEXTS

Published in association with the Herbert D. Katz Center
for Advanced Judaic Studies of the University of
Pennsylvania

Series Editors

Shaul Magid

Francesca Trivellato

Steven Weitzman

A complete list of books in the series is available
from the publisher.

SECRECY AND ESOTERIC WRITING IN KABBALISTIC LITERATURE

Jonathan V. Dauber

UNIVERSITY OF PENNSYLVANIA PRESS

PHILADELPHIA

Copyright © 2022 University of Pennsylvania Press

All rights reserved. Except for brief quotations used for purposes of review or scholarly citation, none of this book may be reproduced in any form by any means without written permission from the publisher.

Published by
University of Pennsylvania Press
Philadelphia, Pennsylvania 19104-4112
www.upenn.edu/pennpress

Printed in the United States of America on acid-free paper
10 9 8 7 6 5 4 3 2 1

A Cataloging-in-Publication record is available from the Library of Congress

Hardcover ISBN: 9781512822748
eBook ISBN: 9781512822762

*This book is dedicated to my parents,
Drs. Kenneth and Antoinette Dauber*

Contents

Acknowledgments — ix

Note on Translations of Biblical Verses — xi

Introduction. The Writing of Secrets — 1

Chapter 1. Secrets and Secretism — 9

Chapter 2. A Typology of Esoteric Writing in Kabbalistic Literature — 27

Chapter 3. Abraham ben David as an Esoteric Writer — 61

Chapter 4. Isaac the Blind's Literary Legacy — 105

Chapter 5. Ezra ben Solomon of Gerona as an Esoteric Writer — 134

Chapter 6. Esotericism and Divine Unity in Asher ben David — 173

Conclusion — 209

Appendix 1 — 215

Appendix 2 — 216

Appendix 3 — 217

Notes	219
Bibliography	263
Index	283

Acknowledgments

I developed the kernel of this book in a seminar titled "Secrecy in Jewish Thought," which I have taught several times at the Bernard Revel Graduate School of Yeshiva University. I am thankful to the many students who participated in this seminar, who, through their engaged participation in classroom discussions, helped me refine various points in this book. I am also thankful for my colleagues at Revel who have helped make Revel an ideal environment to write and to teach in. I am particularly grateful for the leadership and support of David Berger, who was dean of Revel during most of the writing of this book, and to Daniel Rynhold, who became the new dean of Revel as I was revising the manuscript, and successfully guided Revel through a year indelibly marked by the coronavirus pandemic.

I am also thankful for the thoughtful comments of various colleagues with whom I have discussed aspects of this book. I would particularly like to acknowledge the Kabbalah Working Group, organized by the Philip and Muriel Berman Center for Jewish Studies at Lehigh University and convened by my good friend Hartley Lachter, director of the center, which provided a great forum to discuss the ideas in this book. In addition to Hartley, this group included Ellen Haskell, Marla Segol, Eitan Fishbane, Clémence C. Boulouque, Glenn Dynner, Joel Hecker, Nitsa Kann, Nathaniel Berman, and Sharon Koren. The members of this group provided very helpful feedback on aspects of this book. I also would like to acknowledge Joel Hecker, Hartley Lachter, Avishai Bar-Asher, Tzahi Weiss, and Ariel Mayse, who read drafts of portions of this book and offered important suggestions.

In researching this book, I consulted numerous manuscripts. Most of these manuscripts are available online through Ktiv: The International Collection of Digitized Hebrew Manuscripts (https://web.nli.org.il/sites/nlis/en/manuscript). This collection, a project of the National Library of Israel, undertaken in partnership with the Friedberg Jewish Manuscript Society, is a tremendously valuable resource, without which I could not have completed this project. Similarly, I would like to acknowledge Otzar HaHochmah (https://www.otzar.org/otzaren/eodot.asp), a digital library of Jewish books, which includes an excellent collection of kabbalistic works, to which the Yeshiva University library subscribes. This resource allowed me to access works even when libraries were closed due to the pandemic.

Special thanks go to Professor Elliot Wolfson, who was crucial in my intellectual formation and whose imprint can be seen in all my scholarship.

I would like to express my gratitude to the Rakia family for graciously granting me permission to use "Signs," the beautiful painting by David Rakia, to adorn the cover of this book.

My parents, Drs. Kenneth and Antoinette Dauber, to whom this book is dedicated, took the time to carefully read the entire manuscript and provide numerous insightful comments. It is a true blessing to have parents who offer constant encouragement and were happy to discuss the broader implications of a topic that is literally arcane. I am forever grateful.

Finally, I offer my deep thanks to the love of my life—my wife, Sarah—and to my children, Joshua and Zachary, for their encouragement, support, and love.

Note on Translations of Biblical Verses

In translating biblical verses in this book, I consulted various standard translations, such as JPS (1917 and 1985 editions) and NRSV (1989). When necessary, however, my translations of biblical verses are in keeping with the idiosyncratic ways in which they are understood by the figures whom I treat in this work.

Chapter 6 is a revised version of Jonathan V. Dauber, "Esotericism and Divine Unity in R. Asher ben David," *Jewish Studies Quarterly* 21 (2014): 221–60.

Introduction

The Writing of Secrets

Writing always involves decisions about what to include and what to exclude, about where to elaborate and where to be brief, and about how to organize the material. In the case of kabbalistic writing, these decisions take on an added urgency, for according to Kabbalists' own understanding, many kabbalistic ideas are properly secret. The writing of kabbalistic works was always implicitly accompanied, therefore, by a series of questions: Should particular secrets be put into writing at all? If so, should an effort be made to control which audiences gain access to the newly composed texts? Should different types of texts be composed for elite audiences and for popular audiences? Is it possible to compose a single text that will be understood differently by elite and popular audiences?

The secrecy that lies at the heart of kabbalistic discourse is apparent to anyone who has examined kabbalistic literature and has been duly noted by scholars. Indeed, Elliot Wolfson has argued that "nothing is more important for understanding the mentality of the Kabbalist than the emphasis on esotericism" ("Beyond" 170) and has suggested that "Jewish esotericism" is a more apt designation for Kabbalah than the more common "Jewish mysticism" ("Occultation" 113; "Beyond" 168–70). Yet, despite the robust research on the philosophical and social implications of secrecy in Kabbalah that is found in the work of Wolfson,[1] Moshe Idel,[2] Moshe Halbertal (*Concealment*), and Hartley Lachter, to name a few scholars, scant attention has been paid to the relationship between secrecy and the craft of kabbalistic writing. Basic issues, such as the literary techniques that Kabbalists have employed to conceal their secrets, or what determined which ideas they chose to keep secret, have gone largely unstudied.

This marks a striking contrast to the abundant research on the relationship between secrecy and writing in both Jewish and general medieval and early modern philosophic literature, which has largely been carried out under the influence of Leo Strauss.[3] The seemingly strange state of affairs wherein the *literary* dimensions of secrecy in kabbalistic writing have been largely ignored despite the fact that Kabbalah is recognized as an avowedly secret discourse can perhaps be explained by this very recognition. After all, a commitment to study the means by which Kabbalists hid ideas in publicly available texts is predicated on the assumption that these texts also have an exoteric meaning distinct from their esoteric one. Yet, insofar as Kabbalah is viewed, in its entirety, as esoteric knowledge, there might seem to be little to gain by examining the secret dimensions of what is already secret.

In fact, Kabbalists carefully distinguish between ideas that are suitable for a public audience and those that must be reserved for an elite audience. Indeed, kabbalistic literature is replete with references to secret concepts that cannot be recorded, and numerous Kabbalists testify that they adopted strategies of esoteric writing to hide their ideas. These strategies, while intended to keep these ideas from the broad public, were intended, as well, to convey them to a more worthy audience.

It is this interplay between secrecy and communication that I wish to explore. But first, I will clear up some matters that might otherwise be distracting.

Leo Strauss

As intimated, Leo Strauss has played an outsize role in the study of esoteric writing in the Jewish philosophic tradition, primarily through his work on Maimonides.[4] I believe that Strauss's keen observations about the mechanics of esoteric writing in the works of Maimonides and others are useful in the study of kabbalistic esotericism, particularly because, as I will argue, Kabbalists borrowed some of their techniques from Maimonides. At the same time, this book is not a "Straussian" book, nor does paying heightened attention to esoteric writing in kabbalistic works—or even arguing that a Kabbalist's public position contradicts his esoteric one—make one a "Straussian," unless all that Straussianism means is respecting Strauss as a careful reader of old books.[5] This book is not a "Straussian" one in two senses. First, my contention that Strauss offers useful insights into how to decode esoteric texts does not entail the corollary claim that I accept his particular interpretation of this or that esoteric text. For example, I do not have to accept Strauss's particular interpretation of Maimonides (assuming that clarity is reached about what this interpretation is—a difficult proposition, given Strauss's own esoteric style) to believe that his essays offer important clues to deciphering Maimonides's thought. In any case, Strauss did not offer any interpretations of kabbalistic works, which were far from his philosophical agenda, that I would have to accept or reject. Yet his analysis, for instance, of Maimonides's use of the dispersion of knowledge and intentional contradictions—techniques of esoteric writing that I discuss throughout this book—is nevertheless useful in assessing Kabbalists' adoption of these methods of esoteric writing.

Second, while Strauss's rediscovery of esotericism was part of his broader philosophical project, I do not need to subscribe to this project to accept his basic proposition that esoteric writing is ubiquitous and demands careful attention. Thus, for example, Strauss, among other things, was concerned with showing that the existence of esoteric layers in various philosophic texts could serve as an antidote to historicism.[6] Yet I can reject Strauss's particular critique of historicism and its relationship to esoteric writing without discounting the significance of such writing. In fact, as I hope to demonstrate, close attention to esotericism provides us with a much richer sense of the history of Kabbalah than could otherwise be achieved. The words of Arthur Melzer, in his study of esoteric writing in the Western philosophic tradition, are apt here as well: "It should always be firmly kept in mind that whatever one's final view of the complex philosophical issues raised by Strauss, both the historical existence and the scholarly importance of esotericism are facts that stand squarely on their own" (111). Similarly, with or without Strauss, esoteric writing is a major component of kabbalistic literature.

Communicable Secrets

My fundamental concern in this book is with secrets that, while they are withheld from a wide audience, are nevertheless communicable. Accordingly, I will not address kabbalistic secrets that are intrinsically uncommunicable. Often, for example, Kabbalists refer to the essential secrecy of the highest of the ten sefirot, the ten aspects of God that are at the center of kabbalistic theology. As Azriel of Gerona, a thirteenth-century Kabbalist, to whom I will return later, says in reference to this sefirah: "One should not investigate (*laḥkor*) these matters beyond what the power of thought [allows]" (*Commentary* 166). Here, and in numerous similar passages, secrecy is an ontological reality, and the secret remains inaccessible even to the most accomplished Kabbalist.

Indeed, in a certain sense, all kabbalistic secrets have something uncommunicable about them, including those that concern the lower sefirot, which Kabbalists regard as more accessible to human reason. Even the lower sefirot, that is, are part of the infinite God and, as such, remain elusive. Wolfson has argued that in Kabbalah, it is precisely this elusiveness that underwrites the legitimacy of writing about what cannot otherwise be written, since something will inevitably be held back. As Wolfson puts it: "Utterance of the mystery in a linguistic garb, whether oral or written, is possible *because* of the inherent impossibility of its being uttered. It follows that even for the adept, who demonstrates unequivocally that he deserves to be the recipient of the esoteric tradition, there is something of the secret that remains hidden in the act of transmission" (*Open Secret* 33; emphasis added).

Wolfson's work highlights the paradox of the kabbalistic secret that reveals even while it conceals—and conceals even while it reveals.[7] This paradox, however, is not my interest here. No doubt kabbalistic secrets are never fully communicable, and understanding this point is crucial when assessing the phenomenon of secrecy in Kabbalah. Yet whatever may remain hidden, kabbalistic writings about secrets still have clear semantic content. They express ideas, however partial, about the nature of divinity, and Kabbalists who possess them believe that, as partial as they are, they still need to be concealed for various religious and social reasons. Moreover, they conceal these secrets in their works by employing a wide range of techniques of esoteric writing that can be deciphered by those who are worthy. As Wolfson explains, notwithstanding the paradoxical nature of kabbalistic secrecy, Kabbalists "also embraced the rhetoric of esotericism based on the presumption that secrets must be withheld from those not fit to receive them" (33). It is precisely this understudied aspect of kabbalistic secrecy that I explore in this book, as I seek to assess the relationship between the secrets that Kabbalists possessed and the actual practice of writing in kabbalistic literature.

As Idel has argued, there is a "need to distinguish carefully between what was understood as Kabbalah according to Kabbalistic masters, who revealed it only fragmentarily, and what contemporary scholars, who assumed that the discipline was disclosed in written documents, believed to be Kabbalah" (*Kabbalah: New Perspectives* 21–22). Indeed, Idel's point stands not only in the case of ideas that Kabbalists left entirely out of writing but also in the case of ideas that they hid in writing. Uncovering the secrets that Kabbalists concealed in their works will enrich our understanding of the development of kabbalistic thought and practice and help us rewrite the social and intellectual history of Kabbalah. The study of these hidden ideas may allow us to discover beliefs that we did not know Kabbalists held or to discover that ideas that we thought were innovated by later Kabbalists were already present in the works of early Kabbalists. In some situations, we may discover that the hidden ideas may actually conflict with the openly presented ones, such that a particular Kabbalist's true beliefs might be at odds with his stated ones. Moreover, such study will offer insight into why Kabbalists chose to conceal one set of ideas over another and will allow us to reflect on the intellectual or social factors that led a Kabbalist from one time and place to conceal an idea that a Kabbalist from another time and place stated openly.

Work in this vein has been done to good effect. Some studies have attempted to uncover hidden doctrines in kabbalistic and related material by examining the clues that Kabbalists left strewn across their literature.[8] These studies have broadened our understanding of the history of Kabbalah. Yet, since they have not, for the most part, reflected on the relationship between secrecy and the act of writing or on particular techniques of esoteric writing,[9] they do not serve as guides for how to recognize and decode esoteric writing. In the broad study of the techniques of esoteric writing that I offer here, I aim to provide tools that will propel the further study of esoteric ideas hidden between the lines of kabbalistic literature.

In Chapter 1, accordingly, I provide a theoretical framework in which kabbalistic esoteric writing can be studied by examining it in light of what has become a dominant scholarly approach to secrecy, which holds that the content of secrets is ancillary to their social function of establishing the superiority of those "in the know." I argue that kabbalistic secrecy does not always conform to this approach. Rather, the content of kabbalistic secrets often dictates their intended social function. Thus, for example, in what can be termed "defensive esotericism"—esotericism that is the result of fear that outsiders will attack kabbalistic views as heterodox—the doctrines themselves drive the need for concealment. Similarly, when Kabbalists engage in "protective esotericism," which is grounded in the concern that kabbalistic doctrines might prove harmful to the faith of those who are not prepared to understand them, it is apparent that the content of the secrets informs the desired social function. Moreover, kabbalistic esoteric writing is often not grounded in a desire to achieve superiority over others but in a benevolent, if still elitist, drive to spread the "truth" of kabbalistic teachings to as many worthy people as possible.

In Chapter 2, I catalog the various techniques of esoteric writing that Kabbalists employed to guard their secrets during the long course of kabbalistic literature, with the aim of helping scholars identify and decode the esoteric layers of kabbalistic texts. These include ciphers, dispersion of knowledge, intentional contradictions, Zoharic symbolic code, and allusive writing. I present numerous examples of these techniques in kabbalistic texts of different genres and from different periods, from the thirteenth century to the present. I also offer some broader methodological reflections on the study of techniques of esoteric writing in kabbalistic literature.

The first two chapters, then, are a wide examination of esoteric writing across the whole history of Kabbalah. They provide a framework for studying esoteric kabbalistic writing and show how pervasive esoteric writing is in the history of Kabbalah. Yet, by virtue of their broad sweep, these chapters do not provide the opportunity to model how this framework can be applied, in practice, to specific kabbalistic texts. Indeed, since esoteric writers often conceal their ideas by writing "between the lines"—that is, in hints and obscure phrases that are ostensibly marginal to the text at hand—their works demand detailed analysis of what might appear to be minutiae. A synthetic study of the type offered in the first two chapters is necessarily insufficient. Accordingly, in the final four chapters, I turn to consider the literary dimensions of secrecy at the dawn of kabbalistic literary history. In particular, I examine the works of key figures in the earliest history of Kabbalah as a written tradition: Abraham ben David (Rabad) (c. 1125–98), Isaac the Blind (c. 1165–1235), Ezra ben Solomon of Gerona (first half of the thirteenth century), and Asher ben David (thirteenth century). I also provide a briefer analysis of Azriel of Gerona (first half of the thirteenth century). These figures are linked by relationships of familiality, discipleship, or both. Thus Abraham was the father of Isaac. Isaac, in turn, was the teacher of Ezra and the uncle and teacher of Asher. Azriel, while perhaps not the direct disciple of Isaac, may have been Ezra's brother-in-law.[10]

I choose to focus on these figures because while Kabbalists were confronted with the question of whether and how to record secret ideas throughout the history of Kabbalah, the matter was particularly acute at the beginning of Kabbalah's literary history. The first Kabbalists were presented with the task of creating a new literature based on secret ideas. They had to make decisions about what shape this literature would take. Which ideas should they include in writing, and which should they exclude? Should they present the ideas that they chose to include openly, or should they adopt esoteric styles of writing? By examining these figures, I show that esotericism was crucial in determining the particular literary form that kabbalistic writing took at its inception.

At the same time, it should be noted that, for the same reasons, other early Kabbalists, such as Jacob ben Sheshet and Nahmanides, could also have been chosen. By focusing on the figures that I do, I in no way mean to indicate that an examination of the works of other inaugurators of kabbalistic literature would not contribute to our understanding of the relationship between secrecy and writing at the beginning of Kabbalah. While the constraints of space prevent a full treatment of their works, I do refer to them and others when they are helpful in clarifying various aspects of early kabbalistic esotericism.

My examination of these particular works demonstrates that painstaking analysis of the esoteric layers of kabbalistic texts can expand our understanding of the intellectual history of Kabbalah. Hiding and revealing often go hand in hand, and the movement from one to the other is not necessarily linear. For example, though it has been typically assumed that Rabad transmitted his kabbalistic teachings orally, I show that, in fact, he also concealed them within his non-kabbalistic Talmudic and legal writings. Rabad's writings, therefore, represent an unrecognized stage in kabbalistic literary history. While it has generally been assumed that formerly oral kabbalistic ideas were first presented in publicly available texts at the beginning of the thirteenth century, my analysis shows that Kabbalah already had a literary manifestation in the second half of the twelfth century—albeit a very hidden one—in Rabad's widely available works. On the other hand, I also demonstrate that the literary legacy of Rabad's son, Isaac the Blind, a key figure in the development of Kabbalah, is far more meager than has generally been assumed, and much of what has been attributed to him turns out to be the work of later authors. The only works that he did compose are short and highly cryptic and were designed to be incomprehensible to an audience that lacked kabbalistic background. I further argue that the common scholarly presentation of Ezra and Asher as among the first popularizers of Kabbalah needs to be amended. In fact, both these figures employed esoteric styles of writing to conceal their ideas.

The study of the esoteric layers of early kabbalistic literature also provides fresh insights into the social history of Kabbalah at a time for which we lack robust documentary evidence. For example, the fact that the first kabbalistic authors used techniques of esoteric writing suggests that they assumed that there was an audience that could decipher them. Along with other clues, this points to a greater dispersion of esoteric ideas at the earliest period of kabbalistic literature than has generally been assumed. Additionally, the nature of the secrets that the early kabbalists concealed offers insight into the social pressures that they might have felt. As I argue, one closely guarded secret is an idea that would become well known in the subsequent history of Kabbalah: the notion that divine unity is constituted by the sexual union of sefirot. These early Kabbalists, I contend, felt compelled to conceal this idea because of three social factors: (1) internal Jewish pressure to understand divine unity in terms of simplicity (i.e., absence of composition); (2) their wariness that the kabbalistic doctrine of divine unity might undercut Jewish attempts to refute the Trinity; and (3) their fear that this kabbalistic view might appear too close to the views of Cathar heretics.

These and other findings demonstrate the manner in which attentiveness to techniques of esoteric writing can provide new insights into the history and development of Kabbalah. This book, then, is premised on the assumption that to fully appreciate the emergence of Kabbalah as a literary tradition and its subsequent flourishing, it is necessary to attend to the nexus between Kabbalists' commitment to secrecy and the decisions that they made as they constructed kabbalistic literature. As will be seen, these Kabbalists made different—and, at times, opposing—decisions. On the whole, however, their decisions were based on the assumption that kabbalistic secrets could be recorded only with great care.

Chapter 1

Secrets and Secretism

It has by now become a refrain in numerous scholarly analyses that secrecy should primarily be studied as a type of social interaction. The content of the secret, the argument goes, is ancillary to the social function of the very claim of secrecy. This conception builds on the seminal early twentieth-century work of the sociologist Georg Simmel, who was more interested in the social dimensions of secrecy than in the ideational content of secrets. In a highly influential 1906 essay, Simmel argued that the importance of secrets lies chiefly in the sense of exclusivity that the knowledge of secrets brings: "The substantial significance of the facts concealed often enough falls into a significance entirely subordinate to the fact that others are excluded from knowing them" ("Sociology of Secrecy" 464).[1] Developing this insight, scholars have argued that secrecy is best examined as a tool that can be employed to establish group identity and prestige. In this analysis, what is important about secrets is that they are what my group possesses and your group lacks. The content of the secret is of little significance in this dynamic.

Hugh Urban has been especially influential in developing this model of secrecy in numerous studies. As he puts it: "I would suggest that we make a shift from the 'secret' as simply a hidden content and instead investigate the strategies or 'games of truth' through which the complex 'effect' (to use Bruce Lincoln's phrase) of secrecy is constructed. That is, how is a given body of information endowed with the mystery, awe, and value of a 'secret'? Under what circumstances, in what contexts, and through what relations of power is it exchanged? How does possession of that secret information affect the status of the 'one who knows'?" (*Economics* 20).

Borrowing Pierre Bourdieu's notion of "symbolic capital," Urban suggests that secrecy "is a discursive strategy that transforms a given piece of knowledge into a scarce and precious resource, a valuable commodity, the possession of which in turn bestows status, prestige, or symbolic capital on its owner" ("Torment" 210). It is, thus, the very claim that a particular piece of knowledge is secret, rather than the contents of the secret, that is decisive. Accordingly, the contents of the secret itself, while "not, of course, entirely arbitrary or meaningless" ("Adornment" 17), have little bearing on the analysis: "What is important about secrets is not primarily the occult knowledge they profess to contain, but rather, the ways in which secrets are exchanged, the mechanisms of power through which they are conferred, and above all, the kind of status and 'symbolic capital,' which the possession of secret information bestows upon the individual" (17).

Paul Johnson, whose work has also been influential, coined the term "secretism": "Secretism I define as not merely reputation, but the active milling, polishing, and promotion of the reputation of secrets. Secretism is freely and generously shared. Secretism does not diminish a sign's prestige by revealing it, but rather increases it through the promiscuous circulation of its reputation; it is the long shadow that hints of a great massif behind. It is through secretism, the circulation of a secret's inaccessibility, the words and actions that throw that absence into relief, that a secret's power grows, quite independently of whether or not it exists" (3).[2]

"Secretism" describes the mechanism of promoting a secret's value as a commodity. It is the act of advertising the secret to make it seem increasingly valuable. The secret is dangled before the public but never fully revealed. The value of the secret derives from its public absence, not from its content. Indeed, for secretism to be effective, whether the secret has any value or whether there is any secret at all is beside the point.

Urban has employed this model of secrecy, which, for convenience's sake, I will refer to as Urban's model, in studying colonial Bengal and, more recently, new religious movements. Johnson, for his part, has applied it to the Brazilian Candomblé. This model has also influenced scholars working in fields as disparate as ancient Mesopotamia (Lenzi), China during the early imperial era (Campany), Jews in the early Roman Empire (Andrade), and early modern Europe (McCall and Roberts 2–4; Jütte 10–11), to name just a few examples.

Secretism in Kabbalistic Literature

Numerous kabbalistic texts provide good examples of secretism, even in cases where there are no actual secrets. Harley Lachter has shown that this type of secretism was rife in late thirteenth- and early fourteenth-century kabbalistic texts: "The admonitions scattered throughout these texts to conceal such secrets serve more as a mechanism to mark the value of the kabbalistic conception of Judaism rather than as a reflection of a practice of restricting access to kabbalistic ideas" (28). As Lachter explains, the rhetoric of secrecy is used not to conceal actual information but to create a sense of empowerment in the face of both an aggressive Christian majority culture and the inroads of rationalist philosophy in Jewish culture.

Rather than rehearsing the compelling examples that Lachter provides, I will offer an example from a somewhat later period, which can profitably be compared to a particular case of secretism described by Urban. One trick of secretism is to create a sense of an alluring secret, while always deferring its revelation, so that the novice is continuously drawn in by the hope of what is still to come but what never arrives because it does not really exist. As Urban argues, this approach is clear in *The Secret Doctrine*, by Helena Petrovna Blavatsky, who founded the Theosophical Society in New York in 1875.[3] In the opening of the book, Blavatsky proclaims that her work "though giving out many fundamental tenets *from the* SECRET DOCTRINE *of the East*, raises but a small corner of the dark veil. For no one, not even the greatest living adept, would be permitted to, or could—even if he would—give out promiscuously, to a mocking, unbelieving world, that which has been so effectually concealed from it for long aeons and ages" (xvii, emphasis in original). This proclamation, however, is followed by a voluminous and detailed work, which does not hold back. As Urban suggests, we have here "the quintessential example of 'secretism'" ("Secrecy and New" 70). There is a rhetoric of secrecy with no secrets.

Blavatsky's proclamation may be compared to a statement of Ḥayyim Vital, the sixteenth-century Safedian Kabbalist and disciple of Isaac Luria who had a decisive influence on the subsequent history of Kabbalah through his extensive recordings of Luria's teachings. The statement appears in the introduction to *'Ets Ḥayyim*, the work that came to be regarded as the canonical articulation of Luria's thought: "If my intention was to write all that I received from my teacher (Luria), of blessed memory for life in the world to come, the leather of all of the rams of Nebaioth would not suffice, as is known by some, and by those who listen to me in my circle. Rather, my desire is to record in this book some of the most necessary premises that I have been given permission to record and still then with great brevity, like 'peering through the cracks'" (*'Ets Ḥayyim* 22).

The idea that no amount of parchment could possibly encompass all the teachings that Vital heard from his teacher is a prime example of secretism rather than an actual attempt to conceal secrets. Despite the genuine restrictions that Vital put on the dissemination of his work, which I will discuss in Chapter 2, Vital was an extremely prolific writer who left a large corpus of writings. It is quite possible that out of real concerns of esotericism, he left limited teachings out of his writing. The implication, however, that he omitted large swaths of Luria's teachings is analogous to Blavatsky's claim that she will reveal only a fraction of her actual wisdom. Moreover, anyone who is familiar with *'Ets Ḥayyim*—a highly detailed work—realizes that the idea that Vital composed it with "great brevity" borrows rhetorically from a trope of esoteric writing without actually being an example of it. This is a trope, which, in Chapter 2, I will term "allusive writing," which involves writing in a clipped and cryptic fashion that only alludes to ideas without fully describing them.

It is also useful to compare certain kabbalistic texts to the "books of secrets" that were widely printed in sixteenth-century Europe and consisted of "secret" recipes for crafts or medicines. These books were widely distributed and secret in name only. As William Eamon, in his exhaustive study of these works, demonstrates, there is nothing arcane or mysterious about these books (4). Commenting on Eamon's conclusion, the historian of science Koen Vermeir remarks: "To understand such phenomena, it is important not to be misled by the actors' categories and not to take the rhetoric of secrecy at face value. There is nothing paradoxical, per se, in the dissemination of secrecy or the values of secrecy, and many of the secrets transmitted in the books of secrets were 'open secrets' that were already widely known and applied" (180).

In kabbalistic literature, we find parallels in the hundreds, if not thousands, of texts or subsections of texts, many of which are still in manuscript, with titles like the "secret of sacrifice" or the "secret of the Sabbath." For the most part such texts make no effort to conceal the secret meaning of sacrifice or the Sabbath. On the contrary, they typically reveal the secrets quite openly. These texts, that is, adopt a rhetoric of secrecy without actually concealing any information.

On a more micro level, individual kabbalistic texts use the term "secret" (*sod*) ubiquitously to indicate that an object or biblical verse symbolically represents one of the ten manifestations of God known in kabbalistic literature as sefirot. For example, in *Sha'arei orah*, Joseph Gikatilla, the thirteenth-century Castilian Kabbalist, refers to the fact that the "sea" symbolically represents the tenth sefirah: "This is the secret (*sod*) of 'All the rivers flow into the sea' (Eccles. 1:7)" (61). Similarly, another thirteenth-century Castilian Kabbalist, Moses de León, writes: "Know that Rachel is the secret (*sod*) of the *shekhinah* (divine presence), the *shekhinah* is the dimension of west, and Reuven is the secret (*sod*) of the dimension of south" (Tishby, *Studies* 40). In other words, the matriarch Rachel symbolically refers to the tenth sefirah, known as the *shekhinah*. Her nephew Reuven refers to the "dimension of south," that is, the fourth sefirah, *ḥesed*. In these instances, and in countless others, the word "secret" serves as a hermeneutical key to alert the reader to decode the word that follows "secret" as a reference to a sefirah.

On the one hand, it might be argued that in such examples, the term "secret" has no connection to a "secret" defined as intentionally concealed information. Rather, it functions as a kind of technical term to signify that it is not the ordinary meaning of the object or verse that is intended but one based on its deeper meaning. If so, this use of the word "secret" is not relevant for our purposes. On the other hand, I do not think that such semantic hairsplitting is relevant to the experience of most readers. As Kabbalists were surely aware, it is hard for a reader to ignore one of the standard meanings of "secret" when he comes across the word in a kabbalistic text. Whatever its primary meaning in a particular text, the reader who encounters this word is likely to come away with the sense that the text deals with hidden information. This would certainly be the case for a non-Kabbalist reader, but I would venture to say that even a kabbalistically knowledgeable reader, who understands the primary meaning of "secret" in this context, cannot entirely escape the full semantic range of the term. In other words, these examples function as cases of secretism, wherein the reader is drawn in by an atmosphere of mysteriousness when, in fact, nothing is concealed.

In all, then, a "rhetoric of secrecy," even when there are no real secrets, is quite prevalent in kabbalistic literature. I would argue, however, that this prevalence should not obscure the fact that many kabbalistic texts do conceal real secrets. And these real secrets are put into sharp relief when seen in the context of the ubiquity of the rhetoric of secrecy.

Content Drives Social Function

Even when dealing with real secrets, it is surely correct that not only the contents of secrets but also the social effect of their exchange should be studied. Yet it seems that, in many cases, these two aspects of secrecy are intertwined, that the "rhetoric of secrecy" is not merely "rhetoric," and that, in fact, the content regulates the social impact. In contrast, as we have seen, scholars following Urban's model of secrecy have often presented the two as separable and have advocated for a focus on the latter rather than on the former. In the words of scholar of religious studies Kocku von Stuckrad, "As scholars we have to focus less on the content of secret knowledge but on the very fact that this knowledge is claimed" (*Locations* 56).[4]

The analysis of these scholars strikes me as accurate in situations in which the motivation for keeping secrets is to burnish one's reputation. It seems less applicable, however, when secrecy is resorted to for different reasons. Among others, which I will discuss shortly, let us consider self-defense. Heterodox ideas or practices often need to be kept secret from those in authority who might feel challenged by them. This is a type of secrecy that Strauss famously described in *Persecution and the Art of Writing* and that Arthur Melzer, in his masterful work on secret writing in the Western philosophic tradition, terms "defensive esotericism" (127–59; cf. Schwartz, *Contradiction* 15). Urban, too, describes a similar type of secrecy when he notes that "secrecy is by no means always a matter of advertisement, adornment, or displaying one's possession of secret knowledge. On the contrary, it is just as often a matter of camouflage, of concealing one's knowledge and practices from those who might threaten and/or be threatened by them. Secrecy is in fact a key strategy of social and political resistance to, dissent from, and critique of the dominant social and political order" ("Secrecy and New" 73).[5] I would argue that in this type of "defensive esotericism," the content of the secret and its social function are deeply intertwined insofar as it is the particular content of the secret that triggers the need for secrecy.

Kabbalists, at times, engage in "defensive esotericism" when they conceal ideas that are heterodox or that at least might be perceived as such by outsiders. If these ideas were made public, Kabbalists might be subject to persecution. For example, as I will discuss in Chapter 2, Moses de León chooses to conceal certain matters because "his ideas would seem strange in the eyes and ears of other people when they would hear them." He goes on to say that he must keep his secrets so "that those who have toiled in [studying] them all their days will not become a target of an arrow" (141). Similarly, as I will explain at length in Chapters 3 and 6, Abraham ben David and Asher ben David were worried, with good reason, that should the idea that divine unity is contingent on the sexual union of male and female sefirot become public, Kabbalists would be regarded as heretics. I note parenthetically that this is not because these Kabbalists viewed themselves as heretics but because they were worried that this idea would be misunderstood by an uninitiated public.

In these examples, the content of the secret drives the social function of secrecy to keep Kabbalists safe from outsiders. Moreover, without understanding the content of the secret, one would not realize that the particular way in which these Kabbalists present themselves to non-Kabbalists is the direct result of the secret's content. For instance, in the case of Asher, as I will argue, his desire to hide a concept that might be viewed as scandalous led him to present kabbalistic views on divine unity in a duplicitous manner. His public presentation of Kabbalah, then, is conditioned by the content of the secret that he wished to conceal.

The same is true of what Melzer terms "protective esotericism," which he distinguishes from "defensive esotericism" (127–203; cf. Schwartz, *Contradiction* 15). "Protective esotericism" is grounded in the notion that certain esoteric ideas, should they become public, would undermine important social values. Along these lines, some Kabbalists worried that if their ideas were spread too widely, they would be misunderstood and undermine the faith of the uninitiated. Again, it is apparent that in secrecy of this kind, an analysis that ignores the content of the secret would have little ability to grasp its social function. I will discuss "protective esotericism" more fully and present examples in the next section.

In addition to the sociological grounds for focusing on the effects of secrecy rather than on the contents of secrets, Urban also offers pragmatic ones. He argues that this focus is a way of escaping from what he terms a "double bind." As he describes it, the double bind refers to the following predicament: on the one hand, if a religious tradition actively dissimulates, how can the scholar, who is an outsider, ever hope to gain accurate knowledge of the tradition's secrets? On the other hand, if scholars succeed in becoming initiated into the secrets, are they not ethically bound to keep them secret? (*Economics* 15). As he puts it in a recent study on scientology, "This does not mean that the content is nonexistent or unimportant, but rather that it is in many cases unknowable and/or ethically problematic" ("Third Wall" 22). Concentrating on the social ramifications of secrecy rather than on the content of the secrets, he argues, prevents him from becoming entangled in this double bind.

The ethical side of the double bind does not seem relevant to the study of kabbalistic texts. In most instances, the authors of the texts studied by scholars of Kabbalah are long dead, so that exposing the secrets of their texts does not affect them. Moreover, the secrets concealed by one group of Kabbalists are often revealed by a later group, so that the scholar is not revealing new information but merely revising the historical record to show that later ideas were already present earlier.

For some of the same reasons, what might be termed the epistemological side of the double bind, the difficulty of knowing what the group that holds a secret really believes, also does not apply to the study of kabbalistic texts. This is clear if we attend to Urban's own qualification of this side of the double bind in the conclusion of his study. There he notes instances in which the content of the secret is knowable and relevant: "Lastly, I want to acknowledge the limitations of the approach I have outlined here, with its focus on form and strategy rather than content in the study of secrecy. After all, one might legitimately ask: Are there not cases where the content of the secret really is important and really is knowable?" ("Third Wall" 30). His answer is that there indeed are such cases, as in the example of uncovering the Church of Scientology's acts of espionage against the U.S. government (30). He thus concludes: "Yes, there are indeed forms of religious secrecy that require a different methodological approach, and there are many cases where a focus on hidden content would be more directly relevant" (30).

So, too, many kabbalistic works are examples of cases in which the content of the secret, as Urban puts it, "really is knowable" and "directly relevant." Studying the written tradition of Kabbalah (or, for that matter, other esoteric written traditions) is different from engaging in fieldwork with living informants, as Urban did with the Bengali Kartabhaja sect. Live informants, after all, can constantly amend their narrative as the situation warrants, so that it may be difficult to know what their beliefs really are. Kabbalistic texts, by contrast, are fixed and susceptible to scholarly methodologies, such as comparing different works of the same Kabbalist, since he may write more openly in some works than in others, or, for the same reason, different works of members of the same circle. Indeed, from our vantage point in the twenty-first century, where we have easy access to a far greater wealth of kabbalistic texts, including manuscripts, often in digital formats, than in any previous period, we are uniquely positioned to uncover the secrets contained in kabbalistic texts with a reasonable degree of confidence.

Protective Esotericism

Those investigating secrecy according to Urban's model have tended to present it as fundamentally adversarial in that it is a way of burnishing the prestige of a subordinate group over and against groups of higher status or as a way of establishing the superiority of a group over groups of lower stature. As the editors of a collection of essays titled *Visual Cultures of Secrecy in Early Modern Europe* put it: "In place of seeking knowledge of secrets, the authors of these essays begin by examining to whose benefit (and just as importantly to whose detriment) secrets function. We consider asking 'cui malo?' to be as productive as inquiring 'cui bono?'" (McCall and Roberts 8). "Protective esotericism," however, a particular type of secrecy manifest in some kabbalistic works, as well as in other types of literature, has less of an adversarial function.

"Protective esotericism," as mentioned, is grounded in the notion that certain esoteric ideas, should they become public, would undermine important social values. For example, exoterically speaking, Maimonides describes a moral order grounded in revelation, according to which God rewards the righteous and punishes the wicked. Strauss argued, however, that Maimonides hints "between the lines" of his work that he does not believe in such an order. Rather, operating in a tradition of Platonic political thought, as mediated by al-Farabi, Maimonides was forced to engage in a noble lie to preserve a society that required a belief in such an order to function.[6] "Protective esotericism" of the type that Strauss describes may be characterized as a kind of benevolent elitism. It is grounded in the theory that the vast majority of members of a given society need to adhere to false beliefs for that society to function. Those in possession of the truth must, therefore, exercise extreme care to keep it in the hands of the few.

The type of "protective esotericism" that is common in Kabbalah is of a somewhat different order. In Strauss's analysis, philosophers are led to engage in "protective esotericism" for fear that their ideas will fundamentally subvert standard orthodox views, which are necessary for the maintenance of society. In the case of Kabbalists, the matter is more complex. At the risk of an overgeneralization, Kabbalists tend not to believe that their ideas are at odds with core orthodox views. Rather, they worry that should their ideas be made public, they would be likely to be misunderstood as such. I already noted Asher's concern, shared by numerous other Kabbalists, that kabbalistic views regarding gendered and anthropomorphized multiple sefirot will lead to accusations that Kabbalists are heretics. This is an example of "defensive esotericism." Yet Kabbalists—particularly in situations where they wielded significant religious authority—also worry that these same views will lead the noninitiated to believe the heretical ideas that God actually has a body or is really composed of multiple deities when, in fact, these views should not be taken literally but must be understood in various figurative ways. Heresy was viewed as a serious transgression that would lead to divine punishment and would undermine the Torah and God's honor. Keeping such ideas out of the public's hands was, therefore, seen as a way to protect individual Jews, the Torah, and, ultimately, God.

I will limit myself to two examples.[7] In the first example, the mid-thirteenth-century Castilian Kabbalist Todros Abulafia presents "protective esotericism" as the primary motivation to conceal kabbalistic secrets: "This wisdom [Kabbalah] requires the fear of the Lord for it deals with supernal matters that are as exalted as the heart of the heaven, as deep as the great depth and distant from human ratiocination. And should a person come to consider them with his human ratiocination, which is too limited to comprehend and apprehend divine wisdom, he will be led to error and will go astray like Elisha, that is Aḥer. . . . And this is the real reason that those who have understanding conceal this wisdom, so that no mishap will result from it" (*Otsar* 19). As will be seen in Chapter 2, Abulafia himself employed esoteric writing throughout his works. Here he explains that one who rationally speculates about kabbalistic matters is bound to make theological errors and ultimately be led astray—that is, be led towards heresy—much like the arch-heretic of rabbinic literature Elisha ben Abuya, known as Aḥer ("Other"). The Talmud uses the expression "cutting the saplings" to refer to Elisha's heresy (B. Ḥagigah 14b), and, for Abulafia[8] and other kabbalists, it came to mean heretically misunderstanding the nature of the unity of the sefirot. It is likely that in invoking Elisha here, Abulafia intends to allude to such a misunderstanding. In Abulafia's view, it is precisely the desire to prevent such a misunderstanding that leads Kabbalists to conceal their ideas.

Centuries later, the nineteenth-century Kabbalist and halakhic scholar Yosef Ḥayyim of Baghdad, known as Ben Ish Ḥai, shares Abulafia's concern.

In a responsum where he attempts to dissuade an unnamed figure, whom he regards as insufficiently knowledgeable in kabbalistic thought, from teaching Vital's *'Ets Ḥayyim* to others, he writes:

> Even though our teacher, of blessed memory for the world to come [Ḥayyim Vital] spoke his words [in *'Ets Ḥayyim*] in a clear manner, you should, nevertheless, think regarding them that our knowledge about all of these matters, which are closed and sealed with one hundred fetters, is insufficient. For he [Ḥayyim Vital] explicated what is possible to explicate in order to explain the matter to one who listens, but, in truth, he revealed a handbreadth and concealed ten handbreadths regarding each and every matter. Therefore, a simpleton who does not know his worth and is wise in his own eyes and, as a result, opens concealed matters and explicates them based on his own intellect, might come to cut the saplings such that the truly wise one, who sees his words, rends his garment because of them. (3:2b, *Sod yesharim* sec.)[9]

It will be recalled that, in his introduction to *Ets Ḥayyim*, Vital indicates that "if my intention was to write all that I received from my teacher [Luria], of blessed memory for eternal life, the leather of all of the rams of Nebaioth would not suffice, as is known by some, and by those who listen to me in my circle." Above, I characterized these remarks as an example of "secretism," since *'Ets Ḥayyim* is verbose and does not apparently hold back. Yosef Ḥayyim echoes these remarks when he claims that Vital in *'Ets Ḥayyim* "revealed a handbreadth and concealed ten handbreadths regarding each and every matter." Yet he does not marshal this sentiment for "secretism" but to support the need for "protective esotericism." Thus he argues that the fact that Vital allegedly speaks with such brevity means that the work is likely to be misunderstood by the uninitiated. If Vital's work is taught too widely, it will lead to "cutting the saplings," an expression that, as seen, refers to heretically misunderstanding the nature of divine unity. Truly knowledgeable Kabbalists will, as he puts it, rend their garments when they see Kabbalah being misunderstood, not because they are worried about their own honor but because they are worried about the harm to the individual and to the Torah itself. As he explains it in the continuation: "If a person comes to add a reason or explicate something concealed or answer a question [regarding kabbalistic matters] that he is concerned with, he might stray from the truth, and he will be led to cut the saplings and to heresy, and he destroys the foundation of the Torah, God forbid.... It is likely that he will think something that will be imputed to him as the sin of heresy" (2a).

This type of protective esotericism, of course, is elitist and reflects Kabbalists' self-perception as superior to non-Kabbalists, but it is not designed to strengthen this perception but to protect those less fortunate than they. That is, it is not based on an adversarial relationship with non-Kabbalists but on a caring, if paternalistic, one. Here the comments of Edward A. Tiryakian, in his study of the sociology of what he refers to as "esoteric culture," are apt: "Since these secrets are those that reveal the ultimate nature of reality, the concealed forces of the cosmic order, it means that esoteric knowledge is an ultimate source of power, which must be shared and utilized by a relatively small group of initiates. Such power is never justifiable in terms of the enhancement of the material conditions of the esoteric knowers but rather in terms of broad impersonal ends, humanitarian ideals, etc." (501). While I would not apply these comments too broadly,[10] they seem apt in the case of protective esotericism and present a different model of secrecy from the one that has become prevalent in the works of Urban and others.

Esoteric Writing

The preceding accounts of the manner in which certain instances of kabbalistic esotericism do not conform to Urban's model of secrecy are true even when Kabbalists do not engage in strategies of esoteric writing but merely keep secrets out of public circulation. Yet there is a particular manner in which kabbalistic and other forms of esoteric writing break from this model that does not apply to other practices of secrecy, such as sticking to oral transmission or limiting the circulation of manuscripts. In the remainder of this chapter, I will describe the alternate model of secrecy entailed in esoteric writing.

To recapitulate, in Urban's model, one who possesses a secret gains a certain elite status in the eyes of others who know that he possesses it but who do not possess it themselves. If he chooses to reveal his secret to these others, they now become part of his group and become beneficiaries of the status that its possession accords. Moreover, he and those to whom he revealed the secret forge a certain solidarity with one another that comes from the knowledge that they share a secret that others do not have access to. It is the control he exerts over the secret—his ability to reveal it to some and conceal it from others—that allows him to wield it as a commodity that he can capitalize on for personal social gain.

The calculus changes if he decides to disguise his secret, using a technique of esoteric writing, in a public work. If he does not declare in the work that it contains a secret idea "between the lines," it is apparent that he has no desire to turn the secret into a commodity. This situation, accordingly, requires no further consideration. Instead, I will focus on a situation in which he does declare in the work that it contains an encoded secret. Following Urban's model, it might be expected that such a declaration would have two effects. First, it would give his work an allure, thereby drawing readers to it. Second, it would provide him with a certain cachet insofar as it would enhance his reputation as a master of secrets. The matter, however, is more complicated. It is indeed likely that his declaration will increase the book's allure, but, from his point of view, as I will explain, this may not necessarily lead to positive results. Moreover, any potential cachet that he might gain is mitigated, if not fully erased, by various considerations that I will outline. In short, if his goal were to increase his social capital, esoteric writing is not an effective means. In fact, I would argue that the type of secrecy that is reflected in esoteric writing functions quite differently from the type of secrecy described by Urban.

Simmel already pointed out that the act of recording what was formerly an esoteric oral tradition undermines the sense of group identity and exclusivity that those who share secrets might feel:

> The necessity of depending upon tradition from person to person, and the fact that the spring of knowledge flowed only from within the society, not from an objective piece of literature—this attached the individual member with unique intimacy to the community. It gave him the feeling that if he were detached from this substance, he would lose his own, and would never recover it elsewhere. . . . So soon, however, as the labor of the group has capitalized its output in the form of literature, in visible works, and in permanent examples, the former immediate flow of vital fluid between the actual group and the individual member is interrupted. The life-process of the latter no longer binds him continuously and without competition to the former. Instead of that, he can now sustain himself from objective sources, not dependent upon the actual presence of former authoritative persons. ("Sociology of Secrecy" 475–76)

Simmel's comments concern a case in which the written word fully reveals what formerly was a secret passed only orally between members of a group. The same argument, however, can be made about esoteric writing in which the secrecy of the secret is preserved, albeit in a text available to a wider audience. On the one hand, the decision to record the secrets in an encoded manner that only a select audience could successfully decode is obviously elitist. On the other hand, precisely the fact that the writing is intended for a broad audience means that anyone with access to the manuscript can have a go at deciphering its true meaning. As Paul Bagley puts it in reference to exoteric/esoteric literature, his term for esoterically encoded writing: "The motive of conceit associated with teaching esoteric doctrines secretly does not inherently apply to exoteric/esoteric literature. Indeed, since the esoteric teaching in exoteric/esoteric literature, figuratively speaking, 'hides in plain sight,' it always remains accessible to any perspicacious and diligent reader" (239).[11]

In recording a secret through esoteric writing, the author dramatically gives up the control that he (or his group) has over the flow of the secret. Its status as a commodity is thus undermined. Indeed, as much as esoteric writing reflects the elitist view that only the few may gain access to the secret material, it is also egalitarian insofar as it constitutes an implicit invitation to others—those outside one's elite circle; indeed, those whom the author may never meet—to attempt to gain access. In recording his secret through techniques of esoteric writing, he has effectively ceded the control that makes it a valuable commodity. Perhaps if, as in some of the examples that I will describe in Chapter 2, he tries to limit the circulation of the manuscript, he would retain some control. In a situation, though, in which he distributes the manuscript freely, any person who comes into possession of it can attempt to uncover his secret. What is more, he cannot regulate whether this person understands the secret correctly. The person who attempts to decipher the secret might be someone at a great cultural and geographic distance from him or someone who lives many centuries later, such that whatever honor he receives will be unknown to him. The person might even be his adversary and might explain the secret in a manner that is detrimental to him. All these negative effects are magnified by the very fact that his declaration that the work contains secrets will increase its allure, thereby maximizing its readership. In all, his potential to achieve symbolic capital is compromised.

Secretism is effective when the writer advertises a secret that he does not really possess or one that he does not plan to fully reveal but intends only to hint at, tantalizingly, while always leaving the unfulfilled hope that there is more to come. "It is through secretism, the circulation of a secret's inaccessibility, the words and actions that throw that absence into relief, that a secret's power grows, quite independently of whether or not it exists" (Johnson 3). In esoteric writing, secretism does not pertain because the author is not merely hinting and deferring but fully exposing his secret to those with eyes to see. Why, then, does he choose to write in this manner?

The main purpose of employing esoteric writing is pedagogical.[12] It gives a chance to those who are worthy to gain access to the secret. That is, the main goal of the writer is to try to give others access to what he believes to be deep truths. This is in keeping with Elliot Wolfson's observation that "the reluctance of the master to promulgate the secret in writing is entangled inexorably with the expectation that the perspicacious student will be able to extrapolate the matter from the innuendo that is bequeathed in the text" ("Anonymity" 77–78). Herein lies the positive side of the increased readership created by the allure of the declaration that the work contains secrets. More readers may mean more misunderstanding or greater potential persecution, but they also mean a greater chance that those who are worthy will gain access to the secrets.

While the writer is guided by a (from a modern lens, deeply troubling) perspective that society is divided into those who are wise and those who are simple, he does not, on his own, pick and choose who falls into each category. Rather, he disseminates the text and gives all people who are literate a chance to prove that they are among the elite. This might be because he believes that having access to the truth is a fundamental good that he wants to bestow on others while still protecting himself from opprobrium and other members of society from the damaging consequences of knowledge that they are not ready for. In the case of Kabbalah, where the secrets might be of a theurgic nature, he might want to spread the ideas to help accomplish theurgic goals. Whatever his precise reasons, his goal is not self-aggrandizement but to spread the truth to others.

This dynamic is well captured by the comments of Maimonides, in the *Guide of the Perplexed*, who, as I will show, influenced the approach of Kabbalists to esoteric writing: "I am the man who when the concern pressed him and his way was straitened and he could find no other device by which to teach a demonstrated truth other than by giving satisfaction to a single virtuous man while displeasing ten thousand ignoramuses—I am he who prefers to address that single man by himself, and I do not heed the blame of those many creatures. For I claim to liberate that virtuous one from that into which he has sunk, and I shall guide him in his perplexity until he becomes perfect and he finds rest" (*Guide* 16–17, introduction). Maimonides is not concerned about the likelihood that ignoramuses will misunderstand his esoteric hints so long as a single worthy individual understands them properly.

Yet if the pedagogical goal of esoteric writing causes authors to willingly run the risk that readers will misinterpret the secret, seemingly this goal undermines the defensive and protective motivations for keeping the secret in the first place. The defensive motivation is challenged because not only those who would agree with the author's secret positions but also those who might violently disagree may succeed in deciphering them. Moreover, even if they are unable to decipher the secret of the text, what is to prevent opponents from inventing a meaning that will reflect badly on the author? Perhaps the solution to this quandary lies in the fact that esoteric writers may have believed that esoteric writing allowed them to preserve plausible deniability. Any critique can be met with the retort that the critics misunderstood the true secrets of the book.

The protective goal is also challenged because if readers misconstrue the secret, they may inadvertently develop ideas that do as much harm as the real secret would. This dilemma does not have an easy solution. It is possible that esoteric writers tended to tacitly assume that a reader with the intellectual wherewithal even to attempt to solve the secret is one who is least in need of protection.

At this point, we have moved into speculation about the often unstated motivations of esoteric writers, whose approaches, in any case, may dramatically differ from one another. All we can say definitively is that numerous writers—including Kabbalists—make it explicit that they are employing esoteric styles of writing to defend themselves, to protect others, and to spread the truth, and that sometimes these motivations interact in complex ways.

A Knowledgeable Readership

Esoteric writing is a useful tool to disseminate secret ideas only if there are readers who can decipher the clues strewn through the text. Usually, uncovering the true meaning of a text requires more than simply breaking a code. Extensive knowledge of the subject matter at hand is needed to understand the significance of the allusions and how they fit together. This raises a conundrum of esoteric writing: a reader with sufficient knowledge to decipher the hints likely already knows the secret. Esoteric writing is really only useful, therefore, in a situation where the secret is related to a topic that an elite reader knows well but provides some kind of additional insight that the reader is unfamiliar with. By analogy, one who has advanced knowledge of physics might not know how to design a nuclear bomb, but surely an encoded manual on bomb design could be understood only by one with such advanced knowledge.

In the case of secrets encoded in medieval Jewish philosophic texts, the relevant background is extensive knowledge of primarily Aristotelian philosophy, which could be gained by studying widely available Arabic and Hebrew translations of Aristotle's works and their medieval commentaries. In many cases, uncovering the secret meaning of a Jewish philosophical text involves applying this knowledge to decode the author's cryptic comments, which hint that a biblical or rabbinic text must be understood in terms of a particular philosophical principle.

An analogous situation pertains in the case of secrets encoded in kabbalistic texts. Here the reader must have extensive knowledge of kabbalistic theosophy that he can apply to decipher the author's allusions, which often pertain to kabbalistic readings of biblical or rabbinic texts. By the first half of the fourteenth century, extensive materials were available—works like de León's *Shekel ha-kodesh* and Gikatilla's *Sha'arei orah*, as well as many others—that were designed as Kabbalah primers to provide the novice with a basic understanding of kabbalistic thought (Lachter 40–43). Armed with this understanding, the novice could attempt to decipher the cryptic allusions found in kabbalistic texts.

At the very beginning of Kabbalah's literary history, more than a century earlier, this literature did not exist. This makes the use of esoteric writing by the first Kabbalists a more perplexing phenomenon. I will address this problem in subsequent chapters when I turn to esoteric writing in the works of the first Kabbalists. Here, however, I simply want to highlight the fact that esoteric writing requires a knowledgeable readership.

Conclusion

As I have shown in this chapter, plenty of kabbalistic writing can best be explained by Urban's model. Kabbalists frequently employ a rhetoric of secrecy that served to heighten their status as masters of secret knowledge. Even in the contemporary orthodox Jewish world, Kabbalists have retained their status as an elite group entitled to special deference because of their secret knowledge, despite the fact that this secret knowledge is readily accessible in academic studies and even on popular websites. Yet kabbalistic secretism should not make us overlook kabbalistic secrecy. Kabbalists, for various reasons, did, in fact, keep real secrets. Moreover, often their goal was not to wield these secrets to achieve social gain for themselves and their circle. On the contrary, they were, through the agency of esoteric writing, dedicated to spreading their secrets to men of understanding.

In Chapter 2, I show just how pervasive Kabbalists' commitment to keeping secrets really was.

Chapter 2

A Typology of Esoteric Writing in Kabbalistic Literature

It is no secret that Kabbalists keep secrets. Even a casual reader of kabbalistic texts will have likely come across passages in which Kabbalists express their reluctance to reveal a certain idea or in which they explain that a particular concept must be left out of writing. Despite the ubiquity of such passages, there has yet to be a systematic scholarly attempt to describe the various strategies that Kabbalists have employed to conceal their secrets. That is, while it may be obvious that Kabbalists keep secrets, how precisely they do so has never been studied. This chapter represents the first attempt to catalog and describe the techniques that Kabbalists have employed to keep secret ideas out of public hands. In addition to simply leaving their ideas out of writing, or attempting to limit the circulation of their manuscripts, Kabbalists employed techniques of esoteric writing, including various forms of ciphers, dispersion of knowledge, intentional contradictions, Zoharic symbolism, and allusive writing.

The sheer quantity of kabbalistic texts that claim to keep secrets is immense, and I cannot possibly hope to examine every such instance. Instead, I have chosen to describe the various methods by which Kabbalists keep secrets and provide selective illustrative examples for each. I have cast my net as widely as possible so that the examples that I provide come from Kabbalists with different intellectual orientations, who lived in a variety of different locales, and who were active at various times throughout the entire literary history of Kabbalah.

While I will present my examples in chronological order, this chapter is not intended as a history of kabbalistic secrecy. Thus, I will not examine historical trends, such as whether successive Kabbalists in a single tradition adopted more or less pronounced esoteric tendencies over time or whether Kabbalists in one locale treated certain ideas with more secrecy than Kabbalists elsewhere. Rather, this chapter takes a taxonomical approach that is meant to elucidate strategies of esotericism rather than historical developments.

In this chapter, I will not attempt to decipher the ideas that Kabbalists sought to hide. Such an attempt would require painstaking analysis of the arcane details of the theological system of the Kabbalist under consideration as well as those of other members of his circle, as they appear across their entire oeuvre. Indeed, in many cases, uncovering the meaning of a hinted idea in a single example that I will cite would itself require a separate study. This chapter is intended as a reference point for future scholars who seek to decode esoteric kabbalistic texts and for my own work, in Chapters 3–6, where I do attempt to uncover the secret ideas concealed in the works of a number of the first Kabbalists.

Sequestering Secrets

The most straightforward way in which Kabbalists have historically kept secrets from a wider audience is by not committing them to writing. As will be discussed in Chapter 4, at the beginning of the thirteenth century, Kabbalah moved from a strictly oral tradition to a written one. Isaac the Blind, it will be seen, protested this transition and argued that Kabbalah should remain oral. Yet even Kabbalists who did record kabbalistic ideas continued to maintain that certain ideas must remain unwritten. And this is true not only of Kabbalists who, generally speaking, made an effort to conceal their kabbalistic ideas by adopting esoteric modes of writing but also of Kabbalists who typically presented Kabbalah in an accessible fashion.

As examples of the first group, we may consider Nahmanides (1194–1270), perhaps the leading rabbinic authority and Kabbalist of the thirteenth century, and some members of his school. As we will see, these figures were committed to a code of esotericism,[1] which led them to adopt esoteric modes of writing to conceal some of their ideas. Yet, in the case of certain ideas, they chose to remain completely silent and did not even leave hints in written form. As Nahmanides writes regarding the interpretations of certain verses from the book of Job, which apparently concern the secret of metempsychosis, "They are among the secrets of the Torah that were concealed save from those who merited them from a tradition. It is prohibited to explain them in writing, and a hint [regarding them] has no benefit" ("Torat ha-Adam" 2:279).

Similarly, Shem Tov ben Abraham Ibn Gaon, the turn-of-the-fourteenth-century Kabbalist who was a student of Nahmanides's students Shlomo ben Abraham Ibn Adret and Isaac ben Todros, explains in *Keter Shem Tov*—his supercommentary on the kabbalistic secrets found in Nahmanides's *Commentary on Torah*—that "there are also many things that I have received, but I have not hinted at them here for I heard it from their mouths when I received them long ago" (MS Florence, Laurentian Library, Plut.II.20, 88b).

Among the second group of Kabbalists—those who, generally speaking, presented their ideas quite openly but nevertheless chose to keep certain topics out of writing—a good example is the thirteenth-century Castilian Kabbalist Joseph Gikatilla. His *Sha'arei orah* served as a Kabbalah primer for later generations of students because of its clarity of style and organization. Nevertheless, he believed that some topics must be left unwritten. As he puts it in one instance: "I do not have permission to explain more than this in writing" (239), or in another, "I have to enlighten your eyes regarding these matters for they are closed and sealed, and I offer hints in writing, but I will complete [transmitting] all the matters to you in an oral transmission (*be-kabbalah 'al peh*), God willing" (244).[2]

We find a similar state of affairs in *Sefer mishkan ha-'edut* by Gikatilla's contemporary and fellow Castilian Kabbalist Moses de León. On the one hand, de León speaks of the necessity of revealing secrets. For example, in the context of a discussion of the punishment that souls will face in hell, he avers that it is "a mitzvah to bring the deep darkness into light and to reveal the sealed matters that they (the Talmudic sages), of blessed memory, concealed" (118–19).[3] Yet elsewhere in the work, he stresses that certain ideas may not be put into writing at all. For example, in the context of a discussion of the Garden of Eden, in a passage that partially echoes an unrelated statement by Maimonides,[4] he writes:

> From here on, I do not have permission to reveal, for [to do so] would be like sticking a finger in the eye because they are deep secrets and awesome wonders, which I am not permitted to speak of by any means since they (the Talmudic sages) concealed their secrets. Additionally, [I cannot reveal] because they (the secrets) would seem strange in the eyes and ears of other people when they would

hear them. [Moreover, I cannot reveal the secrets] so that those who have toiled in [studying] them all their days will not become a target of an arrow. For not everyone will merit to know their hidden aspects, so that those who are not fitting will not glory in knowledge of the Most High. (141)[5]

Put in other terms, even though de León clearly feels an imperative to reveal esoteric ideas, he nevertheless contends that certain ideas are too sensitive to be recorded.[6] The reasons he provides for keeping secrets—that their revelation might lead to the mocking of Kabbalists—are an example of the defensive esotericism discussed in Chapter 1.

In the later history of kabbalistic literature, we continue to find such statements. One particularly striking much later example is found in a letter that Israel Baal Shem Tov, the figure who inspired eighteenth-century eastern European Hasidism, wrote to his brother-in-law, Gershon of Kutov, in which he recounts his "ascent of the soul," during which he met the messiah in the heavenly realm. While there is some question of whether the passage relevant to my concerns was actually composed by the Baal Shem Tov—it may have been added to the letter by an anonymous later figure[7]—it was certainly accepted as such by Hasidic tradition. In this passage, in the course of meeting the messiah, "three charms and three holy [divine] names" (Mondshine 235) are revealed to him that would magically allow others to easily learn how to perform their own ascents of the soul and gain a high level of Torah knowledge. These achievements, the Baal Shem Tov is told, would hasten the messiah's arrival. The Baal Shem Tov, however, is forbidden to reveal the charms and names: "But I was not given permission all the days of my life to reveal this. And I asked, on your behalf, [for permission] to teach you, but they did not permit me at all, and I am under oath and must remain steadfast regarding this" (235). Here, then, the Baal Shem Tov (or the anonymous author) believes that he possesses knowledge that would lead to messianic redemption but is nevertheless unable to reveal it.

A second approach to keeping secrets from a wide audience was to sequester kabbalistic manuscripts and circulate them only to confidants. A particularly striking example of this is referred to in a letter written to a student by David ben Judah he-Ḥasid, another Castilian Kabbalist, who was active at the beginning of the fourteenth century. There he states: "All of these matters are received by one man from the mouth of another man. They were not meant to be written. Were it not for my love for you, I would not write them down. But since I know that they will remain concealed (*genuzim*) with you, I have written them for you" (Idel, "The Image of Man Above the Sefirot: R. David" 186n22).[8] David, then, regards keeping certain secrets entirely out of writing as the ideal. Given, however, his feelings of affection toward his student and his trust that the student will keep the letter concealed, he is willing to record his esoteric ideas.[9]

We find a similar statement at the conclusion of another letter written in Italy in 1491 by Isaac Mor Hayyim, a Spaniard who visited Italy on the way to the land of Israel at the end of the fifteenth century,[10] to Isaac of Pisa: "I request of your excellence to place this text with the other texts that I sent to your honor. . . . Keep them in the store house so that they do not fall into the hands of one who is not fitted to have them. They will only be seen or found by one who you know is trustworthy of spirit, who conceals matters and loves truth" (Greenup 375).[11]

The idea that certain kabbalistic manuscripts should be sequestered also plays a role in the debate that raged in the mid-sixteenth century over whether the esoteric nature of the ideas in the Zohar, the central text of kabbalistic tradition, should prevent its publication.[12] Jacob Israel Finzi argued against printing on the grounds that until this point, "patrons secretly arranged for it to be written for them for large sums of gold, and they made it available to study by those whose belly was full of Scripture, Mishnah, Talmud, and the fear of God, as well as those who learned Kabbalah through an oral transmission." Previously, "it never occurred to anyone to act in this way and print it" (Assaf 242).[13] That is, Finzi describes a system that was in place to allow only those deemed worthy to gain access to Zoharic manuscripts. From his perspective, this was an ideal situation that the publication of the Zohar would destroy by making the material widely available.

Another notable instance of limiting the circulation of kabbalistic manuscripts involves the teachings of the sixteenth-century Safed Kabbalist Isaac Luria, as recorded by his student Hayyim Vital toward the end of the sixteenth century. Luria's teachings, as recorded by Vital, would eventually transform Kabbalah and come to be regarded as the canonical articulation of kabbalistic thought and practice. Yet Vital was zealous about restricting the distribution of his recordings of Luria's thought. After the death of Luria in 1572, Vital allegedly hid away these writings and those of other students of Luria (Benayahu, *Toledoth ha-Ari* 240–42). He also composed a pledge that was signed by Luria's students "not to reveal to anyone other than him (i.e., Hayyim Vital) any secret that we will hear from his mouth by way of truth (i.e., regarding kabbalistic matters), or anything that he taught us in the past, or even what our teacher, the great Rabbi, the honorable teacher, R. Isaac Luria Ashkenazi, of blessed memory, taught us during that whole period" (Benayahu, "Shitrei ha-hitkasherut" 149).[14] Clearly, this pledge covered oral transmission as well as written accounts of Luria's and Vital's teachings that were carefully guarded and not disseminated.[15]

Finally, a particularly extreme case of an attempt to keep a manuscript of esoteric ideas out of public circulation is the Hasidic master Naḥman of Bratslav's (1772–1810) order to burn a text that he had written, as well as its only duplicate. This text became known in Bratslav tradition as "The Burnt Book."[16]

After the practice of printing kabbalistic works became more widespread, one way to limit the dissemination of kabbalistic secrets was to leave certain sensitive materials out of print, thereby consigning them to manuscripts that were much harder to come by. One well-known example is the fourth and final section of *Sha'arei kedushah*, by the aforementioned Ḥayyim Vital, which was left out of the first edition of the work that was printed early in the eighteenth century and, until recently, of subsequent editions.[17] In lieu of publishing this section, we find this note: "The printer said: This section, the fourth, has not been copied or printed since it is all about [divine] names and combinations [of letters] and hidden secrets, which are not allowed to be put on the altar of printing" (Vital, *Sha'arei kedushah* 35b).[18]

We find evidence even of the attempt to limit the circulation of printed kabbalistic works. In his *Yosher levav*, the eighteenth-century Italian Kabbalist Raphael Immanuel Hai Ricchi describes his internal deliberations regarding whether to write the work, given the lofty nature of its material and the possibility that he might make doctrinal errors. He arrives at an affirmative decision by meditating upon the first two biblical verses that pop into his head upon awaking in the morning (1b). He then wonders whether to print it "so that it will be easily found in the hands of every man who desires life, or whether it is very good that it is hard to come by so that it does not, as a result of its abundant availability, reach the hands of one who is unworthy to see it" (4b). Using a similar technique of meditating on verses, he concludes that printing is appropriate (4b–6a, esp. 4b and 5b). Nevertheless, slightly earlier in the work, he offers the following instructions to those whom the printed book reaches: "I beseech you to always defer my honor in the face of His honor, and, in each and every city that this book reaches, do not give it to nor sell it to any member of the city before it reaches the Rabbi[19] or the appropriate sage in that city. Based on what he says, it will reach the hands of those who ask for it, so that it will not be seen or found in the hands of one who is prohibited by the Rabbi or the sage from reading it" (4a).[20]

We find a similar—if largely unsuccessful—attempt at the beginning of the twentieth century in Jerusalem to limit the circulation of printed versions of prayer books that contained the kabbalistic instructions of the famed eighteenth-century Kabbalist Shalom Sharabi (Meir, *Reḥovot* 124–28). Recent examples of such attempts to limit the circulation of printed books, such as Moses Zacuto's *Shorshei ha-shemot*, can also be identified (Chajes 247–49).[21]

There is even an interesting case of an attempt to limit access to a digital copy of a kabbalistic work. A website that features an English translation of the aforementioned *Sha'arei kedushah* includes the following warning: "*Shaarei Kedusha* (the Gates of Holiness) by Rabbi Chaim Vital deals with supernatural phenomena and is not appropriate for all levels." Accordingly, interested readers must pass an online quiz on various aspects of Jewish law and practice before they are granted access to the work.[22] Once accessed, the reader is instructed to "please guard this ebook from getting out to the mainstream public."[23] The traditionally censored fourth section, referred to above, is only partially translated.[24] There we find notes such as: "Translator's Note: Rest of Gate 1 is not fit for translation due to the danger involved for those who are not fit (i.e., all of us)."[25]

Techniques of Secret Writing

As Isaac the Blind reminds us, "What is written has no master" (T. Weiss, "Letter" 331).[26] Even material that is sequestered away may eventually reach a wider audience. Accordingly, Kabbalists kept secrets not only by preventing their dissemination but also by hiding them in plain sight within their publicly available works by adopting various techniques of esoteric writing, which I will catalog in this section.

Ciphers

In limited instances, Kabbalists employed various types of ciphers, such as letter substitutions, anagrams, and acronyms. For example, in *Keter Shem*

Tov, the aforementioned Ibn Gaon offers the following account of an exchange with his teachers, Shlomo ben Avraham Ibn Adret and Isaac ben Todros, both of whom were disciples of Nahmanides:

> I consulted with them about whether I should write in a hinted fashion—for the sake of remembering [the explanations of Nahmanides's secrets that he learned from them]—about a few of the matters that are hinted at by our teacher (Nahmanides), of blessed memory, and they permitted me to do so. My teacher, R. Isaac ben Todros, may God protect him, even asked me to write for him what we have agreed upon regarding secret matters. Nevertheless, my heart did not allow me write in an explicit fashion (*meforash*) but only with combined hints (*birmazim metsorafim*) and substituted letters (*ve-otiyyot meḥullafot*) in the case of each and every hint and each and every concealment. (MS Florence, Laurentian Library, Plut.II.20, 83a)[27]

The meaning of *birmazim metsorafim*, which I translate as "with combined hints," is not clear.[28] "Substituted letters," however, likely refers to a substitution cipher whereby certain letters stand in the place of the other letters, although it conceivably may refer, instead, to composing words with the letters out of order to create anagrams,[29] as in an example that I will mention below. *Keter Shem Tov* does not include such "substituted letters." It seems likely, rather, that in these remarks, Ibn Gaon is not referring to *Keter Shem Tov* as we have it but to an earlier version of this work that he wrote using these esoteric techniques. We learn of this earlier version from an introductory poem that precedes these remarks. Here, again, referring to his teachers, he writes:

> They permitted me to hint for them, for the sake of remembering, using substitution (*be-ḥilluf*)/ And I wrote in their presence, as I was accustomed, using the wisdom of combining (*ḥokhmat ha-tseruf*)/ And when I left their tent/ After I had thirstily drunk their words/ And I planted the tent of my tabernacle in the Wilderness of Zin [behind] a one-cubit partition/ They commanded me for they undertook to expound (*be'er*)/ But the great stone is upon the well (*be'er*)/ [As a result] I had to change its power/ For "behold its strength is in its loins and its power is in the muscles of its stom-

ach" (Job 40:16)/ And I changed its name from that which I had called it, *Secrets of Secrets* (*sitrei setarim*)/ And I have dubbed it *Keter Shem Tov* amongst the names of books. (82b)

It is difficult to make full sense of Ibn Gaon's dense poetic language, which is replete with biblical allusions. Apparently, his claim is that while he was still studying directly with his teachers, and with their blessing, he wrote a work using the esoteric techniques of "substitution" (*ḥilluf*) and "combining" (*tseruf*). Note that the description of the esoteric style of this work parallels the description in the passage quoted above. In both passages, as well, the reason given for writing the work is to prevent secrets from being forgotten. Yet after he had already departed from his teachers, they became concerned that the style of writing was too concealed.[30] This is the implication of his statement that "the great stone is upon the well." "Well" and "expound" are expressed by the same word in Hebrew, *be'er*, and Ibn Gaon's point is that his work blocked the possibility of a clear exposition, as a stone blocks the opening of a well. The concealed nature of the text is also implied in the quotation from Job: "Its strength is in its loins and its power is in the muscles of its stomach"—that is, its meaning was deeply concealed within its esoteric style of writing. While this is not specified, perhaps his teachers' problem with the deeply concealed nature of the work was that it would not even serve the purpose of aiding in memory, since it would be so difficult to decipher its meaning. Regardless, he explains that in response to his teachers' complaint, he rewrote the work and changed its title from *Secrets of Secrets*, a name appropriate for a deeply encoded work, to *Keter Shem Tov*.[31] Indeed, while *Keter Shem Tov* is still an esoteric work—in it, Ibn Gaon makes clear, as seen above, that certain ideas are left oral and that he adheres to a style of writing in "chapter headings,"[32] which I will describe below—it is more accessible than a truly encoded work like *Secrets of Secrets* must have been.

Given that *Keter Shem Tov* does not include substitution of letters but *Secrets of Secrets* did, it seems likely that in the first passage I quoted, Ibn Gaon was referring to the latter rather than the former.[33] *Secrets of Secrets* is apparently lost, but it is easy to imagine that it was a work, which could have been understood only by someone who possessed the key.

Another text, a series of kabbalistic responsa by a certain R. Isaac,[34] written to Ibn Gaon's teacher, Isaac ben Todros, does employ a version of letter substitution, even though it is impossible to know whether this was the type of letter substitution used by Ibn Gaon.[35] In this text, key words are written in an ancient technique known as ATBaSH, whereby the first letter of the Hebrew alphabet is substituted for the last letter, the second letter for the second to last letter, and so forth. The result is that important words in the text read to the unsuspecting reader like gibberish.[36] As Moshe Idel ("Commentaries" [72] 47n159) has noted, this technique was surely employed as a way to conceal the contents of the text. At the same time, ATBaSH was a very well-known technique, and readers of a fairly moderate level of erudition would have little trouble deciphering it. I will return to this point later in this chapter.

Another example of using the technique of ATBaSH to conceal the contents of the text is referred to in a letter by the turn-of-the-seventeenth-century Lurianic Kabbalist Israel Sarug: "Regarding what his Torah eminence asked about *Derush Aḥim'ats* (The Exposition of Aḥimatz), I am not able to put it in writing, for the matters are ancient, going back more than three hundred generations. When I have free time, God willing, I will write at length using clear language (*be-safah berurah*). Yet it will be written in the *alef bet* of *ATBaSH*. This will be the sign: every letter that is substituted will have a dot over it. Then you will understand what is before you" (Avivi 312).[37] Sarug, then, promises that he will reveal the contents of *Derush Aḥim'ats*, an otherwise unknown text, in clear language. Yet apparently to make up for the clarity of his language, he will disguise the meaning of the text using ATBaSH.[38] A text written in this manner by Sarug is not extant. It seems, however, as Yosef Avivi (312, 425–26) notes, that an extant text by Abraham Yagel (d. c. 1623), which refers to a "letter of the sage Sarug, all of whose words appear in *gematria* (the numerical value of words), *notarikon* (acronyms), and substituted letters (*ḥilluf otiyyot*)[39] of the *alef bet*" (cited in Avivi 425) is an explanation of Sarug's lost letter. Yagel's description of the text suggests that it was truly an encoded document that also used additional techniques beyond ATBaSH.

In a late seventeenth-century manuscript, we find a version of a text originally derived from the circle of the thirteenth-century German Pietists on how to construct a golem. Since this text derives from the German Pietists, it is not kabbalistic in the technical and historical sense of the term. This distinction, however, had little meaning in post-thirteenth-century Kabbalah, when German pietistic and kabbalistic ideas were combined, and, indeed, the manuscript is replete with other kabbalistic materials. Moreover, the esoteric features of the text are apparently the work of the seventeenth-century copyist rather than the original author. Therefore, even though I have generally chosen not to cite German pietistic examples of esoteric writing, of which there are many,[40] it seems appropriate to discuss this text here. This text exists in many earlier manuscripts, as well—starting in the fourteenth century—but as Scholem (*Kitvei* 75) has noted, the seventeenth-century manuscript has a unique feature not found in the earlier versions. This version occasionally scrambles the letters of various words such that they are written in anagrams.[41] This is apparently an attempt to conceal the esoteric contents of the text. As in the case of ATBaSH, however, I would note that these anagrams are not particularly difficult for a diligent reader to decipher.

A final example of the use of encoded styles of writing is the *Scroll of Secrets*, which outlines the messianic vision of the aforementioned Hasidic master Rav Naḥman of Bratslav, as recorded by his student Natan of Nemirov. As Zvi Mark (15–48) details, this text was regarded as deeply secret in Bratslav tradition. It was sequestered and known only by select Bratslav Hasidim through the generations. At the beginning of the current century, Mark was able to gain access to the scroll in various manuscripts through personal contacts with Bratslav Hasidim (15–19). As he explains, many words of the scroll are written in acronyms—the result of an intentional desire to conceal its contents—making it an exceedingly difficult text to decipher (22, 33). As Bratslav tradition testifies, the scroll was doubly secreted: it was both hidden away and encoded (32–33).

Dispersion of Knowledge

"Dispersion of knowledge," a technique of esoteric writing whereby ideas are broken up over the course of single or multiple works rather than presented all at once, has a long history, which has yet to be fully written. It was, for example, already employed by the second-century church father Clement of Alexandria (Lerner, "Dispersal" 30–32; *Playing* 7–8).[42] It was used extensively in the alchemical tradition, where it had a particularly important place in the corpus of works attributed to the eighth-century Islamic alchemist Jābir Ibn Ḥayyān (Kraus 1:xxvii–xxxi, 6–7; Haq 6–7, 12–14; Principe 44–45). It was also employed by the fourteenth-century pseudepigraphic Latin Geber (=Jabir) (Newman 71) and, under his influence, by Heinrich Cornelius Agrippa at the beginning of the sixteenth century (Compagni 162).

In non-kabbalistic Jewish sources, the locus classicus of this technique appears in the introduction to Moses Maimonides's *Guide of the Perplexed*: "You should not ask of me here anything beyond the chapter headings. And even those are not set down in order or arranged in coherent fashion in this Treatise, but rather are scattered and entangled with other subjects that are to be clarified. For my purpose is that the truths be glimpsed and then again be concealed, so as not to oppose that divine purpose which one cannot possibly oppose and which has concealed from the vulgar among the people those truths especially requisite for His apprehension" (*Guide* 6–7, intro). "Chapter headings" are pithy explanations that do not provide all the details, as I will explain below. For our present purposes, I would like to focus on Maimonides's contention that even the "chapter headings" are not presented in a logically contiguous manner in the *Guide*. Rather, they are scattered across the text, and the astute reader must assemble them into a coherent whole. Maimonides expressly indicates that he used this technique to keep certain ideas away from the masses.

Until a full history of this technique is written, it is impossible to offer a complete assessment of the possible influences under which Kabbalists employed it. Given, however, his outsize influence on Jewish thinkers of all stripes, including Kabbalists, it is reasonable to conclude that Maimonides was the most significant influence,[43] even if is difficult to find the imprint of his specific phraseology on the descriptions of the technique of dispersion that I am familiar with in kabbalistic sources.

An early example of a kabbalistic use of this technique is found in *Commentary on Sefer Yetsirah* by the thirteenth-century Kabbalist Barukh Togarmi, a teacher of Abraham Abulafia: "I propose to write, but I am not permitted, so I propose not to write. Yet I cannot put it entirely aside. Therefore, I write and then put it aside, and I return to it again in another place. Such is my method" (Scholem, *Ha-kabbalah shel sefer ha-temunah* 235).[44] For Togarmi, then, using the technique of dispersion was a way of getting around the impermissibility of recording kabbalistic secrets.

Another early example is found in *Sha'ar ha-razim* by the aforementioned mid-thirteenth-century Castilian Kabbalist Todros Abulafia, where, in the poetic opening, he explains that he will use the technique of dispersion: "I have scattered matters that are closely related and gathered together matters which are unrelated, and I placed a space between matters that cleave together so that no foreigner comes close to sacrifice and burn incense" (*Sha'ar ha-razim* 45).⁴⁵ As Abulafia makes clear, the purpose of this technique is to keep the "foreigner"—that is, one who is unqualified—from gaining access to the secrets of the work.

A somewhat different version of the technique of dispersion is employed by de León in his aforementioned *Mishkan ha-'edut*. There he refers to a secret, which the sages "revealed and concealed" (16), regarding the ability of human beings to draw down the tenth sefirah. According to de León, "One who understands its secret will merit a great matter" (16). He does not, however, reveal this secret in *Mishkan ha-'edut*: "It is not fitting to reveal it here, but in the secret of the concealments of *Sefer ha-pardes* that I composed. . . . There, I revealed and hinted at this matter when I expounded the secret of the chariot. Go to it, and there you will find it explained" (16). The approach to dispersion here, which has precedents in the Jabiran corpus,⁴⁶ involves presenting the secret more fully in another work—in this case, the no longer extant *Sefer ha-pardes*⁴⁷—while merely whetting the reader's appetite in the work at hand. To understand the secret in *Mishkan ha-'edut*, the reader would need to have access to *Sefer ha-pardes*, quite possibly a difficult proposition in a period before printing, when manuscripts of kabbalistic texts were scarce and were possibly purposely sequestered.

We find yet another explicit use of dispersion in a commentary on "The Song of Unity," written in Ashkenaz in the first half of the fourteenth century. Addressing his reader, the anonymous author writes, regarding the topic of metempsychosis, that he will "disperse [its discussion] in scattered places, and you must join them together and come to know them. But I warn every foreigner, with the threat of banishment, not to interpret this matter at all, for, God forbid, he might come to speak erroneously about God, and he will not be able to atone for this" (MS Vat. 274, 175a–b).⁴⁸

Similarly, the aforementioned Ibn Gaon, according to his own testimony, also used the technique of dispersion in *Keter Shem Tov*. Once again employing partially rhyming verse, he explains: "If you find within them matters that I have repeated twice and three times, this was not for naught. Rather, it was for one of three reasons: either to make it easy on those who study [my work], or because I did not want to reveal⁴⁹ the entire hidden matter in one place nor in only two places, but [to reveal the matter] in three places is the most honorable [practice], or due to the decrees of our teachers owing to the depth of the matter, [repeating it] is desirable [since] the prospect of forgetting is present" (MS Florence, Laurentian Library, Plut.II.20, 88a–b).

Ibn Gaon thus provides three reasons that certain ideas in his work are repeated more than once. The first reason is so that ideas that are relevant to more than one discussion will appear each time. This will prevent the reader from having to search earlier in the book for an explanation that is also needed later. The third reason is to ensure that certain key ideas will not be forgotten. If the first and third reasons are meant to assist the reader, the second reason is meant to confound him: due to the secrecy of certain ideas, they must be broken up and partially presented in three places in the work, forcing the reader to assemble the full idea on his own.

This technique was also employed by the sixteenth-century Jerusalem Kabbalist Joseph Ibn Sayyah. In the introduction to *Even ha-shoham*, he explains that "what I have hidden in one place, I have revealed in another with a great and subtle hint" (MS Bar-Ilan University, 598, 2a). Later on, he again refers to the technique of dispersion by invoking a phrase from *Sefer Yetsirah*. *Sefer Yetsirah* says of the sefirot that "their end is attached to their beginning and their beginning to their end like a flame that is tied to a coal" (Hayman 74 = 1:7). Turning to the reader, Ibn Sayyah suggests that "he should read it all and thereafter go back and examine it before his Rabbi, for [in the case of] the matters [in this book], their ends are attached to their beginnings and their beginnings to their ends like a flame that is tied to a coal'" (MS Bar-Ilan University, 598, 2a).[50] Apparently, his point is that ideas that appear at the beginning of the work must be understood in light of ideas that appear later, and vice versa.

Finally, in the eighteenth century, in the work of the revered Kabbalist Shalom Sharabi (1720–77), who was born in Sana'a, Yemen, and immigrated to Jerusalem, we still find the practice of "dispersion" in use. In reference to a discussion in his *Hakdamat* ("introduction to") *rehovot ha-nahar*, Sharabi writes: "I wrote with brevity regarding this matter insofar as was possible, for I was afraid that these pages [of the 'introduction'] would fall into the hands of one who has not yet properly studied the words of the ARI (Isaac Luria), of blessed memory, and he will suspect that I have studied other works, but this is not so, as I explained.[51] Therefore, I have written with brevity, and I have scattered (*u-fizzarti*) the matters in the 'introduction.' But everything is written there in the 'introduction,' but a high level of insight is required to understand one matter from another (*lehavin davar mittokh davar*)" (140). Here, then, Sharabi describes his practice of writing with brevity—a style of writing to which I will turn below—and of scattering the components of an idea throughout his work rather than presenting it all at once. Both these practices were intended to ensure that a novice reader would not fully comprehend the text.

Intentional Contradictions

There is also limited evidence that Kabbalists employed the technique of intentional contradictions.[52] Here, too, the influence of Maimonides was apparently paramount. At the conclusion of the introduction to the *Guide*, Maimonides outlines seven reasons that explain why contradictions are found in various works (*Guide* 17–20, introduction). He indicates that in the *Guide* itself, he included contradictions for the previously outlined fifth and seventh reasons (20, introduction). The fifth reason involves pedagogical necessity and need not concern us here (17–18, introduction). The seventh reason, though, is directly relevant to our purposes: Maimonides states that, at times, he purposefully offers contradictory statements as a way of misleading the unsophisticated masses.[53] Leo Strauss famously saw the seventh reason as the key to deciphering the *Guide*'s secrets. According to Strauss, an astute reader of the *Guide* must carefully search for contradictory statements. In his view, it is precisely the out-of-the-way, seemingly innocuous, statement, which, upon reflection, contradicts other more prominent statements, in which Maimonides's true view lies.[54]

The intentional use of contradictions to conceal certain ideas was employed by several Kabbalists, including Abraham Abulafia (second half of the thirteenth century), the founder of ecstatic Kabbalah. This branch of Kabbalah has relatively greater interest in ecstatic mystical experience than the theosophic branch of Kabbalah, which is relatively more concerned with describing the nature of the Godhead. On the one hand, Abulafia preaches the need to reveal secrets and criticizes the reticence of theosophic Kabbalists to disclose secrets (Idel, "On the Secrets" 382–83, 417–18, 445–46; "'In a Whisper'" 512; "From R. Isaac" 12–13). On the other hand, Idel (*Abraham Abulafia's Esotericism* esp. 107–256) argues, at length, that Abulafia adopted Maimonidean strategies of esoteric writing. One of these, according to Idel (142, 295–96), was intentional contradictions. I will have more to say about Abraham Abulafia's use of esoteric writing below.

Another example is found in the work of the late fifteenth- and sixteenth-century Kabbalist Abraham Azulai, who was born in Fez but ultimately settled in Hebron and was a popularizer of Kabbalah.[55] In the introduction to his *Ḥesed le-Avraham*, a work that was to become highly popular in subsequent centuries, he informs the reader that "I did not compose for you, in this book, any deep secret that would require [prior] premises to understand them. Rather, any man of understanding can easily understand this secret on his own" (*Ḥesed le-Avraham* 9). Yet this seemingly exoteric stance may not fully capture his literary approach.[56] In the immediate continuation of the introduction, he adds: "One of things that one who studies this work should not overlook is that many things are said in it in one place following one intention and in another place following a different intention, just as Maimonides, of blessed memory, did in many places in the *Guide*" (9–10). Here Azulai is referring to Maimonides's aforementioned discussion of the reasons that contradictions are found in works of various authors. Azulai, like Maimonides, proceeds to explain why contradictions are found in various works. While he talks in general terms about all authors, it is apparent that he also means for his comments to apply specifically to his own work:

> Therefore, it is fitting that a student should take care in studying the [expositions][57] of the work of any given author so that he does not hastily refute his words[58] before he comprehends the truth of the matter. He should keep in mind that, at times, an author will omit a premise in a particular place since it is self-explanatory, or was already explained elsewhere, or [he will do so] with the intent to conceal the matter (*lehastir ha-ʿinyan*). One who studies the work might think that this is a mistake of the author. . . . He should realize that the author is not one of the simpletons. . . . It is preferable for a person to doubt his own intellect and understanding. (10)

Azulai thus provides three reasons that contradictions might be found in his work and in the work of others. First, a particular idea may seem to contradict another idea because the premise that could have been included to show why the ideas do not, in fact, contradict each other is so self-evident that there is no need for the author to expressly state it. Second, in a similar circumstance, even if perhaps the necessary premise is not self-evident, the author sees no need to state it, for he has already stated it elsewhere in his work. For our purposes, it is Azulai's third reason, which is a version of Maimonides's seventh reason, that is key: a premise that would explain the matter away is not included, out of a desire to conceal. How precisely Azulai imagined this technique being employed by other authors or how he may have employed it himself is unclear. One possibility is that Azulai is referring to a situation in which the author does not want to reveal a premise that would resolve a contradiction between two points in the work because in this resolution lies a secret that the author wishes to conceal. If so, this is a different use of contradictions than that adopted by Maimonides. For Maimonides, at least in Strauss's reading, only one of the contradictory statements is true; but for Azulai, the secret may lie in knowing how to successfully resolve the contradiction. Whatever the particulars of Azulai's technique, it should be stressed that even a work such as *Ḥesed le-Avraham*, which was written to popularize Kabbalah, may have employed the technique of intentional contradictions.

If Azulai is somewhat vague, the aforementioned Joseph Ibn Sayyah explicitly states, in the introduction to *Even ha-shoham*, shortly before the passage cited earlier, that he will use intentional contradictions: "Behold, in it, I have arranged and composed a few matters that appear to be opposite of each other and to contradict each other (*soterim ketsatam liktsatam*) and to be incorrect, in order to hide them from those who do not know. But to those who know, they are proper and subtle matters that shine" (MS Bar-Ilan University, 598, 2a). Ibn Sayyah's approach is similar to Azulai's proposed approach: the contradictions in his work are merely apparent. Those who are worthy will figure out how to reconcile the contradiction to arrive at the correct ideas. The unworthy, in contrast, will be kept from fathoming the true meaning of the text.

In a manner that is closer to the Straussian interpretation, Ḥayyim de la Rosa, one of the chief students of the aforementioned Shalom Sharabi, claims that his teacher deliberately supplied incorrect ideas as a way of concealing his true ideas. As he puts it in one place: "The Rabbi [Sharabi], even writes the opposite of the [correct] matter, and he relies on one who studies [his work] to be aware of this" (126b).[59] In interpretive statements such as these, some care is needed because it is quite possible that de la Rosa is invoking the excuse of intentional esotericism to explain an actual inconsistency in his teacher's work or to disguise a disagreement that he has with him.

Esoteric Writing in the Zohar

Another style of esoteric writing is characteristic of the most influential kabbalistic work, *Sefer ha-zohar*. The Zohar is traditionally attributed to the second-century sage Shimon bar Yoḥai, but according to current scholarly understandings, it is not a work produced by a single author but an anthology to which numerous authors contributed over the course of several generations in the thirteenth and fourteenth centuries.[60] It may not even have taken the form of a coherent work until as late as the sixteenth century.[61] A ramification of the complexity of the Zohar's literary history is that various different styles are employed across the work. A truly exhaustive treatment of esoteric writing in the Zohar would thus require a separate monograph that would be alert to stylistic differences across its literary strata.

At the same time, I accept the views of scholars such as Elliot Wolfson and Eitan Fishbane (*Art* 42–50), who argue, in Wolfson's words, that notwithstanding the textual complexity, "It is still possible to posit a coherent textual sense with respect to the homiletical passages gathered together within the margins of this literary artifact in the course of at least three centuries. In my judgment, we can still profitably refer to these passages as expressive of a singular phenomenon classified as the zoharic Kabbalah" ("Zoharic Literature" 323).[62] The style of esoteric writing that I will describe here is, in my view, an aspect of this "coherent textual sense." Thus, while I do not claim that my comments apply to every passage in the Zohar, I do think that they are relevant to large swaths of the text.

Some scholars depict the Zohar as eschewing esotericism. Yehuda Liebes, for example, points to a number of Zoharic passages that speak of the importance of revealing secrets and avoiding metaphors and riddles when speaking of kabbalistic matters. His conclusion is that "these matters look like a rejection of the spirit of the Middle Ages, which is saturated with concealments and allegories, and a return to the Talmudic path, which is distinguished by primitive directness" ("Zohar ve-eros" 18).[63] Along similar lines, Melila Hellner-Eshed treats the Zohar as a work that "removes the veil of esotericism that characterized the major currents of Jewish thought, both in philosophy and in Kabbalah" (159). In broad terms, I agree with these characterizations, even if the Zohar does, at times, resort to what I will term "allusive writing." My general agreement, however, applies only after the work is decoded, since the Zohar, I would argue, is written in a kind of code.

The Zohar's code involves referring to the sefirot (the ten aspects of God) in a vast array of symbolic terms such that a casual reader will not know which aspects of God a particular passage refers to or even that it refers to God at all. Pinchas Giller's observation that "reading the Zohar is different from reading other Jewish literature, for the Zohar was consciously written in an obscure symbolic code, or 'secret speech'" (*Reading* 5) is apt. It is this characteristic of the Zohar that spawned a genre of Zoharic lexicons designed to assist the reader in decoding the text.[64] This is also the reason that, in the introduction to the first academically rigorous English translation of the Zohar, its main translator, Daniel Matt, says of the earlier 1930s English translation that "since the translation is unaccompanied by a commentary, the symbolism remains impenetrable" (*The Zohar: Pritzker Edition* xix).

To be clear, I do not mean to reduce Zoharic symbolism to a mere code. The symbols chosen for the various sefirot, such as the sun and the moon for the sixth and tenth sefirot, are, in the Zoharic conception, connected thematically and even ontologically to the sefirot that they symbolize. Yet they also function as a code that requires a key to break. And even after the symbolic code is broken, the work does not suddenly become clear. Rather, only a reader with extensive knowledge of the manner in which the different sefirot interact with one another will be able to translate the now-decoded work into a coherent exposition. Beyond the aforementioned lexicons, the best way to gain the knowledge necessary to decode the symbols and understand the function of the sefirot is to read widely in the works of Kabbalists who, scholars believe, may have contributed to the Zohar, such as Moses de León and Joseph Gikatilla.

After the work is unveiled in this manner, I agree that it holds back little and amounts to an extensive project of recording kabbalistic secrets. That is, the Zohar does not make significant efforts to leave out sensitive ideas, as we have seen other kabbalistic works do. Rather, it speaks more expansively than most other kabbalistic works. This may explain why, as Boaz Huss (172) has noted, in the earliest centuries of the Zohar's circulation, it was not regarded as a text that needed to be deciphered by special means. On the contrary, as he points out, Isaac of Acre, in his famous journal entry on the Zohar, which he composed in the first part of the fourteenth century, commented on how accessible the Zohar's teachings were. Isaac recounts the question that he asked those who had Zoharic material in their possession: "From where did they get these wondrous secrets, which are received by oral transmission and which are not to be recorded, but are now found there, explicated for anyone who can read a book?" (in Zacuto 88).[65] Yet Isaac's assessment is patently false, as anyone who has attempted to teach the Zohar to students—even those with broad background in the rabbinic tradition—can testify. Students must be offered extensive introductions to kabbalistic theosophy and systematic decodings of symbolism if they are to make headway. The most that can be said is that for someone like Isaac, who, as a result of deep knowledge of Kabbalah, had the tools to decipher the text, this assessment would appear to be the case.

In the late fifteenth century, according to Huss (172–75), the Zohar began to acquire a reputation as an esoterically encoded work. Yet it is precisely at this time that the influence of the Zohar began to grow (114–47). It does not seem surprising that Kabbalists would begin to take greater note of the esoteric style of the text as it began to spread beyond limited conclaves of Kabbalists, who would find it easiest to understand.

Consider two examples of this assessment of the Zohar as an esoteric work. If, as we saw, Finzi was worried that the publication of the Zohar would make it readily available, a counterargument was that the Zohar's esoteric style of writing renders the text incomprehensible to all but an elite audience, such that publishing the work would not run the risk of exposing secrets to the unworthy. Accordingly, Moses Basola, in remarks printed at the beginning of the Mantua edition of *Tikkunei Zohar* (1557), notes that Mishna Ḥagigah 2:1 forbids teaching "the account of the chariot"—a body of wisdom that Kabbalists identified with Kabbalah—to one "who is not wise and understands on his own" (M. Ḥagigah 2:1). How, then, asks Basola, can the Zohar be published? "How can the Zohar be printed such that it will be available to every man? In fact, this question applies only to one who is not proficient in the Zohar and does not understand its paths. For in truth, when the Zohar speaks of the divine essence and of emanation, it uses mysterious language that only a sage who is 'wise and understands' and knows the path of Kabbalah can understand. Therefore, I say that the Zohar is good for everyone, because those of impoverished knowledge will learn from it the simple meaning of a few verses according to the path of truth" (*Tikkunei Zohar*, first page—unpaginated). From Basola's perspective, only those who are proficient in kabbalistic wisdom will understand the intentionally "mysterious language" that the Zohar adopts. The Zohar's obscure style, however, makes it impenetrable to the layman. Nevertheless, the Zohar will still benefit the layman, as he will learn simple interpretations of biblical verses. In a series of examples that follow, it emerges that these interpretations are novel but do not pertain to the essence of kabbalistic wisdom. When, however, this layman encounters passages that do contain essential kabbalistic wisdom, "the lame man will leap like a deer[66] [over these passages] because, in his eyes, they will be like words of a sealed book, and he will say, I cannot understand for the matters are concealed and sealed" (second page—unpaginated).[67]

In a related fashion, Ḥayyim Vital writes that Shimon bar Yoḥai (Rashbi), the purported author of the Zohar,

> had the ability to cloak (*lehalbish*) the matters and expound upon them in such a manner that even if he expounded upon them before many, only those suited to understand them would understand them. Therefore, permission was granted to him to write the book of the Zohar, while permission was not given to his teachers or to the earlier sages who preceded him to write a book regarding the wisdom of this Zohar. This is despite the fact that they certainly knew more regarding this wisdom than he. . . . In this manner you will understand the extent of the concealment (*godel he'elem*) of the book of the Zohar that Rashbi, of blessed memory, wrote, for not every intellect can comprehend it. (*Sha'ar ha-ma'amarim* 29)

Basola's comments could be dismissed as merely motivated by a desire to the see the work brought to print and not as his heartfelt assessment, and, as Huss (173–75) notes, Vital's emphasis on the concealed nature of the text can be seen as part of an attempt to legitimize the interpretation of his teacher, Isaac Luria, over the interpretation of Moshe Cordovero, who tended to view the Zohar as a more open text. I would not dismiss these possibilities, but it seems to be a situation in which the reality of the text happily coincided with their ulterior motivations. Again, the idea that not everyone can understand the Zohar due to its obscurity is patently true.

Allusive Writing

The techniques of esoteric writing surveyed so far are technical in nature and require specific strategies to decode. A less technical esoteric style is to write in terse, abbreviated, or hinted terms, leaving the reader to fill in the missing gaps. This practice, which I will refer to as "allusive writing," is well attested to by esoteric writers of all stripes (Melzer 306–7). It is certainly the most prevalent form of esoteric writing employed by Kabbalists.

In the case of Jewish tradition, a rabbinic precedent set the stage for later writers. M. Ḥagigah 2:1 severely limits teaching about the "chariot," a reference in the original context to Ezekiel's vision as recounted in Ezekiel 1,[68] but, later on, understood by Maimonides as a reference to philosophic metaphysics and by Kabbalists as a reference to kabbalistic theosophy. In the words of the Mishnah, "One may not expound upon the chariot before one person unless he is wise and understands on his own." According to the ensuing Talmudic discussion, R. Ḥiyya adds the following to this stipulation: "But one may transmit chapter headings (*ra'shei perakim*) to him" (B. Ḥagigah 13a). In its original context, "chapter headings" perhaps refers to "opening phrases from Scripture upon which the student was allowed to introduce his own exposition" (Gruenwald 116).[69] Moreover, these "chapter headings" were conveyed orally by the teacher to the student.

Maimonides, however, understood *ra'shei perakim* as terse allusions and indicated that, in deference to R. Ḥiyya's view, in his own discussions of metaphysics in the *Guide*, he would reveal esoteric ideas only in *ra'shei perakim* (Maimonides, *Guide* 6–7 intro.)—that is, as Strauss (*Leo Strauss on Maimonides* 357–59) has noted, he transferred a practice of oral esotericism into one of written esotericism. Many Kabbalists followed suit in describing their style as one of writing in *ra'shei perakim*.

Another precedent for the use of allusive writing is the Bible commentary of the twelfth-century Jewish Neoplatonist Abraham Ibn Ezra. In his commentary, after presenting a more straightforward interpretation of a verse at hand in reasonably clear language, he often offers an esoteric explanation in veiled language, which he frequently marks with variations of the phrase *ha-maskil yavin* ("the knowledgeable will understand").[70] Many Kabbalists take the same approach and use the same and related phrases, including *veha-mevin yavin* ("the understanding will understand"). It is possible that this last phrase is based on the aforementioned mishnaic warning that the "chariot" may be taught only to one who "is wise and understands (*u-mevin*) on his own." That is, Kabbalists who mark a passage with the phrase *ha-mevin yavin* may intend to imply that only one who fulfills the mishnaic stipulation will comprehend the cryptic language. Variations of *ha-mevin yavin*, such as *ve-haven zeh* ("understand this"), are also common.[71]

Kabbalists use allusive writing in a number of different contexts. Occasionally, we find it employed in the kabbalistic sections of works that are not entirely kabbalistic in nature but include kabbalistic content. While the non-kabbalistic components of such works are written in clear prose, the kabbalistic ideas are presented in cryptic shorthand. The preeminent example of a work that employs this practice is Nahmanides's Bible commentary, which is generally non-kabbalistic in nature but occasionally offers terse and enigmatic kabbalistic interpretations, at times marked by the expression *ha-maskil yavin*.

Another example is the commentary on Song of Songs by the late thirteenth-century Kabbalist Isaac Ibn Sahula, which contains both kabbalistic and non-kabbalistic explanations of the verses of the Canticle. As Arthur Green, its modern editor, notes regarding the kabbalistic portions: "Both in its content and in its brief and vague style, this commentary is reminiscent of the secret matters in Nahmanides's commentary on the Torah, a commentary that itself requires a commentary" ("Rabbi Isaac" 395). Green continues: "It is often truly difficult to understand the hints of Sahula, who has the habit of explaining one verse solely by means of citing other verses. From this combination of texts, the reader accustomed to secrets of the Torah was supposed to grasp the hint to the supernal world, while, at the same time, a reader who has no knowledge in these matters will not come to harm" (395). In one passage, Sahula intimates as much when he states, regarding Song 7:6, "I heard from the mouth of my teachers that in this verse is a wondrous secret and supernal concealment (*sod nifla' ve-seter 'elyon*), which cannot be contained in thought or ideas. Nevertheless, I will hint at its explanation, and I will proceed slowly with regard to it"[72] (474).[73]

More frequently, it is within entirely kabbalistic works that we find the practice of allusive writing. Here we may distinguish between works that are written completely in this style and the more common scenario of works written in a largely exoteric fashion that only occasionally resort to allusive writing.

An example in the former category is *Sefer ha-bahir*, which is rife with obscure phrases that serve more like signposts for the already initiated than expositions for the aspiring student.[74] A second example is a late thirteenth-century text transmitted in the name of an anonymous elder, published and analyzed by Elliot Wolfson. This text argues that it is necessary to write down kabbalistic ideas so as to prevent forgetfulness. Yet, as Wolfson ("Anonymous Chapters" 160) notes, according to the text, such writing can be only in the form of allusions. As the text puts it: "I saw fit to write it in a very concealed hint (*be-remez nistar me'od*) in a greatly concealed allusion out of fear of forgetfulness" (205).[75] Indeed, a perusal of the text reveals that it is written throughout in terse and cryptic terms. A final example in this category is the anonymous *Sefer ha-temunah*, a medieval work whose provenance is disputed.[76] Scholem notes: "It is obvious that the author chose an epigrammatic, often semipoetic, and in any case highly allusive style that conceals more than it reveals in matters of detail" (*Origins* 461).[77]

Works in the second category are extremely numerous. Indeed, this technique is employed even by Kabbalists who are typically regarded as exoteric writers. Since this might seem surprising, in the remainder of this section I will highlight significant examples of Kabbalists who generally composed exoteric works, which nevertheless include allusive writing. An early example is the thirteenth-century southern French Kabbalist Asher ben David. In his otherwise clearly written *Sefer ha-yiḥud*, he employs allusive writing in passages marked with the phrase *ha-maskil yavin*. Asher's work will be treated in detail in Chapter 6.

Another example is Abraham Abulafia, who, as we have seen, sought to popularize his brand of Kabbalah but nevertheless resorted to strategies of esoteric writing. In addition to his use of intentional contradictions (see above), he employed allusive writing. As Wolfson (*Abraham Abulafia* 82) puts it, Abulafia often reverts to an esoteric style of writing, "which embraces the concomitant divulgence and obfuscation," whereby only the worthy are able to fathom the meaning of the text.[78] For instance, amid a discussion of the material composition of the sublunar realm, Abulafia writes that "there is a matter here that we need to discuss following that which we have already discussed. But it is fitting to conceal it, so we will suffice with chapter headings" (*Ner elohim; get ha-shemot* 14, in *Get ha-shemot*). Similarly, elsewhere, speaking to the addressee of one of his works, Abulafia indicates that while he will provide a commentary on *Sefer Yetsirah*, "it is impossible to explain every matter in the book for fear of the eyes of flesh of the blind"—that is, for fear of revealing secrets to the unworthy who are blind to esoteric wisdom. "I will, therefore," he continues, "speak with you regarding this matter in a few chapter headings, and if you want to succeed, complete it on your own, and may God be with you" (*Gan na'ul* 10).[79]

Another exoterically minded Kabbalist who occasionally employs allusive writing is Menahem Recanati, who was active in Italy at the end of the thirteenth and the beginning of the fourteenth centuries.[80] Despite his generally clear prose, he resorts to allusive writing in rare instances. Thus, in his Torah commentary, after providing one explanation of Gen. 1:15, he adds: "Additionally, there is in it a wondrous secret (*sod mufla'*) that I am not permitted to record. You will understand it from the verse, 'In richly-colored robes, she is led to the king' (Ps. 45:15), which is said about the *shekhinah* (i.e., the lowest sefirah)" (1:42). Thus Gen. 1:15 has a secret explanation that Recanati believed he was forbidden from revealing. The knowledgeable reader must reconstruct the secret by attempting to figure out the esoteric idea hinted at in Ps. 45:15.[81] Similarly, in his comments on Lev. 15:19, after providing a kabbalistic explanation for various rules associated with a ritual bath, Recanati states: "But the reason for 40 *se'ah* (the measurement of the minimum amount of water that a ritual bath must contain), I am not permitted to record. The knowledgeable one will understand it from the verse 'And he was there with the Lord for forty days and forty nights' (Exod. 34:28). Each day he [Moses] learned a *se'ah* from the overflow that emerged from the supernal covenant (the sefirah *yesod*) whose measure is 40 *se'ah*, and the knowledgeable one will understand" (2:58). Recanati therefore believed that he could not openly reveal the kabbalistic explanation for the requirement that a ritual bath contain at least forty *se'ah* of water, so instead he hints at it in veiled terms.

Moses ben Jacob of Kiev (1449–c. 1520) also has exoteric tendencies. Indeed, in his *Shoshan sodot*, he at times requests God's forgiveness for revealing too much (102, 117), though it should be said that even in such instances, his expositions are hardly models of clarity. Despite this seeming desire to reveal kabbalistic secrets, he concludes a number of other expositions with variations of the phrase "I am not able to reveal more than this" (80, 110, 168).[82]

Other examples can be seen in the work of the highly influential sixteenth-century Safedian Kabbalist Moshe Cordovero. He is not generally known for adopting esoteric techniques[83] and is among the most verbose kabbalistic authors; but on various occasions, he employs allusive writing. For example, in a passage in *Pardes rimmonim*[84] dealing with an esoteric theory of evil useful in explaining a particular Zoharic passage, Cordovero writes: "Regarding these matters, abbreviated writing (*kitsur*) is proper out of consideration for God's glory" (*Sefer pardes* 34b, gate 7, chap. 4).[85] The details of this theory of evil have been well explicated by Leore Sachs Shmueli (esp. 131–36) and need not concern us here. I would, however, cite her provocative question, which seems to be on the mark: "Do we have here a hint to an esoteric message that does not fit well with his other statements regarding the subject of evil (in the fashion of Leo Strauss), and therefore, he included them without detailing their full meaning?" (135).

A second example can be found in Cordovero's *Sefer shi'ur komah*,[86] following a passage in which he describes the relationship between God and the world: "One who studies [the preceding words] should consider this matter in depth in his intellect [by examining it] to and fro,[87] and he will find that there is something concealed in these words of ours, and it is not fitting to reveal it, even orally. If he merits, he will understand the secret of God on his own. One who merits [the secret] should not let it leave his lips, for this is a matter that the heart should not reveal to the mouth" (*Sefer ha-zohar* 100). Here, again, Cordovero suggests that his remarks allude to a secret that only the worthy will comprehend.[88]

To conclude this section, I will turn to a few examples from eighteenth- and nineteenth-century Hasidic masters. Let me begin by noting that Lithuanian Kabbalists in the so-called mitnagdic (opposition) camp—those who opposed the new Hasidic movement—criticized Hasidism for its exoteric attitude toward Kabbalah and favored restricting the dissemination of kabbalistic material.[89] There is no question that this distinction between closed mitnagdic Kabbalah and open Hasidic Kabbalah is a real one: generally speaking, Hasidic masters did, indeed, assume a more exoteric attitude toward Kabbalah than their mitnagdic counterparts. Indeed, the extreme secrecy, as seen above, with which the Hasidic master Naḥman of Bratslav treated some of his ideas is rather exceptional. At the same time, there were certainly tensions among Hasidic thinkers about the relative merits of spreading kabbalistic teachings,[90] and for our purposes, accordingly, it is important to highlight that Hasidic masters, too, at times, made use of allusive writing.

Before proceeding, a word of caution is in order. Most Hasidic homiletical works do not contain the actual writings of the Hasidic masters to whom they are attributed. Rather, these masters originally presented their teachings on the Sabbath orally and in Yiddish, and they were subsequently translated into Hebrew from memory by a disciple. It is therefore possible that instances of allusive writing in many Hasidic works do not reflect the original oral presentation of the Hasidic master but were added by the disciples.[91] To the extent that this is true—a matter that is usually impossible to verify—it might be due to the fact that the medium of writing requires greater esotericism than an oral presentation because the written text may reach those outside the teacher's circle who are likely to misunderstand the written teaching. In any case, for the purposes of the present analysis, I have largely skirted this issue by choosing writings that were verifiably composed by the figures to whom they are attributed. The only exceptions among the figures whom I consider are Avraham Yehoshuʻa Heshel, who did not compose his own works, and Menachem Mendel Schneerson, from whom we have some materials composed in his own hand, as well as transcriptions and paraphrases.[92]

I begin with the remarks in *Toldot Ya'akov Yosef* of Jacob Joseph of Polnoye, the disciple of Israel Baal Shem Tov, regarding Exod. 6:3 ("And I appeared to Abraham, to Isaac and to Jacob as God ShDY, but My name YHVH I did not make known to them"): "Were I not afraid, [I would have] recorded in writing awesome matters that I heard from my teacher regarding the sweetening of the judgments [known as] 320 and 280 and the sweetening of passing thoughts by means of the [divine name] ShDY and its transposition KHHT as well as by the transposed version of the Tetragrammaton. But I wrote these matters in chapter headings on a separate sheet of paper. In this manner, this verse will also be explained. Understand! And may God grant atonement" (36a). Jacob Joseph indicates his reluctance to fully explicate a teaching of the Baal Shem Tov that would allow for the amelioration of divine judgments and the purification of inappropriate passing thoughts that might enter the mind. Yet he is not entirely silent. Instead, he hints at the teaching, which has been deciphered by Menachem Kallus (52–53nn282–84), in the most obscure of terms ("by means of the [divine name] ShDY and its transposition KHHT as well as by the transposed version of the Tetragrammaton"). Moreover, he indicates that he wrote an apparently fuller explanation on a separate piece of paper, which he presumably intended for private use. This paper has apparently not survived (53n286). Even the explanation on this separate paper was not written in clear terms but only in "chapter headings," such that it would likely be incomprehensible to an untrained reader. Notwithstanding his use of an esoteric style of writing, he feels a need to ask God for forgiveness for recording secretive matters. Whether the forgiveness he seeks is for the comments that he makes here or the ideas that he recorded on the private piece of paper, or both, is not made clear.

Similarly, the Hasidic master Abraham Kalisker (1741–1810), in keeping with his criticism of the founder of Ḥabad Hasidism Shneur Zalman of Lyady (1745–1813) for publicizing Kabbalah,[93] indicates in a letter regarding the mystical ascent of the *tsaddik* (Hasidic leader) that "I have greatly abbreviated matters like these, and 'It is the Glory of God to conceal a matter etc.' (Prov. 25:2)" (Barnay 223).[94]

Another example can be found in *Torat emet*, which contains the teachings of Avraham Yehoshu'a Heshel (ca. 1748–1825), who is known as the Apter Rebbe. There he concludes a terse kabbalistic explanation of a debate between the "House of Hillel" and the "House of Shammai" regarding the date of the new year of the trees (M. Rosh ha-Shanah 2:1) by stating: "The knowledgeable one will understand, for we have written with great brevity (*be-kitsur nimrats*), and we rely on one who is knowledgeable on his own" (*Torat emet* 146, *ḥodesh shevat*).[95]

We find a similar approach in his more well-known *Ohev Yisra'el*. After offering a brief and cryptic analysis of Exod. 33:23, a verse that recounts that God showed Moses his backside,[96] the Apter remarks: "More should not be spoken about this, and 'It is the Glory of God to conceal a matter' (Prov. 25:2). These matters are ancient, closed, and sealed, and one who is wise will understand on his own" (*Ohev Yisra'el* 171, *parashat tissa'*).[97]

Additional examples come from the works of Tsvi Elimelekh Shapira of Dinov (1783–1841).[98] Tsvi Elimelekh is notable for the emphasis that he placed on the importance of spreading kabbalistic wisdom. For example, in his *Ma'ayan ganim*, a commentary on Josef Jabez's (d. 1507) *Or ha-ḥayyim*, he argues that spreading kabbalistic teachings is a way of staving off corrupting forces of the Jewish enlightenment.[99] Referring to Jabez's contention that the esoteric aspects of Torah should not be studied until one has reached old age, Tsvi Elimelekh contends:[100]

> You will see in the writing of the Ari (Isaac Luria), of blessed memory, and of the Ramak (Moshe Cordovero) that all of this no longer applies in our generations, for hidden matters have become like revealed matters for those who desire God's closeness. I say, if only the great sages of our generation would not be lenient regarding [the imperative] to study the holy wisdom (i.e., Kabbalah), and if only they would teach their students the path to engaging in this wisdom, then there surely would be no honor[101] given to external wisdoms. And all wisdoms would be banished before it, like darkness is banished before light. (*Sefer ma'ayan ganim* 12)

Similar affirmations of the importance of spreading Kabbalah can be found throughout his works.[102] Nevertheless, on numerous occasions, Tsvi Elimelekh resorts to allusive writing, which he marks with familiar expressions. Examples include: "the knowledgeable will understand and be silent, and 'It is the Glory of God to conceal a matter etc.'" (Prov. 25:2) (*Agra' de-kallah* 1:384, *parashat va-yigash*; cf. 2:194, *parashat shelaḥ*); "'It is the Glory of God to conceal a matter etc.' (Prov. 25:2), and the good God will forgive us, and our mouths will not say anything against His will" (*Benei Yissakhar* 2:280, *kislev-tevet, ma'amar* 5; cf. 1:404 *tamuz-av, ma'amar* 4); "I will only hint in chapter headings that will be understood by those who are knowledgeable in wisdom" (*Agra' de-kallah* 2:200, *bere'shit—midrash rabbah*); "I will transmit to you in a whisper, 'the secret of the Lord is with them that fear Him'" (Ps. 25:15) (*Sefer ve-heyeh berakhah* 7). Thus, while, generally speaking, Tsvi Elimelekh regards Kabbalah as exoteric knowledge that should be disseminated, he nevertheless retains the notion that certain kabbalistic ideas are suitable only for an elite audience.

Let me turn briefly to a more recent Hasidic example, the messianic pronouncements of Menachem Mendel Schneerson (1902–94), the seventh and final Lubavitcher Rebbe. From one perspective, the Lubavitcher Rebbe was a consummate believer in the need to spread Kabbalah as a way of ushering in the messianic age, a time-honored reason for the revealing of kabbalistic secrets. Schneerson, accordingly, stresses that every Jew should study kabbalistic mysteries.[103] Yet in his masterful study of Schneerson's messianism, Elliot Wolfson, in effect, argues that the Rebbe was the ultimate allusive writer: "What has not been sufficiently appreciated, however, is the extent to which the language of messianism may have been a facet of Schneerson's esoteric dissimulation" (*Open Secret* 4). It is not possible in the current context to go into the details of Schneerson's esoteric view other than to state that instead of the traditional messianic position that he seems to espouse, which involves the reestablishment of the Davidic dynasty and the building of the third temple, he views real redemption as a matter of "being reintegrated into the infinite essence beyond all distinctions, including the distinction between being emancipated and not being emancipated" (293). In contrast to the previous examples that I have considered, Schneerson never indicates that he is an esoteric writer. Yet, as Wolfson notes: "One should never forget that Schneerson was heir to a long-standing esoteric tradition, according to which things are not always as they seem to be, nor do they always seems to be what they are" ("Open Secret in the Rearview" 402). In this tradition, I submit, it is appropriate to look for esoteric writing even when it is not announced.

The Difficulty of Deciphering Esoteric Writing

In the previous sections, I described the various styles of esoteric writing employed by Kabbalists, including letter substitution, ATBaSH, anagrams, acronyms, dispersion, intentional contradictions, Zoharic symbolism, and allusive writing. These various techniques present different levels of challenge to the reader who hopes to gain access to the secret ideas of a work. As we saw, in the case of what I suggested was an early version of Ibn Gaon's *Keter Shem Tov*, the text was apparently encoded in a way that would have made it quite difficult to decipher. The same is true of the acronyms in Rav Naḥman's *Scroll of Secrets*. In contrast, in the other examples that I cited in which ATBaSH or anagrams were used, the barriers to breaking the code were quite low. ATBaSH is a well-known technique already employed by the book of Jeremiah,[104] as an exceptionally popular and decidedly exoteric commentator like Rashi already noted.[105] Anyone with even a modicum of erudition would succeed in deciphering words encoded with ATBaSH. By the same token, unscrambling words of an anagram, especially when, as in the example discussed above, only a few of the words are encoded so that the context is apparent, does not present serious difficulties.

This situation is comparable to what Benedek Láng describes as the state of affairs in late medieval and early modern magical texts that use substitution ciphers:

> They all stay on a relatively simple level, not stepping beyond the usual monoalphabetic system, despite the fact that by this time, the turn of the fifteenth and the sixteenth centuries, homophonic systems complemented with nomenclatures were known. Furthermore, ciphers in magic manuscripts usually encrypt short fragments of texts. . . . Encrypting methods in these cases do not in the least seem to be used as means for hiding information. This is not only because these cipher alphabets are easy to break, but also because the accompanying text, which is left open, clearly reveals what the coded text is about. ("Ciphers in Magic" 135–36; *Ciphers and Secrets* 168–69)

From Láng's perspective, such texts do not constitute serious attempts to conceal material. Rather, he argues, "Their mysterious appearance worked more like a strategy of exposure, an advertisement by means of the rhetoric of secrecy" ("Ciphers in Magic" 136; *Ciphers and Secrets* 169).[106] That is, while he does not use the term, he effectively sees these texts as employing a form of "secretism," in that they are more concerned with capitalizing on the allure of secrecy than in actually keeping secrets.

I largely agree with this analysis, and it seems that, in the case of the kabbalistic analogues, a similar analysis applies. The very act of breaking a code—even if it is an extremely easy one—would likely provide readers with the sense that they are "in" on something special. The code, therefore, creates a sense of mystery without actually concealing anything. Nevertheless, a way remains in which even these fairly simple codes aid the goal of maintaining secrecy: they weed out careless readers. Such readers would be more interested in dabbling than in carefully studying the texts. After all, texts written in these styles cannot merely be skimmed but require effort and care. In other words, such texts may not test the substantial worthiness of their readers but may at least test their seriousness and commitment.

In contrast, the techniques of dispersion and intentional contradictions do seem like better tests of the worthiness of the reader. In the case of the former, the reader must have a substantial level of knowledge to determine, for example, whether a particular passage is a complete exposition of the subject or if the exposition fully emerges only when the original passage is combined with other passages. He must, in turn, determine which passages are the ones that best fit together. In the case of the latter, he must first realize that there is a contradiction and then determine which side of the contradiction is accurate or figure out how to resolve the contradiction. Similarly, when it comes to deciphering the esoteric style of the Zohar, it is not sufficient merely to decode the symbols. Even after the symbols are decoded, extensive knowledge of kabbalistic theosophy is required to make sense of the text. Finally, allusive writing also demands high levels of erudition from the reader. It is only with detailed knowledge of the entire kabbalistic system that a reader can hope to make sense of the obscure hints characteristic of such writing.

Conclusions

A number of conclusions and suggestions for further research emerge from the preceding analysis. First, the acts of leaving certain kabbalistic ideas out of writing or presenting them only through various styles of esoteric writing are ubiquitous in kabbalistic history. These phenomena, as I have shown, are reflected in the works of Kabbalists of all types—such as those associated with theosophic, ecstatic, and Hasidic forms of Kabbalah—and from all locales. While it is certainly not the case of every kabbalistic work, my analysis makes clear that even some Kabbalists who generally preach the need to spread kabbalistic ideas widely still hold on to the notion that certain ideas are not intended for public consumption. From the perspective of its growing influence in the public square, it is true that, over time, Kabbalah became an increasingly exoteric doctrine (Idel, *Kabbalah: New Perspectives* 253–60; "From R. Isaac"; Gondos). This should not be taken to imply that Kabbalists abandoned the sense that certain ideas should remain out of public circulation. Certainly, for example, in the contemporary state of Israel, there has been a striking push to publicly disseminate Kabbalah under the continuing influence of figures like Yehuda Leib Ha-Levi Ashlag (1884–1954), a Polish rabbi who immigrated to Palestine in 1921 and became a leading popularizer of Kabbalah. Not surprisingly, the popularizing tendencies of Ashlag and his followers have been met with opposition from other Kabbalists who have argued for reinstating a more esoteric stance.[107]

Second, the manifold examples that I have provided deal with real secrets and do not merely reflect what might be called a rhetoric of secrecy. To repeat the point that I made in Chapter 1, there is no doubt that various kabbalistic works employ a rhetoric of secrecy but do not actually conceal any information. This reality should not obscure the fact that in the examples that I have provided in this chapter, as well as in countless others, real secrets are concealed.

Third, Kabbalists did not treat all kabbalistic ideas with the same level of secrecy. Throughout the history of Kabbalah, Kabbalists distinguished between kabbalistic ideas that were suitable for public consumption and those that were not. Indeed, I would argue that we must distinguish between exoteric and esoteric Kabbalah. In the study of medieval Jewish philosophy—particularly when it comes to the work of Maimonides—scholars routinely distinguish between esoteric and exoteric ideas. Yet similar analysis has been largely lacking in the case of Kabbalah.

Fourth, trying to uncover the esoteric views of Kabbalists will enhance our understanding of kabbalistic thought and history. This is demonstrated by a number of important studies, such as Haviva Pedaya's work on the circle of Isaac the Blind (*Name*), Moshe Idel's work on David ben Judah he-Ḥasid ("R. David"), and others,[108] which have attempted to "read between the lines" of kabbalistic texts to uncover their hidden ideas. More frequently, esoteric asides, marked by expressions such as "the knowledgeable will understand" and other esoteric strategies of writing, are ignored in scholarly literature. Yet it is possible that precisely the ideas that Kabbalists conceal are the ones that they consider most important. At the very least, there is no reason to believe that the esoteric ideas are any less important than the exoteric ones. I am in full agreement with Idel's contention, which I partially cited in the Introduction, that there is a "need to distinguish carefully between what was understood as Kabbalah according to Kabbalistic masters, who revealed it only fragmentarily, and what contemporary scholars, who assumed that the discipline was disclosed in written documents believed to be Kabbalah. It is reasonable to suppose that those Kabbalistic matters that were kept secret even from younger Kabbalists concerned sensitive pivotal subjects. Hence, if we do not attempt to uncover the hidden problems of the Kabbalists and to decode them, our view of Kabbalah may be, at least to a certain extent, misleading" (*Kabbalah: New Perspectives* 21–22). While Idel's remarks pertain to oral traditions that were left out of writing, they can also apply to kabbalistic ideas that are concealed through various means of esoteric writing. The attempt to uncover the ideas concealed by a Kabbalist must involve extremely close readings of kabbalistic texts that are sensitive to the various strategies of esoteric writing that I outlined above. It must also involve comparisons between the various writings of the Kabbalist in question, since he may be more open in one text than another, or between various Kabbalists of a single circle insofar as one member of the circle may be more open than others, or between earlier and later Kabbalists who are part of a single tradition because the latter may be more open than the former.

Fifth, scholars should examine what motivated various Kabbalists to keep particular ideas secret. Such examination will shed light on the range of factors that helped shape the literary decisions that Kabbalists made in their texts. Such factors might include, to name a few, halakhic considerations, a desire to avoid persecution for heterodox ideas, or a fear that certain ideas are detrimental to the public good. Since such factors are often historically determined, what one Kabbalist may have treated as esoteric may have been viewed as exoteric by another. Again, in the field of medieval Jewish philosophy, the study of such factors is commonplace, but they have been examined only to a limited extent by scholars of Kabbalah.

Sixth, once we have acknowledged a distinction between exoteric and esoteric Kabbalah, we must consider the relationship between them. Are the esoteric ideas merely a more developed and nuanced version of the public ones? Are the esoteric ideas not intrinsically related to exoteric ones?

That is, do they simply concern different topics? Alternatively, do they concern the same topics but offer opposed perspectives such that the secret and public positions stand in contradiction to each other? We have seen some evidence that Kabbalists use the technique of intentional contradictions to conceal their ideas, but it is also possible that, even when this technique is not formally used, the public doctrine of a particular Kabbalist may be diametrically opposed to his private views. In such situations, the examination of the exoteric meaning of a text may distort our understanding of what a given Kabbalist actually believed.

Finally, we must wonder if there are times when even Kabbalists who do not announce that they are employing techniques of esoteric writing may nevertheless do so. In such cases, the very fact that the work contains secrets is concealed. Only a sharp reader who knows how to spot the clues that the author left "between the lines" will fathom the esoteric dimensions of the text. Needless to say, to prove that a seemingly exoteric text has esoteric dimensions is a difficult task, and the interpreter runs the risk of imputing secret ideas to a text in which no such ideas are present. This is a problem that has bedeviled the Straussian enterprise of uncovering the esoteric ideas in philosophical texts and has, to my mind, rightly threatened to undermine some of Strauss's contributions. At the same time, the fact that so many Kabbalists unambiguously announce that they are employing esoteric strategies of writing must at least make us open to the possibility that some kabbalistic texts that lack such announcements may nevertheless engage is esoteric writing, too.

Chapter 3

Abraham ben David as an Esoteric Writer

Many esoteric writers announce that they will employ techniques of esoteric writing in their works. Arguably, however, some writers write esoterically without proclaiming that this is their practice. In this chapter, I will contend that Abraham b. David (Rabad) is a case in point. Any attempt to decode an esoteric text runs the risk of what George Sabine, in a critique of Strauss, referred to as "perverse ingenuity" (220). Hints and clues that the interpreter finds to the secret doctrine of the text might merely be the result of imprecise or careless language. As a more recent critique of Strauss puts it: "Strauss's esoteric interpretations require a writer to be totally careful in every way" (Blau 146). These difficulties are only compounded when dealing with texts that do not claim to be composed esoterically.

Rarely is there the equivalent of a smoking gun, such as when, in a text intended for an elite audience, an author makes one claim, while in a text intended for a wide audience, he makes an opposite claim and there is no reason to believe that his views have shifted over time. Typically, there is no set of objective criteria that can be applied to definitively prove that a particular passage contains an encoded message. More modestly, I would contend that it is possible to prove that it is plausible that the passage contains an esoteric message. This can be done by showing that, given the historical and cultural context of the work and knowledge of the writer's other works and those of members of his circle, it is plausible that certain words or phrases contain hints to this message. Once an esoteric interpretation of a given passage meets the bar of plausibility, the most that an interpreter can hope for is that his particular interpretation will be deemed more convincing by readers than whatever other plausible alternatives may exist. In short, trying to show that a text adopts an esoteric style and trying to decode its esoteric meaning require a hermeneutic of modesty that is aware that the interpretation is not definitive.

Accordingly, in my interpretation of Rabad's work, I aim to show that it is plausible (and, I hope, convincing) that he concealed certain esoteric ideas in his public works.

Esoteric Ideas in Exoteric Works

Rabad was, by far, more prolific than the figures whom I treat in the subsequent chapters—Isaac the Blind, Ezra ben Solomon of Gerona, and Asher ben David. Rabad's works, however, are not theosophical tracts but standard rabbinic writings, which include novellae, topical halakhic works, and commentaries on classical rabbinic texts.[1] He is, accordingly, regarded as "one of the most creative Talmudic scholars" of twelfth-century southern France (Twersky, *Rabad* 2). In fact, he did not leave a single kabbalistic monograph. Yet there is no doubt that Rabad possessed kabbalistic knowledge.[2]

Rabad was the father of Isaac the Blind, the teacher of a number of the first Kabbalists, whose view on esotericism is the subject of Chapter 4. In a famous letter that Isaac wrote to Nahmanides and Jonah Gerondi, which I will discuss more fully in Chapter 4, he indicates regarding his "fathers"—presumably, a reference to Rabad and to Isaac's grandfather and Rabad's father-in law, Abraham ben Isaac of Narbonne, who also seems to have been in possession of esoteric ideas (Scholem, *Origins* 199–205)—that "never did a word [regarding kabbalistic secrets] escape their lips" (T. Weiss, "Letter" 332).[3] This statement both affirms that Rabad was familiar with kabbalistic ideas and that he chose to keep them secret.

Consistent with Isaac's characterization of his father, our knowledge of Rabad's kabbalistic teachings is limited. Our main sources of information about his kabbalistic ideas are fairly brief passages that appear in his name in the works of later Kabbalists or in kabbalistic miscellanies.[4] I will discuss these types of passages below.

In Rabad's own writings, he unambiguously refers to his secret knowledge in only one passage: a lone gloss in his collection of glosses on Maimonides's *Mishneh torah*, which I will also discuss below. Moreover, the gloss does not even rise to the level of allusive writing, since its language reveals nothing of the secret, even in hinted terms. In passages where, I will suggest, he does engage in allusive writing, he also invokes secrecy; but as we will see, he does so ambiguously in a manner that would not lead an unsuspecting reader to look for hidden content.

A statement by the turn-of-the-fourteenth-century Kabbalist Shem Tov ben Abraham Ibn Gaon, whom we already encountered as an esoteric writer in his own right, claims that Rabad occasionally included kabbalistic ideas in his *Commentary on the Talmud*. As he puts it, Rabad "hinted occasionally (*ramaz miktsat*) wherever he deemed it necessary but no more" ("Sefer badei" 19).[5] Since most of the *Commentary* is not extant, we are forced to rely on rather limited textual evidence to assess what Ibn Gaon meant by this claim.

Nowhere in the extant portions of the *Commentary* do we find passages that are obviously kabbalistic or that explicitly refer to secret explanations. While this does not preclude the possibility that such passages existed in nonextant portions, I find it unlikely. If there were such passages, we would expect to find discussions of them in the works of later Kabbalists. Yet we find no such thing.[6]

It is more plausible that Ibn Gaon had in mind a type of passage that we learn of from a text that is appended to *Sefer ha-yiḥud*, a work by Asher ben David, Rabad's grandson. This appended text is apparently also by Asher.[7] In it, Asher cites two passages in the name of Rabad. The sources of these passages, Asher makes clear, are Rabad's now-lost commentaries on tractate Berakhot and tractate Taʻanit, respectively. As he puts it: "In tractate Berakhot: the words of the great Rabbi, Abraham b. David, my grandfather" (141),[8] and as he says of the other, "In tractate Taʻanit: the words of the aforementioned Rabbi, may his name last for eternity" (141). Each of these passages, which I will discuss below, deals with the angel Metatron. It is likely that Ibn Gaon would have viewed these passages as kabbalistic, since the angel Metatron became the subject of intense interest in Kabbalah. Yet Metatron was already the subject of speculation in much older written works, including the Talmud,[9] and Rabad's comments do not overtly add a specifically kabbalistic flavor to the discussion of the angel Metatron based on specific oral traditions that fed nascent Kabbalah. Here it will be recalled that Kabbalah, as it emerged in writing in the thirteenth century, was an amalgam of earlier literature and received oral traditions that are particular to Kabbalists. Accordingly, it may be the case that Rabad was willing to write explicitly in his *Commentary* about themes that already figure in earlier literature but not about particularly kabbalistic themes.

Yet, if it is unlikely that Rabad included overtly kabbalistic passages in his *Commentary*, I will argue that, in both this work and his other rabbinic texts, he did write in what I would term a "concealed" allusive style, whereby he presented secrets in a hinted fashion without unambiguously indicating to the reader that he was doing so. Only the knowledgeable reader would perceive that there even is a secret. It is not impossible that Ibn Gaon also had such passages in mind. In fact, as I will show below, the passages about Metatron might themselves be examples. That is, while the passages ostensibly talk about Metatron in a conventional matter, they may allude to a particularly kabbalistic understanding of this angel.

In the remainder of this chapter, I will examine these and other examples of what I will argue is Rabad's concealed allusive writing. One goal will be to assess the relationship between the hidden ideas and the public ones. As we will see, in some cases the esoteric idea merely deepens the exoteric idea by providing an extra layer of meaning. In at least one case, the esoteric idea apparently contradicts the exoteric one. A second goal will be to analyze the rhetorical strategies that Rabad employed to conceal esoteric ideas. That is, I will analyze his craft as an esoteric writer.

"And the Face and the Back Is a Great Secret"

The only time Rabad unambiguously claims to possess esoteric knowledge is in one of his glosses on *Mishneh torah*, Maimonides's code of Jewish law. Despite the legal nature of the code, its opening chapters deal with matters of religious philosophy, and Rabad's gloss is on a passage from this section of the work. In the passage, Maimonides discusses Moses's request that God show him His glory, as is recounted in Exodus 33:

> What did Moses, our teacher, want to apprehend when he said, "Show me, I pray, Your Glory" (Exod. 33:18)? He wanted to know the truth of the existence of the Holy One, blessed be He, such that it would be known in his heart in the same manner that one knows a particular person whose face he saw and whose likeness was engraved inside him such that the person is distinct in his thought

from all other people. Similarly, Moses, our teacher, wanted the existence of God to be distinct in his heart from all other existences, such that he would know the truth of His existence, as it is. And He, blessed be He, answered him that the intellect of a living human being, who is a combination of a body and a soul, lacks the ability to apprehend this matter with complete clarity. And God informed him of what no man knew before him nor will know after him, such that he apprehended enough of the subject of the truth of His existence such that the Holy One, blessed be He, was distinct in his thought from all other existences, just as a person whose back he saw and whose entire body and clothing he apprehended is differentiated in his thought from the bodies of all other people. Scripture hinted at this matter, saying, "You shall see My back, but My face shall not be seen" (Exod. 33:23). (*Mishneh torah, hilkhot yesodei ha-torah* 1:10)

In Maimonides's reading, when Moses, according to Exod. 33:18, asks to see God's glory, he is seeking knowledge of God's essence. God responds that such knowledge, which Maimonides compares to the type of knowledge that would make it possible to distinguish one person from another on the basis of that person's facial features, is impossible. Instead, the only kind of knowledge that is available to Moses is one that may be compared to knowledge, whereby it is possible to distinguish one person from another on the basis of the form of that person's back. According to Maimonides, it is this analogy of the back and the face that God refers to when He tells Moses, in Exod. 33:23, "You shall see My back, but My face shall not be seen." In short, therefore, "front" and "back" cannot be taken as distinct aspects of God. Given Maimonides's well-known commitment to divine simplicity, such a position would be impossible. Rather, God's "front" and "back" refer to different states— one impossible and one possible—of human apprehension of God.

Maimonides himself is arguably engaged in a form of esoteric writing here insofar as he gives a much fuller and more sophisticated account of this episode in the *Guide of the Perplexed*;[10] but for our purposes, it needs to be underscored that he reads the episode described in Exod. 33:23 and the surrounding verses as a story about Moses's desire to receive metaphysical knowledge of God.

In contrast, Rabad, in his gloss, reads it as an account of Moses's desire to receive assurance that God will accompany the Israelites in the desert despite the sin of the Golden Calf that is recounted in the previous chapter of Exodus. Moses is not looking for intellectual knowledge but for moral support:

> Abraham [ben David] said: I am not satisfied with this. After all, Moses saw at Sinai during the forty days [of preparation] for the tablets [to be given] what no prophet had ever seen—so much so, that the angels became jealous of him and wanted to push him out, until he grasped onto the throne [of glory]. What need would he have for more [knowledge]? Further, if this had been his request, why did He have to say in response, "I will be gracious to whom I will be gracious" (Exod. 33:19). Therefore, it seems to me that since the Holy One, blessed be He, said to him, "I will not go up in your midst," etc. (Exod. 33:3), and Moses asked that He return [to their midst], and he said to Him, "Let me know, I pray, Your ways" (Exod. 33:13), and He said to him, "My face shall go with you (Exod. 33:14), and Moses said, "If your face does not go [do not raise us up from this]" (Exod. 33:15), [Moses intended to say in this conversation], "do not say that when we enter the land, then You will go with us, for we will not move from here until You go with us." And the Holy One, blessed be He, said to him, "I will also do this thing" (Exod. 33:17). And he [Moses] said, "Show me [I pray] Your glory" (Exod. 33:18), that is to say, "I want to see." "And He said, I will make My goodness pass before your face," etc. (Exod. 33:19), and I will let you know when I pass before you. And among the nation who angered Me, there will be those to whom I will be gracious, but not to everyone. And the face and the back is a great secret (*sod gadol*), and it is inappropriate to reveal it to any man, and perhaps the one who made these comments (= Maimonides) did not know it. (printed in *Kesef mishneh*, ad loc)[11]

Partially basing himself on a midrashic source,[12] Rabad, in this complicated gloss, affirms that Moses already knew all he needed to know about God, such that, when he asks to see God's glory, his request must relate to something other than knowledge of God. Moreover, if his request was indeed for metaphysical knowledge, God's response that "I will be gracious to whom I will be gracious" seems out of place. To reach a proper interpretation of "show me, I pray, Your glory" (Exod. 33:18), Rabad begins earlier in chapter 33, with the third verse, in which God tells Moses, "I will not go up in your midst," etc. Rather, as God states, "I will send an angel before you" (Exod. 33:2). According to Rabad, when, subsequently, in verse 13, Moses asks God to "Let me know, I pray, Your ways" (Exod. 33:13), he is trying persuade God to indeed go in the midst of Israel instead of an angel, a proposition that God accepts when He affirms in verse 17, "I will also do this thing." When Moses, then, requests that God show him His glory, he is merely asking, in Rabad's reading, that God make it plain that He will be with the Israelites in the desert. This is indeed what God promises that He will do when He makes His "goodness" pass before Moses—that is, His goodness passing before Moses will serve as a sign that God will accompany the Israelites.

The whole tenor, then, of Rabad's interpretation of this episode is to suggest that Moses was not interested in knowledge of God's nature but in an assurance of God's continued presence. In fact, Rabad's gloss can profitably be read not only as a critique of Maimonides's specific exegesis of Exodus 33 but, in a manner that recalls the sentiments of Judah ha-Levi in *Kuzari*, also as a broader criticism of the philosophical notion that acquiring knowledge of God is the highest human endeavor.[13] Instead of placing value on knowledge of God's nature, Exodus 33, in Rabad's reading, teaches about God's involvement in history, the theme that ha-Levi valorizes as well. It is true that at the beginning of the gloss, Rabad does give credence to Moses's great knowledge. Yet in the context of the gloss as a whole, Rabad's opening remarks seem rather perfunctory, as if to say, "Of course, Moses has great knowledge of God, but that should not be the center of our focus."

I would argue that the esoteric comment at the end of Rabad's gloss shows that the preceding account does not do justice to his full understanding of the episode. That is, the esoteric comment is not simply an afterthought but recasts the way in which the episode should be understood. In what follows, I will attempt both to uncover the contents of Rabad's secret and to determine how the secret relates to the rest of his exposition.

It seems that the aforementioned passage from Rabad's *Commentary on Tractate Berakhot* that was recorded by his grandson, Asher ben David, sheds light on this secret. It concerns the striking rabbinic tradition that God Himself dons tefillin:

> In tractate Berakhot: the words of the great Rabbi, Abraham b. David, my grandfather: "From where do we know that the Holy One, blessed be He, dons tefillin" (B. Berakhot 6a)? This refers to

the minister of the countenance (*sar ha-panim*) whose name is like that of his Master (= Metatron).[14] . . . And he is the one who was revealed to Moses at the burning bush and to Ezekiel "in the image of a man upon it above" (Ezek. 1:26). But the Cause of Causes (*'illat ha-'illot*) has no left and has no right (*lo' be-yamin ve-lo' bi-sm'ol*), has no front and has no back (*lo' be-fanim ve-lo' be-aḥor*). And this is the secret mentioned in *The Account of the Creation*: "Anyone who knows the measurements of the Former of Creation (*yotser bere'shit*) is promised that he will be a member of the world to come. This is [the meaning] of what is written: "Let us make man in our image" (Gen. 1:26). (141)

Adam Afterman (455–56) has noted, in passing, that Rabad's gloss, regarding the secret meaning of God's face and back, and this passage are related. Expanding on his analysis, let me point to two factors that connect these passages. First, according to a Talmudic tradition (B. Berakhot 7a; B. Menaḥot 35b), God's back, which He reveals to Moses, is a reference to the knot on God's tefillin. It is true that this tradition is not directly connected to the Talmudic tradition that God wears tefillin, which is the subject of the present passage. The two traditions, however, appear in tractate Berakhot on adjacent folio pages, and the relationship between them is obvious. Moreover, they are explicitly connected in two sources, which Afterman (454–55) also cites: in *Sefer ha-eshkol*, by Abraham ben Isaac of Narbonne (223), Rabad's father-in-law and a figure whom Rabad cites frequently;[15] and in a passage by Ḥananel ben Ḥushiel, cited by Judah Barzillai in his *Commentary on Sefer Yetsirah* (42–43), a work that Rabad knew.[16] Second, Rabad's particular language in the passage cited by Asher—the Cause of Causes (*'illat ha-'illot*) has no left and has no right (*lo' be-yamin ve-lo' bi-smo'l*), has no front (*panim*; "face") and has no back (*aḥor*)—is apparently borrowed from Maimonides's *Mishneh torah*, where it appears in the very next passage after the one that is the subject of Rabad's gloss. According to Maimonides, God has "no composition and no separation, no place and no measure, no ascent and no descent, no left and no right (*ve-lo' yemin ve-lo' semo'l*), no front (*panim*) and no back (*aḥor*), and no sitting and no standing" (*Hilkhot yesodei ha-torah*, 1:11). As far as I know, this phraseology was coined by Maimonides, and Rabad seems to have borrowed it from him. It seems that Maimonides, in stating that God has "no front and no back," is deliberately referring to Exod. 33:23, "You shall see My back, but My face (*u-fanay*;

"front") shall not be seen," about which he had just written. By the same token, I would suggest that Rabad, in his *Commentary on Tractate Berakhot*, also intends to allude to Exod. 33:23, and perhaps to Maimonides's exposition of it.[17] Even if he did not intentionally mean to direct the reader to Maimonides's exposition, at the very least, the linguistic connection suggests that it was on his mind when he wrote this passage.

What light, then, does the passage cited by Asher from the *Commentary* shed on the gloss? The simple meaning of the passage is straightforward enough: it is not the "Cause of Causes," God Himself, who wears tefillin. Rather, it is "the minister of the countenance (*sar ha-panim*) whose name is like that of his Master." This is a reference to the angel Metatron.[18] Similarly, Moses's vision at the burning bush and Ezekiel's chariot vision were, in fact, of this angel. By the same token, "the measure of the 'Former of Creation'" described in the *Shiʿur komah* tract—a pseudoepigraphic text attributed to second-century rabbinic sages, which ostensibly provides the measurements of the divine body—and the anthropomorphic figure in whose image human beings were created, according to Gen. 1:26, in fact refer to this angel.[19] Thus if we read the gloss in light of this passage, we can assume that the back of God—the knot of the tefillin—refers to Metatron.

The preceding analysis does not directly explain the "secret" of God's face, but we may presume that if the "back" refers to the angel Metatron, then God's face refers to God Himself. Moses, therefore, was able to see the angel but not God Himself. If so, we can readily speculate about why Rabad would have desired to keep this idea secret. It seems to fundamentally alter the meaning of the biblical text as he explained it in the exoteric portion of the gloss. Indeed, it apparently contradicts it. According to the exoteric portion, Moses, when he requests to see God's glory, is seeking a sign that God and not an angel will accompany the Israelites. Yet according to the esoteric portion, he never receives it. On the contrary, all he is permitted to see is an angel, even if it is the greatest angel, Metatron. On this reading, then, the secret does not involve a concealed doctrine but a particular instance of an otherwise revealed one. That is, the idea that various prophetic visions of God are, in fact, of Metatron is one that Rabad presents openly in his *Commentary*. He conceals in the gloss, however, the fact that Moses's particular vision of the back of "God" is an example of such a vision. At the same time, it must be stressed that in identifying God's "back" as an angel, Rabad, like Maimonides—albeit through different means—avoids the challenge to perfect divine unity that would arise if it were assumed that God's back refers to a distinct aspect of God.

This is certainly a possible reading, but one wonders whether it constitutes a "great secret," especially given that the other examples of esoteric writing in Rabad's work, which I will detail below, involve theosophic doctrines. I would like to raise the possibility, therefore, that the passage from the *Commentary* should itself be regarded as an example of esoteric writing that conceals a deeper secret.[20] In particular, perhaps the angel Metatron should be identified with the tenth sefirah[21]—that is, as an aspect of God rather than merely an angel. This identification is one that has a precedent in Ashkenazic sources[22] and is found in early kabbalistic sources.[23] It may, however, have been rejected by Rabad's son, Isaac, a point I will return to below. If this identification is accurate, the secret meaning of the back of God, referred to in the gloss, would also be the tenth sefirah.

In support of this identification, we may point to the aforementioned passage from Rabad's *Commentary on Tractate Ta'anit*, which, like *Commentary on Tractate Berakhot*, is no longer extant. Asher cites this passage immediately after he cited the passage from *Commentary on Tractate Berakhot*, presumably because he saw them as related:

> In tractate Ta'anit: the words of the aforementioned Rabbi, may his name last for eternity: Regarding that which R. Yoḥanan said, 'Three keys were not put into the hands of a messenger' (B. Ta'anit 2a):[24] This shows that three things were not given to the hands of a messenger. He is the minister of the world (*sar ha-'olam* = Metatron), who appeared to the prophets and who ruled over the first chariot (*moshel ba-merkavah ha-ri'shonah*), and the power of the highest one is in him (*ve-khoaḥ ha-'elyon bo*). And he said, 'Let us make man in our image after our likeness'" (Gen. 1:26). (A. ben David 141)

Like the name "Minister of the Countenance" employed in the previous passage, the name "Minister of the World" refers to the angel Metatron.[25] As in the previous passage, the "Minister of the World" appears to prophets and is referred to in the verse "Let us make man in our image" (Gen. 1:26). The "first chariot" is probably a reference Ezekiel's chariot vision as recorded in Ezekiel 1 and is meant to distinguish it from Ezekiel's second chariot vision, as recounted in Ezekiel 10. In other words, the human-like figure of

Ezekiel's vision in Ezekiel 1 was Metatron. Rabad's statement—regarding the "Minister of the World," or Metatron—that "the power of the highest one is in him (*ve-khoaḥ ha-ʿelyon bo*)," is suggestive.[26] It may just be an echoing of the rabbinic statement, quoted by Rabad in the first passage from the *Commentary*, that Metatron's "name is like that of his Master." In this case, *ve-khoaḥ ha-ʿelyon* ("the power of the highest one") is a generic reference to God. Yet it seems stronger than the rabbinic statement because it suggests a metaphysical relationship between Metatron and the "highest one." Moreover, *ve-khoaḥ ha-ʿelyon* might not be a generic reference to God but may refer to the highest sefirah. Indeed, perhaps it should not be translated as the "the power of the highest one" but as "the highest power"—a designation appropriate to the highest sefirah. If so, it may imply that Metatron partakes of the "highest power" insofar as he is an emanation of that power, rather than an angel outside of divinity. This reading is in keeping with my proposed identification of Metatron and the tenth sefirah, since the tenth sefirah is viewed in kabbalistic sources as an aspect of divinity that emanates from the powers above it.[27]

Further evidence for this identification comes from a letter by Samuel ben Mordekhai[28] to a certain Yekutiel ha-Kohen,[29] which was apparently written in southern France in the first half of the-thirteenth century (Roth 83; Porat, *Who* 254). In the letter, Samuel writes of Abraham ben David and the Nazir (apparently, Jacob the Nazarite)[30] that "regarding the tenth sefirah they received that it is that which our Rabbis in one place referred to as 'Minister of the Countenance' and in another place as 'Minister of the World,' and he appeared to the prophets" (Scholem, "Traces" 60). Thus Samuel states explicitly that Rabad identified the "Minister of the Countenance" and "Minister of the World"—the names used to refer to Metatron in Rabad's remarks cited by Asher—as the tenth sefirah. Scholem partially published this letter in an article, "Traces of Gabirol on the Kabbalah," where he notes, in comments that he added to his earlier article after its original publication that were subsequently included in the republished version, that the words "and he appeared to the prophets" are taken from Rabad (65). Scholem does not mention which text of Rabad he had in mind, but I assume that he means the text just cited from Rabad's *Commentary on Tractate Taʿanit*, which, it will be recalled, reads: "He is the minister of the world (*sar ha-ʿolam* = Metatron), who appeared to the prophets." In other words, Samuel ben Mordekhai's comments should be seen as a gloss of this text. At the same time, the extent and accuracy of his kabbalistic knowledge are unclear.[31] His claim that Rabad identified Metatron and the tenth sefirah should not, therefore, be taken as definitive.

Moreover, the likelihood that this identification is correct needs to be weighed against the possibility that, as already alluded to, Isaac, Rabad's son, rejected the identification of Metatron with that sefirah. In one manuscript version of *Commentary on the Talmudic Aggadot*, by Isaac's student Ezra of Gerona, there is a passage, introduced by the remark "I have received from the son of the Rabbi," which refers to Metatron as a name for a class of angelic messengers (MS Vat. 294 48b).[32] If Metatron does not even refer to a specific entity, he certainly cannot be identified with the tenth sefirah. This is a challenge to the claim that Rabad identified Metatron with the tenth sefirah, for to uphold this identification for Rabad, we would need to assume that his son broke with him on this matter, or—although there is admittedly no evidence to support this possibility—that Isaac's position on Metatron, as recorded in the *Commentary on the Talmudic Aggadot*, reflects only his public position. At the same time, it is hard to be sure about the accuracy of this tradition, since it is not found in the other extant versions of the *Commentary on the Talmudic Aggadot*.[33] Moreover, it is not even certain that "the son of the Rabbi" is a reference to Isaac, since Ezra never uses this designation for Isaac elsewhere in his writings.[34] Finally, Ezra himself does identify Metatron and the tenth sefirah.[35]

In any case, this type of dilemma—competing sets of evidence pointing to different conclusions—is a common one faced by those who try to decode esoteric texts. There is often no objective standard to decide what is correct, and the interpreter must ultimately make a subjective decision. In this particular case, it seems that Rabad's indirect but suggestive comments that seem to point to the identification of Metatron and the tenth sefirah carry more weight than a questionable secondhand comment attributed to Rabad's son, Isaac, especially when Isaac's student Ezra accepts the identification.

With this proviso in mind, let me point to the ramification of Rabad's possible identification of Metatron and the tenth sefirah for interpreting his "secret" in his gloss on the passage in Maimonides's code: it emerges that God's "back" does not refer to Metatron qua angel but to Metatron qua sefirah. This identification does not directly tell us how Rabad might have understood the esoteric meaning of God's "face." It stands to reason, though, that if the "back" is the tenth sefirah, then the "face" is one of the higher sefirot—most likely, the sixth sefirah, since the sefirotic dyad of the tenth and sixth sefirot is exceptionally common in kabbalistic thought. Based on this interpretation of the secret of the face and back, Moses is not granted a vision of the sixth sefirah (God's "face") but only of the tenth sefirah (God's "back").

This understanding of the "secret" of the face and the back exposes a crucial theological disagreement with Maimonides. It will be recalled that Maimonides's reading of God's "front" and "back" as different states of human apprehension of God allows him to deny that God has multiple aspects. The explanation of "back" as the angel Metatron, with no sefirotic significance, does not challenge this point. In contrast, the explanation that God's front and back refer to distinct sefirot directly challenges Maimonides by positing that the biblical narrative describes multiple aspects of God.

As will become clear throughout the remaining chapters of this book, one of the key secrets that some of the early Kabbalists tried to conceal was the idea that God was constituted by a multiplicity of sefirot, and especially the idea that the sefirot unite sexually. In this particular instance, there is no hint at the notion of the sexual union between the sefirot. In other passages in Rabad's work, however, as will be seen below, the specifically sexual nature of the union is alluded to. In all, Rabad's secret reading—assuming the correctness of the foregoing interpretation—deepens his opposition to Maimonides's view in a way that would not have been noticed by casual readers.

* * *

Rabad's gloss stands out from the other examples of esoteric writing that I will consider in this chapter insofar as there do not seem to be any clues to the contents of the secret in the exoteric account, such as technical terms that might be read differently by casual and expert readers. Thus in the one place where Rabad announces unambiguously that he possess a secret interpretation, he offers no guide to uncovering it. This raises the possibility that Rabad is engaging in "secretism." It might be speculated that Rabad's goal was to highlight Maimonides's ignorance of an esoteric idea while loudly proclaiming his own esoteric knowledge, even while he had no intention of revealing the secret.

This secretism, while surely present, is attenuated by the fact that the passages from his *Commentary on Tractate Berakhot* and *Commentary on Tractate Ta'anit* do offer clues about the meaning of the gloss. The question is whether Rabad acted intentionally, or if the attenuation of secretism is accidental. The latter scenario seems most likely: if so, it may be true that the passages in the *Commentary* and the gloss deal with related themes, but Rabad did not intend that one should be read in light of the other. But we cannot entirely discount the former scenario, whereby Rabad did intend them to be read in light of each other. If so, Rabad employed the technique of esoteric writing known as dispersion of knowledge, which was described in Chapter 2, wherein ideas are purposely presented out of order or are broken up and scattered across one or several works instead of being presented all at once. It is difficult to verify the chronological order in which Rabad composed the passages from the commentaries and the gloss;[36] but for our purposes, it would not much matter. Rabad could have recorded one or both of the passages first and, later on, written the gloss with the knowledge that the passages would help clarify it, or he could have written one or both of the passages second and have hoped that the readers of the passages would go back to the gloss with new insight. Whatever the specifics, based on this scenario, Rabad left clues that he hoped the assiduous reader would follow.

Written and Oral Traditions

As I explained above, in addition to those passages in his works where, I will argue, Rabad engages in esoteric writing, we also have a number of short passages, in his name, that explicitly deal with theosophic kabbalistic ideas. In Twersky's view, such passages are "oral reports rather than direct literary quotations" (*Rabad* 290n16). In two instances, Twersky is most likely correct. In both, we are dealing with traditions taught by the "Pious One"—a common early kabbalistic designation of Isaac the Blind—in the name of his father, Rabad, that were recorded by later Kabbalists. In his "Sefer ha-emunah veha-bittaḥon," the thirteenth-century Geronese Kabbalist Jacob ben Sheshet attributes a teaching to Rabad, writing, "So I have heard (*shama'ti*) from the mouth (*mi-pi*) of the Pious One, R. Isaac, the son of the great Rabbi, R. Abraham (the memory of the righteous one should be a blessing), in the name of his father" ("Sefer ha-emunah" 357).[37] While it is conceivable that Isaac's own source was textual,[38] the impression that this attribution gives is that Isaac recounted to Jacob something he had heard from his father. The second one, on which I will focus below, is recorded in *Commentary on the Talmudic Aggadot*[39] by Ezra of Gerona, where it is cited as "the Pious One in the name of his father" (MS Vat. 441, 13a; MS Vat. 185, 10a).

In this case, it is difficult to tell whether Ezra had a written source by Isaac, or whether he was recording something that Isaac conveyed verbally.[40] Even if there was a written source, the terminology "in the name of his father," again, gives the impression that it is something that Isaac heard from his father. In any case, given the clear chains of transmission of these traditions, we can be relatively confident that they reliably express Rabad's sentiments. At the same time, they may not reflect Rabad's precise words, since they are twice removed, repeated once by Isaac and once by either Jacob or Ezra.

Yet in the case of passages attributed to Rabad that appear without reliable chains of transmission, such as one regarding Adam and Eve that I will describe below, their reliability cannot be assumed. Rather, it needs to be proved on a case-by-case basis. Moreover, even if the reliability of a particular passage is established, it remains difficult to be sure if it originated in teachings communicated orally by Rabad or if Rabad himself recorded it. In the latter scenario, given his son Isaac's pronouncement about his esotericism, it is unlikely that he would have widely distributed it or other passages that he composed. For the same reason, it is unlikely that some of these passages were originally found in his *Commentary on the Talmud*. Rather, he would have circulated them only to initiates, such as his son. The purpose of such passages would not have been to develop a detailed or systematic account of Kabbalah but to preserve a record of key ideas that his confidants could refer to.

Neither the oral reports nor the possible recorded passages can be regarded as examples of Rabad's esoteric writing, since, in the case of the former, Rabad did not write them, and, in the case of the latter, even if he did write them, they tend to be recorded with relative clarity and show no signs of containing concealed ideas. Insofar as we can verify their reliability, they are useful for our purposes because they give some indication of Rabad's esoteric knowledge and can therefore help us decipher passages in Rabad's public works, in which, as I have been arguing, he did indeed conceal esoteric ideas.

The Sanctus Prayer and the Return of the Divine Presence to Jerusalem

The aforementioned tradition that Ezra records as that of "the Pious One in the name of his father" concerns the Sanctus prayer. It reflects an esoteric kabbalistic teaching that Rabad shared with his son but left out of his public works. In this section, I will describe this rather complex tradition and argue that it allows us to decode an instance of esoteric writing in another one of Rabad's glosses on the *Mishneh torah*.

The Sanctus prayer includes the recitation of three verses: Isa. 6:3 ("Holy, holy, holy, the Lord of hosts, all the world is full of His glory"), Ezek. 3:12 ("Blessed be the glory of the Lord from its place"), and Ps. 146:10 ("The Lord will reign forever; your God, O Zion, from generation to generation"). In the early kabbalistic understanding, prayer functions to theurgically unite the sefirot. This view of prayer is reflected in Rabad's interpretation of the Sanctus as presented by Ezra:

> This is the explanation of the three holies [in Isa. 6:3, which is part of the Sanctus]. And corresponding to them are "the God of Abraham, the God of Isaac, and the God of Jacob." "All (*kol*) the earth is full of His glory" (Isa. 6:3). You already know the meaning of "all." It is the completeness (*shelemut*) of all and gives existence to the world and is its foundation (*yesodo*), as it is written, "The righteous is the foundation (*yesod*) of the world" (Prov. 10:25). "Blessed be the glory of the Lord from its place" (Ezek. 3:12), from the side that receives, and thereafter he joins each one to the other. And according to a haggadah, "When the *shekhinah* returns to the holy of holies, they would say, 'Blessed be the glory of the Lord from its place'" (Ezek. 3:12) (Schäfer, *Synopse* § 538, *Seder rabbah de-bere'shit*). The Pious One in the name of his father. (MS Vat. 185, 10a)[41]

As I will detail in Chapter 5, in his *Commentary on the Talmudic Aggadot*, Ezra adopts an esoteric style of writing, which assumes that the reader will have a significant level of familiarity with kabbalistic symbolism. This style, which includes the ubiquitous use of the words "you already know," is on display here. Thus while, in this passage, he is conveying Rabad's teaching, he is not doing so verbatim but casting it in his own esoteric style. Ezra begins by explaining that the three holies, in the first part of Isa. 6:3, correspond to the three patriarchs: Abraham, Isaac, and Jacob. The reader is expected to come with the knowledge that, decoded sefirotically, Abraham, Isaac, and Jacob represent the fourth, fifth, and sixth sefirot, "lovingkindness," "judgment," and "mercy." He should thus be able to deduce that the three holies represent these three sefirot.

Ezra does not indicate exactly where Rabad's teaching begins, so it is conceivable that this discussion of the Trisagion is Ezra's own. Yet Jacob ben Sheshet reports this same explanation of the Trisagion in the name of Isaac, albeit in more transparent language (*Sefer meshiv* 151, lines 58–59).[42] This suggests that Ezra intended to attribute the entire explanation of the Sanctus to Isaac, in the name of Rabad, and not just the material that immediately precedes the attribution.

Ezra then turns to the word "all," in the second part of Isa. 6:3 ("all [*kol*] the earth is full of His glory"). Note that when he states, "You already know the meaning of 'all,'" he again assumes a community of informed readers. Nevertheless, he provides a few clues. In explaining that "it is the completeness (*shelemut*) of all and gives existence to the world and is its foundation (*yesodo*)," he is intimating that "all" is a reference to the ninth sefirah, which is commonly known as "foundation." This sefirah, according to early kabbalistic sources (as well as countless subsequent ones), serves to unite the sixth and tenth sefirot.[43] He glosses the next verse of the Sanctus, "Blessed be the glory of the Lord from its place" (Ezek. 3:12), with the words "From the side that receives." "The side that receives" is apparently a reference to the tenth sefirah, which receives efflux from the sefirot above it, particularly from the ninth sefirah. This is made explicit in *Commentary on the Talmudic Aggadoth*, by Azriel of Gerona. Azriel's commentary incorporates large sections of Ezra's *Commentary* but often adds clarifications,[44] perhaps suggesting that his intended audience may have been somewhat wider. To Ezra's comment "From the side that receives," Azriel adds, "From the place of His *shekhinah* (= the tenth sefirah), which is everywhere" (119).[45]

Ezra then states: "And thereafter he joins them one to the other." I assume that he is referring to the worshiper's joining of the fourth, fifth, and sixth sefirot, described in the first part of Isa. 6:3, by means of the ninth sefirah, described in the second part of Isa. 6:3, with the tenth sefirah, described in Ezek. 3:12. Therefore, according to Rabad's teaching as transmitted by Ezra, by reciting the Sanctus, the worshiper theurgically unites the sefirot.[46]

The particular union described here develops into a central motif in the subsequent history of Kabbalah, particularly in the Zohar. Indeed, a key goal of kabbalistic theurgy becomes to create this union. According to kabbalistic thought, in the ideal state, the tenth sefirah, which is gendered female, is sexually united with the sixth sefirah, which is gendered male. This union is the key to divine unity. Yet when Israel is exiled from its land, the tenth sefirah is correspondingly exiled from the sixth sefirah, thus compromising divine unity. The sixth sefirah, often referred to as "mercy," is the perfect balance of the fourth and fifth sefirot, lovingkindness and judgment. By extension, therefore, the union of the sixth and tenth sefirot is really the union of the fourth, fifth, and sixth sefirot with the tenth sefirah. Through the performance of the commandments with proper intention, Jews have the ability to theurgically reunite these sefirot, thereby reversing the exile of the tenth sefirah. This occurs through the aegis of the ninth sefirah, which is the phallic aspect of divinity. Ultimately, the union of these sefirot will usher in the messianic period, when Israel will once again be united with its land.[47]

I would argue that much of this motif is already present in Rabad's comments on the Sanctus. For one, I suspect that Rabad also understood the union between the sixth and tenth sefirot in sexualized terms, since we will find the theme of sexual union within God—though perhaps not between these two sefirot—in another passage attributed to him that we will consider below. At any rate, this is certainly how Ezra understood Rabad's teaching. After citing it, he invokes the Song of Songs: "I am my beloved's and my beloved is mine" (Song 6:3): to join them one to the other" (MS Vat. 185, 10a). In Ezra's view, as he explains in his *Commentary on the Song of Songs*, the beloved and the lover of the Canticle are the sixth and tenth sefirot, respectively.[48]

The notion that the unity of these sefirot is a mark of the messianic period is reflected in the conclusion of Rabad's teaching, which presents a citation from a haggadah according to which "When the *shekhinah* returns to the holy of holies, they would say, 'Blessed be the glory of the Lord from its place'" (Ezek. 3:12). This haggadah turns out to be *Seder rabbah de-bere'shit*, a cosmogonic and cosmological work probably from the early Geonic period.[49] According to *Seder rabbah de-bere'shit*, Ezek. 3:12 is recited by the heavenly creatures in the messianic future when the *shekhinah* returns to the holy of holies (Schäfer, *Synopse* § 538, *Seder rabbah de-bere'shit*). The term *shekhinah*, which literally refers to God's indwelling presence, became a common designation for the tenth sefirah in kabbalistic literature. Ezra, in his *Commentary on the Song of Songs*, describes the "holy of holies" as a marriage canopy under which the tenth sefirah is wed—that is, joined with the sixth sefirah.[50] I would suggest that Rabad read the "holy of holies" in the citation from *Seder rabbah de-bere'shit* in the same manner. Thus, in keeping with the explanation of Ezek. 3:12 earlier in the teaching, according to which the verse refers to the tenth sefirah, Rabad presumably understands the citation as indicating that the heavenly creatures recite Ezek. 3:12 at the moment when the *shekhinah*, or the tenth sefirah, returns to the holy of holies to unite with the sixth sefirah. Moreover, since in the original passage in *Seder rabbah de-bere'shit*, the heavenly creatures recite Ezek. 3:12 in the messianic future, the union of tenth and sixth sefirah is apparently part of Rabad's messianic vision, as it would be for many future Kabbalists.

Finally, I would add that while Rabad may have understood the "holy of holies" as some sort of figurative space where the two sefirot unite, it is likely that he simultaneously understood it, literally, as a place within the temple—that is, he may have seen the holy of holies in the temple as a physical site to which the *shekhinah*, or tenth sefirah, will return in the messianic period. This would correct the exile of the *shekhinah*, which, according to rabbinic tradition, occurred after the destruction of the temple.[51] Here, I would suggest that Rabad partially foreshadows a view that, as Haviva Pedaya (*Name* 154–58) shows, was articulated by Ezra and Azriel, perhaps on the basis of a teaching from Isaac, according to which the union of the *shekhinah* and the sixth sefirah triggers the return of the *shekhinah* to Jerusalem. This is another component of the aforementioned kabbalistic motif according to which, in the messianic period, the national restoration of Israel will be marked not only by the perfect unity of the *shekhinah* and the sixth sefirah but also by the renewed presence of the *shekhinah* in Jerusalem.

The teaching of Rabad cited by Ezra is of particular interest for our purposes because it sheds light on Rabad's gloss of a passage in "Laws of the Temple" in Maimonides's *Mishneh torah*. This gloss, which has already been identified as an example of esoteric writing by Pedaya (42–55), concludes with the words "so it was revealed to me as 'a secret of the Lord is with them who fear Him'" (Ps. 25:14). In the passage considered in the previous section, the term *sod* ("secret") clearly refers to an esoteric teaching. In general, however, in various other places in his writings in which he also refers to a *sod* or invokes Ps. 25:14, it is apparent, as Isadore Twersky suggests, that a kabbalistic teaching is not intended. Rather, he merely means to refer to a "hitherto 'concealed' interpretation, entirely devoid of kabbalistic overtones" (*Rabad* 295; cf. 293, 297–99).[52] Pedaya, though, argues that in the gloss at hand, Rabad indeed intends to refer to an esoteric secret. As she notes, this impression is enhanced by the fact that the citation of Ps. 25:14 is prefaced by the words "so it was revealed to me" (*Name* 43–44, 176).[53] Nevertheless, precisely because the usage of Ps. 25:14 need not imply esoteric knowledge, I think it is fair to say that Rabad does not unambiguously announce that he is speaking of an esoteric tradition in the manner that he does in the gloss considered in the previous section. It is thus unsurprising that Twersky does not suspect that any secret ideas are at play.[54] In fact, it is possible that this ambiguity is intentional and may itself be an aspect of Rabad's esoteric style of writing.

The gloss concerns the legal distinction between the first and second consecrations of Jerusalem and the temple, as well as between the first and second consecrations of the remainder of the land of Israel. This distinction is significant, since certain commandments can be performed only in the land of Israel, while others can be performed only in Jerusalem, and still others can be performed only in the temple. Yet this is the case only if these sites are consecrated. If they are not consecrated, these commandments cannot be performed. According to Maimonides, while the first consecration of most of the land of Israel, which was carried out by the biblical Joshua, became void after the destruction of the first temple, the first consecration of Jerusalem and the temple, by King Solomon, will remain in place for eternity. Thus while biblical Ezra's subsequent reconsecration of the land of Israel was necessary, his reconsecration of Jerusalem and the temple was merely a ceremonial act with no legal significance (*Mishneh torah, hilkhot beit he-beḥirah* 6:14–16; Shailat 6:14–17). Maimonides is keen to explain the reason for this distinction between Jerusalem and the temple, on the one hand, and the remainder of the land of Israel, on the other. It is because "the sanctity of the temple and of Jerusalem is a result of the *shekhinah* (divine presence), and the *shekhinah* is never nullified" (6:16; Shailat 6:17). It would take us too far afield to discuss what Maimonides means by the *shekhinah*. Suffice it to say that he was unaware of kabbalistic theosophy, and he certainly did not have the tenth sefirah in mind. Nor could he have maintained any sort of conception of the *shekhinah* as an actual manifestation of God in a particular locale, since this violates his view of God's transcendence and incorporeality. Rather, he understands the *shekhinah* in some sort of allegorical fashion.[55] Be that as it may, since the *shekhinah*, whatever precisely this means, rests specifically on the temple and Jerusalem, rather than on the remainder of the land of Israel, and since this connection can never be nullified, there is no need, nor will there ever be a need, for a new consecration.

Rabad categorically disagrees with Maimonides. I will focus on one aspect of his disagreement: from his point of view, Solomon's consecration of Jerusalem and the temple did become void, and thus Ezra's reconsecration of Jerusalem and the temple was not merely ceremonial but legally significant. Moreover, even Ezra's reconsecration of Jerusalem and the temple was not permanent but became void after the destruction of the second temple:

> Even according to R. Yossi, who said that the second consecration applies in the future (see B. Yevamot 82b), he only said so with regard to the rest of the land of Israel, but he did not say so with regard to Jerusalem and the temple, since Ezra knew (*hayah yodea'*) that in the future, the temple and Jerusalem will change and become sanctified with a different kind of eternal sanctity (*sheha-mikdash virushalayim 'atidim lehishtannot u-lehitkaddesh kiddush aher 'olami*) by the glory of God for eternity (*bikhvod YY le'olam*). So it was revealed to me as "a secret of the Lord is with them that fear Him" (Ps. 25:14). (*Mishneh torah, hilkhot beit ha-behirah* 6:14–16 ad loc)

Rabad argues that "Ezra knew" that the temple and Jerusalem will, in the messianic future, take on a new kind of sanctity. In contrast to Maimonides's view, therefore, the original sanctity of the temple and Jerusalem is not eternal. Pedaya (*Name* 47, 176) highlights the expression "Ezra knew," which, in her view, signifies that Rabad believed that Ezra possessed a particular tradition of knowledge that was identical to his own esoteric tradition. Moreover, she argues that Rabad wrote this passage in an encoded fashion, such that its true meaning will be fathomed only by one who is familiar with a certain set of technical terminology. In particular, she highlights Rabad's choice of words in describing this new sanctity: "will change" (*lehishtannot*), "different kind" (*aher*), and "eternal" (*'olami*). These words, she argues, derive from ancient Jewish apocalyptic literature, where the theme that, in the messianic period, the third temple will descend in a fully built fashion from heaven is prominent. It is to this miraculous descent of the third temple, Pedaya (47–48, 176) suggests, that Rabad alludes when he talks about the "change" and the "different kind" of "eternal" sanctity that will exist in the messianic future.

Pedaya also points to another technical phrase that, she argues, can be explained on the basis of specifically kabbalistic terminology: "by the glory of God for eternity" (*bikhvod YY le-'olam*). The term "glory," in Pedaya's view (48), refers to the lowest sefirah, often termed the *shekhinah* (divine presence). Thus when Rabad writes that "the temple and Jerusalem will change and become sanctified with a different kind of eternal sanctity by the glory of God for eternity," he means to say that part of what will cause the third temple to have this eternal sanctity is the descent of the *shekhinah* into the third temple. As Pedaya explains, from the perspective of Rabad's kabbalistic understanding, the descent of the *shekhinah* into the third temple would also mark the "completeness in the world of the sefirot" (49). To put Pedaya's point into slightly different terms, as we have seen, the messianic period is marked by the return of the *shekhinah* to the temple and by the union of the tenth and sixth sefirot. This union establishes what Pedaya refers to as "completeness in the world of the sefirot" or, in other terms, divine unity. Therefore, the esoteric meaning of the key line of the gloss—"Ezra knew (*yode'a*) that in the future the temple and Jerusalem will change and become sanctified with a different kind of eternal sanctity by the glory of God for eternity"—is that Ezra had esoteric knowledge that the third temple will descend from heaven in the messianic period, accompanied by the descent of the tenth sefirah into the temple.

It would seem that the teaching of Rabad, recorded by Ezra in his *Commentary on the Talmudic Aggadot* and discussed above, corroborates and indeed expands Pedaya's analysis. Pedaya (48–49) stresses that in combining the notion of the temple descending from heaven with the kabbalistic view of the tenth sefirah returning to the temple, Rabad is reading ancient Jewish apocalyptic literature through the lens of sefirotic Kabbalah. Rabad's teaching, as cited by Ezra, concludes with a line from *Seder rabbah de-bere'shit*: "When the *shekhinah* returns to the holy of holies, they would say, 'Blessed be the glory of the Lord from its place' (Ezek. 3:12)." While not an apocalyptic work, *Seder rabbah de-bere'shit* comes out of a milieu of ancient Jewish cosmological speculation of which apocalyptic literature is also a part. Indeed, the work makes note of the heavenly Jerusalem and heavenly temple (Schäfer, *Synopse* § 771), and though it is not stated explicitly, Peter Schäfer ("In Heaven" 249–50) points out that the implication is that they are waiting to descend to earth in the messianic future. Rabad, as I argued, reads the line from *Seder rabbah de-bere'shit* as describing the descent of the lowest sefirah, in the messianic period, into the holy of holies, which occurs when the tenth and sixth sefirot are united. This is precisely the process hinted at in Rabad's gloss. His teaching, therefore, gives tangible evidence of the kind of exegetical process imagined by Pedaya. Thus, once again, the coming together of two aspects of God is a matter that Rabad only alludes to in public works—even while apparently speaking of it openly in his private communications with his confidants.

Recall that, in Maimonides's view, it is the fact that the *shekhinah* eternally dwells upon the temple that obviates the need to reconsecrate it. On the one hand, as noted, it is difficult to square Maimonides's understanding of the *shekhinah*'s dwelling in the Temple with his philosophical belief that God cannot have a specific manifestation in a physical locale. On the other hand, his claim that the *shekhinah* dwells eternally in the temple is in keeping with his philosophical view of the unchanging nature of God and may even be an implicit critique of the rabbinic tradition that the *shekhinah* left the temple after its destruction.[56] I would argue that Rabad's gloss should be seen as a reaction to this point. In contrast to Maimonides's view, the esoteric layer of the gloss hints that the *shekhinah* did indeed leave the temple after its destruction and will return in the messianic period. Rabad was surely aware that Maimonides did not regard the *shekhinah* as the tenth sefirah. Regardless, though, Rabad would have seen Maimonides's view that the *shekhinah*—however Maimonides might have understood it—is eternally present in the temple as contradicting his own kabbalistic position that the *shekhinah* is exiled from the temple and will return in the messianic period. As is well known, Maimonides's static understanding of God is at odds with Kabbalists' dynamic understanding of divinity.[57] Rabad's gloss may be an attempt to signal to his initiated readers that Maimonides's static view needs to be replaced by the dynamic kabbalistic one.

* * *

This gloss may be contrasted with the one on the front and back of God, considered in the previous section, in two ways. First, while in the gloss on the front and back of God, there is arguably tension between the exoteric and esoteric interpretations (according to both possible esoteric interpretations), there is no evidence that the same is true here. Read exoterically, the current gloss teaches that Jerusalem and the temple will have a fundamentally different type of sanctity in the messianic period, but the nature of that sanctity is not explained. The esoteric explanation merely clarifies that this new sanctity involves the unification of two aspects of God and the descent of the *shekhinah* into the third temple but does not alter the basic fact that a new type of sanctity will emerge. Second, while the first gloss does not offer the reader any hints that will allow him to uncover the esoteric meaning, the current one provides the adept reader with rhetorical clues that will aid him in deciphering the esoteric meaning. As Pedaya puts it, the passage employs words that "are loaded with meaning from a different register of knowledge.... The assumption is that the listener knows the entire [linguistic] field to which the register of technical terms belongs and that an entire structure will arise in his thought" (*Name* 47).

The Two-Faced First Human Being

A passage attributed to Rabad in several manuscripts regarding the Talmudic legend that Adam and Eve were originally created as a single two-faced creature[58] has been more heavily discussed by scholars than any other kabbalistic passage attributed to Rabad.[59] While it is not an example of esoteric writing but presents kabbalistic ideas quite openly, it will help us clarify passages in Rabad's public works, in which, I suggest, he concealed esoteric concepts. As noted, in the case of the tradition in Ezra's *Commentary on the Talmudic Aggadot*, considered in the previous section, the lines of transmission are clear: Rabad transmitted it to Isaac, who, in turn, transmitted it to Ezra. In contrast, the origins of this passage, which is extant only in three sixteenth-century kabbalistic miscellanies,[60] are murky. The earliest likely reference to it of which I am aware appears in the fourteenth-century *Explanation of Nahmanides's Torah Commentary* (*Bei'ur le-ferush ha-Ramba"n 'al ha-torah*), a supercommentary on the kabbalistic hints in Nahmanides's Torah commentary. While it is attributed to Meir ben Solomon Ibn Sahula, its real author is the subject of dispute.[61] This work, replete with citations of sometimes otherwise unknown early kabbalistic traditions—especially teachings of Isaac the Blind—refers, in passing, to an explanation that Rabad wrote about the two-faced first human without citing it and without any elaboration (*Bei'ur* 4c).[62] Apparently, the author has our passage in mind. As I will discuss in Chapter 4, many of the attributions to early Kabbalists in this work are spurious. Yet here, it is likely accurate.

Despite the unclear provenance of our passage, the authenticity of its attribution to Rabad has been unanimously accepted by scholars, a conclusion with which I concur. Scholem based this conclusion on the fact that it uses terminology and concepts not found in later thirteenth-century Kabbalah. As Scholem puts it, were it a later forgery, "Forgers of this [later] period would obviously have attributed their own views to the Rabad, much as they did in the case of ever so many pseudoepigraphic writings with regard to other authors" (*Origins* 217).[63] Additional support for the accuracy of the attribution to Rabad comes from the fact that the passage has clear parallels to a non-kabbalistic passage in Rabad's *Ba'alei ha-nefesh*, as I will discuss later in this chapter. Moreover, as I will argue in Chapter 6, Rabad's grandson Asher ben David, while not explicitly referencing this passage, alludes to it in his *Sefer ha-yiḥud*.

Since the notion that Adam and Eve were created two-faced appears in the Babylonian Talmud, Scholem (*Origins* 216) suggests that our passage was originally part of Rabad's *Commentary on the Talmud*. This passage, however, speaks openly of kabbalistic matters. Given Rabad's commitment to esotericism, Scholem's suggestion is unlikely. This leaves two alternatives: either Rabad wrote the passage himself[64] but only intended it for limited circulation, or the ideas were Rabad's own, and he orally transmitted them to a confidant. In this second possibility, the confidant, or he himself, or some later figure further down the oral chain eventually recorded them. In any case, this passage, like the one in Ezra's *Commentary on the Talmudic Aggadot*, provides us with access to Rabad's private kabbalistic ideas that he left out of his public works.

The opening of the passage comments on the social implication of the rabbinic legend that Adam and Eve were originally created as a single two-faced being before they were separated: "Therefore Adam and Eve were created two-faced so that a wife will obey her husband (*tihyeh nishma'at le-va'alah*), for her life is dependent upon him, and so that he does not go one way and she another way (*she-lo' yelekhu zeh le-darko ve-zeh le-darkah*). Rather, there should be closeness and affection between them, and they will not separate, and then there will be peace between them and tranquillity in their palace" (Scholem, *Re'shit* 79n2).[65] The fact that Adam and Eve, the original couple, were originally a single creature implies that there will be a close and affectionate relationship between all future spouses, even while the wife remains subservient to her husband. As the passage puts it, "a wife will obey her husband."

In the immediate continuation, the passage turns to the divine analogue of the original two-faced human:

> And this is also true of the agents of truth (*be-fo'alei ha-emet*) whose action is truth. The reason for the [two] faces is twofold. First, it is

known (*ki yadua' hu'*) that two opposites were emanated, one of complete judgment (*din gamur*) and the other of complete mercy (*raḥamim gemurim*). If they had not been emanated "two-faced," and each of them would act in accordance with its own principle, it would appear as if there were two [independent] powers (*kishtei rashuyyot*), and each would act without being joined to the other and without its assistance. But now that they were created "two-faced," all their action takes place together and with balance, in complete unity, and there is no separation (*perud*) between them. Moreover, if they had not been created "two-faced," no complete unity could be made from them, and the attribute of judgment would not be able to elevate itself to that of mercy, or [vice versa] that of mercy to that of judgment. But now, since they were created "two-faced," each of them comes close to the other and unites itself with the other and longs (*kosef*) and desires (*u-mit'avveh*) to be joined to the other, so that the tabernacle may be one whole (based on Exod. 26:6 or 36:13). A proof for this is that you will find that the [divine] names refer to each other. Thus you will find that YHVH [which usually refers to the attribute of mercy] can refer to the attribute of judgment, and *Elohim* [which usually refers to the attribute judgment] can refer to the attribute of mercy, as in "YHVH rained upon Sodom and Gomorrah" (Gen. 19:24). YHVH rained down[66] and transferred from one attribute to the other. (79n2)[67]

"Complete judgment" and "complete mercy" clearly refer to two aspects of God, but these are unusual terms that do not find parallels in the literature of Isaac and his students. Idel (*Kabbalah and Eros* 63) very plausibly suggests that they should be identified with the fifth and fourth sefirot, respectively.[68] Whatever the appropriate sefirotic identifications, Rabad's basic claim is that these two aspects of God are the divine models for Adam and Eve. Like Adam and Eve, they were originally united and then separated. The original unity of pure mercy and pure judgment is what makes their subsequent union possible. Their union is, in fact, a reunion or, in other terms, a recapitulation of their original unity.

In Rabad's view, certain biblical usages of divine names prove that pure mercy and pure judgment can join. According to rabbinic tradition, the Bible employs YHVH when God exercises mercy and *Elohim* when He exercises judgment.[69] Rabbinic sources also point out that this is reversed in certain exceptional verses[70]—a point that Rabad highlights by citing Gen. 19:24. In this verse, it is YHVH who metes out judgment upon Sodom and Gomorrah. From Rabad's perspective, the reversal of divine names in this verse reflects the fact that mercy and judgment can unite.

It would seem that the comparison of the divine couple to the human one implies that pure mercy and pure judgment are gendered masculine and feminine, respectively. It also implies that their union is a sexual one. Indeed, it is apparent that the sexual union of mercy and judgment is the divine model for that of Adam and Eve, which the latter couple consummated after their own separation. The teaching underscores the sexual nature of the union by stating that mercy and judgment "desire" (*mit'avveh*) to be joined to each other, a term that carries an erotic connotation. This teaching, then, like the one recorded by Ezra, deals with the sexual union of two aspects of God, a theme not openly found in any of Rabad's rabbinic writings.

We should take special note of the comment that if they were not originally united, "it would then appear as if there were two [independent] powers (*kishtei rashuyyot*), and each would act without being joined to the other and without its assistance. But now that they were created 'two-faced,' all their action takes place together and with balance, in complete unity, and there is no separation (*perud*) between them." From this comment, it is apparent that divine unity hinges on the union of these attributes[71]—a conception of divine unity that, as seen, is also reflected in Rabad's position on the Sanctus, even if, in the latter case, different sefirot are involved.[72]

For our purposes, this passage is significant because it allows us to recognize examples of esoteric writing in Rabad's public oeuvre. It enables us, that is, to assume the position of the initiated reader who is able to spot the clues to esoteric ideas that Rabad left in his public works. In the next sections, I will consider three examples of this phenomenon.

Judgment and Mercy

In his *Commentary on Tractate 'Avodah Zarah*, one of the few portions of his Talmudic commentary that has survived, Rabad comments on a passage in B. 'Avodah Zarah 4a in which R. Papa is cited as pointing to a contradiction between Ps. 7:12 and Nah. 1:6. According to the former verse, "God (*el*) has wrath each day"; according to the latter, "Who can stand before His wrath." As Rabad explains the contradiction, in the latter verse, the prophet implies that God does not get angry each day, for He knows that if He did, no one could withstand His anger. This verse is thus at odds with the former one stating that God does get angry each day (*Commentary* 7). R. Papa resolves the contradiction by arguing that the former verse refers to God's anger at the community as a whole while the latter verse refers to His anger at an individual. From Rabad's point of view, this resolution of the contradiction is an affirmation of God's ultimate mercy. God is willing to get angry at an entire community because He knows that the collective prayers of the community will be sufficient to assuage His anger such that He will not destroy them. In the case of an individual who sins, in contrast, there is no collective communal prayer to assuage God's anger. God, therefore, chooses to act mercifully toward the individual:

> Therefore, the Holy One, blessed be He, does not allow his anger to fall on individuals, even at a moment of anger (*afillu bish'at ha-ka'as*). He, rather, acts toward them at every moment (*kol sha'ah*) with the attribute of mercy (*middat ha-raḥamim*) and [as though it is] a time of favor (*ve-'et ratson*). A being of flesh and blood, in contrast, cannot act with these two attributes (*bishtei middot hallalu*). It is written of the Holy One, blessed be He: "The Lord (YHVH) is a man of war; the Lord (YHVH) is His name" (Exod. 15:3). It is expounded in the *Mekhilta*,[73] "When jealousy and power overtake a strong man in the nation, he will even go and strike his father and his loved one with anger. This is not the case for the Holy One, blessed be He. Rather, 'The Lord (YHVH) is a man of war' (Exod. 15:3) who fights Egypt; 'The Lord (YHVH) is His name' (ibid.), for he shows mercy upon the creatures, as it is written, 'The Lord (YHVH), a God (*el*) merciful [and gracious]' (Exod. 34:6)." (7–8)

On their face, Rabad's comments read like a paean to God's mercy—to His ability to overcome His anger and act mercifully even to those who anger Him. Eli Ḥadad (491–94), however, has contended that this passage needs to be read in light of the passage on the two-faced first human and that, when read in this manner, it refers to the ability of God's attributes of mercy and justice to unite. In what follows, I further develop his analysis and consider its implications for Rabad's approach to esoteric writing.

For one with knowledge of Rabad's teaching on the two-faced first human, this passage takes on a more technical meaning. It describes the process in which the aspect of God associated with anger, which is identical to judgment (arguably, the fifth sefirah), unites with that associated with mercy (arguably, the fourth sefirah), so that the former is mitigated.

A close reading suggests that the implication of Rabad's comments is not merely that God is able to forget His anger and replace it with mercy but that His anger is combined with His mercy—that is, anger and mercy are two aspects of God that unite, such that the latter mitigates the former. This, I think, is the force of his remarks that "God does not allow his anger to fall on individuals, even at a moment of anger (*afillu bish'at ha-ka'as*). He, rather, acts toward them at every moment with the attribute of mercy (*middat ha-raḥamim*) and [as though it is] a time of favor (*ve-'et ratson*)." His anger does not disappear in face of His mercy, but "even at a moment of anger," He acts as though it is a "moment" of mercy. In other words, His anger and mercy operate in a state of unity whereby the anger is mitigated. This becomes even clearer from Rabad's comparison of God to a human being. Note that he does not claim that a human is unable to overcome his anger while God can but that the human is unable to hold both attributes, mercy and anger, together while God can: "A being of flesh and blood, in contrast, cannot act with these two attributes (*bishtei middot hallalu*)."

Admittedly, one not versed in kabbalistic tradition may end up reading the text as I just explicated it and assume that Rabad is making a point about God's psychology: God is able to hold together conflicting emotions. Yet I would contend that one with prior knowledge of Rabad's passage regarding the two-faced human, or similar kabbalistic traditions, would immediately realize that Rabad is not merely making a psychological point but a theosophic one about "the agents of truth," to use the language from the passage.

I would also add that a version of Rabad's proof, in the passage on the two-faced human, that mercy and judgment can unite—the fact that YHVH, which usually refers to the attribute of mercy, can refer to the attribute of judgment—also appears in the citation from *Mekhilta de-Rabbi Ishmael* in the current passage: "YHVH is a man of war" (Exod. 15:3) who fights Egypt"—that is, the name usually associated with mercy, YHVH, becomes the name of judgment when God fights Egypt. Read through Rabad's theosophic lens, this shift in the meaning of YHVH is possible because the attribute of mercy can combine with the attribute of judgment to form a unity.

Finally, there is perhaps one terminological clue in the passage that would further alert the astute reader to its theosophic meaning: the phrase "a time of favor" (*'et ratson*). In Chapter 4, I will highlight a teaching of Rabad's son, Isaac, according to which a variation of this phrase ("a time of unity and favor") functions as a *terminus technicus* for the coming together of two aspects of God—in that case, the sixth and the tenth sefirot. The exact phrase ("a time of favor"), I will show in Chapter 6, was understood in the same manner by Rabad's grandson Asher and other early Kabbalists in Isaac's circle. It is possible that the phrase functions in the same manner for Rabad. If so, this would be a clue to the esoteric underpinnings of the passage that would be picked up only by those deeply familiar with Rabad's kabbalistic terminology.

As a model of esoteric writing, this passage is more subtle than the others considered thus far. Rabad does not mention a secret—that is, he never announces, even if only in an ambiguous manner, that an esoteric teaching is concealed here. It is up to the reader to realize that an esoteric idea lurks behind this passage.

In this case, there also does not seem to be any tension between the exoteric and esoteric interpretations. It might be said that the esoteric interpretation provides a theosophic explanation for a psychological phenomenon. The psychological interpretation is accurate insofar as it properly captures God's behavior. It just lacks the theosophical explanation of this behavior.

"How Wondrous Are the Works of the Creator, and Who Can Comprehend Their Secret"

The passage on the two-faced human also sheds light on another instance of esoteric writing in Rabad's work, which is found in his *Ba'alei ha-nefesh*, a halakhic work dealing with the laws of menstruation. In the introduction to the work, he describes the ideal relationship between a husband and his wife:

> How wondrous are the works of the Creator, and who can comprehend their secret (*u-mi yavin sodam*): for all the creatures were created male and female, whereas Adam was created singular, and thereafter He created out of him a helper suitable for him. Who can know the depth of His wonders and reach the purpose of His wisdom, the wisdom of His actions. . . . Had they been created male and female (that is, separately) from the earth in the manner that

the rest of the creatures were created ... each one would turn to
their own way (*ve-ish le-darko yifnu*). ... Therefore, the Creator
saw what Adam needed and what was necessary for his enjoyment,
and He created him as single creature, and took one of his ribs, and
built the woman from it, and He brought her to Adam to be his
wife and to be a help and a support for him, since she is considered
to him as one of his limbs who was created to serve him. And a man
will rule over her in the manner that he rules over his limbs. ...
Therefore it is fitting for a man to love his wife as his own body
and honor her, and be merciful toward her, and protect her as he
would protect one of his limbs, and similarly she is obligated to
serve him and to honor him, and to love him as she loves herself for
from him was she taken. (*Ba'alei ha-nefesh* 14–15)[74]

As other scholars have already noted, we recognize the sentiments here from the passage regarding the two-faced human.[75] In both texts, we find the idea that the original unity of Adam and Eve is what allows for the proper relationship between a husband and wife in which there is mutual love and respect between them, even while the wife is subservient to her husband.[76] There is even, as Idel (*Kabbalah and Eros* 271n24) noticed, a linguistic link between the passages, which further shows their interrelatedness. In the passage on the two-faced human, the original unity is presented as ensuring that "he does not go one way and she another way" (*she-lo' yelekhu ze le-darko ve-ze le-darkah*) while in the passage from *Ba'alei ha-nefesh*, Rabad explains that were it not for this unity, "each one would turn to their own way" (*ve-ish le-darko yifnu*). Even if Rabad is not the actual author of the passage on the two-faced human, the terminological link shows that both passages are operating with similar conceptions of the nature of the relationship between a husband and wife.

There is, however, a major distinction between the two passages. In the one, a married couple's ideal relationship is grounded in the theosophic reality of the unity of mercy and judgment. It might be said that the relationship between the human husband and wife is a reflection of the relationship between these gendered aspects of divinity.[77] Yet in the other, the theosophic background of this relationship is omitted. Isadore Twersky (*Rabad* 291n20) has alluded to the likelihood that this is a case of esoteric writing in which Rabad chose to conceal the theosophic background of a social ideal in a work that was intended for public consumption.

Note that the passage in *Ba'alei ha-nefesh* begins, "How wondrous are the works of the Creator, and who can comprehend their secret" (*u-mi yavin sodam*). Certainly, the primary sense in which Rabad uses the term "secret," in this context, is not to refer to an esoteric tradition but to evoke the wonder of God's creation. Perhaps, however, Rabad also means to allude to the idea, which would later be attributed to Isaac both by Ezra and by the author of the aforementioned *Explanation of Nahmanides's Torah Commentary*, that everything in the created world derives from and is modeled after the sefirot.[78] That is, the "secret" of God's works—what makes them wondrous— is their connection to a divine model. On this reading, the relationship of a husband and wife, described in the remainder of the passage, is just one instance of this broader idea insofar as it is modeled after the relationship of divine mercy and judgment. Notably, immediately after citing, in Isaac's name, the idea that the world is modeled after the sefirot, the author of *Explanation of Nahmanides's Torah Commentary* adds, in a passage referred to above, "And behold, the human was created like a model (*ke'ein dugm'a*). Male and female were two-faced. And Rabad, of blessed memory, already wrote the explanation of the matter" (*Bei'ur* 4c). *Explanation* provides no elaboration of the contents of Rabad's teaching, but apparently it is referring to Rabad's explanation of the two-faced first human that has concerned us here. This author, then, apparently also sees Rabad's teaching as an example of the broader principle according to which what is below is modeled on what is above. If my analysis is correct, Rabad in *Ba'alei ha-nefesh* alludes to these same ideas, if only in the most subtle of ways. Beyond this one line, the remarks do not appear to contain any technical terminology that would focus the knowledgeable reader on its esoteric meaning.

In this example, too, the exoteric and esoteric explanations are not at odds. The simple reader is not left with misinformation. Rather, he is left without a complete understanding of the full reason behind Rabad's account of the appropriate behavior between spouses.

Competing Views of Divine Unity

So far, we have seen that in esoteric traditions apparently intended only for limited audiences, Rabad espouses the notion that God consists of multiple aspects that unite sexually. In the case of the passage on the two-faced human, he presents the union as definitional of divine unity. This is also implied in the tradition on the Sanctus prayer. These esoteric traditions allowed us to read between the lines of certain passages in Rabad's public writings to uncover related ideas. We have seen varying levels of tension between the exoteric and esoteric readings of these passages. We have yet to see, however, any passage in Rabad's public work that is at odds with the basic idea that God consists of multiple interacting aspects. This is precisely what we find in the final passage that I will consider. This passage, which appears at the conclusion of *Ba'alei ha-nefesh*, does not contain allusions to esoteric ideas but rather argues for a position that apparently directly contradicts them.

For the most part, Rabad avoids theological discussions in his work. This passage is an important exception: "Every created being should know that he is neither separated (*nifrad*) from the Maker nor compounded (*meḥubbar*) with Him, for any compound (*meḥubbar*) is delimited (*mugbal*), and anything delimited is created. But the Creator has none of these attributes, for He precedes all. He is neither delimited nor created" (127). Here Rabad argues that no created being may be compounded with God, since compounds are delimited and hence created—two characteristics that do not apply to God. If created things cannot be compounded with God, then, of course (and for the same reasons), God Himself cannot be a compound. In essence, Rabad accepts the definition of divine unity as simplicity or as the absence of composition that was prevalent in Jewish philosophical sources. According to this definition, God is not one being with multiple components. God's oneness is such, rather, that it is completely free of any composition. Certainly, according to this definition, God does not have multiple aspects that are joined together but is, rather, a perfect unity, free of any multiplicity. This understanding of divine unity is directly at odds with Rabad's esoteric conception of God.

That Rabad's publicly stated position here is at odds with his esoteric one comes into sharper focus when we realize that his above-mentioned remarks are based on Baḥya Ibn Pakuda's *Duties of the Heart*.[79] Originally composed in Arabic, which Rabad did not read, this philosophic work was translated by Judah Ibn Tibbon into Hebrew in 1161 as part of a general project, starting in the second half of the twelfth century, to translate classical works of Jewish philosophy into Hebrew for southern French Jews whose cultural language was Hebrew and who did not have access to Arabic.[80] Judah initially translated just the first section of the work, which addresses divine unity, but, at Rabad's urging, he completed the translation.[81] Thus, we cannot doubt Rabad's keen interest in this work. The passages from

Duties of the Heart that are in the background of Rabad's remarks all argue for divine simplicity and appear in the seventh chapter of the opening section of the work, a chapter that offers seven philosophical proofs that there is only one God.[82] For the sake of clarifying their relationship to Rabad's remarks, I present them out of order:

1. As part of the fourth proof, Bahya offers the following explanation (in Ibn Tibbon's translation): "Anything distinguishable is delimited (*mugbal*), and anything delimited is finite, and anything finite is a compound (*meḥubbar*), and anything that is a compound is created (*meḥuddash*), and anything created has a Creator (*meḥaddesh*). Thus, one who thinks that the Creator is more than one, necessitates that He was created" (Ibn Pakuda 128).
2. In the seventh proof, Bahya offers this contention: "Anything finite has a boundary (*gevul*), and anything that has a boundary is a compound (*meḥubbar*), and anything that is a compound is created (*meḥuddash*), and anything created has a Creator (*meḥaddesh*)" (130).
3. In the fifth proof, Bahya specifies that God's unity "is a complete unity and separateness (*u-vedidut*), which has no composition (*ḥibbur*), or any image at all, or multiplicity, or any number whatsoever, and it is not compounded (*hitḥabber*) with another thing, or separated from (*hitpared*) another thing" (129).

Rabad's dependence on these passages, in which Bahya argues for divine simplicity, is apparent. Terminologically, the words "compound" (*meḥubbar*), "created" (*meḥuddash*), and "delimited" (*mugbal*), which appear in Rabad's statement, are also prominent in these passages. Thematically, Rabad's reasoning is based on them. Thus, according to the first and second of the passages by Bahya, something finite must be a compound, and, insofar as an agent has to bring together the multiple components of a compound, any compound is, of necessity, created. Since, however, God is not created, God cannot be a compound; put in other terms, God's oneness is characterized by simplicity. Rabad repeats this line of reasoning in his statement that "any compound (*meḥubbar*) is delimited (*mugbal*), and anything delimited is created. But the Creator has none of these attributes."

Of the three passages, Bahya's position on simplicity is stated most clearly in the third, according to which, to repeat, God "is a complete unity and separateness (*u-vedidut*), which has no composition (*ḥibbur*), or any image at all, or multiplicity, or any number whatsoever, and it is not compounded (*hitḥabber*) with another thing, or separated from (*hitpared*) another thing." It is easy to see that Rabad is following Baḥya when he states that "every created being should know that he is neither separated (*nifrad*) from the Maker nor compounded (*meḥubbar*) with Him" (129).

As I will discuss below, and as numerous scholars have outlined, philosophical material translated into Hebrew, including *Duties of the Heart*—the first major example of such a translation—was of great interest to the intellectual elite of southern French Jews to which Rabad belonged. Readers of *Ba'alei ha-nefesh*, therefore, would certainly have realized the literary source of Rabad's comments. In short, readers of these comments would readily understand that they imply an argument for divine simplicity.

It is apparent that the notion of divine unity as simplicity to which these comments allude rules out multiple aspects of God interacting with one another. It sharply contradicts the various esoteric ideas that we have been considering that depict multiple aspects of God. The possibility must be considered, therefore, that Rabad's comments in *Ba'alei ha-nefesh* represent his exoteric position on divine unity and are meant for public consumption.

While the passage in *Ba'alei ha-nefesh* does not itself contain esoteric allusions, its placement, at the end of the final chapter of the work, is revealing. This chapter, titled "The Gate of Holiness," is devoted to the ideal sexual relationship of a married couple. As we have seen in the passage on the two-faced human, the union of a married human couple is a mirror of the union of the divine couple, and the union of the divine couple is constitutive of divine unity. Rabad, then, chooses to stress divine simplicity precisely in the chapter that describes the union that is the analogue of his esoteric conception of divine unity. This might very well be intended as a clue to the initiated reader meant to highlight the disparity between the esoteric and exoteric views.

Perhaps, for a public audience, Rabad declares his allegiance to the philosophic view of divine unity even while secretly alluding to traditions that divine unity is constituted by the sexual union of multiple aspects of God. As I will argue, this pattern repeats in the work of his grandson, Asher ben David. It remains an open question as to whether Rabad entirely rejected the exoteric account. Might he have nevertheless seen a way of reconciling the esoteric traditions with the exoteric view? There is simply not enough evidence to answer this question. In the case of Asher, as I will argue, it is possible that the answer is affirmative.

Rabad's Readership

If Rabad included esoteric hints in his works, he must have believed that there was a readership who might successfully decipher them. Since esoteric writing is a useful tool to disseminate secret ideas only if there are readers who have the requisite background knowledge to decode the clues that the author left in his text, this readership must have been a knowledgeable one. Yet this had to be a readership who were not part of his immediate circle of confidants, for esoteric information could be passed on to them in person. My finding, therefore, that Rabad was an esoteric writer points to a wider dissemination of kabbalistic ideas in the twelfth century than might otherwise be assumed.

According to Kabbalists' own historiography, Kabbalah emerged from one family—that of Rabad—from which it spread widely. A number of late thirteenth- and early fourteenth-century kabbalistic sources depict an apparently closed chain of transmission from Rabad's father-in-law (Abraham ben Isaac), to Rabad, to Rabad's son (Isaac the Blind), and to Isaac's students Ezra and Azriel.[83] In such a closed chain, it is unclear who the intended readership of Rabad's hints might be.

Yet in addition to the very fact that Rabad wrote esoterically, other factors point to the existence of a wider readership who might have been able to understand Rabad's clues. For starters, the sources that depict this closed chain are relatively late and therefore may not be accurate accounts of the situation in the twelfth century. Moreover, as Oded Yisraeli ("Jewish Medieval" 23–31) has shown, these sources may have had a polemical intent of legitimizing the tradition of southern French and Geronese Kabbalah over and against newly ascendant Castilian Kabbalah. As such, they should not be seen as expressing a historical reality.

We do get a sense of a closed tradition from what is ostensibly a more reliable source: Isaac's aforementioned letter to Nahmanides and Jonah Gerondi. There, it will be recalled, Isaac says of his fathers that "never did a word [regarding kabbalistic secrets] escape their lips, and they conducted themselves with them as with people who were not versed in the [higher]

Wisdom" (T. Weiss, "Letter" 332). By his fathers, Isaac has in mind his father, Rabad, and his grandfather Abraham ben Isaac. The impression that Isaac's remarks give, therefore, is that there would have been no readers able to decipher Rabad's esoteric hints outside those in his own closed circle. Yet it is quite possible that Isaac's comments are self-serving and meant to bolster his own kabbalistic teachings over those of other groups, particularly given that, in the same letter (332), he criticizes unknown figures in Burgos for circulating heretical kabbalistic beliefs. That is, when read with a critical eye, Isaac's remarks may point to a wider audience for Rabad's kabbalistic hints than they first appear to.

My suggestion that Rabad was aware of a broader readership is also bolstered by the research of Idel, who argues that the differences of opinion that we find in the earliest kabbalistic writings point to the existence of closely related but distinct traditions that must have existed prior to the emergence of Kabbalah as a literary tradition:

> The multiplicity of opinions, regarding a number of subjects, which are already revealed in the earliest stages of Kabbalah . . . teaches, in my opinion, that there were processes that caused the differentiation of views, which existed earlier, into various directions, on the basis of a shared platform concerning a number of topics. The fact that it is possible to discern a few common denominators in the various early kabbalistic schools, such as the assumption of a set of ten sefirot with a dynamic character, which are called by abstract names, or the ditheistic or binitarian conception—occasionally characterized by sexual polarity—of the meaning of ritual and especially of its theurgic character, teaches that there were processes of conceptual differentiation in the periods that preceded the appearance of the literary platform of Kabbalah. ("Commentaries" 5–6)[84]

Thus, even in Rabad's time—that is, prior to the literary emergence of Kabbalah—there were already differentiated but closely related esoteric traditions that help explain the differences of opinion in the earliest kabbalistic texts. Rabad's Kabbalah reflected one such nonliterary tradition. To the extent that Rabad was aware of multiple esoteric traditions that were distinct from, yet still close to, his own, we can imagine a situation in which he might have held the hope of various readerships grasping his esoteric clues.[85]

Social Factors Driving Rabad's Esotericism

Why did Rabad resort to esoteric writing instead of merely keeping silent or fully expounding his ideas? As my analysis shows, he had a particular desire to conceal the idea of two aspects of God that unite. All the main examples of esoteric writing that we considered relate to this idea, with the exception of the gloss regarding the front and back of God. Even this gloss, at least in one explanation, deals with two aspects of God, though it does not relate to their union. In the passage dealing with the two-faced human, the union is evidently understood as sexual in nature, and this is the way that Ezra interprets the teaching regarding the Sanctus prayer that he received from Isaac, in Rabad's name. Finally, the passage regarding the two-faced human makes it clear that the union of the two aspects of God is necessary for divine unity. This is not made evident in the other passages, but it is reasonable to assume that it is part of the subtext.

As we have noted, Rabad operated in an intellectual climate stimulated by the translation of the classics of Jewish philosophy into Hebrew by Judah Ibn Tibbon—the so-called father of the translators—and others for a southern French audience without access to the original Arabic. A key characteristic of this philosophic literature was an understanding of divine unity as the absence of composition or simplicity. As scholars have documented, these translations were part of a cultural shift in southern France beginning in the mid-twelfth century in which, as Isadore Twersky put it: "A Torah-centered community, widely respected throughout Jewish Europe for its wide-ranging rabbinic scholarship and deep-rooted piety, whose sages were constantly beseeched for scholarly advice and learned guidance, turned with remarkable zest and gusto to the cultivation of philosophy and other extra-Talmudic disciplines" ("Aspects" 190–91).[86]

It is true that *Ba'alei ha-nefesh*, the one work in which Rabad (indirectly) presents the view of simplicity, was written somewhat early in this process. Judah's first translation was of the first treatise of *Duties of the Heart*—the section of the work from which Rabad borrowed in *Ba'alei ha-nefesh*. He completed it in 1161, so Rabad could not have composed the work prior to this year, but he apparently did not write the work too long after that. Twersky (*Rabad* 86–88) offers two possible dates for *Ba'alei ha-nefesh*—prior to 1170 or around 1180—without adjudicating between them. Whatever the precise date, in this late twelfth-century time frame, philosophical sources involving divine simplicity available to southern French Jews were fairly limited. Nevertheless, the evidence suggests that the concept of divine simplicity caught on at a very early date among a circle of scholars with whom Rabad associated. Rabad was a student of Meshullam ben Jacob, who is regarded by modern scholars as a key catalyst for the emerging interest in philosophy in southern France.[87] He was the figure who encouraged Judah to translate the first treatise of *Duties of the Heart*. As Gad Freudenthal ("Abraham Ibn Ezra" 68, 72–73 "Causes" 651–52, 658) points out, it was the fact that this treatise deals with divine unity that spurred Meshullam's interest in the work in the first place. Judah makes this explicit in his translator's introduction to the work: "Having now learnt that one of the sages of Sefarad, namely Rabbi Baḥya son of Joseph of blessed memory, wrote a book about the doctrine of the duties of the heart, based on the idea of the unity of God, he [Meshullam] craved to see it. . . . Having heard its words and its discourse, his spirit did not rest until he had it copied, and he ordered me to translate for him the First Gate, namely the one on the unity of God" (Ibn Pakuda 57–58).[88]

Further evidence of the interest in divine unity among this circle of scholars is found in Judah's letter to Asher, one of Meshullam's sons, which is appended to Judah's translation of Solomon Ibn Gabirol's *Improvement of the Moral Qualities of the Soul*.[89] There Judah writes, "Recall: You and I were studying that gate [i.e., the first treatise of *Duties of the Heart*] in his presence" (Freudenthal, "Causes" 668).[90] Judah is referring to a study session with Meshullam. He proceeds to explain to Asher that Gabirol's work could serve as a fine abbreviation of the remaining treatises of *Duties of the Heart* (668–69). He concludes: "At that time you committed me to translate it for you after I completed [the translation of] that gate [on the Unity of God]" (669).[91] As Freudenthal ("Abraham Ibn Ezra" 70) explains, this letter suggests that "even before the translation of the 'Gate' on the Unity of God was complete, Judah Ibn Tibbon studied the text—i.e., taught it—'in front of' R. Meshullam, that is, in a session at which the latter presided, probably in his yeshiva. This class on a work-in-progress was presumably attended not only by R. Meshullam and his son, but also by other Lunel scholars and students." Thus, the very section of *Duties of the Heart* from which Rabad borrowed was studied in the yeshiva in Lunel. While Rabad was no longer in Lunel by the time of the study session, he was relatively nearby, in Nîmes,[92] and presumably was in contact with people who were there. Indeed, Rabad enjoyed a personal relationship with the teacher of this session, Judah himself, as we know from the fact, mentioned above, that he pushed Judah to complete the translation of *Duties of the Heart*. Rabad was thus active in an environment where the view of divine unity as simplicity had generated intense interest.

Given this state of affairs, we can understand why Rabad would be particularly wary of publicly exposing his esoteric tradition, which suggested that multiple aspects of God unite. Rabad was surely aware of the contradiction between his traditions and the newly available philosophical views, and we can imagine that he worried about the derision that his traditions would have received from figures who were part of his circle of acquaintances.

He may have had additional overlapping reasons for keeping his traditions secret that did not concern his personal relationships but involved larger communal pressures faced by southern French Jews. Freudenthal has suggested that the move to translate works of philosophy into Hebrew starting in the mid-twelfth century was partly spurred by newly emerging Christian polemics against Judaism that resorted to rational philosophical argumentation in its attacks. Jews, Freudenthal ("Arabic") argues, felt a need to respond in kind and thus required access to philosophical material.[93] This might explain, Freudenthal notes, Meshullam's particular interest in a philosophical account of divine unity. Such an account might aid Jews in refuting the idea of the Trinity ("Arabic" 132; "Philosophy" 42). One piece of evidence that Freudenthal marshals in support of his claim is the fact that Jacob ben Ruben, as he recounts in his *Milḥamot ha-shem*, composed in 1170, engaged in a debate with a Christian priest that relied heavily on rational argumentation in criticizing the Trinity ("Arabic" 130–33; "Philosophy" 44–57). As Freudenthal adds it is clear from *Milḥamot ha-shem* that he drew on the newly translated *Duties of the Heart* in making his defense of Judaism ("Arabic" 132; "Philosophy" 42–43, 45, 63). In fact, in two different places in *Milḥamot ha-shem* (10, 42; see also 9), in the course of critiquing the idea of the Trinity, he employs one of the very same passages that I showed Rabad employed.[94] It is therefore possible that Rabad's concern about hiding his esoteric traditions might have been heightened by a fear that they might seem to undercut Jewish critiques of the Trinity or, conversely, add ammunition to Christian polemics, since, after all, they posit a conception of God that would seem to allow for a certain multiplicity. Against this backdrop, his choice to adopt a philosophical account of divine unity in his *Ba'alei ha-nefesh* takes on added significance.

There is also the possibility that Rabad's fear of Christian polemics may have been intertwined with another contemporary religious threat: the dualistic Cathar heresy. Perhaps Rabad was concerned that the idea that God had aspects of "judgment" and "mercy" could be mistakenly interpreted as a dualistic one concerning an evil God and a good God. Indeed, this concern may be reflected in the wording of the tradition about the two-faced first human (again, provided that the passage very directly reflects Rabad's sentiments, even if he didn't record it himself). Hence, it stresses that if "complete judgment" and "complete mercy" were not originally from a single entity, it would appear as though they were two powers (*shetei rashuyyot*). The phrase *shetei rashuyyot* is a much older one; but in a late twelfth-century southern French context, it is easy to see how it might be associated with the *duo principia* in which Cathars believed. Notably, as we will see, Rabad's grandson Asher also worried that Kabbalists might erroneously be understood as believing in "two powers" (A. ben David 120). His use of the phrase, too, as Joseph Shatzmiller (80–81) suggested,[95] may refer to Cathar theology. Rabad's esotericism, then, may partly be due to a worry that his traditions might be taken to imply excessive similarity between Jewish tradition and the faith of his Cathari neighbors. This would not only have been undesirable in and of itself but also might have caused his tradition to be lumped with those of Cathars by the church, which was taking an increasingly strident approach to heresy in southern France.

Indeed, the fear of being caught up in church persecutions against the Cathar heresy might have seemed very real to Rabad because of his relationship with Roger II Trencavel, the viscount of Béziers. It appears that Rabad was under the personal protection of the viscount, and the viscount intervened on Rabad's behalf in a dispute that the latter had with the former's vassal (Twersky, *Rabad* 35–38). Roger himself was the target of the campaign against heresy. In 1178, accompanied by a small army, Henri of Marci, the abbot of Clairvaux, traveled to Albi to try to free its bishop, who had been imprisoned by Roger. Roger was forced to retreat, and in the aftermath, Henri declared him a heretic. In his account of the events, Henri describes Roger as "an agent of evil" as well as a "traitor and heretic" (Moore, *Birth* 121). Before arriving at Albi, Henri encountered two accused heretics: Raymond de Baimac and Bernard Raymond. They were allowed to defend themselves at a public hearing in Saint-Étienne, where they denied any heretical beliefs, including the belief in two principles. Later, in nearby Saint-Jacques, they again publicly defended themselves, but the assembled crowd accused them of lying. According to the account of Cardinal Peter of Saint Chrysogonus, who led the questioning of the heretics, "Some of those present steadfastly maintained that they had heard from some of the heretics that there are two Gods, one good and one evil" (115).

In 1181, Henri, now a cardinal, returned with a larger army and laid siege to Lavaur, which was under the control of Roger's wife, Adelaide. Roger was forced to surrender and renounce his alleged heresy. Additionally, he agreed to give up Raymond de Baimac and Bernard Raymond, the aforementioned heretics, who had taken refuge in Lavaur. The two men now confessed to their heretical ideas, which included a belief in dualism.[96] Rabad surely would have been aware of these events, and his fear of persecution by the church, should his ideas seem connected to those of the heretics, may have been one motivation for his esotericism in works that he composed from this period forward, which might include *Ba'alei ha-nefesh* (see above) and certainly includes his glosses on Maimonides's *Mishneh torah* (Twersky, *Rabad* 125).

It is true that R. I. Moore (*War*), in his influential work, has questioned whether dualism had really taken hold in southern France prior to the thirteenth century—as the standard account has it—and, indeed, whether Catharism existed as a coherent movement at this early period.[97] Part of Moore's argument lies in suggesting that the standard view is more a product of church propaganda than historical reality. In the case, for instance, of the confession of Raymond de Baimac and Bernard Raymond to believing in dualism, Moore suggests that it is possible "that they hoped to win pardon and favour (as, in fact, they did) by confirming the expectations of their interrogators" (*War* 219). Even if Moore is correct, from Rabad's perspective, the perception of the church would have mattered more than the reality on the ground and, as suggested, may have provided a compelling reason to maintain a code of secrecy.

Therefore Rabad had ample reason to keep his traditions secret and even to publicly present a point of view on divine unity that seems to contradict these traditions. His decision to conceal his secrets can be understood as a form of "defensive esotericism" necessitated by multiple threats of persecution, as in the model famously articulated by Strauss in *Persecution and the Art of Writing*.

The Emergence of Kabbalah as a Written Tradition

My contention that Rabad engaged in esoteric writing helps reshape our understanding of the emergence of Kabbalah as a literary tradition in one additional way. The writing of the first kabbalistic monographs has often been presented in recent scholarship as marking, at least in part, a move from an oral to a written tradition. That is, the assumption has been that Kabbalah existed in some form as an esoteric oral tradition that was first put into writing at the beginning of the thirteenth century.[98] The analysis in this chapter introduces an intermediate stage in which this tradition had begun to be put into writing already in the twelfth century, but only in veiled terms. The opening act of Kabbalah as a literary tradition is therefore not the recording of esoteric ideas but the recording of allusions to esoteric ideas in otherwise exoteric texts.

Yet if we can understand the social pressures that likely prevented Rabad from openly revealing his traditions, it is less clear what motivated Rabad to allude to them through esoteric writing. If, as I am contending, this is a new approach, which marks the beginning of Kabbalah as a literary tradition, we must wonder what pushed him to innovate in this manner. Insofar as Rabad, for the most part, did not advertise the fact that his works contained concealed traditions, we can eliminate the possibility that it was an act of "secretism" meant to bolster his social standing. Such an act, in any case, flies in the face of the defensive motivation for which I have argued.

Instead, I would suggest that it is possible that the very same social factors that made esotericism necessary also led Rabad to become the first figure to allude to kabbalistic secrets in writing. Perhaps the coalescence of threats to his traditions in the form of newly emergent Jewish philosophy, a church that also employed philosophy, and the spread of Cathar theology led to conflicting impulses. On the one hand, these threats may have underscored the need to keep his traditions silent. On the other hand, they may have also provoked the fear that, if they were not somehow publicized, they would be overwhelmed by outside forces and eventually lost, even by those who sought to preserve them. Esoteric writing might therefore represent a compromise position wherein Rabad could preserve his tradition in a public forum but also maintain its basic secrecy.[99] In the Introduction, I argued that esoteric writing serves a pedagogic function of spreading secret ideas to those who are worthy of understanding them. This motivation may be especially compelling in times when the traditions themselves are under threat. At this point, though, we have entered into conjectures about Rabad's psychological motivations, which, absent textual evidence, remain speculative.

Chapter 4

Isaac the Blind's Literary Legacy

At first blush, Rabad's son, Isaac the Blind, appears to be a contradictory figure. On the one hand, he is the author of the aforementioned letter to Nahmanides and Jonah Gerondi in which he decries the publicizing of kabbalistic material and claims that he followed the approach of his fathers not to reveal even the very fact that he possessed esoteric knowledge. This letter is surely the most explicit denunciation of the public dissemination of Kabbalah that we have from the first generation of kabbalistic literary activity. On the other hand, there are numerous kabbalistic teachings in his name, far more than those in the name of his father. Some of these teachings purport to be Isaac's oral lessons recorded by other figures. In such instances, we might reasonably suggest that Isaac never intended his oral teachings to be made public and that they were recorded without his authorization. Yet we also have a fair amount of material allegedly written by him. Such material seems to stand in conflict with his stance in the letter, where he criticized "sages, wise men, and pious men who were lengthy in their language and extended their hands to write about great and sublime matters (*gedolot ve-nora'ot*) in their books and letters" (T. Weiss, "Letter" 331). Scholem ("Te'udah" 13–16; *Origins* 394) surmised that he is likely referring to Ezra and Azriel of Gerona—a point that is difficult to prove and may or may not be accurate.[1] Regardless of the identity of these scholars, their behavior is problematic from Isaac's point of view because "what is written has no master; often these things are lost or their owners die, and the writings fall into the hands of fools or scoffers, and the name of heaven is thus profaned" (T. Weiss, "Letter" 331). As Idel puts it: "The concept of a profound concern with esotericism in the circle of Isaac the Blind is exclusively based upon some statements in the epistle. . . . However, the authentic remnants of Sagi Nahor's (= Isaac the Blind's) writings, both those that are printed or discussed by Scholem and those that are found in manuscripts and were not the subject of analysis, do not concur with his pose" ("Nahmanides" 37; parentheses added).²

Idel does not offer a way of resolving these apparently contradictory stances. Ram Ben-Shalom (*Jews of Provence* 571–72) offers a number of possible explanations. Among others, he suggests that Isaac began to write kabbalistic texts only after he saw that his campaign against kabbalistic writing had failed and there was a need for accurate kabbalistic writings to combat the misleading kabbalistic works that others had already composed. Similarly, he raises the possibility that once Isaac saw that, through their writings, others had made names for themselves as Kabbalists, he felt compelled to make a name for himself as a central bearer of kabbalistic tradition. As interesting as these and other possibilities that Ben-Shalom raises are, I will argue that a simpler solution readily presents itself. This solution is twofold. First, as I will show, there is good reason to be skeptical about the authenticity of much of Isaac's alleged literary legacy,³ and, in many cases, the attributions to Isaac appear to be spurious. Second, to the extent that he nevertheless occasionally put his kabbalistic ideas into writing, he did so only in very brief texts, which were composed in a highly allusive style and likely circulated only to initiates. Isaac, I will suggest, did not see this style of writing as violating his commitment to esotericism because even if such material were to fall into the hands of uninitiated readers, its cryptic nature would prevent them from deciphering his ideas.

Reevaluating Isaac's Literary Legacy

Our understanding of Isaac's literary output has been dramatically altered by a highly compelling recent study by Avishai Bar-Asher ("Illusion"). While his study is devoted to proving that the universally accepted attribution of *Commentary on Sefer Yetsirah* to Isaac is spurious, he also highlights the need to reassess Isaac's entire literary legacy and suggests that he did not compose any extended works (281–83). Bar-Asher astutely notes that we can definitively state that Isaac was the author of only one text: the letter to Nahmanides and Jonah Gerondi that I have already cited (272–73). This is the only extant text in which Isaac definitively identifies himself as the author within the text itself. At the end of the letter, he signs off by writing, "and you know that it is I who speak to you, Isaac, the son of the Rabbi, R. Abraham" (T. Weiss, "Letter" 334).

A second text, which has also been widely assumed to be by Isaac, also includes a self-identification. I refer to a non-kabbalistic responsum dealing with the halakhic question of whether one of the blessings of the *Shemoneh 'Esreh* prayer—the centerpiece of the traditional liturgy—should end "Builder of Jerusalem" or "God of David and Builder of Jerusalem."[4] At the beginning of the responsum, we read: "I, Isaac, the son of the Pious One, the memory of the righteous one will be a blessing, bring a proof" (Abramson, *'Inyyanut* 152). The author of the letter signs off with the same name (153). As Bar-Asher ("Illusion" 273n11) points out, however, it is uncertain that "Isaac, the son of the Pious one" should be identified with Isaac the Blind.[5] Indeed, as far as I know, Isaac is never identified in this manner in any other source. I would add that a primary reason that this Isaac has been identified with Isaac the Blind is the fact that Jacob ben Sheshet, a Kabbalist who received teachings directly from Isaac the Blind, states that the latter used the ending "God of David and Builder of Jerusalem" ("Sefer ha-emunah" 396).[6] Ben Sheshet's comments, though, do not help us identify the author of the responsum, since the responsum, itself does not resolve which ending is the correct one but presents arguments for both positions. Yet, even if the responsum is by Isaac the Blind, it does not concern kabbalistic matters[7] and does not, therefore, conflict with his opposition to the dissemination of kabbalistic ideas.[8]

The remaining teachings attributed to Isaac do not include such self-identifications. Rather, they are identified as deriving from Isaac by other Kabbalists or by later copyists. Indeed, dozens of such teachings are extant in printed kabbalistic texts or in manuscript,[9] and they have served as the basis of numerous scholarly analyses of early Kabbalah.[10] For our purposes, we must ask two questions about the nature of the attributions to Isaac found in these texts. First, does the particular text claim that it is recording Isaac's oral teaching, or does it claim that Isaac himself actually put pen to paper? This distinction has not been of particular importance to previous scholarship whose goal has been to characterize Isaac's thought and trace his influence. For such research, once it is established that the ideas in a given text reflect Isaac's thought, it matters little whether he was their actual author. For our purposes, where the goal is to examine esoteric writing, the question of actual authorship is significant. Second, in the cases of texts that claim direct authorship, how much credence should we give these claims? As we will see, scholars have often too readily accepted attributions to Isaac.

In what follows, I will analyze various teachings attributed to Isaac with the aim of answering these questions. Given the quantity of such teachings, I cannot hope to analyze each one.[11] Instead, I will focus on a large selection of such teachings that have generally been deemed authentic and that are broadly representative of Isaac's supposed oeuvre.

Isaac's Alleged Major Works

By far the longest text attributed to Isaac is *Commentary on Sefer Yetsirah*.[12] It has served generations of scholars as the major source for understanding Isaac's thought, even if there was some disagreement as to whether Isaac was the actual author or if the text merely reflected his teachings and was recorded by one his students.[13] In his aforementioned study, however, which primarily focuses on this text, Bar-Asher compellingly demonstrates that it was composed neither by Isaac nor by one of his students but, in all likelihood, by an anonymous figure in the last third of the thirteenth century. It thus reflects a considerably later stage in the history of Kabbalah. I will not rehearse Bar-Asher's extended and comprehensive argument; highlighting his key findings will suffice: (1) There is not a single citation of this text by the first Kabbalists, who otherwise quote teachings of Isaac; (2) In important recensions of the text, the attribution to Isaac is missing; and (3) Some of the first Kabbalists to cite the text, who were active at the turn of the fourteenth century, know nothing of the attribution to Isaac and, indeed, contrast its ideas with traditions that they had regarding Isaac's understanding of *Sefer Yetsirah*. In light of Bar-Asher's study, I am convinced that we can eliminate this text from our discussion.

No other text attributed to Isaac is nearly as extensive as *Commentary on Sefer Yetsirah*, which runs some 5,500 words. After the *Commentary on Sefer Yetsirah*, the next two longest texts attributed to Isaac are: (1) A commentary on the creation narrative ("Commentary on Creation"), which is first found in Ezra of Gerona's *Commentary on the Talmudic Aggadot* (*Aggadot Commentary*) and runs about 1,300 words; and (2) An explanation of the kabbalistic significance of temple sacrifice ("Commentary on Sacrifice"), which is found in *Explanation of Nahmanides's Torah Commentary* (*Explanation/Bei'ur*), a text composed at the turn of the fourteenth century by a student of Rashba. In its current form, it runs about 980 words but, as I will show below, was originally longer.[14] The former text includes the label "the words of the Pious One" (*leshon he-ḥasid*), the standard designation for Isaac in kabbalistic literature. The latter text is described by the author of *Explanation* as a text that "the Pious One wrote." After these two texts, the length of the remainder of the material attributed to Isaac drops precipitously.[15]

In the course of my discussion below, I will treat the numerous other teachings that are attributed to Isaac in *Aggadot Commentary* and in *Explanation*. Given the more substantial size of "Commentary on Creation" and "Commentary on Sacrifice," they merit separate study. Unfortunately, the confines of space prevent me from fully expounding on both texts. In the case of the "Commentary on Creation," I will suffice with pointing out that while both older and more recent scholarship has widely assumed that "Commentary on Creation" was composed by Isaac,[16] Efraim Gottlieb already showed in 1968 that this is not the case. He points out that, based on the copy of "Commentary on Creation" found in the text of *Aggadot Commentary* included in MS Vat. 441, 24a–32a, it is clear that only two brief passages of the longer commentary derive from Isaac (*Studies* 60–61).[17] Gottlieb's accurate observation is supported by a fuller investigation of the available manuscript evidence that I will publish elsewhere. Here, I will focus on "Commentary on Sacrifice," whose attribution to Isaac has yet to be subjected to critical scrutiny.

Commentary on Sacrifice

As noted, "Commentary on Sacrifice" appears in *Explanation of Nahmanides's Commentary on the Torah*, a turn-of-the-fourteenth-century supercommentary that focuses on explaining the kabbalistic hints that Nahmanides strewed through his Torah commentary. The identity of *Explanation*'s author has yet to be settled. While it is attributed to Meir Ibn Sahula, a student of Shlomo ben Adret (Rashba), Scholem claimed that the true author is another student of Rashba, Joshua Ibn Shuaib. Scholem's position has not been met with universal acceptance. Regardless of the specific author, the scholarly consensus is that it is a work by a student of Rashba.[18] This fact, according to Scholem (*Origins* 258), provides a potential explanation for how the author came to possess traditions of Isaac that are not found in earlier works: they may have been in the possession of his teacher, Rashba, who received them from Nahmanides, who was in contact with Isaac. A close examination, however, of the numerous passages in

Isaac's name that are included in *Explanation* raises questions about the accuracy of these attributions. I will discuss these passages more fully below. For now, I will focus on the longest of these passages, "Commentary on Sacrifice."[19]

In the printed edition of *Explanation* and in some manuscripts, the author introduces it in the following manner: "Though the meaning of sacrifice is concealed and hidden, and the Rabbi (Nahmanides) only hinted at it in a manner that is sufficient for the understanding, it remains for me to explain a little more, so that the matter becomes clearer according to the conception of the Rabbi (Nahmanides), of blessed memory, based on what I found written by the Rabbi, the Pious One (Isaac the Blind)" (*Bei'ur* 23b).[20] In other manuscripts, an additional comment appears immediately after these remarks: "I will write it using his language, even though I will shorten it, but I will write its essence."[21] According to this line, the author did not transcribe Isaac's entire text but only presented it in an abbreviated form, even if he was careful not to change Isaac's wording. Assuming that this version is accurate, the text before the author of *Explanation* was even longer than the text that he included. If, therefore, "Commentary on Sacrifice" was indeed by Isaac, it was a substantial composition.

Two other recensions of the text, which contain significant differences, also exist. One is found in *Me'irat 'einayim*, by the late thirteenth- to mid-fourteenth-century Kabbalist Isaac of Acre (Goldreich 139–41).[22] There, Isaac attributes it to an anthology of various early kabbalistic texts prepared by an unnamed *ḥakham maskil* ("knowledgeable sage"), a source he cites frequently.[23] It is also found, independently of *Me'irat 'einayim*, in a number of manuscripts that contain versions of this anthology.[24] The third recension, which I have printed in a separate study ("Early Kabbalistic Explanation," 75–79), is found without attribution in a number of manuscripts.[25] In this context, I will not comment on the relationship between the three recensions, which I have already done in the above study (58–62), other than to note that my analysis suggests that neither of the other two recensions is dependent on the one in *Explanation*, nor is the one in *Explanation* dependent on them. Significantly for our purposes, the attribution to Isaac is found only in the recension in *Explanation*.

While the attribution to Isaac has generally been accepted by scholars,[26] it is very difficult to uphold. A number of factors lead me to this conclusion. First, to my knowledge, this attribution does not appear in any other manuscript of either of the other recensions. Given Isaac's central place in

Kabbalists' self-understanding of the history of Kabbalah, a text attributed to him would surely have been seen as valuable. Accordingly, it seems more likely that this attribution was added to the text (perhaps by *Explanation*'s source) than that it was removed from the text. Second, the substantial length of the text (particularly considering that the version in *Explanation* is abridged) argues against its attribution to Isaac because, as we will see, according to his letter to Nahmanides and Jonah, he found only brief kabbalistic expositions acceptable. Finally, in "Commentary on Sacrifice" an exegesis of a rabbinic teaching regarding sacrifice from the halakhic midrash, *Sifra*, appears prominently. Yet in *Commentary on the Song of Songs* (*Song Commentary* 499), Ezra cites a different explanation by Isaac of the same rabbinic teaching. While the two explanations are thematically related insofar as both imagine a process whereby sacrifice theurgically causes the lowest sefirah to ascend to one of the higher sefirot and draw down efflux, there is no linguistic overlap between them. Moreover, the references to corporeality, which are prominent in the passage in *Song Commentary*, are missing in the exegesis of this statement in "Commentary on Sacrifice." Since Ezra heard teachings directly from Isaac, the statements that he cites in Isaac's name carry a fairly high level of reliability. The fact that the exegesis that he provides in Isaac's name of the passage in *Sifra* is different from that in "Commentary on Sacrifice" further calls into question the reliability of the attribution to Isaac in the latter.

At the same time, parts of "Commentary on Sacrifice" are clearly based on material in Ezra's works that he never ascribes to Isaac. In particular, "Commentary on Sacrifice" shares material with Ezra's "Excursus on the Commandments," a text that he appended to *Song Commentary*,[27] and with *Aggadot Commentary*.[28]

Indeed, I would suggest that "Commentary on Sacrifice" derives in some form from the writings of Ezra of Gerona or from members of his immediate circle. Thus, "Commentary on Sacrifice" also shares clear linguistic similarities with a short text on sacrifice attributed to Azriel of Gerona in several manuscripts.[29] Additionally, there is linguistic overlap between "Commentary on Sacrifice" and an extended discussion of sacrifice that appears in manuscripts before Azriel's aforementioned text.[30] While this discussion is unattributed, scholars have generally assumed that it, too, is by Azriel.[31] Joseph Dan (*History* 8:250n45), for his part, offers the suggestion that it is by Ezra. Neither suggestion can be verified, but, judging from the style of the passages, both are certainly possible.

While it is conceivable that all these recensions of "Commentary on Sacrifice" and all the related passages by Ezra or Azriel draw on an earlier text by Isaac, it is highly unlikely. Not a single one of them, with the exception of the one found in *Explanation*, includes any attribution to Isaac, as we would have expected if they were borrowing from his work. Indeed, as noted, the only time in his work that Ezra cites a teaching by Isaac regarding sacrifice, it does not appear in any of these passages. In the final analysis, it may be best to view "Commentary on Sacrifice," as it appears in *Explanation*, as one example of a genre of interrelated early kabbalistic speculation about sacrifices of which the various other recensions, as well as the other related passages that I have described, are other examples. This possibility is in keeping with Daniel Abrams's (*Kabbalistic Manuscripts* 439–54, esp. 450–51) insightful observation that there was a high level of textual fluidity in early Kabbalah, in which one Kabbalist reworked the work of another, or one and the same Kabbalist produced multiple versions of the same text.[32] There is no evidence, however, that Isaac himself contributed to this genre.

* * *

Thus, the three longest texts attributed to Isaac were, in all likelihood, not composed by him. Indeed, I see no evidence that would allow us to conclude that Isaac ever composed extended kabbalistic texts. The question remains as to whether Isaac composed shorter pieces. Here the answer is affirmative because, as we will see, in the one text that he definitively wrote—his letter to Jonah and Nahmanides—he includes a brief commentary on Psalm 150. Did Isaac compose other such brief kabbalistic pieces? To answer this question, I propose to closely examine the material attributed to Isaac by the three Kabbalists who most frequently cite kabbalistic teachings in his name: Ezra, Jacob ben Sheshet, and the author of *Explanation*.

Teachings Attributed to Isaac by Ezra ben Solomon of Gerona, Jacob ben Sheshet, and the Author of *Explanation*

Ezra ben Solomon of Gerona

As already seen, Ezra ben Solomon of Gerona frequently cites Isaac, using the appellative "the Pious One." In his extant works, Ezra definitively cites

Isaac fifteen times. Two additional citations may also derive from Isaac. Since Ezra studied with Isaac, his citations carry particular authority and warrant close inspection. A number of questions emerge about the sources of these citations. Should they be taken as verbatim citations of Isaac's teachings—in which case, they provide a window into Isaac's manner of expression, or should they be regarded as periphrastic? Were the teachings conveyed to Ezra orally by Isaac? Beyond any oral teachings that he may have received, did Ezra also have textual material upon which he drew, and, if so, was it by Isaac or by a third party? If it is not possible to conclusively answer all these questions, a close examination of these citations allows us to make some headway.

I will begin by listing the places in which Ezra cites Isaac, while paying particular attention to the precise language of the attribution to Isaac, since the specific language may provide a clue to the nature of its source.[33] Let me, however, offer a proviso. As Elliot Wolfson ("Beyond" 196–97) has noted, in kabbalistic literature, at times, even expressions that seem to describe pure oral transmission, such as "I have received" or "I have heard," can convey the transmission of written documents. Yet in the particular citations of Isaac that I describe in this chapter, from Ezra and other figures, I find no evidence that this is the case. Wolfson's broader claim (193–206), however, that these terms may involve the transmission of oral traditions about written sources, is often true of these citations.[34]

In a letter that he wrote to a certain R. Abraham, Ezra cites a teaching of Isaac with the phrase "the Pious One hinted" (*ramaz*) (Scholem, "Te'udah" 26). The term *ramaz* is ambiguous and, on its own, does not allow us to determine whether we are dealing with a written or an oral tradition or whether it is a verbatim citation of Isaac's words. There is nevertheless some evidence that it is a verbatim citation.[35]

In his *Song Commentary*, Ezra cites his teacher twice. Once, he does so in the body of the commentary with the phrase "our Rabbi, the Pious One, explicated" (*peiresh rabbenu he-ḥasid*) (*Song Commentary*, 499; MS Vat. 86, 38a; MS Vienna 148, 1a–47a). This is the passage regarding sacrifice that I mentioned above. The word "explicated" also leaves it ambiguous as to whether Ezra is paraphrasing Isaac or citing his exact words. Even if the latter is correct, for which there is some evidence,[36] it is difficult to know whether he is citing Isaac's words from an oral teaching that he heard directly from Isaac, or whether he is citing a text written by Isaac. The second time he cites Isaac is in the "Excursus on the Commandments," which Ezra appended to *Song Commentary*. There, he writes: "And our Rabbi, the Pious One, of blessed memory, said" (*ve-amar*) (Travis 6–7). This phrase might imply that he is using Isaac's precise terminology but does not allow us to determine whether the source is oral or written.[37]

Most of Ezra's citations of his teacher appear in *Aggadot Commentary*. Here is a complete list of the various ways in which Ezra words the attribution:

1. A passage in which Ezra states, regarding a text in *Bere'shit rabba'*, "I have received this version (*girsa'*) [of the passage] from the mouth (*mi-pi*) of the Pious One, may God protect him" (MS Vat. 441, 31b).[38] This passage obviously involves an oral communication and may suggest that Ezra and Isaac studied this text together.
2. The passage considered in the last chapter regarding the Sanctus, which Ezra attributes to Isaac as "the Pious One in the name of his father" (MS Vat. 441, 13a; 185, 10a). There is no way to tell whether Isaac recorded the passage in a text that Ezra had access to, or whether he transmitted the ideas orally to Isaac. As I suggested in Chapter 3, he did not record it verbatim, since the teaching is presented in Ezra's own esoteric style, with his telltale expression "you already know," which assumes that the reader comes with prior kabbalistic knowledge.
3. A passage described as "the opinion (*da'at*) of the Pious One" (MS Vat. 441, 33a).[39] This language may very well reflect an oral teaching but is ultimately ambiguous.
4. In one of the extant manuscripts of *Aggadot Commentary*, Vat. 294, 48b, two passages are perhaps attributed to Isaac that do not appear in any of the other versions. Tishby (Azriel of Gerona, *Commentary* 27) suggests that they may ultimately derive from unknown writings of Ezra but were not originally part of *Aggadot Commentary*. One passage is introduced as "I have heard (*shama'ti*) in the name of my Rabbi."[40] There is no way to determine whether the Rabbi is, in fact, Isaac. The second passage is introduced as "I have received (*mekubbelani*) from the son of the Rabbi." The "son of the Rabbi" may be a reference to Isaac but, given that this is not Ezra's typical designation for his teacher, it is difficult to be sure. In any case,

both passages seem to involve oral traditions, although the former was apparently not transmitted directly but through a third party.

5. The majority of the citations—nine, to be precise—are attributed to Isaac with the phrase "the words of the Pious One" (*leshon he-ḥasid*).[41] At a minimum, this terminology implies that the teachings reflect Isaac's actual words.[42] Like all the teachings cited by Ezra in Isaac's name, those described as "the language of the Pious One" are quite short—just a few lines—and could plausibly be direct quotations of Isaac's oral teachings that Ezra jotted down. Alternatively, they might be based on some sort of document(s) in which Isaac recorded brief ideas about certain topics.[43]

Therefore, of the fifteen times that Ezra cites Isaac, we can conclude with reasonable confidence that nine of them reflect verbatim transcriptions of Isaac's words. Of the fifteen citations, Ezra definitively describes only one as an oral tradition that he heard directly from Isaac. For all the other fourteen instances, it remains an open question as to whether they are based on a document composed by Isaac that Ezra had in his possession or an oral tradition that Ezra heard directly or indirectly from Isaac.

Let me also comment on the character of these citations. They are all quite brief; the longest one is only eighty-one words.[44] Moreover, they are written in a condensed and allusive style, which requires considerable background knowledge on the part of the reader who hopes to understand them. That is, they have the character of communications intended for a select audience rather than public teachings meant to transmit Kabbalah to a wider group. I will provide an example so that the tenor of these passages becomes apparent.

In *Aggadot Commentary*, Ezra first cites a passage from *Bere'shit rabba'*: "Rabbi Pinḥas in the name of Rabbi Hoshaya: The space between the earth and the firmament is equivalent to the space between the firmament and the upper waters. [As it is written]: 'Let there be a firmament in the midst of the waters [that it may divide waters from waters]' (Gen. 1:6)—halfway between them.[45] Rabbi Ḥanina said:[46] And their fruits are the rains" (MS Vat. 185, 17a; MS Vat. 294, 34b; MS Vat. 441a, 20a).[47] Immediately after citing this midrash, Ezra records a tradition in the name of Isaac: "For they are sent from the cause (*sibbah*) at the time of unity and will (*be-'et ha-yiḥud veha-ratson*). The words of the Pious One" (MS Vat. 185, 17a; MS Vat. 441, 20a).[48] I will return to this passage at greater length in Chapter 6, since it will prove useful in decoding an esoteric hint in Asher ben David's work. For now, I will briefly decipher this passage with an eye toward its terse and cryptic style. My exegesis of the passage is based on two other passages in Ezra's and Azriel's work, respectively, that also deal with "rain."[49] On the basis of these "rain passages," which I will describe in detail in Chapter 6, it becomes apparent that this short teaching intimates a fuller teaching regarding the sexual union of male and female sefirot. According to the passage in *Bere'shit rabba'*, the firmament divides between the upper waters and the lower waters.[50] As the fuller exposition will indicate, Isaac identifies the "upper waters" with the efflux of the male sixth sefirah and the "lower waters" with the efflux of the female tenth sefirah.[51] These effluxes emerge and combine with each other when the sixth and tenth sefirot unite sexually. These combined effluxes are the rains: that is, they are the emanative flow that sustains the human world, or, in the idiom of the passage from *Bere'shit rabba'*, the rains are the "fruits" of this union.

This entire teaching is hinted at in the cryptic citation of Isaac. The "cause" (*sibbah*), from which the rains are sent, is the tenth sefirah, since it is from this sefirah that the mixture of male and female waters ultimately descends to the human realm. "The time of unity and will" is a *terminus technicus* for the union of the sixth and tenth sefirot.

For our current purposes, more important than the actual details of the teaching is the fact that these details are not elaborated but presented in a terse shorthand, using technical terminology like "cause" (*sibbah*) and "the time of unity and will" (*be-'et ha-yiḥud veha-ratson*). The brief teaching, then, is comprehensible only to one with detailed knowledge of this terminology and of the workings of the sefirot that this terminology alludes to. I am able to decipher this teaching only by consulting the "rain passages." Yet these passages are hardly models of clarity. On the contrary, it is only because I have access to later kabbalistic works that explain kabbalistic terminology more openly and because I am the beneficiary of extensive modern scholarship on kabbalistic doctrine that I am able to decipher them and, in turn, use them to elucidate Isaac's teaching. Needless to say, these tools were not available in the first half of the thirteenth century.

This teaching is hardly exceptional. A similar analysis could be applied to the other teachings that Ezra records in Isaac's name. To repeat, it is unclear whether Isaac conveyed these teachings orally or whether he wrote them down. Let me begin with the former possibility. We have no knowledge about the manner in which Isaac might have orally transmitted his teachings to his students. It is possible, however, that, in keeping with the Talmudic dictum, Isaac conveyed some of his teachings as "chapter headings" and would have expected his students to fill in the details. If so, Isaac may have conveyed these teachings just as Ezra cites them, without any accompanying explanation. If, rather, Isaac recorded his teachings, Ezra's citations of them show that the former's written style was characterized by terseness and obscurity. In either scenario, it should be apparent that when Isaac transmitted these teachings, his intended audience must have been quite limited.

Jacob ben Sheshet

A combined total of eleven citations are found in Isaac's name in "Sefer ha-emunah veha-bittaḥon" and *Sefer meshiv devarim nekhoḥim*, the main works of Jacob ben Sheshet, another Geronese Kabbalist who knew Isaac personally. As is true of the citations in Ezra's work, on the basis of these citations, which are quite short (consisting of only a line or two of text), it cannot be established with any certainly that ben Sheshet had access to written materials by Isaac. Nor is it apparent, in most cases, whether he is citing Isaac's words verbatim or merely paraphrasing him. Nevertheless, here, too, closely inspecting the language of the attributions provides limited answers.[52]

I will begin with the most unambiguous cases. In one instance, ben Sheshet clearly employs a written source. The source, however, is not a text by Isaac but Ezra's *Aggadot Commentary*: "The sage R. Ezra wrote regarding this statement . . . the preceding was the language of the Pious One" ("Sefer ha-emunah" 410).[53] In two other places, he describes teachings that he heard directly from Isaac. In one, he writes: "So I have heard (*shama'ti*) from the mouth (*mi-pi*) of the Pious One, R. Isaac, the son of the great Rabbi, R. Abraham (the memory of the righteous one should be a blessing), in the name of his father" (357). In the second, he writes: "I heard (*shama'ti*) these words (*ha-lashon*) from the mouth of (*mi-pi*) of the Pious One, R. Isaac, the son of the great Rabbi, R. Abraham, the memory of the righteous and holy one should be a blessing" (*Sefer meshiv* 177, lines 59–60).[54] In both instances, the terminology "from the mouth" indicates a direct oral transmission.[55] In the second instance, it is apparent that he is offering a verbatim citation, although this may be implied in the first instance as well. In any case, these passages show that, at some point in his career, he encountered Isaac, who personally taught him kabbalistic ideas.

In three other instances, ben Sheshet employs variations of "I have heard (*shama'ti*) these words (*zeh ha-lashon*) in the name of (*be-shem*) the Pious One, R. Isaac, the son of the great Rabbi, R. Abraham (the memory of the righteous one should be for a blessing)."[56] The terminology of "I have heard these words . . . in the name of" suggests that these teachings are based on oral reports of Isaac's views from a third party. The terminology may also imply that the third party conveyed Isaac's words verbatim, but this is not certain.

Elsewhere, it is unclear whether ben Sheshet was using a written or an oral tradition. In one instance, ben Sheshet introduces one of Isaac's teachings with "and the Pious One, R. Isaac, of blessed memory, the son of the great Rabbi, R. Abraham (the memory of the righteous should be a blessing) said" (*ve-amar*) (*Sefer meshiv* 164, lines 31–32). The term "said" could conceivably refer to a teaching that he heard directly from Isaac, but it might also reflect an indirect oral transmission. It may even refer to a textual transmission, directly by Isaac or from a third party, since the term "said" need not be taken as a literal act of speaking but may refer to something said in a text. It may or may not also imply a verbatim citation.

In another instance, he writes: "So I have received (*kibbalti*) in the name of (*be-shem*) the Pious One, R. Isaac, the son of the great Rabbi, R. Abraham, of blessed memory" ("Sefer ha-emunah" 401). "I have received" may imply a written or an oral report, but "in the name of" suggests that he was referring neither to a teaching that he heard directly from Isaac nor to a text written by Isaac himself. Whether these are Isaac's precise words is also unclear.

In yet another passage, he refers to "the opinion of the Pious One, R. Isaac, the son of the great Rabbi, R. Abraham (the memory of a righteous and holy one should be a blessing), as I have recorded his words (*katavti leshono*) in the second chapter regarding the verse, 'Hear O Israel'" (*Sefer meshiv* 72, lines 43–44). The wording *katavti leshono* seems to suggest a verbatim transcription of Isaac's words. This passage appears in ben Sheshet's *Meshiv devarim nekhoḥim*. Yet no such teaching is found in the extant versions of chapter 2 of this work. This led Ephraim Gottlieb (*Sefer meshiv* 14) to suggest that ben Sheshet may have been referring to the teaching regarding "Hear, O Israel" that is found in ben Sheshet's "Sefer ha-emunah veha-bittaḥon." This teaching is one of those referred to above, which ben Sheshet attributed to Isaac as "I have heard (*shama'ti*) this language in the name of the Pious One" (362). Thus, if Gottlieb is correct, we are not dealing with a teaching written by Isaac. At the same time, it must be noted that in "Sefer ha-emunah veha-bittaḥon," the teaching is found in the third rather than the second chapter. This calls Gottlieb's contention into question and at least leaves open the possibility that ben Sheshet had a written source. Of course, we cannot be certain that such a source was composed by Isaac himself.

At first glance, other instances do seem as though they are based on a text written by Isaac. Closer inspection, however, calls this possibility into question. Ben Sheshet twice mentions explications by Isaac of *Sefer Yetsirah*. Yet this fact in no way contradicts Bar-Asher's argument that the attribution to Isaac of the *Commentary to Sefer Yetsirah* is spurious, and, as he shows, there is no evidence that either of these explications refers to ideas in the *Commentary* ("Illusion" 363–73, 374–75). Rather, as Bar-Asher suggests (366–67), it seems that authentic explications by Isaac of parts of *Sefer Yetsirah* were known to the first Kabbalists, including ben Sheshet. The question remains as to whether these explications derive from a source that Isaac or someone else composed or whether they circulated orally.

The first explication pertains to a passage in *Sefer Yetsirah* 1:3, which insists that there are exactly ten sefirot—no more and no fewer: "ten and not nine." Ben Sheshet does not share the contents of Isaac's explanation. Rather, he merely notes that Isaac had an explanation that was different from his own: "The Pious One, R. Isaac, son of the holy Rabbi, R. Abraham—the memory of the righteous and holy one shall be a blessing—explicated (*peiresh*) 'ten and not nine' in a different manner" ("Sefer ha-emunah" 362).[57] As Bar-Asher ("Illusion" 366–68) points out, Isaac explains the phrase "ten and not nine" in his letter to Nahmanides and Jonah. It is not impossible, therefore, that this written source lies behind ben Sheshet's citation of Isaac. It is equally possible that ben Sheshet received this explication orally, either directly from Isaac or through an intermediary. It is similarly possible that Isaac communicated the explication in another written work that has not survived—perhaps even a letter to ben Sheshet himself.

The fact that he does not cite Isaac's explication should not be regarded as an act of esotericism because ben Sheshet is not reluctant to reveal Isaac's teachings elsewhere. Perhaps the seeming reluctance here stems from the fact that he disagrees with Isaac and, because of Isaac's stature, was uneager to publicize the details of this disagreement. It is also possible that Isaac's explication was well known, and ben Sheshet therefore felt no need to record it. If so, this implies that Isaac's explication of this passage and perhaps of other passages of *Sefer Yetsirah*, in whatever form they took, were diffused fairly widely.[58]

Ben Sheshet attributes to Isaac the second explanation of a passage in *Sefer Yetsirah* in the same manner as the first one: "'Two—air from spirit: He carved and hewed in it the twenty-two basic letters, three primary letters and seven double letters, and twelve simple letters. And the spirit is one of them' (*Sefer Yetsirah* 1:9): The Pious one, Rabbi Isaac son of Abraham—the memory of the righteous and holy one shall be a blessing—explicated (*peiresh*)" ("Sefer ha-emunah" 364). The details of this explication need not concern us here,[59] but suffice it to say that they are not found in the *Commentary on Sefer Yetsirah* attributed to Isaac. Again, however, it cannot be determined whether ben Sheshet derived it from a written text.

Still elsewhere, ben Sheshet writes: "The Pious One, Rabbi Isaac, of blessed memory, was accustomed to saying 'God of David and builder of Jerusalem'" ("Sefer ha-emunah" 396).[60] Above, I mentioned the responsum attributed by scholars to Isaac regarding whether these words or the shorter formula, "builder of Jerusalem," was the appropriate ending of one of the blessings of the *Shemoneh 'Esreh* prayer. Even if this responsum really is by Isaac—a questionable proposition—it could not have been ben Sheshet's source, since, as noted, it presents both views without taking a stance. This does not rule out the possibility that ben Sheshet had a different written source. It is equally possible, however, that ben Sheshet learned of Isaac's practice directly from Isaac or from a third party.[61]

On the basis of ben Sheshet's citations of Isaac, there is no clear evidence that he had access to material written by Isaac, even if this possibility cannot be ruled out. Like the citations recorded by Ezra, those recorded by ben Sheshet are pithy and obscure and would likely be understood only by someone with significant previous knowledge of Kabbalah.

Let me provide an example that illustrates the tenor of these passages. In "Sefer ha-emunah veha-bittaḥon," ben Sheshet offers the following teaching in Isaac's name: "This is similar to the explanation of [the rabbinic statement that] 'He was contemplating Torah.'[62] He saw the essences (*havvayot*) in Himself, for they were essences of wisdom, and from within these essences, which are the essences of wisdom, He discerned that they would in the future be revealed. I have heard (*shama'ti*) this language (*zeh ha-lashon*) in the name of (be-shem) the Pious One, R. Isaac, the son of the Rabbi, R. Abraham, of blessed memory" ("Sefer ha-emunah" 409).[63] Here, ben Sheshet quotes Isaac as offering a kabbalistic explanation of the rabbinic notion that in the course of creating the world, God contemplated the Torah as though it were a blueprint. Yet a reader with any hope of deciphering this explanation would require significant background knowledge. He would have to know that the term "wisdom" refers to the second sefirah; he would have to know the function of this sefirah, and he would have to be familiar with the nature of the "essences" within this sefirah. Only then would he understand that through Isaac's kabbalistic lens, the Torah becomes the second sefirah, "wisdom," and God's contemplation of the Torah becomes His contemplation of the essences within this sefirah.

Explanation of Nahmanides's Torah Commentary

As noted, *Explanation* (*Bei'ur*) was composed at the turn of the fourteenth century by a student of Rashba. The author of this work cites teachings or practices of Isaac seventeen times.[64] Some of the teachings are quite short—one is only five words (*Bei'ur* 5b)—while others are significantly longer. The longest, as mentioned, is "Commentary on Sacrifice," but there are a number of other extended passages, including one that exceeds 250 words (4c)[65] and one that is at least 150 words (25c).[66] Indeed, some of the teachings that the author of *Explanation* records in Isaac's name are longer and more developed than those found in any previous text.

In some cases, it seems that he is not basing himself on written material but on oral traditions about Isaac's opinions or practices. In one instance, he writes, regarding the kabbalistic significance of the priestly blessing, "I heard (*ve-shama'ti*) in the name (*be-shem*) of the Pious One" (29b). Elsewhere, he writes: "I heard (*ve-shama'ti*) that the Rabbi, the Pious One, of blessed memory, would make sure that a person should only write [the divine name in the form of three *yods*] one next to the other [in the mezuzah scroll]" (15c).[67] In another instance, he writes, "I have heard that the opinion of the Pious One regarding fire offerings is" (MS Parma 2704, 37a[68]). In yet another instance, he writes, regarding proper intentions during the *Shema'* prayer: "And if what I heard in the name of the Pious One, of blessed memory, is true (*be'emet*)" (*Bei'ur* 32d). Here, he regards the attribution of what may be a teaching to Isaac as hearsay and expresses doubt about whether the attribution is accurate. The turns of phrase in these attributions to Isaac suggest that the author was operating in an environment in which Isaac's ideas and behaviors remained important to the intellectual and religious agenda of Kabbalists who, like the author of *Explanation*, were connected to Rashba and that various statements and practices in his name circulated among them.

This sense of Isaac's importance implied by such turns of phrase is in line with what we know about Isaac's exalted status in Rashba's circle, which cultivated the historically dubious notion[69] that Nahmanides, Rashba's teacher, was Isaac the Blind's student. Such a chain of transmission is stated by the anonymous author of *Or ha-ganuz*,[70] a commentary on *Sefer ha-bahir*, who describes himself as the student of both Joshua Ibn Shuaib, the possible author of *Explanation*, and of Rashba: "[I have interpreted the *Bahir*] as I have received and understood from the mouths of my Rabbis, R. Joshua Ibn Shuaib and from the mouth of R. Solomon of Barcelona (=Rashba), who received from Nahmanides, and he received from R. Isaac the Blind, the son of Rabad, of blessed memory, and he received from Elijah the prophet" (Margaliot 94, *Bahir* sec.).[71] Isaac's stature is also reflected in the fact that Rashba's students circulated legendary stories about Isaac's supernatural abilities. Thus, in his *Keter Shem Tov*, Shem Tov ben Abraham Ibn Gaon, another student of Rashba, writes: "Isaac, the son of the Rabbi, of blessed memory, was able to discern through feeling the air, even though he was blind, and would say, 'So and so will live and so and so will die'" (MS Vat. 211, 113b).

In light of the special status accorded to Isaac, it is not surprising that his teachings and practices would be of special interest to this circle. Yet by the same token, the very fact that Isaac's teachings may have had a special cachet also raises the possibility that false rumors about them could easily spread. Caution—which, as we have seen, in one case the author of *Explanation* himself expresses—is therefore in order when it comes to assessing the reliability of the oral traditions about Isaac's teachings or practices reported in *Explanation*.

In seven other instances, the author explicitly claims that he had in his possession textual material that Isaac actually "wrote."[72] Other examples are more ambiguous but may also involve material that the author believed that Isaac wrote. In three cases, he remarks that Isaac "explicated," using versions of the Hebrew root *PRSh*, in reference to a biblical verse.[73] This language is somewhat ambiguous, but in one of these cases, after first stating that Isaac "explicated," he later adds: "He additionally wrote" (*Bei'ur* 17a).[74]

This suggests that he regarded the whole passage as having been written by Isaac. Assuming that his terminology is consistent, it is likely that the two other instances in which he uses the term "explicated" also refer to a text that he believed Isaac wrote. In another instance, comparing Isaac and Nahmanides, the author indicates that "the Pious One also took this approach" (34a)—that is, Isaac's approach is similar to that of Nahmanides. Here, it is unclear whether the author is drawing on a text composed by Isaac, but this is certainly possible. In yet another instance, he writes regarding sacrifice to Moloch: "I have found it written in the name of the Pious One, of blessed memory, regarding the explanation of this verse, and these are his words" (25c). Here, he may be referring to a text that quotes Isaac rather than a text composed by Isaac himself. Still, the text purports to be the words of Isaac, so we are dealing with an alleged verbatim quotation of Isaac's words in a text that was in the possession of the author of *Explanation*. It is possible that this text claimed to be based on material composed by Isaac. This possibility gains support from a parallel passage in another work, as I will discuss below.

In most, and perhaps all, of these cases, we are not dealing with rumors or hearsay but with texts that apparently contained an indication that they were composed by Isaac. Here, too, caution is required. Below, I will cast doubt on the reliability of the attribution to Isaac in the case of a few of these texts. Before I do so, let me highlight that there is good reason to distrust the reliability of attributions to other figures that the author makes throughout *Explanation*. In one passage, he notes that despite the fact that Nahmanides claimed in his Torah commentary not to possess a tradition regarding the kabbalistic meaning of forbidden incestuous relationships, there is nevertheless "a scroll of secrets" written in Nahmanides's own handwriting that explains their meaning (25b). He proceeds to quote from this scroll. Another student of Rashba, Ibn Gaon, quotes the same text in his *Keter Shem Tov*. In introducing the text, he notes that his teachers, Rashba and Isaac ben Todros, never received a tradition from Nahmanides regarding the explanation of incestuous relationships. He then adds: "And I have found [an explanation] of the meaning of the prohibition of incestuous relationships" (*Keter* 51), without any mention of Nahmanides.[75] Ibn Gaon, then, seems to know nothing of the attribution of this text to Nahmanides. In yet another work, an anonymous commentary on the Pentateuch written by someone in Rashba's circle (from here on, *Anonymous Commentary*), the text is incorporated into the main commentary without any mention that it is taken from another source[76]—a move that would be quite strange if the author believed that it had been written by Nahmanides, given Nahmanides's towering status in Rashba's circle. As Idel has conclusively shown, the text is indeed not by Nahmanides. It is, rather, the work of a certain R. Meshullam, who composed it as part of a letter to an unnamed figure, which is extant in a Vatican manuscript ("Kabbalistic Interpretation" 141–47).[77] It seems, therefore, that even when it comes to writings of his teacher's teacher, Nahmanides, the author of *Explanation* is unreliable.

We can identify another instance of misattribution. The author of *Explanation* cites teachings of Ezra of Gerona on numerous occasions. It is possible to locate all these passages in Ezra's extant work,[78] save one instance, in which the author offers an exegesis of Exod. 30:19, after which he writes: "I have copied this from the words of the sage, R. Ezra, of blessed memory" (*Bei'ur* 19d). Since this exegesis includes comments on a passage from *Sefer Yetsirah*, Tishby (Azriel of Gerona, *Commentary* 50) raises the possibility that it comes from a no longer extant commentary on *Sefer Yetsirah* that, according to Abraham Abulafia, Ezra wrote.[79] This possibility is called into question by a passage in the aforementioned *Anonymous Commentary*, a highly important work for the study of Kabbalah in Rashba's circle, which has not been sufficiently mined by scholarship.[80] As Zechariah Holzer (319–22), editor of the first volume of *Anonymous Commentary*, already noted, this work includes the same exegesis of Exod. 30:19 (see D. Holzer 352–55 on Exod. 30:19). Its author never mentions the attribution to Ezra. On the contrary, three times in the course of the exegesis, he states the ideas as "in my opinion" (*mida'ati*). It is difficult to ascertain whether he means to claim that the whole explanation is his own or only the parts that appear immediately after he states "in my opinion."[81] Yet even these parts appear word for word in *Explanation* as part of the citation of Ezra.

The relationship between *Explanation* and *Anonymous Commentary* is complicated and requires further study. The citation of Ezra is not the only place in which there is overlap between the two texts, and Idel ("An Anonymous Commentary" 9–17) has argued, based on limited examples (without reference to this citation), that *Anonymous Commentary* draws from *Explanation*. Subsequent to Idel's discussion of the relationship between the two texts, the first two volumes of *Anonymous Commentary* were published. In the first volume, Zechariah Holzer, the editor, argues against Idel, on the basis of many more examples, that it was the author of *Explanation* who borrowed from *Anonymous Commentary* rather than the reverse, or that, at the very least, they both took from a third source (27–29, 314–27). In my view, the question of the relationship between the two works is not fully settled and requires a fresh examination beyond the purview of the present study. Suffice it to say that in the current passage, given that *Anonymous Commentary* refers to at least some of the material as "my opinion," it is quite difficult to uphold the contention that the author of *Anonymous Commentary* borrowed from *Explanation*. In this case, we seem to have a situation whereby, through processes that are currently unknown, an exegesis from *Anonymous Commentary* came to be attributed to Ezra and found its way into *Explanation*. Once again, then, an attribution found in the *Explanation* proves to be unreliable. I would add parenthetically that the exegesis allegedly by Ezra in *Explanation* mentions, in passing, that Isaac had a particular variant of a passage in *Sefer Yetsirah*. Isaac is not, however, mentioned in the parallel in *Anonymous Commentary*.[82] The source of this addition and how it came to be part of the passage in *Explanation* is unclear.[83]

To be clear, my claim is not that the author of *Explanation* was fraudulently misattributing material. Rather, it seems that he operated in an environment in which texts circulated with misattributions such that two members of the same general circle might each have had access to the same text even while their respective versions carried different attributions, leaving it to contemporary scholarship to verify which attributions are reliable. If this is true of material that the author of *Explanation* had in the name of Nahmanides and Ezra, it may also have been true of material that he had in Isaac's name.

Indeed, a closer look at some of the teachings allegedly composed by Isaac that the author of *Explanation* cites confirms this suspicion. I have already shown that the longest of these teachings, "Commentary on Sacrifice," was unlikely to have been composed by Isaac but was probably based on Ezra's writings. We can say this definitively in the case of another one of the teachings attributed to Isaac. In relation to the question of why, according to biblical law, a woman who gives birth to a female remains ritually impure longer than a woman who gives birth to a male, the author of *Explanation* cites a teaching of Isaac. In introducing this teaching, he writes: "I have received (*ve-kibbalti*) that the Rabbi, the Pious One, of blessed memory, wrote [the following], and these are his words (*ve-zeh leshono*). It is adduced by Ezra, of blessed memory, in his *Commentary on the Song of Songs*, and these are the words (*ve-zehu leshon*) of the Pious One, of blessed memory" (*Bei'ur* 24b). As these introductory remarks indicate, the passage that follows is, indeed, a slightly expanded version of a passage that appears in the excursus on the commandments that Ezra appended to *Song Commentary* (Travis 33–34). In the excursus in *Song Commentary*, however, the passage is not attributed to Isaac.[84] Note the stylistic awkwardness of the introductory remarks in *Explanation*. It begins, "I have received (*ve-kibbalti*) that the Rabbi, the Pious One, of blessed memory, wrote [the following], and these are his words" (*ve-zeh leshono*). After "and these are his words," we would expect the immediate citation of Isaac's remarks. Instead, we find the following line: "It is adduced by Ezra, of blessed memory, in his *Commentary on the Song of Songs*, and these are the words (*ve-zehu leshon*) of the Pious One, of blessed memory." It is only at this point that the citation actually begins. This line, therefore, has the hallmark of a later interpolation. Indeed, while this line does appear in most of the manuscripts that I consulted,[85] it is missing in one early manuscript.[86] I would suggest, therefore, that this line was added by a later author who noticed the similarity to Ezra's text and not by the original author of *Explanation*. If so, it seems that the original author had in his possession a text of Ezra that was erroneously attributed to Isaac. The author of *Explanation* quotes from both Ezra's *Aggadot Commentary* and *Song Commentary* on numerous occasions.[87] None of these quotations necessarily comes from the excursus on the reasons for the commandments. It is therefore possible that the author had access to a version of *Song Commentary* that did not include the excursus,[88] and the author of *Explanation* was thus unaware that the passage at hand was by Ezra. Given the fact that "Commentary on Sacrifices" also seems to draw from the excursus, we might wonder if ideas from the excursus were erroneously circulating in Isaac's name.

Yet another passage raises suspicions. Here the author of *Explanation* introduces a commentary on Lev. 18:21 ("You shall not give any of your offspring to be offered up to Moloch") by writing: "I have found it written in the name of the Pious One, of blessed memory, regarding the explanation of this verse, and these are his words" (*Bei'ur* 25c). Idel ("Commentaries" 28n90) has already called the authenticity of this attribution into question, suggesting that it is an adaptation of a much shorter statement attributed to Isaac, which he deems authentic, found in an anonymous collection of kabbalistic passages that are extant in a number of manuscripts. It seems to me that the reverse is true, and the shorter statement is based on the underlying source of the passage in *Explanation*. The shorter statement reads: "[Regarding] that which the Rabbi, the Pious One (= Isaac the Blind), of blessed memory, wrote about the matter of Moloch, in reference to those insolent ones in the generation: And he mentioned the midrash of our Rabbis, of blessed memory, who said that 'He stood and planted them in each and every generation' (see B. Ḥagigah 13b–14a). His intention was to hint to the generation of Enoch, who were insolent, and they come and return in each and every generation" (MS Vat. 202, 62a).[89]

I will not attempt to decipher these remarks here. Rather, I merely wish to highlight that the wording makes clear that the author of this passage is not citing Isaac's remarks but is recounting and explaining the fact that Isaac used a rabbinic midrash from B. Ḥagigah 13b–14a in a separate passage that the author had before him; hence his statements that "he mentioned the midrash" and "his intention was."[90] I suggest that the passage that the author had before him is the one that also is cited in *Explanation*. Two points lead me to this conclusion. First, in the passage in *Explanation*, this midrash plays a prominent role in the explanation of sacrifice to Moloch. Second, like the author of *Explanation*, the author of this anonymous collection of kabbalistic passages was a student of Rashba, whom he refers to as "our teacher" (MS Vat. 202, 62a). This makes it likely that they both had access to the same material. Indeed, scholars have suggested that the author of the anonymous collection is Joshua Ibn Shuaib (Scholem, "An Inquiry" 263),[91] the possible author of *Explanation*. Thus, the two authors may even have been one and the same figure. In short, the author of the anonymous collection is referring to a text that is cited in full in *Explanation*.

Above, I noted that the author of *Explanation*'s introduction of the passage with "I have found it written in the name of the Pious One" is somewhat ambiguous. While it seems to refer to a work that cites Isaac rather than a work composed by Isaac himself, it is unclear whether this former work claims to cite material that Isaac wrote or merely to present an oral tradition in Isaac's name. Given that the author of the anonymous collection states that Isaac wrote the passage regarding Moloch, we can assume that the first possibility is correct.

Yet none of this implies that the attribution to Isaac in the text in *Explanation* is accurate. On the contrary, it is highly doubtful for a number of reasons. First, the text begins with a non-kabbalistic explanation of the prohibition of sacrificing one's offspring to Moloch, according to which this prohibition is juxtaposed in the biblical text to the prohibition of adultery (see Lev. 18:20), because God regards Israel's worship of Moloch in the same manner that a man regards his wife's adulterous relationship (*Bei'ur* 25c). It is only after this mundane explanation that the text turns to a kabbalistic one. There is no evidence anywhere else that Isaac ever composed or even orally transmitted an exoteric commentary on any part of scripture. Second, the kabbalistic portion of the text seems to hint at metempsychosis. Yet, as Idel argues, the evidence suggests that Isaac and members of his circle rejected the doctrine of metempsychosis.[92] Finally, the same passage appears, with only slight differences, in the aforementioned *Anonymous Commentary*, with absolutely no attribution and no indication that it was taken from an outside source (MS Estense University Library, O.7.26, 117b–118a; MS Munich Cod. hebr. 26, 277b).[93] Of course, it is possible that the author of *Anonymous Commentary* borrowed from a text supposedly by Isaac but failed to identify it as such, or even that he borrowed from *Explanation*. Still, the possibility must be considered that once again a passage found in *Anonymous Commentary* somehow became misidentified as the work of Isaac.

I have called into question the attribution to Isaac in the case of three of the passages in *Explanation* that Isaac supposedly wrote. This does not necessarily mean that the remaining passages are also misattributed. It is certainly possible, however, that future research will lead to the questioning of the attributions to Isaac of these passages as well.[94]

Esotericism vs. Exotericism

At the opening of this chapter, I asked how we might reconcile the seeming tension between Isaac's strong opposition to recording kabbalistic secrets, as reflected in his letter to Nahmanides and Jonah, and his apparently relatively extensive literary legacy. The foregoing analysis provides a partial answer: his literary legacy is far more meager than has generally been assumed. As I have argued, a close examination of the teachings attributed to Isaac shows that, in many cases, we are dealing with oral traditions recorded by others. In other cases, the attribution to Isaac of actual compositions appears to be spurious.

At the same time, I was not able to rule out the possibility that at least some of the material attributed to Isaac was actually recorded by him; again, I would recall that the only piece definitively by Isaac, the aforementioned letter, includes a brief kabbalistic commentary on Psalm 150. This in and of itself presents a conundrum: in the very text in which he rails against kabbalistic writing, he includes kabbalistic writing. The key to resolving this conundrum lies in a close examination of the letter.

Since it is one of the few texts that sheds light on the social and historical circumstances of the early history of Kabbalah, it has been treated in numerous studies.[95] Scholars have not, however, examined the contributions that this letter makes to understanding Isaac's perspective on esoteric writing. In the letter, to repeat, Isaac complains about the inappropriate dissemination of kabbalistic secrets by "sages, wise men, and pious men who were lengthy (*she-he'erikhu*) in their language and extended their hands to write about great and sublime matters (*gedolot ve-nora'ot*) in their books and letters" (T. Weiss, "Letter" 331). The behavior of these scholars, who, as seen, may or may not be Ezra and Azriel, is problematic from Isaac's point of view because "what is written has no master; often these things are lost or their owners die, and the writings fall into the hands of fools or scoffers, and the name of heaven is thus profaned" (331). Here, Isaac's esotericism seems to be of both a defensive and a protective nature. From a defensive perspective, Isaac seems to be concerned that these fools and scoffers might attack Kabbalists for their views (whether their actual views or a misunderstanding of their views). As we will see in Chapter 6, Isaac's nephew Asher indicates that this is indeed what happened. From a protective perspective, the ridicule of kabbalistic ideas, which focus on the true nature of God, would lead to a profanation of God's name, a state of affairs that might harm the faith of the uninitiated.[96]

In the continuation (331–32), Isaac proceeds to contrast the approach of these "pious men" who record kabbalistic wisdom, with his own approach, which he claims follows that of his fathers—as mentioned, presumably his father, Rabad, and his grandfather Abraham ben Isaac of Narbonne—who exercised extreme secrecy when it came to kabbalistic ideas.

Note should be taken of the precise type of kabbalistic writing that Isaac objects to: writing that is "lengthy." Later in the letter, he makes the same point again when he tells his addressees that "I will not be able to offer a *lengthy* (*leha'arikh*) written exposition regarding what you asked" (332). The implication seems to be that Naḥmanides and Jonah had, in a no longer extant letter to Isaac, asked a question regarding a kabbalistic matter (apparently, the esoteric meaning of Psalm 150, as becomes immediately clear), but Isaac felt that it would be inappropriate to write a lengthy answer. He does, however, provide a short answer. Thus he continues:

But the ten praises [in Psalm 150] correspond to the ten sefirot, and scripture has arranged them from top to bottom. "Hallelujah" (Ps. 150:1): by way of wisdom. "[Praise (*halelu*)] God in his sanctuary" (ibid. 150:1): understanding within mercy, for there is a great difference between "in His sanctuary" (*be-kodsho*) and "in the sanctuary" (*ba-kodesh*), for the language of blessing goes with "in the sanctuary" (*ba-kodesh*), as is written, "Lift up your hands to the sanctuary (*kodesh*) [and bless the Lord]" (Ps. 134:2). "Praise" (*vehilul*) goes with the language of "His sanctuary" (*kodsho*), as it is written, "Receive praise (*hithalelu*) in His holy name (*be-shem kodsho*)" (Ps. 105:3). It is also stated, "You shall not profane My holy [name] ([*shem*] *kodshi*)" (Lev. 22:32). And the explanation of the language of praise (*ha-hilul*) cannot be put into writing. "Praise Him (*haleluhu*) in His mighty firmament" (Ps. 150:1) as is written, "Strength and splendor (*tiferet*) are in His sanctuary (*be-mikdasho*)" (Ps. 96:6): righteousness within truth. After the text mentioned mercy and judgment, it mentioned the causes of judgment and the causes of mercy: "Praise Him (*haleluhu*) in His mighty acts; Praise Him (*haleluhu*) according to His abundant greatness" (Ps. 150:2). The reason "might" was stated in the plural is that mercy is also from judgment. "Greatness" is in the singular [because] lovingkindness is above judgment. Therefore, the effects of mercy overrule judgment when Israel repents, and with their good deeds, and when they recall the merit of their forefathers, as is written, "Give truth to Jacob and lovingkindness to Abraham [as You have sworn to our forefathers]" (Mic. 7:20). Where did he swear? "By Myself, I swear, says the Lord" (Gen. 22:16). This means, in the things that are unified in Me. Up until this point [in Psalm 150] is the general principle of the things. From here and on, it details the effects until ten is reached. Just as it concluded with judgment in a general way, so it concluded with their details. At the end of the whole matter, it repeated and said, "Let every soul praise (*tehallel*) the Lord" (Ps. 150:6). "Every soul" is "understanding." "Praise the Lord" is "wisdom." The general rule is "ten and not nine and not eleven" (*Sefer Yetsirah*, 1:4). (333–34)

Scholem ("Te'udah" 24) offers only a few tentative interpretive comments and stresses that Isaac, here, "greatly concealed his words." Recently, Avishai Bar-Asher ("Isaac") has offered a compelling interpretation of this cryptic passage that challenges Scholem's assumptions. While Scholem ("Te'udah" 24–25) saw the passage as offering an account of the stages of the emanation of the sefirot, Bar-Asher shows that it ultimately concerns theurgically uniting the sefirot through liturgical practice. He, too, stresses that Isaac "locked" his interpretation of Psalm 150 "in allusions" ("Isaac" 420). I will not reproduce Bar-Asher's intricate interpretation here. Rather, I will focus on what this letter can teach us about Isaac's approach to kabbalistic writing. Isaac's statement that he cannot provide a "lengthy written exposition" explains the terse style of the interpretation.[97] For our purposes, it must be stressed that by writing in this style, Isaac avoids violating the code of esotericism that he highlights in the letter. Unlike the Kabbalists he criticizes, he is not lengthy in his language, and therefore he feels comfortable recording a kabbalistic teaching in the letter. The terseness of Isaac's explanation is not just a matter of less detail. Note how suffused this passage is with technical terminology like the names for the sefirot such as "understanding" and "mercy," which would look like generic terms to a non-Kabbalist, or phrases like "causes (sibbot) of judgment and causes (sibbot) of mercy," which would similarly befuddle the non-Kabbalist. Even after these terms are deciphered, the passage, as Bar-Asher's analysis shows, is full of hints and allusions that would surely escape the notice of most readers. To take one example, discussed by Bar-Asher (426–27), hidden in the statement that the "language of blessing goes with 'in the sanctuary' (ba-kodesh)" is a reference to the priest focusing on the tenth sefirah, also known as kodesh, when reciting the priestly blessing, as alluded to in the verse, ""Lift up your hands to the sanctuary (kodesh) [and bless the Lord]" (Ps. 134:2). Clearly, this meaning would be missed by most readers. In short, it seems to me, the entire passage is an example of allusive writing, which Isaac assumed that the addressees of the letter, Jonah and Nahmanides, would understand, but not the uninitiated.

Note that even within his already-cryptic interpretation of Psalm 150, Isaac highlights a matter that cannot be divulged in writing: "And the explanation of the language of praise cannot be put into writing." Apparently, a certain hierarchy is at play in Isaac's approach to esoteric writing. Some ideas can be recorded, if only in a terse cryptic style, while other ideas must remain altogether unwritten.

The fact that Isaac is employing allusive writing explains why he is not worried that the letter would "fall into the hands of fools or scoffers, and the name of heaven is thus profaned." The potential fools and scoffers would not succeed in deciphering the passage.

I would suggest that insofar as Isaac did leave a literary legacy beyond this passage, he composed it in a similarly allusive style. In at least some cases, I was able to show that teachings attributed to Isaac—those labeled "the language of Isaac"—were likely verbatim renditions of his exact words. As I suggested, it is possible that some of these teachings derive from material written by Isaac. An examination of these teachings demonstrates that they, too, use the allusive form of language characteristic of his comments on Psalm 150. They are brief and, as I indicated in my earlier discussion, full of technical terminology like "time of unity and will" and "essences of wisdom," which could be deciphered only by those with knowledge of kabbalistic thought. The primary intent of such passages was likely to jog readers' memory about various kabbalistic concepts with which they were already familiar or to gently point them toward new explanations of biblical verses and rabbinic statements on the basis of concepts that they already knew. It was certainly not to provide an accessible or systematic account of Kabbalah.

Notably, this was also the impression of an early reader of the material. Immediately after he cites one of the passages found in *Aggadot Commentary* as "the words of the Pious One," Todros Abulafia, the mid-thirteenth-century Castilian Kabbalist, remarks: "How precious are his figurative expressions (*melitsato*); how pleasant are his parables and riddles (*meshalav ve-ḥidotav*)" (*Otsar*, Warsaw 46).[98] The ultimate source of the terms "figurative expressions," "parables," and "riddles" is Prov. 1:6: "To understand a parable, and a figurative expression; the words of the wise, and their riddles." But when it comes to esoteric writing, Abulafia takes his cue from Maimonides (Wolfson, "Wings" 216–17), and I presume that Abulafia is employing these terms (particularly "parables" and "riddles") following the precedent of Maimonides in the *Guide of the Perplexed* (in Samuel Ibn Tibbon's translation), who uses them in reference to the style employed by those who wish to teach esoteric matters without openly revealing them.[99] That is, Abulafia sees Isaac's comments as composed in an esoteric style.

Abulafia's remarks foreshadow those of Gershom Scholem: "[Isaac's] *ipissima* [sic] *verba*, to the extent they have been preserved, are mysteriously formulated and exceedingly difficult to understand. I myself cannot pretend to have understood more than half the material transmitted in his name. He has a peculiar way of expressing himself, the syntax of his sentences is in part impenetrable, particularly in the longest of the extant texts, and he often expounds opaque ideas without explaining them. Much of what he says, therefore, remains enigmatic" (*Origins* 253). Even taking into account the fact that Scholem overestimated the extent of Isaac's literary legacy, his comments are supported by my analysis.

As Isaac indicates in his letter, other Kabbalists broke with this approach and did record lengthy kabbalistic works. A prime example is Ezra of Gerona, who composed two lengthy kabbalistic works: *Song Commentary* and *Aggadot Commentary*. Nevertheless, as I will argue in Chapter 5, Ezra did not fully abandon Isaac's code of esotericism.

Chapter 5

Ezra ben Solomon of Gerona as an Esoteric Writer

The First Kabbalistic Monographs

We have seen that Rabad offered hints to kabbalistic ideas in his halakhic writings and perhaps composed short kabbalistic passages. Isaac the Blind, for his part, at most recorded terse and cryptic kabbalistic traditions that were likely closely guarded. As far as we know, it was Ezra ben Solomon of Gerona who was the author of the first kabbalistic monographs. As we have already seen, Ezra, who can be counted among the first known Kabbalists, was in contact with Isaac and records a number of kabbalistic teachings in Isaac's name.[1] Ezra's monographs include *Commentary on the Song of Songs* (*Song Commentary*)[2] and *Commentary on the Talmudic Aggadot* (*Aggadot Commentary*),[3] although it is unclear which of the two he composed first.[4] It is possible that Ezra was also the author of a third monograph, a commentary on *Sefer Yetsirah*, which has not been preserved.[5] Beyond these two longer texts, Ezra is also the author of two letters to a certain R. Abraham on assorted kabbalistic matters.[6] There are also a number of traditions preserved in his name, including extended comments on the Edenic Tree of Life.[7]

There are significant stylistic differences between his two extant monographs. *Song Commentary* includes an introduction in which Ezra explains his decision to write the work, followed by a relatively elaborate verse-by-verse interpretation of the Song of Songs. *Aggadot Commentary*, in contrast, lacks an introduction, and its interpretations of the various aggadot are often quite fragmentary. Nevertheless, both works can be described as systematic insofar as both provide running commentaries, respectively, of the Song of Songs and of the Talmudic aggadot, which Ezra comments on tractate by tractate in the order in which they appear in the Babylonian Talmud.[8] Moreover, as I will elaborate, while *Aggadot Commentary* seems more directed at initiates, *Song Commentary* includes an introduction directed at a broader audience, even if the body of the text would remain obscure to most readers. This work, therefore, marks the emergence of Kabbalah into the public arena. Ezra, then, was the first kabbalistic author to have to confront the question of how to present Kabbalah to a popular audience.

Scholem (*Origins* 396–97) depicted Ezra as breaking with Isaac's code of esotericism and publicizing Kabbalah for the first time.[9] At the same time, he admits that Ezra was not an entirely transparent author. As he puts the matter, in reference to the works of both Ezra and his townsman Azriel, who will be treated separately at the end of this chapter: "Although their books are shorter and more condensed than we would wish, the fact remains that for Isaac's period they were the first to treat kabbalistic themes in public and in a relatively explicit fashion" (397). Other scholars have placed a somewhat greater emphasis on the esoteric dimensions of his work. Georges Vajda (24) comments that Ezra writes for initiates, such that he does not feel a need to demonstrate the basic postulates of his kabbalistic system but assumes that the readers of his work will come with this knowledge. This tendency, according to Vajda, is more pronounced in *Aggadot Commentary* than in his more exoteric *Song Commentary*. Similarly, Pedaya ("Spiritual" 248–49) stresses that Ezra adopts an esoteric style in his writings. She, too, though, sees *Song Commentary* as a more transparent work than his other writings.

Prior to the analysis that I undertake here, no scholar has offered a comprehensive examination of Ezra's craft as an esoteric writer. In this chapter, I argue that Ezra's esotericism is more pervasive than has been realized by previous scholars. Indeed, while *Aggadot Commentary* may be a less accessible book than *Song Commentary*, the latter work was also composed in such a way that would make it inaccessible to a wide audience. I will argue that his role as a popularizer of Kabbalah needs to be presented with nuance. It was a role largely limited to announcing the existence of Kabbalah to a broader public. He was, however, willing to present actual kabbalistic content only in veiled terms that would not have been understood by most readers.

Anti-Maimonidean Agitation

Though *Song Commentary*'s precise date of composition is uncertain, Ezra likely wrote it around the time of the Maimonidean controversy, which reached a high point at the beginning of the 1230s.[10] The controversy roiled

Jewish communities in southern France and Catalonia and divided them into pro- and anti-Maimonidean camps.[11] In the introduction to *Song Commentary*, Ezra explains that he wrote the work to combat "interpreters" who have distorted Jewish tradition. As I have argued in another study (*Knowledge* 34–41), these interpreters are followers of Maimonides who, from Ezra's point of view, were usurping ancient Jewish esotericism by replacing it with philosophical wisdom. In contrast, Ezra proclaims Kabbalah as authentic Jewish esoteric thought.[12]

I also noted there that my argument that Ezra wrote *Song Commentary* in response to Maimonideans accords well with Moshe Idel's observation that the emergence of Kabbalah can partly be explained as a reaction of the first Kabbalists to Maimonides's claim that the ancient esoteric subjects of the "account of creation" and the "account of the chariot" should be identified with Aristotelian physics and metaphysics, respectively. The first Kabbalists, Idel ("Maimonides") argues, worked to set the record straight by recording and developing their traditions, which they regarded as the true "account of creation" and "account of the chariot."[13] In this context, I will both summarize and extend my earlier analysis.

In the first part of the introduction to *Song Commentary*, Ezra traces the transmission of kabbalistic wisdom from the time of Enoch to the destruction of the second temple. According to Ezra, as a result of the deteriorating conditions that Jews faced after the destruction of the second temple, kabbalistic wisdom was increasingly forgotten:

> The exile continues to worsen and our sufferings proceed, indeed undergoing constant renewal, there being neither anyone to impart knowledge nor comprehend tradition. And thus this wisdom ceased from Israel. Wisdom was lost and with it Torah. No one knew its interpretations and subtleties, its exegesis, and the reason for its commandments. For a powerful connection exists between the commandments' meanings and the interpretation of the words of Torah, Prophets and Hagiographa, [on the one hand] and this wisdom [on the other hand]. Many passages of Scripture are based on this wisdom. (489; Brody 22)

In his own days, not only was it forgotten, but it was also in danger of being usurped:

> Interpreters arose possessing neither wisdom nor insight, whether they turned toward the right or toward the left. They turned words of holiness into profanity, diminishing Scripture, adding, detracting, enhancing, interpreting passages spoken through the holy spirit, from a quarry of sacred gems, in terms never to be entertained by human consciousness, let alone spoken, and how much more so transcribed in a book. I call such interpreters those who "overturn the words of the living God, the Lord of Hosts" (based on Jer. 23:36). Concerning this dual cessation of wisdom and its nullification in Israel, the prophet, trembling, devastated, and sighing, said: "Many are the days which will pass in Israel without the God of truth and without Torah" (based on 2 Chron. 15:3). By the phrase "without the God of truth," he referred to the interruption of the knowledge of God, may He be blessed (*hefsek yedi'at hashem yitbarakh*), in Israel. (489; Brody 22–23)

There is little doubt that the interpreters he refers to here are Maimonideans. The themes of his comments in these citations are familiar from the polemical literature of the anti-Maimonidean camp during the Maimonidean controversy. Thus, the notion that the "interpreters" "turned words of holiness into profanity" likely refers to the common critique that the Maimonideans allegorized the Bible.[14] Kabbalah, which has a "powerful connection" to the "interpretation of the words of Torah, Prophets and Hagiographa," offers the antidote to such Maimonidean modes of exegesis. Along similar lines, he emphasizes the necessity of kabbalistic wisdom for understanding the meaning of the commandments. Here he is apparently attempting to position Kabbalah as an antidote to the lax ritual observance that members of the anti-Maimonidean camp claimed that Maimonides's interpretations of the commandments was causing.[15] It is probably for the same reason that Ezra attached an excursus to the commentary dedicated to providing the kabbalistic rationale for the commandments.[16]

His contention, which he exegetically ties to 2 Chron. 15:3, that there has been an "interruption of the knowledge of God" is especially significant. As per Idel's argument, it alludes to the fact that kabbalistic theosophy (true knowledge of God) has been replaced by Maimonidean metaphysics (false knowledge of God).

Despite the fact that Kabbalah was largely forgotten, it was not entirely forgotten. Ezra believed that the traditions that his teachers taught him were continuous with the knowledge that had been transmitted since Enoch's time. In the continuation of his remarks, Ezra explains that on account of his encroaching old age, he felt compelled to leave a written record of kabbalistic wisdom in the form of a commentary on Song of Songs, before it was too late.

> So I have seen again and again over the course of many years. Yet I kept my silence, placing hand to mouth until I reached my fifth rung—one year of the years of my life (*shanah eḥad mi-shenot ḥayyai*)[17]—and saw that the days of my life were setting before me and that old age was rapidly approaching. Therefore, I pressed forward to interpret one of Scripture's twenty-four books, encompassing every delight, bespeaking matters weighty, mysteries and secrets whose memory was lost to Scripture's interpreters, neglecting its perdurance and splendor: That is the Song of Songs. In accord with my strength, I have interpreted it as I have received it from my Rabbis.[18] (479–80; Brody 24)

Apparently, Ezra was concerned that unless he put kabbalistic material into writing, this wisdom would be entirely overwhelmed by Maimonidean interpreters.

Two Types of Readers

The first part of the introduction to *Song Commentary* leaves no doubt that Ezra intended this work to be read by a broad audience. Fellow Kabbalists already knew that Kabbalah was an ancient tradition that had been transmitted across the centuries and that it was the key to understanding the meaning of scriptural passages and the reasons for the commandments. These messages, rather, were directed at a popular audience. *Song Commentary*, accordingly, was not a work that was meant to be sequestered for use by a closed circle of Kabbalists. It was, rather, a public-facing one that was meant to announce the existence of Kabbalah as an alternative to Maimonidean thought in the context of a deep communal divide over the veracity of that thought.

As we have seen in his letter to Nahmanides and Jonah Gerondi, Isaac chastised unnamed scholars for their literary efforts. He thus laments that they were "lengthy (*she-he'erikhu*) in their language and extended their hands to write about great and sublime matters (*gedolot ve-nora'ot*) in their books and letters." He concludes by noting that "what is written has no master; often these things are lost or their owners die, and the writings fall into the hands of fools or scoffers, and the name of heaven is thus profaned" (T. Weiss, "Letter" 331). Scholem (*Origins* 396–97) assumed that Isaac's targets were Ezra and Azriel. This assumption, as noted, may or may not be correct; but even if it is correct, it need not imply that Ezra entirely rejected Isaac's esotericism. It is true that the very fact that Ezra proclaimed the existence of Kabbalah amounts to a rejection of Isaac's desire to conceal this fact entirely. Moreover, as seen, Isaac stressed the need for terseness when it comes to recording kabbalistic teachings. Yet Ezra composed fairly lengthy monographs. Finally, while Isaac was worried about kabbalistic texts reaching the hands of fools and scoffers, Ezra made no effort to sequester *Song Commentary*. All this means that Ezra risked opening up Kabbalah to precisely the misunderstanding and ridicule that Isaac was worried about. Nevertheless, as I will argue, this does not imply that Ezra rejected the notion that kabbalistic wisdom was bound in secrecy. On the contrary, he adopted esoteric forms of writing to conceal the contents of his kabbalistic knowledge. Ezra's decision to record kabbalistic wisdom was, then, a calculated risk necessitated by the rise of Maimonideanism.

In composing *Song Commentary*, Ezra had two audiences in view: kabbalistic initiates; and a much larger public with no prior access to Kabbalah.[19] Readers of the first group, who could penetrate Ezra's allusive style, would gain a great deal of knowledge about kabbalistic wisdom from Ezra's *Song Commentary*. Ezra might have imagined that even such an audience—or, perhaps, precisely such an audience, since it presumably comprised intellectually inclined readers—might be susceptible to the blandishments of Maimonidean thought and could therefore use a refresher or a deepening of their kabbalistic knowledge. In contrast, while readers of the second group would easily understand the first part of the introduction, they would lack the ability to understand the specific teachings of *Song Commentary* introduced later on in the introduction and in the body of the work. For them, *Song Commentary* would function not as a source of kabbalistic knowledge but as an announcement that such knowledge exists. As I will argue, Ezra may have believed that public knowledge of the very existence of Kabbalah, even without a corollary understanding of its contents, could serve as a bulwark against Maimonideanism.

Keeping Secrets Out of Writing

The signs that Ezra was committed to preserving the secrecy of kabbalistic ideas abound in all his writings. At times, he is explicit about this commitment. Thus, in two separate instances, he indicates that a certain idea cannot be communicated in writing or, at least, not in a text that is likely to become publicly available. The first one appears in a letter in which Ezra answers questions posed by a certain R. Abraham. There, he writes: "Regarding the explanation of the midrash on 'blessings are on the head of the righteous' (Prov. 10:6), which seems to contradict the midrash on 'whenever we call Him' (Deut. 4:7), I will inform you of a wondrous matter when I speak to you face to face, which I wrote about three years ago in a *megillat setarim* (scroll of concealments), and then you will know and comprehend the intention of the sage" (Scholem, "Te'udah" 33).

Here is a case where Ezra, out of a desire to keep an esoteric matter out of the letter, states that he will reveal the secret doctrine, which will presumably reconcile the two apparently contradictory midrashic statements, only in person. Notably, Ezra does not specifically identify the two midrashic passages on Prov. 10:6 and Deut. 4:7, respectively, that seem to contradict each other. It is possible that Abraham, in the no longer extant letter that he must have written to Ezra in which he posed his questions, had asked Ezra about a contradiction between two specific midrashic passages. It is also conceivable that not identifying the passages was itself an esoteric technique. If so, to even understand the problem that Ezra was willing to reveal only in person, Abraham would have had to figure out which passages Ezra had in mind and how they contradict each other. As we will see, Ezra uses a similar technique in *Aggadot Commentary*.

Indeed, since Ezra leaves us so little to go on, there is no way to be certain which contradictory passages he had in mind. A possibility is that the contradiction involves two passages with ostensibly differing ideas about how prayer reaches God. A midrash on Prov. 10:6 explains that an angel collects Jewish prayers only after the final congregation has finished worshiping and forms them into a crown, which it places on God's head. In contrast, a midrash on Deut. 4:7 suggests that prayers are received immediately and directly by God.[20] Yet even if this is a correct identification of the passages that Ezra had in mind, how he might have resolved this contradiction between them remains allusive.

Significantly, despite the fact that Ezra was unwilling to record the secret in the letter, he indicates that he had nevertheless written it down earlier in a *megillat setarim*, a scroll of concealments. The term *megillat setarim* already appears in the Babylonian Talmud, where it does not refer to a document containing esoteric materials but to one that contained halakhic notes intended for private use.[21] In other words, the term *setarim* ("concealments") refers to the text itself, which is concealed from public circulation, rather than to the contents of the text. A similar use of the title can also be found in some medieval sources.[22] It is likely that Ezra had in mind something analogous to the halakhic "hidden scrolls": kabbalistic teachings that he recorded for strictly private use; although, in his case, *setarim* may refer not only to the fact that the scroll was private but also to the fact that its contents were esoteric.

Apparently, Ezra was concerned that even a personal letter might be seen by people other than the addressee, and he thus exercised caution in what he revealed. In contrast, the *megillat setarim* would be kept private or shown only to very select individuals.[23] In this manner, Ezra's practice recalls that of Isaac the Blind, who, even in his private letter to Nahmanides and Jonah, was unwilling to reveal a particular detail in the course of his explanation of Psalm 150. Moreover, it is possible that Ezra's *megillat setarim* would have been analogous to the brief expositions that, as I argued, Isaac may have authored.

The second instance in which Ezra states that a teaching cannot be put into writing appears in *Aggadot Commentary*. In this case, Ezra provides sufficient hints to allow me to tentatively suggest a fuller exposition. Ezra first cites a rabbinic statement from *Bere'shit rabba'* 21:9 (ed. Theodor-Albeck 204) according to which the flaming sword that guards the Tree of Life, as described in Gen. 3:24, refers to a sword with which to perform circumcision. Immediately thereafter, he remarks: "I cannot inform you of the explanation of circumcision even in a hint" (*afillu be-remez*) (MS Vat. 294, 42b; MS Vat. 441, 30a).[24] Nevertheless, in contrast to the example from the letter, Ezra does provide a clue. Thus after his emphatic statement that he will not offer even a hint, he continues: "In *Avot de-Rabbi Natan* and in *Bere'shit rabba'* (MS Vat. 441, 30a: chap. 50), if you inquire about it like silver, then you will understand fear of the Lord" (MS Vat. 294, 42b; MS Vat. 441, 30a)—that is to say, while he is not willing to offer a hint himself, he instructs the reader to search for a hint in two midrashic sources. Note, though, that while he identifies the names of works in which the passages appear, he does not specify which passages he has in mind. He then proceeds to cite verbatim, without further explanation, a number of other rabbinic sources that refer to circumcision. These passages, I will show, should be seen as further clues, whose meaning comes into focus after the passages in *Avot de-Rabbi Natan* and in *Bere'shit rabba'* are identified and correctly interpreted.

In what follows, I will attempt to uncover the secret. This attempt will shed light on the specific technique of esoteric writing that Ezra employs here and allow us to observe his art as an esoteric writer. Moreover, arriving at an understanding of the content of the secret will allow me to speculate why Ezra refused to commit it to writing. My analysis begins with Ezra's comment that "in *Avot de-Rabbi Natan* and in *Bere'shit rabba'* (MS Vat. 441, 30a: chap. 50), if you inquire about it like silver, then you will understand fear of the Lord." The statement "If you inquire about it like silver, then you will understand fear of the Lord" is derived from Prov. 2:4–5. As we will see, a related statement, "You will understand the fear of Lord and will find the knowledge of the holy ones," which is a conflation of Prov. 2:5 and Prov. 9:10, is used elsewhere by Ezra in *Aggadot Commentary* to signal that he is employing the technique of dispersion—that is, to signal that the reader must look elsewhere in the work to understand the full meaning of the passage that he is currently studying. (As I will discuss, this related version of the statement may have an esoteric meaning beyond indicating the technique of dispersion. This does not seem to be true of the version of the statement that is used in the present context regarding circumcision.) The version of the statement as it is used in the present context appears to similarly refer to the technique of dispersion. In this case, the explanation of the secret meaning of circumcision is not dispersed within *Aggadot Commentary* but in two passages in two specific works of rabbinic literature. In a manner that recalls the case of the letter to Abraham, part of Ezra's esoteric technique is not to reveal to the reader which particular passages within these works he has in mind.

The passage from *Aggadot Commentary* is extant in two manuscripts. In one, MS Vat. 441, we are provided with a little more information. Here, the reader is given the additional clue that the passage in *Bere'shit rabba'* appears in chapter 50 of the work. This indication is missing in the version in the other manuscript, MS Vat. 294, so it is unclear whether it was originally supplied by Ezra or was added by a later copyist. Therefore, to uncover the secret meaning of circumcision, the reader will have to search through *Avot de-Rabbi Natan* and through all of *Bere'shit rabba'*, or perhaps just chapter 50—a significantly easier task—to decipher Ezra's secret.

The noted scholar of rabbinics Shraga Abramson has already suggested which passages Ezra had in mind. In a footnote in one of his studies on the early Kabbalists Ezra and Azriel, Tishby (*Studies* 31n3) remarks that Abramson suggested to him that Ezra intended two passages—one in each rabbinic work—each of which contains a version of the rabbinic motif that certain biblical figures were born already circumcised.[25] I believe that Abramson's identification of the passage in *Avot de-Rabbi Natan*, which I will cite below, is very plausible. In the case of *Bere'shit rabba'*, I agree that Ezra had in mind a passage regarding a biblical figure who was born circumcised. This motif, however, appears a few times in *Bere'shit rabba'* (26:3, 46:6, 63:6, 74:6, ed. Theodor-Albeck 245–46, 420, 685, 1007), and I think that the one that Ezra intended is not the one suggested by Abramson. I will also cite this passage below.

Of course, identifying the passages is not sufficient. The reader also has to be able to fathom the kabbalistic implication of these passages and how this implication helps explain the meaning of circumcision. Indeed, one way the reader can assess whether he has identified the passages correctly is to determine whether there is a kabbalistic strategy for reading them that might shed light on the meaning of circumcision. Needless to say, only a kabbalistically informed reader could hope to be successful. As we will see, this is precisely the type of reader for whom *Aggadot Commentary* was intended. In fact, a leitmotif of *Aggadot Commentary* is the repeated phrase "you already know," which indicates that only one with considerable background knowledge of kabbalistic thought will succeed in understanding the work. As a contemporary scholar of Kabbalah, I am able to assume this role of a knowledgeable reader because I have access to other later kabbalistic literature, which is more open and provides the necessary background, and to outstanding secondary literature, which clarifies basic kabbalistic concepts—in this case, the extensive work of Elliot Wolfson on the kabbalistic meaning of circumcision.[26] *Aggadot Commentary*, however, was written at the very beginning of Kabbalah's literary history, when the only way to acquire the necessary background knowledge was directly from a teacher.

Abramson suggests that Ezra was alluding to the following passage in *Avot de-Rabbi Natan*:

What is the meaning of "a blameless and upright man" (Job 1:8)? It teaches that Job emerged circumcised. Similarly, Adam emerged circumcised, as it is written, "God created man in His image" (Gen. 1:27). Similarly, Seth emerged circumcised, as it is written, "[And Adam lived a hundred and thirty years,] and he begot a son after his own likeness, in his image" (Gen. 5:3). Similarly, Noah emerged circumcised, as it is written, "A righteous man, blameless in his generation" (Gen. 6:9). Similarly, Shem emerged circumcised as it is written, "Melchizedek king of Shalem (= wholeness)" (Gen. 14:18). (In the continuation, further biblical characters who were born circumcised are mentioned.) (version A, chap. 2; Schechter 12)

I believe that the prooftext for Adam having been created already circumcised—"God created man in His image" (Gen. 1:27)—is especially significant for deciphering Ezra's secret. According to this prooftext, the fact that Adam—the first human—was created already circumcised signifies that he was God-like. Insofar as Adam begot Seth in his own image, the fact that Seth was born already circumcised signifies that he was also God-like. In all likelihood, Ezra did not understand the God-like nature of Adam and Seth in some generic way but in a specifically kabbalistic manner. As Wolfson has discussed at length, from a kabbalistic perspective, the ninth sefirah is the phallic element of the Godhead, which is imagined as circumcised. The circumcision of the eight-day old Jewish male is thus an act of *imitatio dei*.[27] In *Avot de-Rabbi Natan*, therefore, the fact that Adam and Seth were created circumcised would, for Ezra, have marked the manner in which their circumcised sex organs are a reflection of the ninth sefirah. That this was Ezra's understanding may perhaps be derived from the second rabbinic passage that he mentions, without identifying—the one from *Ber'eshit rabba'*.

A number of passages in *Bere'shit rabba'* refer to biblical characters who were born circumcised. Abramson singles out one from chapter 43 of the work, which states, without further elaboration, that the biblical king Melchizedek was born circumcised (chap. 43:6, ed. Theodor-Albeck 420). It seems to me, however, that the passage that Ezra had in mind is one in chapter 26, which describes Noah's son Shem as being born circumcised and contains imagery that is ripe for a kabbalistic interpretation.[28] As noted, in the version of *Aggadot Commentary* that appears in MS Vat. 441, the unspecified passage in *Bere'shit rabba'* is identified as found in chapter 50. This identification is missing in the version in MS Vat. 294. An examination of chapter 50, however, turns up nothing relevant to circumcision. I would note that it is not impossible that the letter *nun* with an apostrophe above it (נ׳), used in MS Vat. 441, following standard Hebrew notation, to refer to the number 50, could be a corruption of the letters *kaf* and *vav* (כו), which would be used to refer to the number 26 in standard Hebrew notation. In Hebrew, the letters *kaf* and *nun* are easily confused, and, in this scenario, at some point in the transmission of the text, the *vav* was inadvertently shortened such that it looked like an apostrophe. Here, then, is the passage in chapter 26:3: "'Shem, Ham, and Japheth' (Gen. 6:10): But Japheth was the oldest (so why was Shem mentioned first)? Rather, you first look for he who was righteous (*tsaddik*), he who was born circumcised, he upon whom the Holy One, blessed be He, particularly placed His name, he from whom Abraham was descended, he who served in the high priesthood, and he in whose domain the temple was built" (ed. Theodor-Albeck 245–46). The significance of this passage from Ezra's kabbalistic point of view may be the fact that the statement that Shem was born circumcised is sandwiched between the notion that he was righteous and the notion that God placed His name upon him. It is quite possible that Ezra understood the term "righteous" symbolically as a reference to the aforementioned ninth sefirah, since this is a very common kabbalistic designation of this sefirah. The passage in *Avot de-Rabbi Natan*, even on a kabbalistic reading, did not mention the ninth sefirah; but here, given a kabbalistic reading, it is clearly indicated. An astute reader therefore might be able to extrapolate from this passage back to the passage in *Avot de-Rabbi Natan*. This would allow him to realize that in that passage, the God-like nature of Adam and Seth is connected to the manner in which their circumcised sex organs reflect this sefirah.

On the basis of the passage from *Bere'shit rabba'*, this reader might come to understand another dimension of the fact that Seth being born already circumcised renders him God-like. He would reach this understanding by observing the juxtaposition of the notion that God placed His name upon Shem[29] to the idea that he was circumcised. In later medieval kabbalistic literature, partially following rabbinic precedents, circumcision was seen as an inscribing of the divine name on the human body.[30] Wolfson, reflecting on a passage by Moses de León, comments: "The Jew, by bearing the sign of circumcision—the Tetragrammaton—on his phallus, participates in that very divine gradation which is in the position of the male organ" ("Circumcision and the Divine" 101). It is certainly possible that this conception was already current among the first Kabbalists and that Ezra hoped that by carefully considering the kabbalistic implications of this passage and using it to reflect back on the passage in *Avot de-Rabbi Natan*, astute readers of *Aggadot Commentary* would be led to the conclusion that Adam and Seth, in being born circumcised, bore the divine name on their body. Presumably, Ezra's secret of circumcision was not limited to Adam and Seth and other biblical figures who were born already circumcised. These figures may have a special status, since they were born circumcised, but any Jewish male who is circumcised on the eighth day of his life also becomes God-like by reflecting the ninth sefirah and inscribing the divine name on his body.

If we turn now to the rabbinic passages that Ezra does not merely allude to but actually cites, we can see that the same theme is present in them but in a more muted fashion. It is therefore possible that Ezra wanted the perspicacious reader to first identify the passages in *Avot de-Rabbi Natan* and *Bere'shit rabba'* and interpret them kabbalistically and then use this kabbalistic interpretation to interpret the passages that he cites verbatim.

Ezra begins with a passage from *Midrash tanḥuma* according to which Ps. 25:14—"The secret of the Lord is with them who fear Him; He makes his covenant (*u-verito*) known to them"—refers to the secret of circumcision. This exegesis, which is based on the fact that the Hebrew word for circumcision (*berit*) means "covenant," serves a greater purpose for Ezra than merely to establish that the Talmudic Rabbis viewed circumcision as containing a secret. Its continuation, when read through a kabbalistic lens, also helps uncover the content of the secret. It continues by noting that God revealed the secret of circumcision to Abraham. The reasoning behind God's decision to reveal this secret to Abraham is that "it is sufficient for the slave to be like his Master." This line of reasoning is clarified on the basis of a parable of a king who has a wealthy friend to whom he desired to give a gift. The king realized that, given his friend's wealth, there would be no point in providing him with expensive goods. Instead, he gives his friend his armor. Similarly, "The Holy One, blessed be He, called to Abraham, and said to him, 'What shall I give you? You already have plenty of silver and gold. It is sufficient for you to be like Me, as it is written, I will make My covenant [between Me and you]' (Gen. 17:2)" (MS Vat. 294, 42b).[31]

According to this rabbinic passage, one who is circumcised becomes similar to God. Taken without a kabbalistic overlay, it implies that circumcision marks the Jewish male as God's emissary in whom God invests authority, just as the king invests authority in his friend by supplying him with his armor. Read kabbalistically, this seems like a somewhat more muted version of the notion already suggested by *Avot de-Rabbi Natan* and *Bere'shit rabba'* that the sex organ of one who is circumcised corresponds to the ninth sefirah, which, as noted, in standard kabbalist symbolism is identified with God's sexual organ. That is, the armor that the king gives to his friend symbolically stands for the divine phallus, which the circumcised Jew now bears on his flesh. A reader who has successfully deciphered the *Avot de-Rabbi Natan* and *Bere'shit rabba'* passages might be able to decode the kabbalistic meaning of this passage.

Ezra then cites another rabbinic passage whose source I have not been able to identify: "An aggadah: the Holy One, blessed be He, created ten fingers on the hands above and ten fingers on the feet below, and He created a finger (MS Vat. 441, 30a: the membrum) between them and crowned it with a crown to be a king (MS Vat. 441, 30a: to rule) over them" (MS Vat. 294, 42b; MS Vat. 441, 30a). This passage, which may be an elaboration of a somewhat similar passage in *Sefer Yetsirah* (Hayman 67 = 1:3), describes the male sex organ as positioned between the ten fingers and ten toes. Unlike the other rabbinic passages that Ezra cited, this one does not explicitly mention circumcision. It is likely, however, that Ezra understood the motif of the crowning of the sex organ as an allusion to circumcision, since the removal of the foreskin reveals the corona of the penis. I would raise the possibility that Ezra read this passage in light of a fuller kabbalistic mythos surrounding circumcision that would perhaps have been on the mind of one who understood that the passages in *Avot de-Rabbi Natan* and *Bere'shit rabba'* described a homology between the circumcised sex organ and the ninth sefirah. As Wolfson has elaborated, in later kabbalistic literature the corona of the penis symbolically stands for the feminine tenth sefirah, also known as "kingship," which is united to the phallic ninth sefirah.[32] Circumcision, which reveals the corona, thus symbolically alludes to the sexual union of the two sefirot. It is possible that this mythos already existed at the very beginning of kabbalah's literary history and that Ezra saw it reflected in the rabbinic passage.

Next, Ezra cites another passage from *Midrash tanḥuma* according to which "Adam was born circumcised, and his son Seth [was born] circumcised, as it is written, 'And he begot a son after his own likeness, in his image' (Gen. 5:3). Moses [was born] circumcised, as it is written, 'She saw that he was good' (Exod. 2:2)" (MS Vat. 294, 42b; MS Vat. 441, 30a).[33] This passage is a parallel to the passage from *Avot de-Rabbi Natan*. Unlike the latter passage, however, this one does not provide the explanation of why Adam was created circumcised. It notes that Seth was created circumcised because he was begotten in Adam's image, but it does not explicitly mention that the reason Adam was created circumcised was that he himself was created in God's image. Reading this passage, then, in light of the passage from *Avot de-Rabbi Natan* would allow the knowledgeable reader to fill in the gap and realize that Adam's, as well as Seth's and Moses's, circumcisions reflect the ninth sefirah. Finally, Ezra cites yet another passage from *Midrash tanḥuma*:

> "It (the sacrificial animal) will remain seven days in the care of its mother" (Lev. 22:27): R. Joshua of Sikhnin said in the name of R. Levi, "A parable of a king who entered a kingdom and issued a proclamation and said, 'All the innkeepers that are here will not see me without first seeing the face of the queen (*matrona*).' Similarly, the Holy One, blessed be He, said, 'Do not offer a sacrifice before me until the Sabbath passes, for there is no offering[34] without Sabbath and no circumcision without Sabbath.'" R. Isaac said,[35] "The law regarding a person is that 'on the eighth day he should be circumcised' (Lev. 12:3), and the law regarding the animal is 'from the eighth day onward' (Lev. 22:7)." (MS Vat. 294, 42b; MS Vat. 441, 30a)[36]

Here, again, Ezra may have understood, and hoped that his reader would also understand, this passage in light of the relationship between the circumcised sex organ of the Jewish male and the ninth sefirah that the passages in *Avot de-Rabbi Natan* and *Bere'shit rabba'* may have called to mind. To a trained Kabbalist, the "queen" is an obvious reference to the tenth sefirah. Decoded kabbalistically, the parable of the king suggests that access to the male aspect of God (the king) can be gained only by going through the tenth sefirah (the queen)—a very common kabbalistic notion already reflected in nascent form in *Sefer ha-Bahir*.[37] Similarly, it would seem that the Sabbath that must pass before circumcision should be associated with the tenth sefirah, while the circumcision itself should be associated with the ninth sefirah or perhaps even with the union of the ninth and tenth sefirot, as mentioned above.

Let me round out the discussion by turning to the explanation for circumcision that Ezra provides in the excursus on the kabbalistic meaning of the commandments that he attached to *Song Commentary*. The content of his explanation comprises an abbreviated citation of the first of the rabbinic passages on circumcision that Ezra cited verbatim in *Aggadot Commentary* and a full citation of the last passage that he cited in *Aggadot Commentary* (Travis 14–15). The only substantive exegetical remark comes right before the first citation: "Circumcision is also part of the secret of the ways of God" (15). He does not explain how this is so, but in light of my exposition of *Aggadot Commentary*, it should be apparent that circumcision is a reflection of the secret ways of God because it is an imitation of God's own phallus, that is, the ninth sefirah.

To repeat, it would seem that, for Ezra, the secret of circumcision involved the fact that the circumcised male organ is a reflection of the ninth sefirah. It is not hard to speculate about why Ezra would have been reluctant to place this secret in writing. To say the least, it runs the risk of giving the impression that Ezra corporealized God in the grossest of ways by assigning a male sex organ to Him. I say, "runs the risk" because clearly, Ezra did not maintain a corporeal conception of God, even esoterically. Such a view would place him entirely outside the kabbalistic norm, wherein the anthropomorphic imagery used to describe the sefirot is not taken literally. (An exposition of the precise manner in which Ezra understood such imagery would take us too far afield.)[38] His decision to keep secret his view that the circumcised male penis is a reflection of the ninth sefirah was therefore most likely an attempt to keep out of the public sphere a view that was likely to be misunderstood.

We do not know exactly when Ezra composed *Aggadot Commentary*, but whatever the precise date, the arguments that raged during the so-called Maimonidean controversy of the early 1230s were surely on the communal agenda. From the literature of this controversy, it is clear that the question of whether God had a body was a live issue, with Maimonideans accusing anti-Maimonideans of corporealizing God[39] and anonymous northern French rabbis accusing Maimonides of rejecting corporealized representations of God.[40] In such a context, we can imagine Ezra wanting to tread carefully. His decision to keep the explanation of circumcision secret may have been a defensive move designed to prevent giving Maimonideans a line of attack against Kabbalists for what might look like a particularly crude form of anthropomorphism. By the same token, it may have been a protective move intended to shield what he would have considered less sophisticated anti-Maimonideans from the theological error that would result from their accepting such crude anthropomorphism. Of course, those with kabbalistic background, who were aware of the nonliteral status of kabbalistic anthropomorphic interpretations of the sefirot, would not fall into this trap even if they did succeed in deciphering his hints.

Ezra's reluctance to place the secret of circumcision in writing is brought into relief when it is compared to a concept that Ezra cites openly in a number of places in his work: "the human being comprises all the spiritual entities" (ha-devarim ha-ruḥaniyyim) (MS Vat. 441, 46a).[41] According to this concept, the human being is a microcosm of the sefirot. It seems to me that the correspondence between the circumcised human penis and the ninth sefirah should be viewed as a particular example of the broader concept that human beings are a microcosm of the sefirot. Yet I would suggest that Ezra was willing to openly state the general concept because, unlike the particular example, it cannot, even erroneously, be taken to imply a somatic relationship between a human being and God. On the contrary, according to the general concept, it is spiritual entities (ha-devarim ha-ruḥaniyyim) that constitute the human being rather than physical aspects of God. This concept, then, is in accord with the nonliteral understanding of the anthropomorphic depictions of the sefirot that he surely espouses. Certainly, Maimonideans would not have approved of the general concept, either, even if they perhaps might not think it was quite as objectionable as the seemingly crude particular case of the homology between the tenth sefirah and the circumcised penis. After all, it both presents God as composed of ten essences—a conception that would be anathema to Maimonideans' commitment to a strict notion of divine simplicity—and it suggests a closer relationship between humans and God than Maimonidean thought would allow. My claim is not, therefore, that Ezra's goal was to appease Maimonideans. On the contrary, as we saw from the introduction to *Song Commentary*, he was willing to confront them. My point is that Ezra did not want to leave himself open to criticism for a crudely anthropomorphic view that he did not hold, nor did he want such a view to become entrenched in the anti-Maimonidean camp.

Let me finally comment on an interesting testimony regarding Ezra's observance of secrecy by the poet Meshullam da Piera, his friend and student, which may pertain to circumcision and other kabbalistic concepts that might be taken to imply a crudely anthropomorphic conception of God. In one of his anti-Maimonidean poems, da Piera writes the following of Ezra, Azriel, and "the rest of his friends": "They were cautious about explicating that which is precious/ They know the measure of their Creator (*shiʿur yotseram*), but they held back their words for fear of heretics" (H. Brody 104, lines 85–89). Here, Ezra is presented as not openly revealing secrets regarding the measurements of God, a reference to the ancient *Shiʿur komah* tract, which ostensibly presents the measurements of the divine stature.[42] As we have seen, this is an issue regarding which Rabad possessed kabbalistic traditions, and it is possible that Ezra and his fellow Kabbalists were aware of these traditions and the attendant esotericism that surrounded them.[43] It may also be the case that da Piera had in mind kabbalistic traditions that seem to give God a body, such as anthropomorphic descriptions in the Song of Songs whose meaning, according to Ezra, are known "to the understanding—the Kabbalists" (*Song Commentary* 495 on Song 4:1)[44]—as well as the secret of circumcision. Notably, the rationale that da Piera imputes to Ezra for keeping this matter concealed is, in keeping with my suggestion above, one of defensive esotericism: if it were presented openly, heretics—presumably Maimonideans—would attack them.

The Technique of Dispersion

In addition to leaving certain ideas out of his writing, Ezra employed the technique of dispersion, which I discussed in the Introduction, whereby an idea is broken up across a work, leaving the reader to assemble its various components. As far as I can tell, his use of this technique is limited to *Aggadot Commentary*, where his approach is to make known in one location that a particular rabbinic aggadah contains a secret explanation that he will explain more fully (although still only in the form of hints) in another location. There are a number of examples of the use of this technique in *Aggadot Commentary*.[45] For the sake of illustration, I will closely follow one example. While I cannot claim to have fully unraveled the secrets contained in this example, I will offer tentative suggestions (some of which will appear in the endnotes). This example will still serve to further showcase Ezra's craft as an esoteric writer.

He begins by citing a passage from B. Berakhot 34b that offers an explanation of Isa. 64:3: "no eye has seen, O God, beside You."[46] This passage offers two different views of what Isa. 64:3 refers to. That is, what is it that "no eye has seen," other than God's? R. Joshua's view is that it refers to special "wine preserved in its grapes from the time of creation." R. Shimʿon ben

Lakish argues, in contrast, that it refers to "Eden." Read in context, these two views are opinions about the reward of the righteous in the "world to come." Thus, earlier in the Talmudic discussion, the view of R. Yoḥanan is cited that Isa. 64:3 refers to the reward of Torah scholars in the "world to come." Our passage describes the nature of this reward. According to the first opinion, these scholars will be nourished by the special wine; according to the second, they will dwell in Eden. After quoting the passage, Ezra remarks: "I will not be able to offer you a hint here (*lirmoz lekha be-kha'n*) regarding this secret, but, with the help of God, in the chapter titled 'one who hires a worker,' you will understand the fear of the Lord and will find the knowledge of the holy ones" (MS Vat. 441, 6a; MS Vat. 294, 27a; MS Vat. 185, 4b). "One who hires a worker" is the fifth chapter of tractate 'Avodah Zarah of the Babylonian Talmud. Ezra's point is that while he will not explain the secret kabbalistic meaning of B. Berakhot's explanation of Isa. 64:3 here, he will explain it in the context of his remarks on the fifth chapter of 'Avodah Zarah.

Yet even before he reaches the fifth chapter of 'Avodah Zarah, we find another reference to the remarks that will be found there. This time, it comes in the context of a discussion of a passage in B. Sanhedrin 99a, a passage virtually identical to the original passage in B. Berakhot 34b. Here, after quoting the view of R. Yoḥanan, who, as seen above, associates Isa. 64:3 with the world to come, Ezra states: "The explanation of this statement is in [tractate] Berakhot in a hinted fashion (*be-remez*), and it is our intention to hint regarding it in [tractate] 'Avodah Zarah" (MS Vat. 441, 68a). Thus, as he did in his comments on Berakhot, Ezra states that he will reveal something of the secret rabbinic explanation of Isa. 64:3 in the section of *Aggadot Commentary* on 'Avodah Zarah. Yet, while in his original comment on the passage in Berakhot, he professes that he "will not be able to offer you a hint here (*lirmoz lekha be-kha'n*) regarding this secret," he now claims that he has already hinted at the secret in Berakhot. Thus, the reader who might originally have read the comment in Berakhot without particular care, expecting that the explanation would come in 'Avodah Zarah, now has to reckon with the possibility that the initial comments in Berakhot already contained some sort of hint about the meaning.[47] Thus, Ezra only reveals that an earlier passage contains an esoteric hint later on in his work.

Finally, in the section in *Aggadot Commentary* on the fifth chapter of 'Avodah Zarah—the promised location of the additional information about the meaning of the earlier passage—Ezra cites a passage from B. 'Avodah

Zarah 65a, which recounts the story of the Jewish sage Rava, who brought a gift to a non-Jewish official named Bar Sheshakh. When he arrives at Bar Sheshakh's residence, he finds him bathing in rosewater with naked prostitutes around him. Bar Sheshakh, upon seeing Rava, asks him if the Jewish world to come has anything finer—to which Rava responds that in the world to come, there is no fear of the king (i.e., the earthly ruler); in contrast, Bar Sheshakh must constantly fear the king, even in his present blissful state. The Talmud, though, continues by suggesting other responses that Rava could have given to Bar Sheshakh's question. According to R. Papi, he could have quoted Ps. 45:10: "The kings' daughters are among your honored ladies; at your right hand stands the queen in gold of Ophir." According to R. Naḥman bar Yitsḥak, he could have quoted Isa. 64:3: "No eye has seen, O God, beside You." Naḥman's statement thus brings the discussion back to Isa. 64:3, the verse that was the subject of the original passage in B. Berakhot 34b.

After some cryptic remarks—which I will not dwell on here but which are typical of *Aggadot Commentary*—Ezra writes:

> And whenever you see in the Talmud, "No eye has seen, O God, beside You" (Isa. 64:3), you should know that its meaning is in accordance with what the two leading sages of the generation said in [tractate] Berakhot, for they do not disagree with each other. One says it is wine preserved in its grapes, and one says it is Eden, which no eye has ever seen. And in *Bere'shit rabba'*, they said, "'She took from its fruit and ate' (Gen. 3:6): she squeezed grapes and gave it to him" (*Bere'shit rabba'* 19:5, ed. Theodor-Albeck 174). This is the opposite of the wine preserved in its grapes from the six days of creation. Behold it has been made clear. (Almalikh 20b)[48]

According to Ezra, the two seemingly opposed positions of R. Joshua and R. Shim'on ben Lakish regarding the nature of the reward in the world to come referred to in Isa. 64:3, as described in the original passage in B. Berakhot 34b, are in keeping with each other. In other words, Joshua's view that the reward is "wine preserved in its grapes from the time of creation" does not contradict Shim'on ben Lakish's view that it is "Eden." Whatever other hints are contained in Ezra's extended discussion, in this last statement we have the clearest example of a new piece of information that was not disclosed in the original discussion in Berakhot.

I would suggest that the congruence of the two views can be understood on the basis of Ezra's kabbalistic symbolism. According to this symbolism, "Eden" is a reference to the second sefirah (wisdom), and the "wine preserved in its grapes" is a reference to the emanative light that emerges from this sefirah.[49] Thus "Eden" and the "wine preserved in its grapes" are not really separable. Ezra, then, may be hinting at an eschatological state in which the soul is nourished by the emanative light that has its source in the second sefirah and is manifest in the third.[50]

There is perhaps an additional piece of information that we gain from the discussion in 'Avodah Zarah. The juxtaposition of the statement about the congruence of the two views with the passage about Bar Sheshakh may suggest that this eschatological vision should be understood in an erotic key. That is, the physical eros of Bar Sheshakh and his prostitutes is replaced by a spiritual eros, in which the emanative flow from the second sefirah, which the righteous receive, is identified with the divine seminal fluid. This possibility is in keeping with the fact that, elsewhere in *Aggadot Commentary* (MS Vat. 441, 53a; Almalikh 14a–b), Ezra follows the Galenic view that sperm originates in the brain and, in the same context, states explicitly that the divine brain is the second and third sefirot.[51] The implication is that the emanative flow from these sefirot is equivalent to divine seed. I would add that the idea that even male Jews will receive the divine seed in the world to come is in keeping with the latent homoeroticism that Wolfson has shown is present in Kabbalah.[52]

If this interpretation is correct, we can understand why Ezra was reluctant to disclose this idea. Once again, we may turn to the disputes of the Maimonidean controversy. One major point of contention was the nature of the world to come, with some in the anti-Maimonidean camp describing it as an embodied state with physical pleasures, including drinking the "wine preserved in its grapes from the six days of creation." Others, even in the anti-Maimonidean camp, rejected such literal interpretations. For example, Meir Abulafia, who did accept a bodily notion of the world to come, nevertheless saw rabbinic descriptions of physical pleasures, including the preserved wine, as metaphorical.[53] Against this backdrop, Ezra, who had a non-bodily view of the world to come (Idel, "Be-or") but who still may have imagined a spiritualized erotic experience awaiting the soul, may have felt a need to tread carefully. Had he openly described his view, he might have given fuel to a corporeal conception of the world to come that he wanted to avoid.

My analysis demonstrates that Ezra is a writer who engaged in an elaborate strategy of dispersion that forces the reader to assemble multiple strands and reflect on how they inform one another. This is an approach that discourages dilettantes, for it requires patience and close attention to textual details.

Let me conclude by pointing out that Ezra also assumes that the Talmudic Rabbis use the technique of dispersion. For example, in the introduction to *Song Commentary*, he writes of the Rabbis: "They scattered (*u-fizzru*) one here and one there so as to hide their place" (489; Brody 23–24). Ezra, therefore, may have seen himself as following a traditional approach. As Wolfson ("Beyond" 177–78; "Wings" 220–21) has noted, in these comments Ezra draws on Maimonidean language and on a Maimonidean hermeneutic, according to which the Rabbis dispersed their esoteric ideas rather than presenting them all at once.[54] This demonstrates that despite his general antagonism toward Maimonides, he was willing to accept a Maimonidean position—an attitude that we find in other instances as well.[55] Maimonides, it might be said, mimicked the approach that he attributed to the Rabbis in his own work.[56] Ezra's approach was different from Maimonides's and ultimately easier to follow, in that he offered the reader guidance of where to look for the various pieces of the puzzle, while Maimonides (*Guide*, I: introduction; Pines 8) simply states that he will use the technique of dispersion without providing any such pointers. Nevertheless, arguably following Maimonides, Ezra also mimicked the rabbinic style.

In *Aggadot Commentary*, Ezra makes the following comment: "You should know the reason for the sacrifice that Adam sacrificed, even though there was not yet any idolatry in the world.[57] The reason is known from the words of our Sages, of blessed memory: it is scattered (*mefuzzar*) among their words in the Talmud. I will collect them and gather them (MS Vat. 298: 'identify them') here" (MS Vat. 441, 27a; MS Vat. 298, 39b).[58] Ezra, then, indicates that he will do the work of assembling the scattered rabbinic traditions. It would seem that the reader must take the same approach when studying *Aggadot Commentary*.

Allusive Writing in *Aggadot Commentary*

The technique of dispersion is a rather technical one, but the technique that Ezra used most frequently is the less technical one of allusive writing.

In fact, I would argue that both *Aggadot Commentary* and *Song Commentary* are written entirely in this style. In a few instances in his work, Ezra explicitly states that he is writing in a laconic, allusive style. One example is found in the introduction to *Song Commentary*, where he indicates that he will compose his exegesis of the Canticle "in a hinted fashion" (*be-remez*) (480). I will return to this passage in the next section. Another example is found in his first letter to Abraham, which he begins by stating that all of Abraham's questions relate to the divine name. Yet, rather than offering a full exposition of this matter, Ezra writes that "since a person is not permitted to speak about this matter and multiply words, but must cover and conceal, I will answer you briefly" (Scholem, "Te'udah" 26).[59] Significantly, in *Song Commentary*, he defines Kabbalah as knowledge of the divine name (478; Brody 20).[60] Thus, in a real sense, Kabbalah is essentially an esoteric matter that he is not willing to fully convey, even in an apparently private letter. Notably, Ezra's approach here seems to be in accord with Isaac's plea for Kabbalists not to be "lengthy in their exposition."

Other examples in which Ezra explicitly states that he will employ allusive writing are found in *Aggadot Commentary*.[61] I will consider one of them, in which he comments on a passage from B. Bava Batra 74b according to which Rav stated: "Everything that the Holy One, blessed be He, created in this world, He created male and female." The Talmudic passage continues by noting that even the creatures Leviathan and Behemoth were created in male and female couples. Ezra's comments on this passage are extant in two versions of *Aggadot Commentary*. After a very brief explanation, consisting of six words in one version of *Aggadot Commentary* and seven in the other, Ezra concludes: "This is the truth (Almalikh: this was stated) according to the path of Kabbalah, and it should not be stated at length" (*ve-ein leha'arikh*) (MS Vat. 441, 61a; Almalikh 17b). Compounding its cryptic nature is the likelihood that the text of the explanation is corrupt, and I have not been able to determine how Ezra understands the midrashic text.[62]

Ezra only states that he is using allusive writing in limited instances; but in practice, he employs this technique throughout his work. I will discuss *Aggadot Commentary* here and *Song Commentary* in the next section. As Tishby noted, *Aggadot Commentary* provides very little actual explanation. Rather, Ezra "assumed, with regard to most of the aggadot, that his readers would discover their mystical content without clarification or explanation" (*Studies* 31).[63] Often, Ezra will simply quote a rabbinic aggadah, and the mere quotation is meant to alert the reader that it has a kabbalistic meaning.[64] In a related fashion, throughout *Aggadot Commentary*, Ezra uses the expressions "you already know" (*kevar yadaʿta*), or "you must know" (*tsarikh attah ladaʿat*). These expressions are used in place of explanation to refer to knowledge that the reader must come with if he is to understand the text. For example, regarding the statement in B. Sabbath 55a that "the seal of the Holy One, blessed be He, is truth," Ezra writes that "you already know [the identity of] what is called the seal" (MS Vat. 441, 47b). He provides no further explanation but presumes that the reader is already familiar with the sefirotic referent of the term "seal." Elsewhere, Ezra quotes Mal. 2:11: "Judah has desecrated the holiness of the Lord, which he loved, and married the daughter of a foreign God." Without providing further explanation, he writes: "You must know who is called 'the holiness of the Lord, which he loved,' and what is 'the daughter of a foreign God'" (67a). Such examples could be multiplied many times over.

While Tishby makes note of this laconic style, he does not see it as a technique of esotericism. Indeed, after providing examples of the sort that I have offered here, he explains that "concealment is not a significant principle for R. Ezra" (Azriel of Gerona, *Commentary* 43). Tishby contrasts Nahmanides, who scattered esoteric hints marked by phrases such as "by way of truth" throughout his biblical commentary, with Ezra, on the grounds that Nahmanides's commentary was written for a public audience and hence concealment was crucial, while Ezra's *Aggadot Commentary* was written for an elite audience such that there would have been no need to hide ideas from a broader audience. Ezra's terseness, in Tishby's view, was grounded not in esotericism but in the assumption that the work would have a limited readership (43).

In contrast to Tishby, I would argue that this terse style should be viewed as part of a strategy of esoteric writing. I have no doubt that Ezra intended *Aggadot Commentary* for a limited audience. Thus contra *Song Commentary*, in which the first part of the introduction is public-facing (even if, as we will see, he wrote the remainder of the introduction and the body of the work allusively), *Aggadot Commentary* does not include any components that were intended for a broader audience. Yet I would argue that Ezra was aware that his work might nevertheless reach a wider non-kabbalistic audience. Indeed, it might be said that Ezra was cognizant of Isaac's warning that "what is written has no master" (T. Weiss, "Letter" 331). It is for this reason that he chose to write allusively. As seen, there are several instances in *Aggadot Commentary* where Ezra employs the technique of dispersion, which is self-evidently an esoteric style of writing. As also seen, there are other instances where he explicitly states that he is writing tersely, where his desire to conceal an idea is apparent. Tishby admits that Ezra uses esoteric techniques but downplays their significance by claiming that they are infrequent (Azriel of Gerona, *Commentary* 43). Effectively, in his view, they are aberrations from Ezra's standard exoteric approach. To my mind, the very fact that Ezra employed such techniques suggests that he knew that outsiders might read *Aggadot Commentary*, even if they were not the primary audience for the work. Otherwise, why employ such techniques at all?

Once it is acknowledged that Ezra knew that his work might be read by outsiders, it becomes likely that his consistent evocations of the knowledge that the reader must bring to *Aggadot Commentary*, as well as his accompanying allusive writing style, are part of an intentionally esoteric style.[65]

It is possible that Ezra takes a hierarchical approach to kabbalistic secrecy in *Aggadot Commentary*. All of *Aggadot Commentary*, as I have suggested, is written in an intentionally allusive style, but certain ideas are presented in even more deeply encoded terms through the technique of dispersion. Possibly, he deemed the ideas hidden through this technique as especially in need of concealment. If my analysis is correct, two such ideas involve anthropomorphic conceptions of God and the nature of the world to come—both topics that, in Ezra's historical context, may have been particularly sensitive. In the case of such ideas, even a reader with kabbalistic background knowledge would be forced to work hard to decipher Ezra's hints.

Allusive Writing in *Song Commentary*

If Ezra was aware that non-Kabbalists might read *Aggadot Commentary* despite the fact that they were not the primary audience of this work, the first part of the introduction to *Song Commentary*, as seen, was clearly directed at precisely such an audience. As Vajda (24) briefly noted, without fully explaining, despite the predominantly public nature of this part of the introduction, Ezra wrote *Song Commentary* for initiates. Here I will elaborate on Vajda's observation by showing that while *Song Commentary* lacks overt forms of esoteric writing like "dispersion" and asides like "you already know," Ezra composed his kabbalistic interpretations of the Canticle in a manner that could be understood only by readers with significant prior knowledge of Kabbalah. Ezra says as much when he writes in the introduction: "I have decided in my heart and my thought to reveal its explanation[66] in a hinted fashion (*legallot be-remez perusho*), according to the true principle that the Rabbis, of blessed memory, have given us. And I have established it upon the pillars of their words and supported it upon the foundations of their homilies. And the knowledgeable will understand (*veha-maskilim yavinu*)" (480). Ezra is explicit that the kabbalistic interpretation of the Song of Songs will be revealed only in hints. In other words, he is stating that he will write allusively rather than offer a complete explanation.[67] Note, as well, his use of the phrase "the knowledgeable will understand," which implies that only those with prior kabbalistic knowledge will succeed in understanding *Song Commentary*.

That prior knowledge of Kabbalah is needed to understand *Song Commentary* might easily be missed by modern scholars who come with extensive knowledge of kabbalistic symbolism, which they have gleaned from later kabbalistic works that systematically present kabbalistic thought, such as Moses de León's *Shekel ha-kodesh* or Joseph Gikatilla's *Sha'arei orah*. It must be recalled, however, that Ezra was apparently the very first author of a kabbalistic monograph. At this early period in kabbalistic history, the only way to get access to kabbalistic ideas was through a personal teacher. An untrained reader—even a member of the rabbinic elite—would therefore have significant trouble understanding the meaning of *Song Commentary*. Even very basic terms, such as "sefirot," would prove problematic for this reader. He would likely be familiar with the term "sefirot" from the widely diffused *Sefer Yetsirah*, which contains the earliest mention of the term. But its meaning in the context of *Sefer Yetsirah* is hardly clear, and it does not self-evidently refer to ten aspects of God, as it does for Kabbalists. On the contrary, other works, which a reader of *Song Commentary* might have been familiar with, such as Judah ha-Levi's *Sefer ha-Kuzari* or Judah ben Barzillai's *Commentary on Sefer Yetsirah*, do not understand the term theosophically.[68] Yet Ezra makes no effort to introduce the reader to the kabbalistic understanding of the nature of the sefirot. Moreover, Ezra speaks of the sefirot in a wide variety of symbolic designations but does not offer any clarification of this symbolism. Without such background information, *Song Commentary* is unapproachable.

The type of allusive writing—the hints—that Ezra states he will employ in *Song Commentary* does not involve shorthand and sparse details, as it does in *Aggadot Commentary*. Ezra writes *Song Commentary* with full sentences that include relevant details. In this regard, the situation is partially akin to an advanced physics textbook that would be virtually meaningless to a reader without background knowledge of physics and mathematics. The textbook contains all the relevant details but is written with the assumption that not every concept and term must be explained. Yet the analogy is not perfect, for the physics textbook would not have been composed in an intentionally esoteric manner. The author would be well aware that introductory physics courses and books would be readily available to an aspiring student, and he presumes that the potential reader would have availed himself of these resources. Indeed, his choice not to provide full explanations of the basic ideas and themes necessary to understand the advanced concepts is guided by this presumption. In contrast, no resources were readily available for an aspiring reader of *Song Commentary*. Ezra's choice not to provide explanatory details therefore should be seen as an act of intentional esotericism. That this is the case comes into clearer focus precisely when we take into account that, as seen, Ezra wrote the introduction to *Song Commentary* with a public audience in mind in which he extolled the supreme value of the wisdom that he would convey in the body of the commentary. If the work were intended only for an elite audience, barring other overt signs of esotericism of the kind found in *Aggadot Commentary*, we might assume that Ezra chose not to explain the basics in *Song Commentary* because such explanations would not have been required by the audience. Yet the public audience to whom the first part of the introduction to *Song Commentary* was directed would have needed such explanations. The choice not to include them seems, therefore, to be a choice to hide kabbalistic ideas from all but a select few readers.

I will illustrate Ezra's esoteric style in *Song Commentary* by considering examples from the text. As seen, in the opening of the introduction, Ezra first recounts the history of transmission of Kabbalah and then launches a critique against Maimonideans. He does all this in an accessible style. In the continuation of the introduction, he provides three principles that underlie the Song of Songs. According to the first principle, the book encodes the sacred history of Israel, culminating in the redemption (*Song Commentary* 480; Brody 27–28). This principle is, for the most part, straightforward[69] and would also be clear to an uninitiated reader—indeed, it is in keeping with the manner in which Song of Songs was read in familiar midrashic literature, where the "lover" in the Song of Songs is God while his "beloved" is the people of Israel, and the arc of Jewish history follows the ups and downs of their relationship.[70]

Yet Ezra's accessible style, which characterizes the beginning of the introduction, now rapidly fades. Starting with the second principle, Ezra's esoteric style comes into view: "The second principle 'lets you know the certainty of true words' (Prov. 22:21): this text (Song of Songs) possesses words that have no parallels that would explain their meaning.[71] The foundation of its parable and edifice is based on them" (481; Brody 30). He proceeds to explain that the meaning of some of these words is gleaned only from traditions—that is, by received oral teachings—while others may be figured out from clues scattered in rabbinic literature (481; Brody 30). He makes clear that there is no written record clearly explaining the meaning of certain words in the Song of Songs. Given this fact, we might expect Ezra to offer detailed explanations of these words. This is not, however, what we find. He continues: "Regarding, the following words—'of wood from Lebanon' (Song 3:9), 'the scent of Lebanon' (Song 4:11), 'Come with me from Lebanon' (Song 4:8), 'flowing streams from Lebanon' (Song 4:15)— we have received that they refer to wisdom" (*ḥokhmah*) (481; Brody 30).

A reader with knowledge of kabbalistic symbolism would know that "wisdom" refers to the second sefirah. He would know that the sefirot are aspects of God and would know the precise function of this sefirah. Moreover, he would understand the methodology of kabbalistic exegesis, according to which seemingly mundane terms are read as symbolic references to the sefirot. In this case, he would realize that Lebanon symbolically refers to the second sefirah. In contrast, an uninitiated reader would be puzzled. To what, he might wonder, does "wisdom" refer? Is it to human wisdom? Is it to God's wisdom, and, if so, is it a generic term for God's knowledge, or does it have some sort of technical meaning? Why would the word "Lebanon," which seems to refer to a place, be connected to any kind of wisdom? These problems do not get solved in the course of the work. On the contrary, new problems would emerge for the uninitiated reader at every turn as the text continues to offer explanations based on kabbalistic symbolism but never clarifies this symbolism.

Even passages that might seem relatively explicit to the knowledgeable reader might confound one with no kabbalistic background. In the excursus on the reasons for the commandments, which Ezra appended to *Song Commentary*, he offers the following explanation of the biblical verses that are found in the head tefillin that is worn during the morning prayer service:

> The meaning of the head tefillin's four chambers: The first, [which contains the passage] "You shall sanctify every first born to Me" (Exod. 13:1–10), pertains to the "beginning is wisdom" (*ḥokhmah*)[72] (Ps. 111:10). The second, [which contains the passage "And when you shall come" (Exod. 13:11–16)], enjoining one to contemplate (*le-hitbonen*) the Exodus from Egypt, pertains to "understanding" (*binah*). The third, *shema'* [including the verse "And you shall love YHVH your God with all of your heart" (Deut. 6:4–9)], pertains to "love of lovingkindness" (*ahavat ḥesed*) (Mic. 6:8). The fourth, [containing] "And if you will" (Deut. 11:13–21), pertains to the attribute of hard judgment (*din ha-kasheh*). This is the meaning of [the Holy One, blessed be He,] donning tefillin[73]—for He is composed of and crowned by all [these attributes] (*kalul u-mukhtar min hakkol*).[74] And because the first sefirah surrounds (*sovevet*) and sets forth them all, it is called "crown" (*keter*). (Travis, 13–14, Hebr. sec.; 197, Eng. sec.)[75]

Here Ezra explains that the four scriptural texts, written on parchment and placed in the four chambers of the head tefillin, correspond to "wisdom," "understanding," "lovingkindness," and "the attribute of hard justice." Yet the reader with no kabbalistic knowledge would have no way of knowing that these terms refer to the second, third, fourth, and fifth sefirot, respectively. Even if he were supplied with this information, he would be little helped because, as seen, he would not have been familiar with the kabbalistic understanding of the term "sefirot." Thus he would also be at a loss to understand the meaning of the statement that the first sefirah, known as crown, "surrounds and sets them all forth."

Similarly, the uninitiated reader would not succeed in understanding an important thesis of *Song Commentary*: that the male and female characters in the Canticle represent the sixth and tenth sefirot, respectively, and that the work is therefore an account of intra-divine love.[76] Indeed, I am able to make the statement that this is an important thesis of the work only because I have familiarity with kabbalistic language and have knowledge of the history of kabbalistic interpretations of the Canticle where this interpretation becomes prevalent.[77] I have already mentioned the traditional rabbinic view that the "lover" refers to God while his "beloved" refers to the people of Israel. As we have seen, Ezra does not reject this reading. Yet, kabbalistically speaking, the lowest sefirah is the representative of the people of Israel on high, and the fates of the earthly and divine Israel are accordingly intertwined. This allows Kabbalists to accept the rabbinic reading while simultaneously adding an additional kabbalistic layer of meaning.[78] For this reason, uninitiated readers of *Song Commentary* might assume, in the case of certain passages, that Ezra is merely following the rabbinic understanding without being aware of the kabbalistic overlay.

Consider Ezra's comments: "'Ah, you are beautiful' (Song 1:15): This refers to the construction of the tabernacle and the entrance into the bridal canopy. As the Sages, of blessed memory, said,[79] 'It was the day in which Moses completed (*KaLOT*) the tabernacle' (Num. 7:1): It is written *KaLaT* ('bride of'), for it is like the day in which the bride (*kallah*) enters into her wedding canopy" (489; Brody 53).[80] Ezra, here, cites a rabbinic play on words, which may have been familiar to a learned non-Kabbalist, according to which the text should be read *KaLaT* ("bride of") rather than *KaLOT* ("completed"). At the basis of this wordplay is the notion that the tabernacle functioned as the wedding canopy wherein the bride (the people of Israel) figuratively wed God. To the uninitiated reader, then, it would look as though Ezra is drawing on the rabbinic passage to underscore the central theme of the traditional rabbinic reading of the Song of Songs: that it refers to the love relationship between the people of Israel and God. Yet the reader with kabbalistic knowledge understands that this theme also needs to be read in a kabbalistic key. Transposed kabbalistically, the bride becomes the tenth sefirah who weds the sixth sefirah, and this passage describes their sacred union.

Elsewhere in *Song Commentary*, Ezra refers to the sixth sefirah as the "glory" (*kavod*) and the tenth sefirah as the "divine presence" (*shekhinah*). In such instances, an uninitiated reader would find it difficult to interpret Ezra's remarks through the standard rabbinic lens. The words "glory" and "presence" would be familiar to him as terms describing God's manifestation in the human realm. Quite possibly, he would have assumed that the terms were synonymous, in keeping with a common assumption in medieval Jewish philosophic literature.[81] Indeed, if he were philosophically inclined, he might assume that these terms refer to a created supernal entity, which Saadia Gaon referred to as both the "glory" and the "divine presence" (see, e.g., *Book of Beliefs and Opinions* 2:10; Rosenblatt 121). Yet he would be befuddled by the manner in which Ezra employs them. From the plain meaning of *Song Commentary*, it would be apparent to him that they refer to two different entities that are figuratively described as the beloved and his lover in the Song of Songs, but he would have no way of understanding the nature of these entities. What, he might wonder, differentiates the "glory" from the "divine presence"? How, precisely, do they relate to God?

For example, regarding Song 4:1, "How beautiful you are, my love," Ezra writes: "These are the words of the glory when he was with the mighty divine presence in the house that Solomon built. For that generation was perfect, and it was a period of peace and joy; anguish and sighing were put to flight" (*Song Commentary* 495; Brody 74). The initiated reader would discern that Ezra construes the words of Song 4:1 as those of the sixth sefirah praising the tenth sefirah. He would realize that the perfection of the generation at the time of Solomon's Temple is what theurgically made their union possible and that the period of peace and joy is a result of the divine efflux that sustains the world and flows properly only when these sefirot are sexually united. The uninitiated reader, in contrast, would be unaware of all these details and would not know what to make of the text.

Later on, regarding verse 4:9, "You have ravished my heart, my sister, my bride," Ezra writes: "As a result of my great desire for you, you have stolen my heart . . . for desire and will and their union and coming close is in accordance with the perfection of the generation[82] and its level" (495; Brody 75–76). Here, again, the knowledgeable reader would understand that Ezra reads verse 4:9 as the words of the sixth sefirah describing his intense sexual desire for the tenth sefirah. He would further realize that, in Ezra's view, the good behavior of the Jewish people can theurgically effect the union of these two sefirot. In the absence of any detailed explanation, the novice would be at a loss to understand the meaning of these comments.

Concealed and Revealed

How are we to understand Ezra's decision to begin *Song Commentary* with an introduction intended for a popular audience while simultaneously concealing the contents of his kabbalistic exegesis from that same audience? I would suggest that this decision was tied to his desire to combat Maimonidean philosophy while still preserving the secrecy of kabbalistic traditions or, in other terms, while still remaining faithful to Isaac the Blind's tradition of secrecy. Effectively, in the introduction to *Song Commentary*, Ezra publicly announces that there is an authentic alternative to Maimonidean thought. Yet he does not see a need to make the contents of that tradition publicly available. He may have felt that public knowledge of the existence of an authentic tradition was sufficient to turn people away from Maimonideanism, even if knowledge of its contents was withheld. He thus may be conceived as mobilizing Kabbalah to do battle with Maimonidean thought, even while striving to preserve its fundamental secrecy.

My analysis of Ezra is quite similar to Moshe Idel's analysis of Nahmanides, Ezra's younger contemporary and fellow resident of Gerona. As indicated, Nahmanides, perhaps the leading rabbinic authority of his time, famously scattered cryptic kabbalistic hints in his otherwise popularly directed commentary on the Pentateuch. Idel notes that Nahmanides intended to make his readers aware of an alternative to philosophical exegesis: "Hints of the existence of another speculative alternative, *Kabbalah*, as the real interpretation of Judaism, was necessary to prevent leaving a void as to the depth of the Jewish tradition. . . . Nahmanides intended to restrict the diffusion of *Kabbalah* to a very limited group of people, while at the same time letting the people know that Jewish tradition is fraught with much deeper significance than people regularly assumed" ("Nahmanides" 61–62).[83]

Yet Idel sees Nahmanides's attitude as distinct from that of the other Geronese Kabbalists, such as Ezra and Azriel: "Basically, Nahmanides remained faithful to the rabbinic interdiction against discussing esotericism in public, an interdiction that was manifestly violated by his Geronese colleagues" (76). For Idel, this distinction is part of his broader claim that Nahmanides represents a different tradition of Kabbalah from that espoused by the other Geronese Kabbalists.[84] Without taking a stand on the general correctness of this claim,[85] in the case of this particular issue, it needs to be revised. The respective attitudes toward esotericism of these early Kabbalists line up differently from the way Idel suggests. There may be differences of gradation between Nahmanides and Ezra; but the former, broadly speaking, shares the view of the latter, while Azriel took a significantly more exoteric approach to Kabbalah.[86] Both Ezra and Nahmanides desired to present Kabbalah as an alternative to Maimonideanism, even while preserving its secrecy.

Azriel of Gerona and Esotericism

Ezra did not completely adhere to Isaac's strict standards of esotericism. In contrast to Isaac, who hid the very existence of Kabbalah from a public audience, Ezra saw fit to publicly proclaim in writing the existence of Kabbalah. Yet, as I have argued, he remained essentially committed to the secrecy of kabbalistic traditions and developed esoteric styles of writing to preserve this secrecy. A more fundamental rejection of the secrecy of Kabbalah can be found in the writings of Ezra's townsman Azriel of Gerona.

A full treatment of Azriel of Gerona's more exoteric approach to Kabbalah requires a separate study, which I will not undertake here.[87] I do, however, want to focus on a specific way in which Azriel breached the boundaries of esotericism set by Ezra. Despite the widely held scholarly view to the contrary (Tishby, *Studies* 5–6; Scholem, *Origins* 396; Porat, *Kabbalistic* 8, 10), there is no reliable evidence that Azriel, who was apparently Ezra's brother-in-law (Tishby, *Studies* 3–5), personally studied with Isaac.[88] There is only one direct reference to Isaac in Azriel's writings: in his own *Commentary on the Talmudic Aggadoth*, he cites a teaching in the name of the "Pious One" that he describes as "his language" (*leshono*) (173). Yet this citation does not prove direct contact between Isaac and Azriel because the same teaching is found in Isaac's name in Ezra's *Aggadot Commentary* (MS Vat. 441, 19a), a work that Azriel expanded and developed in his own *Commentary*.[89] Thus, there is a possibility, as Pedaya (*Name* 67) has raised, that whatever influence Isaac's teachings did exert on Azriel was of an indirect nature. This would have occurred either through written sources or discussions with Ezra. If so, perhaps his lack of a direct relationship to Isaac made him feel less restrained by Isaac's code of esotericism than Ezra was.

If the extant textual evidence presents an accurate picture, Azriel, who, like Ezra, devoted his literary energies exclusively to Kabbalah, was a more prolific author than Ezra. As noted, he is the author of the *Commentary on the Talmudic Aggadoth* (which incorporates and expands upon Ezra's *Aggadot Commentary*). He also wrote *Commentary on Sefer Yetsirah* (which covers the first three chapters of the work), *Commentary on the Liturgy*, a work called *Sha'ar ha-sho'el* (which includes questions and answers about the sefirot), an extended letter to Jews living in the Castilian city of Burgos, and a number of shorter texts.[90] It seems that his relative productivity may, in and of itself, attest to his more exoteric posture and his greater willingness to disseminate kabbalistic ideas. Moreover, as far as I can tell, these works eschew specific esoteric strategies such as dispersion or allusive writing.

Azriel's short work *Sha'ar ha-sho'el* deserves special consideration, for he seems to have composed it as a primer to explain Kabbalah to a popular audience. While Ezra wrote *Song Commentary* with a wide audience in mind, he nevertheless presented its ideas in a markedly esoteric style. No such dichotomy is found in *Sha'ar ha-sho'el*. As Scholem remarked: "The catechism in the form of questions and answers by which Azriel expounded the doctrine of the sefiroth for novices in the Kabbalah was surely not composed for the use of kabbalistic initiates; its goal was to familiarize others with their opinions" (*Origins* 375). Similarly, Halbertal regards the text as one involved in "the breaching of the restrictions of secrecy" (*Concealment* 78).

In this work, using the literary device of answering the questions of an imagined interlocutor curious about Kabbalah, Azriel attempts to offer what is best termed a "defense" of kabbalistic ideas based on philosophical argumentation.[91] As such, it is a work that is meant to be understood by an educated reader even if his education did not include training in kabbalistic thought.

That Azriel's goal is to defend Kabbalah is clear from the accusatory tone of the interlocutor's questions. Thus the interlocutor asks such questions as, "Who will force me to believe in *Ein Sof*?" (Porat, *Kabbalistic* 19) and "Why do you say that the sefirot are emanated and not created?" (20). In these and other questions, the interlocutor takes on the tone of an antagonist against Kabbalah who needs to be logically convinced of its truth. As I have argued elsewhere, this interlocutor should be regarded as a Maimonidean who doubts the veracity of kabbalistic ideas ("Competing" 69–71). This is especially clear in the sixth question, where Azriel has the interlocutor ask: "How can we say that He, may He be exalted, is one, but ten in number (i.e., ten sefirot) are unified in Him? By this, we guard the belief of our heart but not the statement of our mouth" (*nishmor emunat*[92] *levaveinu ve-lo' nishmor ma'amar pinu*) (Porat, *Kabbalistic* 21). Here Azriel is adopting language used by Maimonides in the *Guide of the Perplexed*, as translated by Judah Alḥarizi:

> Anyone who believes that the Creator is one but has many attributes—he states that He is one but believes in his heart that He is many. This is similar to what the non-Jews [the Christians][93] say: He is one, but is three, and the three are one. It is also similar to the statement of he who says that He is one, but He has many attributes and that He and His attributes are one, while simultaneously distancing from Him any corporeality and believing that He is truly simple. It is as though our will and our object is to guard the statements of our mouth and not guard the belief in our hearts

(*lishmor ma'amar pinu lo' she-nishmor emunat libbenu*). (Scheyer and Munk 1:49, p. 181)

Note that Azriel's wording of the question ("By this, we guard the belief of our heart but not the statement of our mouth") is apparently derived from Alḥarizi's translation of Maimonides ("It is as though our will and our object is to guard the statements of our mouth and not guard the belief in our hearts"), even if the wording is reversed. In early kabbalistic literature, the term "attributes" is often used for the sefirot. Maimonides's passage, which argues that the idea of multiple divine attributes is at odds with divine unity, therefore can be read as an attack on the kabbalistic doctrine of the sefirot as effectively endorsing belief in multiple gods, even though this, of course, was not Maimonides's original intention. Azriel's questioner should thus be seen as a supporter of Maimonides who uses Maimonidean language to criticize the kabbalistic notion of the sefirot as at odds with divine unity.

We cannot be sure exactly when Azriel composed *Sha'ar ha-sho'el*, but, based on the unstated assumption that is operative in the work, it seems that it was after Ezra composed *Song Commentary*. Whereas Ezra writes as though he is introducing Kabbalah for the first time, Azriel writes as though the basic doctrines of Kabbalah are well known, if imprecisely understood—hence his need to clarify and defend them. In other words, in the intervening years between the composition of the two texts, some of the doctrines of Kabbalah must have become sufficiently public, but still imprecisely known, such that a text like Azriel's was both possible and required. I would say that Azriel's text itself serves the function of making earlier material like *Song Commentary* more accessible to someone without access to a teacher of kabbalistic ideas.

If Azriel's text should be seen as defending against a Maimonidean critique of Kabbalah, it can be profitably compared to Ezra's *Song Commentary*. Like Azriel, Ezra wrote in response to followers of Maimonides. His response, however, was not intended to answer a critique of Kabbalah. Ezra, rather, takes an offensive stance against what he perceived to be Maimonidean perversity, rather than a defensive stance. His goal was to demonstrate that there was a true alternative to Maimonidean thought—Kabbalah—but he saw no need to open the contents of this thought to a wider audience. Azriel, in contrast, was defending against a Maimonidean attack. His goal was not merely to show that Kabbalah existed as an alternative to Maimonideanism, even if this may have been part of his intention. Rather, he also wanted to convince a Maimonidean reader that his attacks on Kabbalah were logically flawed and that Kabbalah was logically defensible. To do so, he had to speak openly about kabbalistic doctrine.

In *Sha'ar ha-sho'el*, Azriel therefore presents an organized account of kabbalistic doctrine, which, while terse, would provide the uninformed reader with working knowledge of kabbalistic ideas. A variety of key themes are presented in a logical order. The text begins with an argument for the existence of God (Porat, *Kabbalistic* 19). It goes on to describe the nature of God, focusing first on the concealed aspect, *Ein Sof*, and then on the revealed aspect, the sefirot (19–20). It proceeds to describe the sefirot in greater detail, beginning with an explanation of why they are ten (20), continuing with explanations of why they were emanated rather than created (20–21), the nature of their unity, their material nature (21), when they came into existence (21–22), their essential nature, their names and organization, and their nature as bestowers and receivers of divine efflux (22). We know of no previous kabbalistic text that offers such a systematic account in which one idea logically follows from the previous one, such that the earlier portions of the text prepare the reader to understand the later portions.

This account is useful not only as an introduction to Kabbalah but also as a tool for deciphering other more esoteric kabbalistic texts. For example, it might help a reader understand a work like Ezra's *Song Commentary*. As explained, a reader without broad knowledge of the whole kabbalistic system would find much of *Song Commentary* obscure. A reader who had read Azriel's systematic account, however, would likely be able to make greater sense of it.

Azriel's commentary is especially useful in deciphering a work like *Song Commentary* because it is the first kabbalistic text, as far as we know, that provides a glossary of kabbalistic symbols, if only a rudimentary one. At the end of the text, Azriel returns to the questions he had answered earlier in the text and shows that those answers are also rooted in traditional biblical and rabbinic material (23–26). Earlier in the text, in response to a question asking the names and the order of the sefirot, Azriel had provided their standard names, such as *binah* ("understanding") for the third sefirah and *ḥesed* (lovingkindness) for the fourth sefirah (22). At the end of the text, he proceeds, sefirah by sefirah, to identify terms by which the sefirot are named in biblical and rabbinic passages (25–26).

From a critical viewpoint, these biblical and rabbinic terms have nothing to do with the sefirot, which were unknown to biblical and classical rabbinic authors. From a kabbalistic viewpoint, however, these authors were well aware of the sefirot and discussed them in an encoded fashion. According to this viewpoint, sometimes they use the standard terms for the sefirot, without identifying that they have sefirot in mind; at other times, they use alternate terminology. Accordingly, in the case of some sefirot, Azriel merely points to rabbinic passages that use the standard term for the sefirah. For example, he cites various verses and rabbinic statements that refer to "lovingkindness" (25), which he earlier identified as the fourth sefirah. The reader is thus made aware that in these sources, a seemingly commonplace term like "lovingkindness" has a technical meaning as a reference to the fourth sefirah. That is, Azriel has provided a key to read certain rabbinic passages kabbalistically. In so doing, he has effectively provided the reader with at least the beginnings of the means to engage in the kind of interpretive work that Ezra performed in *Aggadot Commentary*.

In the case of other sefirot, Azriel informs the reader of the multiplicity of terms by which the particular sefirot are designated in traditional sources. That is, he reveals that the original list of names that he provided for the sefirot is just one set of names, and, in fact, a variety of names are attached to the sefirot. Consider Azriel's comments regarding the fifth sefirah, which he identified in the original list of names as "fear": "Fear: as it is written '[If] the fear of Isaac had not been on my side' (Gen. 31:42). Regarding it, we say, 'Answer us, the fear of Isaac, answer us' (*seliḥot* service). It is written, 'Judge me by Your might' (*uvi-gvuratekha*) (Ps. 54:3) . . . . This is in keeping with that which they said, '[The eternal covenant] between God and between every living creature that is upon the land' (Gen. 9:15). 'Between God': this is the attribute of judgment that is above, which is strong. 'And between every living creature': this is the attribute of judgment that is below which is weak" (*Bere'shit rabba'* 35:3, ed. Theodor-Albeck 333) (Porat, *Kabbalistic* 25).

In this fairly brief passage, Azriel has revealed that the fifth sefirah can be referred to not only by the term "fear" but also by "fear of Isaac," "might," and "the attribute of judgment above" (in the original list of sefirotic names, Azriel explains that the tenth sefirah is "the attribute of judgment that is below" [22]). The reader now knows that a variety of terms refer to the same sefirah. He can now read scripture and rabbinic literature with eyes open to the possibility that when these terms appear in such material, they might have a technical sense. Moreover, he can read kabbalistic literature, such as Ezra's *Song Commentary*, with new understanding.

Consider the insight that a reader would gain into the aforementioned passage in *Song Commentary* about the tefillin by reading Azriel's commentary. I cite it again here:

> The meaning of the head tefillin's four chambers: The first, [which contains the passage] "You shall sanctify every first born to Me" (Exod. 13:1–10), pertains to the "beginning is wisdom" (*ḥokhmah*) (Ps. 111:10). The second, [which contains the passage "And when you shall come" (Exod. 13:11–16)], enjoining one to contemplate (*le-hitbonen*) the Exodus from Egypt, pertains to "understanding" (*binah*). The third, *shema'* [including the verse "And you shall love YHVH your God with all of your heart" (Deut. 6:4–9)], pertains to "love of lovingkindness" (*ahavat ḥesed*) (Mic. 6:8). The fourth, [containing] "And if you will" (Deut. 11:13–21), pertains to the attribute of hard judgment (*din ha-kasheh*). This is the meaning of [the Holy One, blessed be He,] donning tefillin—for He is composed of and crowned by all [these attributes] (*kalul u-mukhtar min hakkol*). And because the first *sefirah* surrounds (*sovevet*) and sets forth them all, it is called "crown" (*keter*). (Travis 13–14, Hebr. sec.; 197, Eng. sec.)

Having read Azriel's *Commentary*, a reader would now readily recognize that the terms "wisdom," "understanding," and "lovingkindness" refer to the second, third, and fourth sefirot, respectively, since Azriel lists them as the primary names of these sefirot (Porat, *Kabbalistic* 22). Similarly, based on the passage by Azriel cited above, the reader would know that "the attribute of hard judgment" refers to the fifth sefirah.[94] Moreover, he would know what sefirot are and how they function. While Azriel's text does not mention the identification of crown and the first sefirah, nor does it explain the precise manner in which the first "*sefirah* surrounds (*sovevet*) and sets forth them all," after reading his text, the reader would be aware that the other sefirot emanate from the first one and thus might be able to surmise that Ezra's comments pertain to the emanation of the sefirot from the highest one.[95]

Azriel's *Commentary* is the most explicit "guide" to kabbalistic symbolism from this period of which we are aware. A number of other texts from the same period, such as two poetic accounts of the ten sefirot composed, respectively, by two other Geronese Kabbalists, Jacob ben Sheshet ("Sha'ar ha-shamayim") and R. Barzillai (Bos and Pellow),[96] would also have aided a novice reader in decoding cryptic kabbalistic material. This material set a precedent for the far more extensive guides that would begin to appear toward the end of the thirteenth century. These works, hundreds of which exist, go sefirah by sefirah, clarifying the basic function of each one and describing its symbolism.[97] They can be described as Kabbalah primers with a goal of making kabbalistic ideas accessible to wider audiences and, as such, are hallmarks of kabbalistic exotericism. This seems to be the goal of Azriel's work as well.

Chapter 6

Esotericism and Divine Unity in Asher ben David

Asher ben David and Esotericism

Like Ezra ben Solomon, Asher ben David has been depicted by scholars as breaching Isaac the Blind's code of esotericism by composing a public-facing kabbalistic work.[1] This breach is particularly striking because in his letter to Nahmanides and Jonah Gerondi (discussed in Chapter 4), Isaac depicts his nephew Asher as his confidant and follower: "He also knows and saw my behavior and how, from my birth until today, I conducted myself with my companions" (T. Weiss, "Letter" 335). Apparently, Isaac is referring to the fact that Asher was witness to the manner in which he conducted himself with others when it came to kabbalistic ideas—that is, with utmost discretion. He goes so far as to tell his addressees that "if Asher, the son of my esteemed brother, the Sage, R. David, of blessed memory, comes to you, follow every counsel that he gives you" (334–35). While the precise nature of the counsel that Asher was supposed to provide is unclear, it stands to reason that it involved some kind of response to the ill-advised writing of lengthy kabbalistic documents that Isaac criticizes in the opening of his letter.[2] Yet, despite the trust that Isaac placed in him, Asher composed an extended kabbalistic work, *Sefer ha-yiḥud* (*Book of Unity*),[3] which is, as far as we know, the only significant text that he composed.[4]

Scholars have found a ready explanation for Asher's apparent break with his uncle. In the conclusion of this aptly named work, Asher explains that he composed it in response to unnamed critics who accused the Kabbalists of denying divine unity and corporealizing God. As we will see, in Asher's telling, the attacks were so harsh that it almost came to a point that the Kabbalists' teachers were physically assaulted (A. ben David 120). In such a heated environment, with nascent Kabbalah under attack, Asher felt the need to publicly defend Kabbalah, an act that required writing frankly about kabbalistic doctrine. As Scholem puts the matter: "Apparently, as he himself testifies, he wrote his rather lengthy expositions of the doctrine of the sefiroth only when these conflicts and scandals made it necessary to combat the misunderstandings. This explains why he abandoned the reserve shown by his uncle—a reserve that, under the circumstances, was impossible to maintain" (*Origins* 401).

In general, scholars have highlighted the exoteric nature of Asher's *Sefer ha-yihud*. Idel argues, in reference to Asher: "Though several times the latter does employ the formula *ha-Maskil Yavin*,[5] his *Kabbalah* is rather transparent, in any event, much more so than that of his uncle, and its esoteric essence cannot be compared to that of Nahmanides. In any case, the concept that there are basic kabbalistic topics that are not to be disclosed does not play any crucial role in the writings of this kabbalist" ("Nahmanides" 37). Moshe Halbertal is even more emphatic in stressing the exoteric nature of Asher's work: "The writings of Asher ben David reveal far more than what was breached by Rabbi Ezra and Rabbi Azriel; in their explicit, didactic nature, they are quite distant from the strict esotericism of the kabbalists of Provence, among them the Ravad, the grandfather of Rabbi Asher ben David" (*Concealment* 72).

In contrast to these assessments, I will argue that Asher was a consummate esoteric writer. On the face of things, these scholars are correct in highlighting the exoteric nature of *Sefer ha-yihud*. Ostensibly, a major goal of the work is to show that the doctrine of the ten sefirot does not contradict divine unity. Adopting the terminology of Jewish philosophers, such as Bahya Ibn Pakuda and Maimonides, Asher repeatedly tries to show that the doctrine of the sefirot is compatible with the philosophic understanding of divine unity as simplicity, even if, as I will argue, his account would not fully satisfy philosophers. His expositions on this topic are clear and would be accessible to a wide, if educated, audience.

Yet between the lines, Asher also alludes to the apparently diametrically opposed understanding according to which divine unity is constituted by the sexual union of masculine and feminine sefirot. He conceals this idea by employing elaborate techniques of esoteric writing, which I will describe in this chapter. Only the most astute readers with extensive knowledge of kabbalistic thought would be able to follow Asher's cryptic hints. Asher thus follows in his grandfather Rabad's footsteps by presenting two ostensibly contradictory doctrines of divine unity: one for the "understanding" and one for a general audience. Rabad, however, was able to do so without ever revealing that he had any knowledge of kabbalistic lore because he was writing prior to the widespread knowledge of the existence of Kabbalah. By Asher's time, Kabbalah was already a known entity that was debated in the public square. Accordingly, Asher chose to create two *kabbalot*—a public and a private one. In contrast to Ezra, who, even in his publicly directed *Song Commentary*, presented Kabbalah in a manner that would be accessible only to those with significant background knowledge, the public face of Asher's writing would have been understood by a significantly broader audience. Yet his writing also had a private face directed at a much more limited audience. How Asher's public and private accounts of divine unity relate to each other is a difficult question, which I will address at the end of this chapter.

As I will show, Asher should not be seen as breaking with Isaac's esotericism. Rather, he acted pragmatically to defend Kabbalah in the public square even while carefully alluding to kabbalistic secrets.

Asher's Defense of Kabbalah

In a key passage in the conclusion of *Sefer ha-yiḥud* (120), Asher explains that he chose to write the work in response to the intense criticism under which Kabbalists had come. As Scholem (*Re'shit* 159; *Ha-kabbalah be-gerona* 99; *Origins* 402) suggests, Asher may be referring to the anti-kabbalistic missive, written shortly before 1240,[6] by Meir ben Simeon of Narbonne, a leading thirteenth-century rabbinic authority,[7] as well as similar attacks on Kabbalah that we can presume existed at the time. If so, we can date the final edition of *Sefer ha-yiḥud* to around this time.[8] Leading up to this passage, a few lines have misled previous scholarship:

> Regarding all these matters (i.e., divine unity), I have written again and again and again, always recounting their explanation when I mention them. For should anyone who sees this book not find the explanation when I mention them, he will not notice it and will stop reading. When, however, he finds [that there is an explanation that is] sufficient to satisfy him, he will study it [i.e., *Sefer ha-yiḥud*] and decide to read it from beginning to end. Therefore, I have lengthened my exposition in a few places, even though I should have spoken with greater brevity (*'al ken hirḥavti lesapper be-kammah mekomot af 'al pi she-hayah li lekatser*), were it not for things, strong in haughtiness and contempt, that were said at great length. (120)

Scholars (Scholem, *Origins* 481; Halbertal, *Concealment* 73) have read this passage as Asher confessing that he will reveal esoteric matters that should properly remain concealed, so as to respond to the accusations against his fellow Kabbalists that are mentioned in the subsequent passage. This reading makes sense only if Asher's statement in the quotation above that "therefore, I have lengthened my exposition in a few places, even though I should have spoken with greater brevity" is read in isolation. Immediately prior to this statement, Asher notes that he has deliberately been repetitive in his book, regarding the fact that the sefirot are unified ("I have written again and again and again") to ensure that the kabbalistic view is not misunderstood. As he explains, the repetitive nature of his writing style ensured that the reader would not have to spend time searching through the book to find an account of the correct view of divine unity, since such accounts are presented frequently. (A perusal of *Sefer ha-yihud* confirms that this is indeed the case.) Thus, when Asher states that he lengthened his exposition when he should have been briefer, he is not confessing to abandoning his family's esotericism. He is, rather, apologizing for the stylistic awkwardness of his verbosity, which he feels is necessary to ensure that his point comes across with clarity. Moreover, the need for clarity is especially acute, given that, as he remarks in the continuation, unnamed people have unfairly attacked the kabbalistic stance on divine unity. His poor style of writing is therefore justified by his desire to ensure that the true kabbalistic point of view is readily understandable.

Asher then turns to the details of these attacks on Kabbalah. The critics "spoke things that are not so regarding the pleasant and lovely students.... They spread many false ideas about them, and they almost came to [violently] extend their hands against the teachers [of the Kabbalists]" (120). In the continuation, he makes clear that certain Kabbalists themselves are to blame for this criticism:

> It is possible that they brought it upon themselves, since they were not precise in their language, whether in their writing or in their speaking before any which person. And even though they were well intentioned, their lips are profane and their wisdom is spurned, since they neither have the ability to speak nor to write with their hands, in a way that is in accord with the sufficiency of the knowledgeable one and the deficiency of the simpleton (*la-maskil dei sippuko vela-peti dei mahsoro*) so that neither one makes a mistake

regarding matters that have multiple sides. And when they conceal their words in the wrong places or when they explain too much in a place where it is appropriate to hide their secrets, then those who see their books or hear from them do not understand what they mean and err regarding their intentions, and they imagine in their hearts that they [the Kabbalists] believe in two powers, and they become in their eyes like those who deny the wisdom of faith and materialize the Cause of Causes in order to revel in artifice. And everything which they thought of them, they spoke of them, and they said that they are placing a mediator[9] between them and their Creator. (120)

Asher's concern is that kabbalistic secrets are being misunderstood such that some have erroneously thought that Kabbalists "believe in two powers" and corporealize God. This state of affairs is the result of the fact that while certain unnamed Kabbalists have good intentions, they have failed to write "in a way that is in accord with the sufficiency of the knowledgeable one and the deficiency of the simpleton so that neither one makes a mistake regarding matters that have multiple sides." As Haviva Pedaya (*Name* 65–66) has astutely noted, his critique of these Kabbalists is that they did not write in an esoteric manner.[10] Proper esoteric writing, Asher suggests, involves writing for two audiences—a knowledgeable one and a simple one—at once. The writing in a well-constructed esoteric text must be calibrated in such a way that the knowledgeable and the simple will each read the same material but arrive at different understandings. This style of writing, Asher argues, is necessary in the case of ideas "that have multiple sides," that is, particularly complex ideas that are likely to be misunderstood. Yet the Kabbalists whom Asher criticizes made bad judgments; apparently, they wrote too openly precisely in cases that demanded greater discretion and were overly discreet in situations where there was no particular need to conceal.

In Scholem's view, these unnamed Kabbalists were Ezra and Azriel—the same figures whom he thought Isaac targeted in his letter to Nahmanides and Jonah Gerondi, such that the letter and Asher's comments should be read as mutually reinforcing each other (*Origins* 402). I am not sure that we know enough about the early kabbalistic landscape to assess with any certainty that Ezra and Azriel were indeed Asher's targets, rather than other Kabbalists whose memory has been lost.[11] Asher's characterization of these Kabbalists as not knowing the art of esoteric writing clashes with my analysis of Ezra in Chapter 5, where I argued that he employed a style of allusive writing that would make kabbalistic ideas inaccessible to an audience without appropriate background knowledge. If, however, Scholem is correct, we might imagine a scenario where, despite the esoteric style of Ezra's work, the exoteric writings of Azriel and other Kabbalists (as described in Chapter 5) made Ezra's work accessible enough to be the target of anti-kabbalistic agitation,[12] even if current knowledge of Kabbalah was still hazy. What to Ezra, who did not anticipate the composition of works like Azriel's *Sha'ar ha-sho'el* (which, as seen, provides a sort of key to decipher Ezra's works), might have seemed like an effective method of preserving kabbalistic secrecy may have now appeared to Asher as naive and misguided.

Whoever these anonymous Kabbalists were, I will show that Asher avoids their mistakes by crafting an esoteric work that would be understood differently by different audiences. In fact, his approach to esoteric writing differs markedly from that of Ezra. Ezra occasionally used the technique of dispersion, which would present an interpretive puzzle even to one who did have background knowledge in kabbalistic thought; but for the most part, he employed a style of allusive writing that is rather easy to decipher for one with fluency in kabbalistic thought. He employed this style throughout his entire oeuvre, such that none of his work was exoteric. Asher, in contrast, wrote most of *Sefer ha-yiḥud* in an exoteric style and employed esoteric techniques only in particular parts of the work. Effectively, therefore, in *Sefer ha-yiḥud*, he offered both exoteric Kabbalah to the general reader and esoteric Kabbalah to the trained Kabbalist. In recording his esoteric Kabbalah, he employed particular techniques of esoteric writing that even the trained Kabbalist could penetrate only with careful and exacting study, thereby ensuring that a novice, who knew some Kabbalah only from works like Azriel's *Sha'ar ha-sho'el* but lacked an authoritative teacher, would not gain access to his most esoteric ideas. Asher's style, then, is appropriate to a period when kabbalistic thought had become more accessible, and there was a need for a kind of triage that would determine what information could be presented publicly and what must remain concealed. Asher composed his work early enough in the literary history of Kabbalah that he may have believed that he could still control the public narrative of what constituted kabbalistic doctrine, since there were not many works that could provide a counternarrative. The exoteric aspects of his work were his attempt to set the way he wanted Kabbalah to be perceived publicly while the esoteric aspects of his work conceal ideas that are appropriate only for a select few.

Asher employed three particular techniques of esoteric writing: (1) a style of allusive writing that is different from that of Ezra; (2) dispersion; and (3) intentional contradictions.

Allusive Writing

Whereas Ezra wrote relatively expansively because he knew that an average reader would not understand his basic terms, Asher's allusive writing involves condensed, elliptical phrases that require the reader to creatively reconstruct the fuller ideas that they conceal. He employs this method in seventeen short passages in *Sefer ha-yiḥud*, which he marks with the phrase *veha-maskil yavin* ("and the knowledgeable will understand").[13] It is possible that Asher borrowed this technique from the twelfth-century Jewish Neoplatonist Abraham Ibn Ezra, who, as seen in Chapter 2, after presenting a straightforward interpretation of the verse at hand, often offers an esoteric one in brief, clipped language. Setting a precedent for Asher, Ibn Ezra marks these passages with variations of the phrase *ha-maskil yavin*.

Dispersion

Pedaya (*Name* 129) has noted that Asher employed "dispersion," whereby he scattered different components of an idea throughout his work, rather than presenting it all at once.[14] As seen in Chapter 2, this technique has a long history. In Jewish sources, it was used most prominently by Maimonides in the *Guide of the Perplexed*, where he explicitly states that he employs it (*Guide*, intro.; Pines 6–7). Asher does not make such a pronouncement, but I believe that it is clearly reflected in his work, and his proximate source was likely Maimonides's *Guide*.

Intentional Contradictions

The technique of "intentional contradictions" involves introducing contradictory viewpoints without calling attention to the contradictions. Asher likely borrowed this technique, as well, from Maimonides, who, as discussed in Chapter 2, at the end of the *Guide*'s introduction, indicates that he writes in contradictory statements, where one side of the contradiction is intended for the masses while the other side reflects the philosophic truth (*Guide*, intro.; Pines 17–20).

There may be no way to definitively prove that Asher derived the techniques of dispersion and intentional contradictions from Maimonides. There is no question, however, that Asher borrowed Maimonides's general approach to understanding the Bible as an esoteric document.[15] Without mentioning his source, he borrows Maimonides's famous interpretation of "a word fitly spoken is like golden apples in silver filigree" (Prov. 25:11) from the introduction to the *Guide* (Pines 11–12). Following Maimonides, Asher explains that the golden apple is the esoteric meaning of the Torah that might be missed by one who observes only the silver filigree covering it:

> The words of Torah are comparable to a golden apple in silver filigree. The simple meaning of the text is comparable to silver, which is easy to understand, and is clarified like silver, and it is true. But if one delves deeply in the words of Torah so as to understand its hidden and concealed matters, then you will find precious and very deep matters. At times, they will be hinted in one letter; at times, in one word of a complete verse; at times, in the way in which the word is written but not in the way it is pronounced, and, at times, in the way that the word is pronounced and not in the way it is written. "They are more precious than gold, than pure gold" (Ps. 19:11). These matters are called apples of gold. (76)

Leo Strauss (*Persecution* 60–78) argues that Maimonides attempted to emulate the Torah's mode of esoteric writing in the *Guide*. I suggest that Asher tried to do the same in *Sefer ha-yiḥud*. Throughout the work, he employs the three aforementioned techniques of esoteric writing to conceal the doctrine that divine unity is constituted by the sexual union of male and female sefirot even while exoterically arguing that the sefirot are compatible with divine simplicity. In general, I will show that *Sefer ha-yiḥud* merits the type of reading that Strauss applied to Maimonides's *Guide*, wherein close attention is paid to textual inconsistencies and seemingly incidental textual features.

Esoteric and Exoteric Accounts of Divine Unity

I will begin my analysis by considering Asher's exoteric and esoteric readings of 1 Chron. 29:11—"Yours, Lord, are greatness, might, splendor, triumph, and majesty—yes, all (*ki khol*) that is in heaven and on earth." Here we find an example of a place in his work where seemingly opposed views of divine unity are juxtaposed. First the exoteric reading: "It is a tradition (*kabbalah*) in our hands that the [letter] *vav* of the explicit name, which is YHVH and is called the Tetragrammaton, hints at the six extremities (*shesh ketsavvot*), and on each and every extremity is one sefirah of the ten sefirot, and these six sefirot are hinted at in the verse 'Yours, Lord, are greatness, might, splendor, triumph, and majesty—yes, all (*ki khol*) that is in heaven and on earth'" (1 Chron. 29:11) (101). Asher begins by explaining that the third letter of the Tetragrammaton, the letter *vav*, which has a numerical value of six, represents the six extremities, or six of the lower sefirot.[16] He then adds that these same sefirot are hinted at by the various divine attributes listed in 1 Chron. 29:11.[17]

In the discussion that follows, Asher elaborates upon the precise correspondences between the verse and the six sefirot. In particular, "Greatness, might, splendor, triumph, and majesty" refer to the fourth, fifth, sixth, seventh, and eighth sefirot, respectively. The term "all" (*khol*), in the second part of the verse ("Yes, all [*ki khol*]"), refers to the tenth sefirah. As Asher puts it: "'Yes, all' (*ki khol*) is an attribute (*middah*) and might (*u-gevurah*) that completes each and every activity below and above, and this is the meaning of the text, 'Yes, all (*ki khol*) that is in heaven and on earth'" (101).[18] His intention in stating that this sefirah "completes each and every activity below and above" is to highlight its role as the intermediary between the divine realm and what is below it. The second part of 1 Chron. 29:11, "yes, all (*ki khol*) that is in heaven and on earth," suggests, therefore, that the role of "all" is in both heaven and the earth.[19]

Asher's comments are not exactly a model of clarity, but he makes no deliberate effort to obscure. On the contrary, they would be readily grasped by a diligent reader who had read through *Sefer ha-yihud* up to this point. Yet after this exoteric explanation of 1 Chron. 29:11, Asher provides an alternate esoteric reading of the second part of the verse ("yes, all [*ki khol*] that is in heaven and on earth"), which he marks with the phrase *veha-maskil yavin*, "and the knowledgeable will understand." I will return to this reading below. First, though, it is necessary to consider the discussion that appears shortly after the esoteric reading, which is, once again, based on the exoteric reading of the verse and concerns the nature of divine unity:

> And those sefirot that were mentioned [in the exoteric reading of 1 Chron. 29:11] are all connected (*adukot*) one to another without any

separation (*perud*). . . . An analogy (*ve-siman*) for the fact that these seven extremities are connected (*adukot*) one to another without the compounding (*belo' ḥibbur*) of individual components one with another is the candelabra, which is made entirely—"its base and its shaft, its cups, calyxes, and petals, were of one piece with it" (Exod. 37:17; cf. Exod. 25:31)—from one block alone, without any compounding from another place. . . . And an analogy for the flow that flows to them from *Ein Sof* is the light, which is the oil placed in each and every shaft [of the candelabra], and through it they are lit and shine, and an analogy and hint to the middle line, which sustains everything, is the oil in the center shaft. (102)

Various scholars have argued that Asher seems to adopt an early version of the fourteenth-century position that the sefirot are not part of God's essence (*'atsmut*) but are his *kelim*: both the vessels that receive His efflux and the instruments through which He acts (Gottlieb, *Studies* 311–12; Idel, *Kabbalah* 142; Hallamish 160–61). This reading is supported by the analogy of the candelabra. The seven shafts of the candelabra stand for "the seven extremities,"[20] a phrase that, in Asher's view, refers to the lower six sefirot, mentioned in 1 Chron. 29:11 ("the six extremities"), together with the first sefirah.[21] At the conclusion of the analogy, Asher compares the efflux that flows to the sefirot from *Ein Sof*, their endless source, to the oil that flows through the shafts. On this model, the shafts, or six lower sefirot, are *kelim* (vessels) that receive the efflux.

In keeping with the *kelim* reading reflected here, elsewhere in *Sefer ha-yiḥud* we get the impression that the sefirot are outside of God. Thus, for example, Asher contends that prayer must be directed to God Himself and not to the sefirot (75, 81). Indeed, this view allows Asher to argue for divine unity elsewhere in the work, on the grounds that, while there may be multiple sefirot through which the efflux flows, there is, after all, only one efflux (see, e.g., 71).

Yet Asher is not content with this exoteric account of divine unity. In the first part of the analogy, he provides another exoteric account, according to which the sefirot are united with one another and with *Ein Sof* and according to which this unity is defined by the absence of composition. That Asher desired to offer such an account suggests that he did, from a certain perspective, view the sefirot as part of the divine essence (*'atsmut*). In fact, the two accounts are not mutually exclusive, as I will explain below.

In the first part of the analogy, Asher notes that, according to biblical law, the various components of the candelabra were not conjoined together but were carved out of one block of solid gold. It appears that the block of gold should be identified with *Ein Sof*.[22] According to Asher, this analogy is fitting for divine unity because it does not involve "the compounding of individual components one with another." The seven sefirot are not, in fact, multiple components that come together with one another and with *Ein Sof*. Rather, they should be viewed as having been carved out of the underlying substance of *Ein Sof*. This carving out describes the mechanism of emanation. Just as the carving out of the candelabra from a solid block of gold does not suddenly turn the gold into an object that comprises several elements, so the carving out/emanation of the sefirot from *Ein Sof* does not lead to composition within God. Divine unity is therefore the absence of composition. With this analogy, then, Asher is trying to align the idea of the sefirot with the philosophic doctrine of divine simplicity—albeit, as we will presently see, in a manner that would certainly not satisfy philosophers.

In Sandra Valabregue-Perry's impressive study of *Ein Sof* in early Kabbalah, she downplays the indebtedness of Asher and some of the other first Kabbalists to philosophic accounts of divine unity. Referring to his view of emanation (in reference to a different passage in *Sefer ha-yiḥud*), she notes that "the internality that spreads out from a uniform and infinite source allows, precisely, for the existence of multiplicity and allows for multiplicity to be seen as subjugated to unity" (148), a view of divine unity at odds with the philosophical one. To the extent that philosophers, such as Baḥya Ibn Pakuda or Maimonides, would not be satisfied with Asher's account of divine unity, I agree with Valabregue-Perry. In fact, the analogy of the candelabra ultimately breaks down in a fashion that supports her contention. A block of gold is, of course, finite. Yet a basic thesis of the philosophic view of divine unity—a thesis that, as we will see below, Asher also maintains—is that anything finite is at least theoretically divisible and hence not simple. In response to such an objection, Asher might contend that he is offering only an analogy. In fact, *Ein Sof* is infinite and therefore is not actually comparable to a block of gold. Thus, the carving of the sefirot out of *Ein Sof* does not, literally speaking, involve shaping a limited object in the way that carving a candelabra out of a block of gold does.

Yet such a response would prove inadequate because the carving of the sefirot out of *Ein Sof* does, in fact, fail to meet the philosophic understanding of divine unity. If we attempt to move from the analogy to the actual sefirot, we realize that what is really entailed is the carving out of aspects of limitation—the sefirot—within limitlessness. This produces a state of affairs in which the sefirot are, on the one hand, aspects of *Ein Sof* and, on the other, have a certain discreteness within *Ein Sof*. In other terms, they are simultaneously limited and limitless. Asher does not fully spell this out here, but he does express this understanding in a number of other ways elsewhere in his work, such as when he refers to the sefirot as "not delimited (*mugbalot*) from the perspective of their beginning for they are a dimension without a dimension" (*middah belo' middah*) (66).[23] Other articulations that suggest this viewpoint will be examined below. In the final analysis, it seems that it is only insofar as the sefirot have a limitless aspect that Asher is able to claim that divine unity is that of simplicity: since the sefirot are limitless, they are identical to *Ein Sof*, and divine unity is thus defined as the absence of composition. Yet the fact that the sefirot also have an aspect of discreteness makes it clear that Asher's viewpoint is ultimately incompatible with the philosophic account of divine unity.

This viewpoint, incidentally, allows us to understand why Asher seems to view the sefirot both as the vessels and the essence of God. For Asher, these positions are two sides of the same coin. Insofar as the sefirot are limitless and identical to *Ein Sof*, they may be seen as God's essence. Insofar as they are limited, however, they may be seen as the vessels of *Ein Sof* that receive *Ein Sof*'s efflux. This point was made by Elliot Wolfson in slightly different terms. According to him, for Asher and other early Kabbalists, the fourteenth-century distinction between the sefirot as vessels and as essence was not operable, since "the sefirot are the delimited predication of the unlimited" ("Negative" xi).[24]

To repeat: Asher's presentation of divine unity is not fully in keeping with the philosophic one. Nevertheless, for our purposes, it is significant that he makes a conscious effort to provide an explanation that would align the doctrine of the sefirot with the doctrine of simplicity—one that shows, to use his terminology, that divine unity does not consist of "the compounding of individual components one with another." This account of divine unity would certainly seem to be at odds with the view that divine unity is constituted by the sexual union of male and female sefirot, which manifestly involves the compounding of individual components one with another. An unsuspecting reader would conclude that this constitutes Asher's full statement on divine unity. Yet a reader who pays attention to Asher's esoteric hints learns that, alongside this statement, Asher also proffers the view that divine unity is precisely constituted by the sexual union of male and female sefirot.

He expresses this view, among other places, in his esoteric interpretation of 1 Chron. 29:11, which is sandwiched between the exoteric interpretation and the account of divine unity just detailed: "Another explanation: Heaven and earth are two attributes. It is called 'earth' (*erets*); this refers to a desired earth (*erets ḥefets*), and it is linguistically derived from 'will' (*ratson*). And the attribute of 'all' adjudicates (*makhra'at*) between them, and it is for this reason that Scripture combined them (*zivvegam*), and the knowledgeable will understand (*veha-maskil yavin*)" (101). In contrast to the relative clarity of exposition that characterizes the exoteric reading, this passage is intentionally obscure and is a prime example of Asher's style of allusive writing. To unpack this cryptic passage, it is necessary to examine other esoteric passages in *Sefer ha-yiḥud*. Here, then, we have allusive writing combined with a form of the technique of dispersion. Each passage reveals a component of the esoteric idea, and only if we read them in light of one another does the full idea emerge.

Let us start piecing them together. In the passage above, Asher's concern is with the terms "heaven" and "earth" that appear at the end of the verse ("yes, all [*ki khol*] that is in heaven and on earth"). He begins by identifying "heaven" and "earth" with two attributes but does not indicate which ones. As we know from another esoteric passage, which we will examine below, these two attributes are the sixth and tenth sefirot, respectively. Furthermore, since he also refers to earth as "a desired earth" (a phrase by which the people of Israel are called in Mal. 3:12),[25] it is apparent that this "desired earth" is another designation of the tenth sefirah. Thus, while in the exoteric explanation of 1 Chron. 29:11, the words "heaven" and "earth" are taken literally as referents to the divine and earthly realms, here these terms are read as referring to aspects of the intra-divine realm.

Asher further creatively claims that there is a linguistic connection between "earth" (*erets*) and "will" (*ratson*). Significantly, he also points out this linguistic connection in an exoteric context elsewhere in *Sefer ha-yiḥud*. There, without offering any indication that he is revealing a secret matter, he comments on Job 37:13: "Whether as a scourge, or for His earth, or for lovingkindness." According to Asher, "'as a scourge' is analogous to judgment (the fifth sefirah). 'For His earth' (*le-artso*) is analogous to mercy (the sixth sefirah), which is linguistically derived from will (*ratson*). 'Lovingkindness' is according to its meaning (the fourth sefirah)" (64).[26] Note that in the esoteric passage, "earth" refers to the tenth sefirah, and in the exoteric interpretation of 1 Chron. 29:11, it refers to the actual earth; but in the current exoteric passage, it refers to the sixth sefirah: mercy. Moreover, in the current exoteric passage, the linguistic connection that Asher draws between "earth" and "will" makes a certain sense insofar as the term "will" may evoke God's goodwill, which is related to His mercy. Ostensibly, however, it does not make sense in the esoteric passage, since the tenth sefirah is identified by Asher, as will be seen, with God's judgment.[27] This matter will be clarified on the basis of another esoteric passage to be discussed below.

In the continuation of the esoteric passage, Asher apparently reads the word "all" as a reference to the ninth sefirah. As we saw in Chapter 3, the term "all" is also understood in this manner in the tradition about the Sanctus prayer that Ezra records in *Aggadot Commentary* in the name of Isaac, who attributed it to his father.[28] One function of this sefirah is to unite the sixth and tenth sefirot. Asher, here, alludes to this function when he states that it "adjudicates" between heaven (the sixth sefirah) and earth (the tenth sefirah). It seems therefore, that, according to the exoteric reading, "all" refers to the tenth sefirah; and in the esoteric reading, it refers to the ninth sefirah.

Additionally, a hint that the sixth and tenth sefirot are gendered and that their union is sexual in nature may be present in Asher's comment that "it is for this reason that scripture combined them" (*zivvegam*). "Combined them" ostensibly refers merely to the combining of the words "yes, all that is in heaven and on earth" in the biblical verse, a combining that indicates that "all" "adjudicates" between "heaven" and "earth." Perhaps, however, the term "combined them" refers to the sexual union, the *zivvug* (coupling) of the sixth and tenth sefirot—which, in keeping with numerous other early kabbalistic examples, should be gendered male and female, respectively—through the ninth sefirah, which can therefore be said to have a phallic function—its key function, according to numerous kabbalistic sources.

Some of the hints in this passage are clarified by examining another esoteric passage in *Sefer ha-yiḥud* that is similarly marked by the phrase "and the knowledgeable will understand." This second passage is concerned with the biblical account of the extraordinary vision of Aaron, his sons, and the seventy elders: "And they saw the God of Israel; and there was under His feet the likeness of a pavement of sapphire, and the like of the very heaven for clearness" (Exod. 24:10). According to Asher, their vision was of the tenth sefirah, which the verse refers to as "under his feet."[29] He continues: "Regarding this (i.e., the phrase 'under his feet'), it is said, 'The heaven is My throne, and the earth My footstool' (Isa. 66:1). The heaven is the attribute of mercy, which is the throne of mercy, and the earth is the tenth sefirah. The word 'earth' (*erets*) is linguistically derived from 'will' (*ratson*). And the knowledgeable will understand" (114).[30] This passage clarifies the first esoteric passage, which neglected to give the theosophic meaning of heaven and earth. Here, Asher explains that "earth" is the tenth sefirah and "heaven" is the attribute of mercy, that is, the sixth sefirah. As in the first passage, he makes special mention of the linguistic association between earth and will—again, without explanation.

A third esoteric passage helps explain this linguistic link and clarifies other aspects of the first two passages. This passage appears earlier in the text than the other two. At the same time, it is not understandable without them. In what may be another element of his technique of dispersion, Asher, it seems, scatters hints throughout *Sefer ha-yiḥud* without regard for logical order.

Before we turn to the hint itself, it will prove instructive to examine a passage that comes shortly before it. In this passage, which shows no signs of a deliberate effort to conceal and thus may be regarded as exoteric, Asher notes that when God created the world, "The attribute of judgment was joined (*nishtattefah*) to the attribute of mercy" (63)[31]—that is, the fifth and sixth sefirot were joined.[32] Apparently, he is alluding to a rabbinic exegesis of Gen. 2:4,[33] a verse that reads: "In the day that the Lord (YHVH) God (*Elohim*) made earth and heaven," an exegesis that Asher cites in another exoteric context in *Sefer ha-yiḥud* (108). According to this exegesis, the use of the double divine name YHVH *Elohim*, in Gen. 2:4, indicates that God "joined" (*ve-shittefah*) the attribute of mercy to the attribute of judgment when He created the world. This exegesis is itself based on the rabbinic idea, encountered earlier, that YHVH refers to the attribute of mercy, and *Elohim* refers to the attribute of judgment.[34]

In this passage, when Asher speaks of the joining of the attributes of mercy and judgment, he does not have in mind the coming together of two entities. Rather, to understand his intention, we need to return to the exoteric model of divine unity outlined above. It will be recalled that while Asher attempts to align the sefirot with the theory of divine simplicity, he still views them as discrete in a certain sense. It seems that this view serves as the basis of his exoteric theory of divine action. This theory, in turn, helps clarify his exoteric understanding of the unification of the sefirot. On numerous occasions and using roughly the same wording each time, Asher describes the manner in which God acts. For example, in reference to the fourth, fifth, and sixth sefirot, to which he accords particular importance throughout *Sefer ha-yiḥud*, he notes: "God, may He be blessed, acts in all of them as one, or in a few of them, or in one of the three while encompassing within it (*ve-kholel bah*) all of them" (52). In the current context, in reference to the unification of mercy and judgment, he puts it in the following manner: "He joined (*ve-shittef*) the attribute of mercy with the attribute of judgment so as to say that all is unified, and He acts in both of them as one, just as through one He acts in them all" (63). These descriptions of divine action are understandable in light of his exoteric metaphysics. Given the sefirot's discreteness, God can act through an individual sefirah. Since, however, they are also perfectly unified, His action through one sefirah can also encompass other sefirot, or, to put the matter conversely, His action through multiple sefirot is no different from His action through one sefirah. Thus, Asher is able to speak about the unification of sefirot without having to subscribe to the position that different aspects of God are actually brought together. When Asher says that God "joined the attribute of mercy with the attribute of judgment," he apparently merely means that God took advantage of His own metaphysical reality. He is thus able to retain the rabbinic language, cited above, while couching it in terms of a philosophically inspired metaphysics.

Against this backdrop, we turn to the esoteric hint: "[The joining of mercy and judgment] is analogous to the beginning of the creation of the world, and the time when He appears thus (i.e., in a state in which mercy and judgment are joined) is called a time of will (*'et ratson*). And the knowledgeable will understand" (64–65).[35] This passage suggests that Asher understands "a time of will" (a phrase from Ps. 69:14) as a *terminus technicus* for the joining of the sixth and tenth sefirot. The reference to the creation of the world is apparently to Gen. 2:4: "When the Lord (YHVH) God (*Elohim*) made earth and heaven." Its significance lies in the fact that this verse uses the divine names YHVH and *Elohim* together. Since these two names refer to mercy and judgment, respectively, this verse alludes to the union of sixth and tenth sefirot. (On the basis of parallels with the other passages that I will detail below, it is clear that judgment here refers to the tenth sefirah and not to the fifth sefirah.) Ostensibly, the reading of the verse here is similar to the exoteric one, with the exception that in the exoteric one, judgment is a reference to the fifth sefirah. As we will see, in contrast to the exoteric reading, here the union involves two aspects actually coming together.

The parallels between this esoteric passage and the other two are apparent. First, in the other two passages, Asher linked heaven and earth to the sixth and the tenth sefirot. Similarly, heaven and earth are alluded to in the third passage: in addition to using the two divine names, Gen. 2:4 refers to the creation of heaven and earth.

Second, the two other passages linguistically connected "earth" (*erets*) to "will" (*ratson*). The third passage refers to the union of "mercy" and "judgment" as "a time of will" (*'et ratson*). This phraseology, I suggest, helps us make sense of this strange linguistic connection. Esoterically, "earth" refers to judgment, the tenth sefirah. Earlier, we saw, however, that according to one of Asher's exoteric expositions, it refers to mercy, the sixth sefirah. We also saw in the same exoteric exposition that "earth" and "will" are linked. We suggested that this linkage makes sense because "will" suggests divine goodwill, a characteristic related to mercy. Yet what are we to make of the esoteric linkage of "earth" and "will," where earth refers to the tenth sefirah (judgment), rather than to the sixth sefirah (mercy)? I suggest that, on the esoteric level, this linkage may be explained by the fact that when the tenth sefirah unites with the sixth sefirah, its character of judgment is transformed into that of mercy. Thus, the phrase "a time of will," esoterically understood, captures the moment of this transformation—the moment of the union of these sefirot. From another perspective, it might be said that the exoteric understanding both of "earth" and of the connection between "earth" and "will" refers to the situation after the unification has occurred. As a result of the unification, "earth" understood as the tenth sefirah is transformed into "earth" understood as the sixth sefirah—at which point, the relationship between "earth" and "(good)will" is readily understandable. If, however, there is a real transformation of judgment to mercy, it seems that we are dealing with a situation in which two aspects of God actually come together, leading one to take on the character of the other.

The impression that we are dealing with two aspects of God actually coming together is strengthened when we examine three other passages, found in other early kabbalistic works, which share some central ideas with this cluster of esoteric passages in *Sefer ha-yiḥud*. The first is the teaching regarding emanative rains, briefly discussed in Chapter 3, which Ezra recorded in *Aggadot Commentary* in the name of Isaac. The other two passages help clarify Isaac's cryptic remarks. One of them appears in "Commentary on

Creation" (found in *Aggadot Commentary*), which, as I suggested, was erroneously attributed to Isaac but is really the work of Ezra.[36] The second one is found in *Commentary on the Talmudic Aggadoth*, by Azriel (93–94). This passage is mostly Azriel's own remarks, but, as Azriel was wont to do in his *Commentary*, he also incorporated comments from yet another place in Ezra's *Aggadot Commentary*. All three passages deal with the production of rain, where rain must be understood as divine efflux; accordingly, I will refer to them as the rain passages. Since the latter two rain passages are elaborations of the first,[37] in one way or another, all three are based on ideas transmitted by Isaac. While the esoteric passages in *Sefer ha-yihud* do not deal with rain, they share other themes with these passages. Given this fact, it seems to me that Asher's passages might be based on ideas that he learned from his uncle. Let me summarize the main themes that the rain passages share with *Sefer ha-yihud*:

1. In the passage in Azriel's *Commentary on the Talmudic Aggadoth*, we learn that "heaven" stands for the sixth sefirah and "earth" stands for the tenth sefirah.[38] The manner in which heaven and earth are interpreted in the passage in the "Commentary on Creation" is less certain, but on balance, there, too, they seem to refer to the sixth and tenth sefirot.[39] As we saw, they are interpreted in the same manner in the esoteric passages in *Sefer ha-yihud*.
2. The "Commentary on Creation" implies that Gen. 2:4 ("In the day that YHVH *Elohim* made earth and heaven") doubly reflects the union of the sixth and tenth sefirot, since it uses the double divine name and mentions heaven and earth.[40] As we saw, the same reading of the verse appears prominently in the esoteric passages in *Sefer ha-yihud*.[41]
3. The teaching that Ezra records in *Aggadot Commentary* in the name of Isaac the Blind reads, as we saw, "For they [the rains] are sent from the cause (*sibbah*) at the time of unity and will (*be-'et ha-yihud veha-ratson*). The words of the Pious One" (MS Vat. 185, 17a; MS Vat. 441, 20a). According to this passage, rain will fall "at the time of unity and will." The phrase "at the time of unity and will" is related to the phrase "a time of will," which appears in one of the esoteric passages in *Sefer ha-yihud*. As pointed out in Chapter 4, based on the other two rain passages,

which clarify this one, it emerges that this rain falls as a result of the union of the sixth and tenth sefirot.[42] Thus, we can infer that "at the time of unity and will" refers to the moment of union. This phrase thus carries the same meaning as the phrase employed by Asher.[43]

4. In the passage in Azriel's *Commentary on the Talmudic Aggadoth*, it is made explicit that the sixth sefirah is gendered male and the tenth sefirah is gendered female and that their union is sexual in nature.[44] We saw that the sexual nature of the union is perhaps also hinted at in one of the esoteric passages in *Sefer ha-yiḥud*. Indeed, given the other similarities between the esoteric passages in *Sefer ha-yiḥud* and the rain passages, it may be possible to extrapolate from the latter to the former and conclude more definitively that Asher, too, saw the union in sexual terms. Insofar as this is the case, it is obvious that, esoterically speaking, he sees the union of the sixth and tenth sefirot as the actual coming together of two aspects of God. That this sexual reading is appropriate will become even clearer below.

5. In the section of the passage in Azriel's *Commentary on the Talmudic Aggadoth* that incorporates remarks of Ezra from *Aggadot Commentary*, the union of the sixth and tenth sefirot is referred to as the time in which "the building [= the sefirot] returns to its original and unified state" (94). These remarks, taken together with Isaac's characterization of the union "as the time of unity and will," highlight the fact that this union is crucial for divine unity. The idea of sefirot uniting sexually certainly seems to be at odds with divine simplicity. Yet in the esoteric passages in *Sefer ha-yiḥud* considered thus far, Asher never explicitly takes the next step and states that this union is required for divine unity. Again, however, insofar as we can extrapolate from the rain passages to the esoteric passages in *Sefer ha-yiḥud*, we can conclude that according to the esoteric passages, too, this union is required for divine unity. Further evidence for this will be presented below.

These parallels suggest that Asher's esoteric passages are based on ideas that he learned from his uncle. Yet the tradition in Rabad's name, regarding the two-faced first human, which was discussed in Chapter 3, allows us to trace some of these ideas back at least one generation further. To facilitate my analysis, I will cite this tradition again here:

> Therefore, Adam and Eve were created two-faced so that a wife will obey her husband (*tihyeh nishma'at le-va'alah*), for her life is dependent upon him, and so that he does not go one way and she another way (*she-lo' yelekhu zeh le-darko ve-zeh le-darkah*). Rather, there should be closeness and affection between them, and they will not separate, and then there will be peace between them and tranquillity in their palace. And this is also true of the agents of truth (*be-fo'alei ha-emet*) whose action is truth. The reason for the [two] faces is twofold. First, it is known (*ki yadua' hu'*) that two opposites were emanated, one of complete judgment (*din gamur*) and the other of complete mercy (*rahamim gemurim*). If they had not been emanated "two-faced," and each of them would act in accordance with its own principle, then it would appear as if there were two [independent] authorities (*kishtei rashuyyot*), and each would act without being joined to the other and without its assistance. But now that they were created "two-faced," all their action takes place together and with balance, in complete unity, and there is no separation (*perud*) between them. Moreover, if they had not been created "two-faced," no complete unity could be made from them, and the attribute of judgment would not be able to elevate itself to that of mercy, or [vice versa] that of mercy to that of judgment. But now, since they were created "two-faced," each of them comes close to the other and unites itself with the other and longs (*kosef*) and desires (*u-mit'avveh*) to be joined to the other, so that the tabernacle may be one whole (based on Exod. 26:6 or 36:13). A proof for this is that you will find that the [divine] names refer to each other. Thus you will find that YHVH, [which usually refers to the attribute of mercy], can refer to the attribute of judgment, and *Elohim* [which usually refers to the attribute judgment] can refer to the attribute of mercy, as in "YHVH rained upon Sodom and Gomorrah" (Gen. 19:24). YHVH rained down and transferred from one attribute to the other. (Scholem, *Re'shit* 79n2)

As seen, it is possible that mercy and judgment should be identified with the fourth and fifth sefirot. If so, the sefirotic identifications of mercy and judgment are different from those employed in the rain passages and in Asher's esoteric passages. Nevertheless, the similarities between the basic theme of this tradition, on the one hand, and that of the rain passages and Asher's esoteric passages, on the other, are striking enough to suggest that they are related, even if we have to assume that the sefirotic identifications shifted over time.

According to Rabad, just as the first humans were originally created two-faced—that is, as a single entity—so, too, mercy and judgment were originally joined. Like Adam and Eve, they were then separated. Their subsequent union is thus a recapitulation of their original unity. Given the comparison to Adam and Eve, it is apparent that mercy is gendered masculine, while judgment is gendered feminine, and that their union is sexual in nature. Rabad, as I suggested, highlights the sexual nature of the union of mercy and judgment by using the verb "desires" (*u-mit'avveh*), which has an erotic connotation. While he does not state so explicitly, it seems that the sexual union of mercy and judgment is parallel to the sexual union of Adam and Eve, which they consummated after their own separation.

Furthermore, in Rabad's view, certain biblical usages of divine names prove that mercy and judgment can join together. As noted, according to rabbinic tradition, the Bible employs YHVH when God exercises mercy and *Elohim* when God exercises judgment. Yet certain rabbinic sources point to counterexamples of exceptional verses in which this is reversed—a point that Rabad highlights by citing Gen. 19:24. In this verse, it is YHVH, not *Elohim*, who rained down judgment upon Sodom and Gomorrah. From Rabad's perspective, the reversal of divine names in this verse demonstrates that mercy and judgment can unite. The similarities between Rabad's tradition, on the one hand, and the rain passages and Asher's esoteric passages, on the other, are apparent:

1. All concern the union of YHVH (mercy) and *Elohim* (judgment).
2. As with the rain passages, Rabad's tradition also sees this union as sexual in nature. This provides further evidence that this is the full meaning of the esoteric passages in *Sefer ha-yiḥud*.
3. Again, as with the rain passages, Rabad's tradition makes clear that the sexual union of mercy and judgment is required for divine unity. This is the force of Rabad's comment that "all their action takes place in an evenly balanced manner in complete unity and without separation."

Here, "without separation" does not imply absence of composition but a lack of separation that is the result of two entities joining together. (Rabad also compares the union of the two attributes to the tabernacle, a point I will return to below.) This increases the likelihood that, according to Asher's esoteric passages, as well, this union leads to divine unity. Therefore, it seems reasonable to conclude that the esoteric passages in *Sefer ha-yiḥud* that we have examined so far were based on traditions passed down along family lines.

Taken altogether, the analysis above suggests that Asher's esoteric position on divine unity is diametrically opposed to his exoteric one. It is worth highlighting just how different these two positions are. In the latter, to say that two sefirot are united is not to suggest that two aspects were brought together, since, according to his exoteric metaphysics, they were already united. In contrast, in the former, their union involves an intra-divine process in which two components of God actually unite. Against this backdrop, it hardly seems accidental that Asher juxtaposed the first of the esoteric passages, discussed above, to a statement that argues for his modified understanding of divine simplicity. Indeed, this seems like a use of the technique of intentional contradiction. By placing his esoteric hint in this context, Asher highlights, for the adept, the seeming disparity between the competing views of divine unity. This is not an isolated case. In a number of instances in *Sefer ha-yiḥud*, Asher alludes to the union of the sixth and tenth sefirot in the course of discussions of divine simplicity. At times, as in the example above and another example to be considered below, he juxtaposes esoteric passages and discussions of divine simplicity. In two other instances, however, in the very midst of a passage that seeks to reconcile the doctrine of the sefirot with divine simplicity, he inserts a comment that ostensibly proves his point but, in fact, alludes to the sexual union of these two sefirot.

Esoteric and Exoteric Accounts of Divine Unity: Further Examples

In the following passage, Asher argues for divine simplicity more emphatically than he did in the previous passage that we considered:

> How could it be that there are limited (*ketsuvot*) and determined (*va-ḥalutot*) attributes that are nevertheless compounded (*meḥubbarot*) with the Cause of Causes and the Foundation of Foundations? For,

in truth, everything delimited (*mugbal*) has a beginning and an end, and anything with shape has a body, and anything delimited can be disturbed, and any compound (*meḥubbar*) can be separated. And I will testify to this with the heaven and the earth, regarding which it is said, "Thus said God the Lord who created the heavens and stretched them out, who spread out the earth" (Isa. 42:5). And it is said, "Gauged the heavens with a span and meted earth's dust with a measure" (Isa. 40:12). And elsewhere it is said, "The heavens should melt away like smoke and the earth wear out like a garment" (Isa. 51:6). And it is further said, "Long ago You established the earth; the heavens are the work of Your hands. They shall perish but You shall endure" (Ps. 102:26–27). And since they are compounds (*meḥubbarim*)—some out of two and some out of four elements—therefore they will mix and will change. And God forbid that we speak this way regarding the Rider of the Heavens or regarding His aforementioned attributes, for who could say that they are limited or compounded (*meḥubbarot*) with Him? (119)[45]

Asher's comments are apparently influenced by the very same passages in Baḥya's *Duties of the Heart* (128, 129, 130) that, as seen in Chapter 3, influenced Rabad's exoteric view of divine unity. Like Baḥya's and Rabad's remarks, Asher's view is predicated on the assumption that God's unity is that of simplicity. He contends that the attributes or sefirot cannot be delimited entities. Anything delimited has a beginning and an end or, in other terms, is a body. God, however, cannot be a body. Moreover, anything delimited can, at least theoretically, be broken into multiple parts, and if it can be broken into multiple parts, it must be composed of multiple parts. This, however, is not in keeping with God's perfect unity. In the second half of the passage, Asher cites a number of biblical verses concerning heaven and earth to back up his position regarding divine unity. I will return to these verses shortly.

After making this statement, Asher offers another statement that seems to back off somewhat from a conception of divine simplicity:

Therefore it is fitting for every knowledgeable one[46] to understand and know that every attribute of which we have heard is [mentioned in the Bible] to allay the ear that hears. But there cannot be in Him a limited (*ketsuvah*) and determined (*va-ḥalutah*) attribute, since He is one and He unites in all of them, and He acts through all of them as one or through one of them and includes all of them in it. Additionally, through one, He does the act [associated with that one] and [that associated] with its opposite, as one, since the power of one is in the other, as I have explained and have offered clear proofs regarding this. (119)

Valabregue-Perry (147) highlights this statement as evidence that Asher's view is far from the philosophic position regarding divine unity, and she is right to do so. It explains that the notion of distinct sefirot is just an accommodation to the limited human perspective, designed to allay the human ear, which cannot process God's perfect unity. Yet in the same breath, it also describes God, in the familiar wording, as acting through particular attributes even while including the other attributes in the one in which He acts. As we saw, this description is based on Asher's exoteric metaphysics that attempts to uphold simultaneously that divine unity is defined by simplicity and that the sefirot are, in a certain sense, discrete. This theory, as we have seen, strays from the philosophic perspective.

Nevertheless, for our purposes, it needs to be highlighted, once again, that Asher is motivated by an attempt—however imperfect—to align his view with the philosophic one. We already saw that he draws on Bahya's presentation of divine simplicity in formulating his view. Moreover, in comments that follow the statement above, he again draws on a philosophic position: "It is according to His actions upon us that they are called attributes: not from His perspective but from our perspective, since He is one from every side. He is mercy, He is judgment, [and He is] lovingkindness" (119). Asher argues that descriptions of God's attributes, or sefirot (he refers, in particular, to the fourth, fifth, and sixth sefirot), refer to His actions as perceived from a human perspective, rather than to His essence. As other scholars have noted, he is drawing on a philosophic line of thinking (Scholem, *Origins* 284–85; Sendor 303–4). As a way of reconciling multiple divine attributes with simplicity, some of the philosophic works available to Asher in Hebrew employ the notion that certain divine attributes, mentioned in the Bible, refer to God's actions, as perceived by human beings, rather than to His essence.[47] I would add that Asher's specific terminology shows the imprint of a philosophically inspired source: "One from every side" is borrowed from Maimonides, who employs it to describe God's simplicity.[48]

Yet, amid this line of reasoning, he hints at the seemingly opposed esoteric idea that we have been examining. In the passage in which he draws on Baḥya, Asher cites various biblical verses that describe the way in which God can change heaven and earth. Ostensibly, they are intended to prove that divine unity is absolute. As he explains, heaven and earth are subject to change because they were formed by the compounding of the various elements. Every compound is subject to being separated and hence subject to change. The type of unity manifest in heaven and earth is therefore fundamentally different from God's absolute unity. Yet in the esoteric passages from *Sefer ha-yiḥud*, discussed above, Asher identifies heaven and earth with the sixth and tenth sefirot, which unite to form divine unity. The use of these terms amid a discussion of divine unity would remind the adept reader of the secret idea regarding the union of these sefirot.

We cannot dismiss Asher's invocation of heaven and earth as coincidental and assume that he did not really intend to allude to the esoteric doctrine, because we find the same pattern repeated in his discussion of Deut. 6:4, the biblical verse that opens the *Shemaʿ* prayer, the quintessential declaration of divine unity. He provides both an exoteric and an esoteric interpretation of the verse. The former proclaims the absolute unity of God, but within it is an allusion to the esoteric doctrine. As if to underscore this point, the exoteric reading is followed by an esoteric one that also concerns this doctrine.

He begins his exoteric interpretation by explaining that the three divine names in Deut. 6:4 ("Hear, O Israel, YHVH is our God [*Elohenu*], the YHVH is one") designate the fourth, fifth, and sixth sefirot. This interpretation, however, would seem to indicate that a multiplicity of attributes inhere in God. For this reason, Asher argues, the verse proclaims that the Lord is one:

> And should you say, perhaps there are many powers since there are many attributes? Therefore, we unify thereafter and say "one," in order to say that His attributes are neither divided (*ḥalukot*), nor separated (*ve-nifradot*), nor even compounded (*meḥubbarot*). Rather, they are all one, and each one is included in the other. And He, may He be blessed, acts in all of them as one or in one and includes within it all of them. Even though each one is the heading of its attribute (*rosh le-middatah*), its entire force is in this one, since all is one thing for the reason that we mentioned. And even though we have found many things compounded together that are called one, as it is written, for example, regarding the building of the tabernacle,

"And couple the tent together so that it becomes one whole" (Exod. 26:11), and also "And couple the cloths to one another with the clasps, so that the tabernacle becomes one whole" (*ve-hayah ha-mishkan ehad*) (Exod. 26:6): This compound (*hibbur*) [of the parts of the tabernacle] is not like this compound [of the attributes of God]. Because the tabernacle compound was of individual parts (*mi-devarim ahadim*), and, when they were compounded one with the other, it was as though it was one. But this is not the case because this compound could be divided and become as it was in the beginning, and there would be many individual parts.[49] The same is the case in "so that they become one flesh" (Gen. 2:24). But the "one" in the verse, "Hear, O Israel," is one from every side, in all its attributes, without any separation and without any composition (*belo' shum perud u-velo' shum hibbur*). (61–62)[50]

When Asher states that "He, may He be blessed, acts in all of them as one or in one and includes within it all of them," he is drawing on his exoteric metaphysics, which accords the sefirot a certain discreteness. Nevertheless, his main focus is on divine simplicity. Asher argues that the distinction between the fourth, fifth, and sixth sefirot is illusory. God's unity is that of simplicity, not of composition. As Asher puts it: "But the 'one' in the verse 'Hear, O Israel' is one from every side, in all its attributes without any separation and without any composition." Here he combines Maimonides's phrase "one from every side" with another Maimonidean wording, "without any composition and without any separation" (*Hilkhot yesodei ha-torah* 1:11).[51]

Yet within this very passage are two allusions to the esoteric doctrine of the union of the sefirot. Ostensibly for the sake of greater clarity, Asher provides two counterexamples that demonstrate what divine unity is not. The first is the unity of the parts of the tabernacle. In contrast to divine unity, the unity of the tabernacle is the result of the compounding of numerous parts and thus could, at least theoretically, be separated again into its original components. The second is the union of a man and a woman. When conjoined, they are as "one flesh" (language taken from Gen. 2:24), but intrinsically they are individuals and can be separated. An astute reader might see in this second counterexample an allusion to the esoteric idea of the sexual union of the male and female sefirot.

The matter can be taken even further. By using these counterexamples, Asher, I suggest, intended to allude to the tradition of his grandfather, cited above, regarding the two-faced primeval human being. After all, the two counterexamples provided by Asher to explain what divine unity is not were provided by Rabad to explain what divine unity is. In his tradition, it will be recalled, Rabad applied to the divine attributes of mercy and judgment the rabbinic legend that the first human being was originally created as a two-faced creature. Like Adam and Eve, mercy and judgment were first a single entity before they were separated. Moreover, the subsequent sexual union of mercy and judgment, which marks divine unity, parallels that of Adam and Eve. I suggest that Asher's use of Gen. 2:24 was calculated to evoke Rabad's tradition. While Gen. 2:24 speaks of the sexual union of human beings in general terms, the immediate context is, of course, the story of Adam and Eve, as would have been obvious to any reader of *Sefer ha-yihud*. A kabbalistic adept, however, might have been led to recall Rabad's tradition more specifically. Thus, when Asher quotes Gen. 2:24 as an example of what divine unity is not, he is, I suggest, alluding to the fact that Rabad used the same motif for the opposite purpose.

This suggestion gains more weight when we realize that the first counterexample, regarding the unity of the parts of the tabernacle, may also allude to Rabad's tradition. In describing the union of mercy and judgment, Rabad explained that "each of them is close to the other and unites itself with the other and longs (*kosef*) and desires (*u-mit'avveh*) to be joined to the other, so that the tabernacle may be one whole" (*lihyot ha-mishkan ehad*). Rabad's wording regarding the tabernacle is apparently based on Exod. 26:6 (*ve-hayah ha-mishkan ehad*) or Exod. 36:13 (*vayhi ha-mishkan ehad*). Yet Asher employs the image of the tabernacle—citing Exod. 26:6—to demonstrate what the nature of divine unity is not. Once again, in the course of offering an account that attempts to square the sefirot with divine simplicity, Asher alludes to a tradition that seemingly has a very different sense of divine unity. As I indicated in Chapter 3, Rabad's tradition might very well have been intended for private circulation among various early Kabbalists. My assumption is that Asher therefore knew that at least some of his readers would pick up on his allusions.

Shortly following the exoteric interpretation of Deut. 6:4, Asher offers an esoteric one that pertains to the sexual union of the sixth and tenth sefirot: "And similarly [in the Sanctus prayer], after saying, 'Holy, holy, holy' (Isa. 6:3), we say, 'Blessed be the glory of the Lord from its place' (Ezek. 3:12), which is comparable to 'Blessed be the name of the glory of His kingdom' that is said after 'Hear, O Israel.' And this and this are a complete unification. And the knowledgeable will understand" (62).[52] Immediately, we notice that this passage, like the other esoteric passages in *Sefer ha-yiḥud*, is intentionally cryptic. In it, Asher draws a parallel between the recitation, during the *Shemaʿ*, of Deut. 6:4 ("Hear, O Israel") followed by the rabbinic formula "Blessed be the name of the glory of His kingdom," on the one hand, and the recitation, during the Sanctus, of Isa. 6:3 ("Holy, holy, holy"), followed by Ezek. 3:12 ("Blessed be the glory of the Lord from its place"), on the other.

It will be recalled, from Chapter 3, that the Sanctus was the subject of a teaching of Isaac the Blind in the name of Isaac's father, Rabad, recorded by Ezra in *Aggadot Commentary*. It seems to me that Asher's cryptic explanation of the Sanctus is parallel to the explanation that Ezra records in Rabad's name, and it is likely that Asher learned this explanation from his uncle Isaac. In Rabad's teaching, the thrice-repeated "holy" refers to the fourth, fifth, and sixth sefirot, respectively. I suggest that Asher interprets the Trisagion in the same manner here. Accordingly, since, in Asher's view, the Trisagion is parallel to Deut. 6:4, it seems that just as the Trisagion refers to the fourth, fifth, and sixth sefirot, so do the three divine names in Deut. 6:4 (YHVH, *Elohenu*, and YHVH).[53] If so, Asher's esoteric and exoteric readings of Deut. 6:4 are identical. Yet if the overall point of the exoteric reading was to show that the seeming multiplicity within God is illusory, a different impression emerges from the esoteric reading—as will become clear below.

In Isaac's teaching, Ezek. 3:12 ("Blessed be the glory of the Lord from its place"), the second component of the Sanctus, refers to the tenth sefirah. I assume that Asher understands the verse in the same manner. Since Asher sees Ezek. 3:12 as parallel to the formula recited after Deut. 6:4 ("Blessed be the name of the Glory of His kingdom") during the *Shemaʿ*, he presumably also sees the latter as referring to the tenth sefirah.

According to Rabad's teaching, as it is conveyed in *Aggadot Commentary*, the recitation of Isa. 6:3 followed by Ezek. 3:12 theurgically effects the union of the sixth sefirah (which is the perfect balance of the fourth and the fifth sefirot) with the tenth sefirah. It therefore follows that for Asher, the recitation of Deut. 6:4 followed by the recitation of the formula "Blessed be the name of the Glory of His kingdom" achieves the same purpose. Moreover, Ezra makes clear that the union, described by Rabad's teaching, is sexual in nature. Thus, it will be recalled that after recounting it, he writes: "I am my beloved's and my beloved is mine (Song 6:3): to join them one to the other" (MS Vat. 185, 10a). His citation of the words of the female lover of the Canticle to her beloved highlights the erotic character of the sefirotic union. This adds to the likelihood that Asher saw the union in sexual terms as well.

In the other esoteric passages, the relationship between the union of the sefirot and divine unity was not made explicit, even if such a linkage is difficult to escape. Here, the fact that the esoteric passage concerns the *Shema'*—a proclamation of divine unity—leaves no doubt that its subject is divine unity.

In the foregoing analysis, I have shown how paying careful attention to *Sefer ha-yiḥud*'s esoteric allusions uncovers unexpected facets of the work. On the basis of this reading, we are left with a curious state of affairs in which a presentation of divine unity as the absence of composition is juxtaposed to the seemingly opposed notion of male and female sefirot uniting sexually. Moreover, even the exoteric presentation of divine unity contains allusions to the union of the sefirot. Asher thus emerges as an accomplished esoteric writer who proffers one view openly while concealing another.

The Social Factors Behind Asher's Esotericism

It is possible that Asher may have seen the phrase "the knowledgeable will understand" as a way of burnishing the reputation of Kabbalists as an elite group with special knowledge. The social benefits of secrecy, however, do not explain Asher's use of techniques like intentional contradiction, which he does not announce. Moreover, regardless of any potential social capital that he might have accrued by his use of this phrase, it is clear that *Sefer ha-yiḥud* is not a mere exercise in "secretism" but conceals actual secrets about sexual union within God. These were secrets that Asher, I suggest, had very good reason to conceal: they were likely to lead to the persecution of Kabbalists. As was true for his grandfather Rabad, Asher's use of esoteric writing can best be characterized as an act of "defensive esotericism."

The secret that divine unity is constituted by the union of multiple sefirot was the same one that Rabad concealed through esoteric styles of writing. As will be recalled, Rabad's defensive esotericism was likely driven by three factors: (1) internal Jewish pressure to understand divine unity in terms of simplicity; (2) Rabad's wariness that the kabbalistic doctrine of divine unity may undercut Jewish attempts to refute the Trinity; and (3) his fear that the kabbalistic view might appear too close to the views of Cathar heretics.

The pressures that were behind these three factors had become only more intense in Asher's time, and I suggest that they may have driven his choice to engage in defensive esotericism. Other than the intensification of these pressures, a major difference between Rabad's time and Asher's was that in the earlier generation, kabbalistic doctrine was still closely held; by Asher's time, it circulated more widely and was openly attacked. In such an environment, merely pretending to espouse a non-kabbalistic doctrine of divine unity in the manner of Rabad would not have sufficed to protect Kabbalah. Asher, rather, had to present an exoteric doctrine of Kabbalah that could explain Kabbalah in terms that would adequately protect it from these pressures, while hiding the doctrine of multiple powers uniting within God.

First and foremost, Asher was clearly worried about an internal Jewish threat. As we saw, he explains that Kabbalists were being openly criticized for believing in "two powers." According to Asher, the agitation against Kabbalists was so strong that it almost led to physical assaults against them. Asher, however, was not merely content to argue that Kabbalists believed in one God but claimed that they believed in a version of divine simplicity. He did so by drawing on Baḥya's *Duties of the Heart*, the very same work that Rabad drew on when he formulated his own exoteric account of divine simplicity. The fact that belief in divine simplicity had penetrated Rabad's circle might explain why Rabad exoterically purported to accept this position. Two generations later, to judge from Meir ben Simeon of Narbonne's critique of Kabbalah, it was the belief of Kabbalah's bitter opponents. Not only does Meir support divine simplicity across his work,[54] in his criticism of Kabbalah he specifically accuses Kabbalists of denying it: "they said in their folly that all of them [i.e., the sefirot] cleave one with another and they are all one" (T. Weiss, "Their Heart" 334). Hence Asher provided an exoteric account of Kabbalah according to which the sefirot could be reconciled with divine simplicity.

Asher also may have feared that kabbalistic doctrine would undermine Jewish attempts to refute the Trinity at a time when the church took a more active approach to proselytizing in Jewish communities than it had in Rabad's time. As historians have documented, the church became increasingly aggressive in its proselytizing of Jews in the thirteenth century.[55] In Paris, the Talmud was put on trial in 1240 (right around the time that Asher likely composed the final version of *Sefer ha-yiḥud*) and subsequently burned,[56] an event that Jews in southern France were surely aware of. Closer to home, Meir ben Simeon described a sermon by a Christian cleric in the synagogue of Narbonne that Jews were forced to attend.[57] (We are not certain of the precise date of this sermon.) Events like these may have made Asher quite wary of publicly presenting a doctrine that suggests multiplicity within God. In public disputations and in Jewish polemical literature, discussions of the Trinity were common. In these contexts, Jews attempted to argue for divine simplicity as a way of refuting the Trinity. Thus, Meir in *Milḥemet Mitsvah*, to counter the idea of the Trinity, states emphatically that God is a "single existent in every aspect of singularity" and that "He is a true unity, for there is no true unity beside Him" (Herskowitz 122). Meir also makes clear in his anti-kabbalistic letter that he viewed the kabbalistic understanding of the divine as even more misguided than that of Christians.[58] Asher therefore may have been reluctant to openly express an idea that might lend support to Christian polemicists.

Finally, in addition to the factors above, Asher may have wanted to avoid giving the impression that kabbalistic thought had commonalities with Cathar thought. Joseph Shatzmiller (80–81) suggests that the internal Jewish attack on Kabbalists, as reported by Asher, for believing in "two powers," shows that Asher was aware that kabbalistic thought could be interpreted along dualistic Cathari lines.[59] If in Rabad's time, church persecution of the dualistic heresy was in its infancy, Asher was living in the aftermath of the crusade against the Cathars. Shatzmiller (71), in explaining the anti-Cathar tone that Jews of the thirteenth century took in their disputes with Christians, noted that in the post-crusade climate, in which Cathars were pursued by the inquisition, a perceived similarity between Judaism and Catharism could spell disaster for Jewish communities. It is possible that Asher's desire to conceal the kabbalistic view of divine unity, which could be perceived as a form of dualism, was partly motivated by the same fear.

The Relationship Between the Esoteric and Exoteric Account of Divine Unity

How are we to understand the relationship between the esoteric and exoteric accounts of divine unity in *Sefer ha-yiḥud*? I will offer two possible explanations without attempting to decide between them. The most obvious explanation is that the esoteric account represents Asher's true view while the exoteric one reflects a false view intended for non-Kabbalists. This was the approach that I took in the case of Rabad. The difference between Rabad's work and Asher's work is that for the former, the esoteric account is kabbalistic and the exoteric one is philosophical; for the latter, both the esoteric and exoteric accounts are kabbalistic. Historically, as I noted, this is not surprising because in Rabad's time, kabbalistic thought was not yet publicly known; in Asher's time, it was the subject of public controversy. Accordingly, Asher could not ignore Kabbalah in his exoteric account but had to offer an analysis of the manner in which kabbalistic views of divine unity align with philosophic views. Following the explanation that the exoteric account was merely a facade that covered the true esoteric one, this alignment was completely manufactured. Asher has no sincere interest in a philosophical account of divine unity. He, in fact, rejects such an account in its entirety and prefers the more mythological account, according to which divine unity is constituted by the sexual union of male and female sefirot.

Herbert Davidson pointed out that the logical consequence of the Straussian reading of Maimonides's *Guide* is that "the 470-page volume was written in order to conceal a few ethereal clues that overturn virtually every word in the book" (*Moses Maimonides* 402). This explanation of *Sefer ha-yiḥud* would lead to a similar conclusion. In trying to reconstruct Asher's views on divine unity, we would be forced to ignore a large portion of what he actually wrote.

A potential difficulty with this explanation is that if Asher's goal was merely to appear to conform to an orthodoxy according to which divine unity is defined as simplicity, we might expect that he would present the doctrine of the sefirot as fully consonant with divine simplicity. Such a presentation might, for example, amount to a kind of nominalism in which the reality of the sefirot is denied. However, this is not what we find. Asher does not reject the reality of the sefirot. Instead, he argues for a type of simplicity that nevertheless allows for a certain discreteness between the sefirot, which, as I have stressed, is a view that would not have passed philosophic muster. No philosopher who subscribed to the notion of divine simplicity would allow for any sort of discreteness within God. If Asher's attempt to square the doctrine of the sefirot and divine simplicity was merely an exoteric screen, why would he not have done a better job of it? Following the first explanation, we might suggest that a kabbalistic doctrine in which the reality of the sefirot was taken for granted was sufficiently well known that Asher could not merely pretend that it did not exist by appealing to something like nominalism.

There is, however, another possible explanation of why Asher did not do a better job of reconciling the sefirot with divine unity. According to this explanation, Asher's attempted synthesis was genuine. Davidson makes the following observation regarding Maimonides's "secret" view of creation: "A wily philosopher with esoteric beliefs might, as a stratagem, rehearse familiar and commonplace arguments that run counter to his secret position. We can hardly conceive, though of a philosopher's taking pains to fashion and publish brand new arguments that undermine his position" ("Maimonides' Secret" 36).[60] A similar observation can perhaps be made with respect to Asher. His attempts to align the doctrine of the sefirot with divine simplicity are complex and highly creative. This makes it more difficult to imagine that they were just a smoke screen.

Let me propose a hypothetical alternative approach to resolving the seeming contradiction between the exoteric and esoteric presentations of divine unity in *Sefer ha-yiḥud*. As scholars have increasingly come to understand, the development of Kabbalah was a dynamic and creative process. Kabbalistic literature is not simply a record of materials that had been transmitted orally for centuries, nor is it a wholesale invention by figures in the second half of the twelfth and first half of the thirteenth centuries. Rather, as Idel has stressed, it emerged from the synthesis of numerous and even contradictory streams.[61] My suggestion is that the doctrines found in the esoteric passages reflect one of these streams—oral traditions transmitted along family lines, perhaps over many generations. That we are dealing with traditions passed along family lines is clear from the fact that I have been able to trace the key themes of Asher's esoteric passages to Isaac and Rabad. The connection between some of Asher's esoteric ideas and Rabad's passage regarding the two-faced first human being is especially significant, since both Wolfson (*Language* 142–74) and Idel (*Kabbalah and Eros* 22–73; *Kabbalah* 128–36; "Kabbalistic Prayer" 268–77) have marshaled a range of early sources that demonstrate the antiquity of the themes in this passage.[62] This may suggest that we are dealing with far more ancient ideas, even if, no doubt, these ideas changed over time, both before and after they reached Rabad.

If it is correct to assume that the esoteric passages in *Sefer ha-yiḥud* reflect older traditions, the following reconstruction of the factors that contributed to Asher's esoteric stance may be suggested. Perhaps his attempt to align the sefirot with the doctrine of divine simplicity was not a screen meant to hide his true view from the masses. On the contrary, Asher may have been legitimately attracted to the conception of divine unity proffered in the philosophic literature. At the same time, he was confronted by the fact that his own received traditions seemed to present a dramatically different sense of the nature of divine unity. In this regard, his predicament was quite similar to the one faced by Jewish philosophers: How could they square philosophic ideas with traditional sources that seemed at odds with those ideas? An important difference is that Asher had an additional set of traditional materials, unavailable to philosophers, to which he accorded great authority: his received traditions.

From a Straussian perspective, the solution that Maimonides offered to this predicament was merely a ruse, since no real synthesis between Athens and Jerusalem is possible. In contrast, perhaps, the synthesis that Asher looked to create reflected a real conviction that harmonization was possible.

Against this backdrop, the relevant question becomes a hermeneutical one: How did Asher interpret his own traditions in light of philosophic views, so as to achieve this harmonization? It is possible that he did not read them literally, or, rather, that he read them literally only to a point. My suggestion is that while he was drawn to the philosophic view of divine simplicity, he could not escape entirely from the literal sense of his own traditions, according to which multiple elements inhere in God. At the same time, given the weight of philosophic arguments for divine simplicity, he could not read his traditions fully literally, either. Rather, he chose to accommodate his traditions as much as possible to philosophic understandings of divine simplicity. This required arguing for divine simplicity but nevertheless maintaining that the sefirot are in some manner discrete. Accordingly, it likely would also have required assuming that the gendered and sexual imagery should not be taken literally, although how, in more precise terms, Asher felt this imagery should be taken is unclear. Similarly, it is unclear as to how the notion of theurgy would fit into his understanding. On this reading, Asher looks more like Maimonides as interpreted by various critics of Strauss, according to whom Maimonides genuinely sought to reconcile philosophy and Jewish tradition.[63]

If this line of reasoning is accepted, we can point to the following dilemma that Asher may have faced. The traditions he received had historically been kept secret. Yet, as we saw, he indicates that, as a result of other Kabbalists being too loose with esoteric traditions, there were those who accused the Kabbalists of denying divine unity. Driven by his belief that it is possible to square these traditions with divine simplicity, he wanted to set the record straight. If, however, he openly recorded his esoteric traditions—even with the goal of properly explaining them—he would be defying his uncle's esoteric code. Even if he could justify doing so as necessary to defend Kabbalah, there was nevertheless a chance that readers would seize on the traditions themselves—perhaps reading them literally—and ignore his explanations.

It is possible that Asher's response to this dilemma was to offer a book that could be read on two levels. For the general reader, he provided his considered view of divine unity. He obscured from this reader, however, that this view was based on a hermeneutical engagement with his own traditions. In contrast, for the adept reader, he hinted at the esoteric traditions—at times, in the very passages in which he tried to present a conception of divine unity that was in line with the philosophic one. In so doing, he may have been trying to signal to this reader that the esoteric traditions must be interpreted through the lens of the exoteric presentation.

A weakness of this hypothesis is that nothing in Rabad's extant writings leads us to believe that he had developed a similar idea of divine unity. On this analysis, we would have to assume, therefore, that Asher broke with Rabad's view. Rabad's towering stature might suggest that Asher would have been unlikely to reject his grandfather's view.

These, then, are two possible ways of understanding the relationship between Asher's esoteric and exoteric accounts of divine unity. Whether either of these explanations, or an entirely other one, is correct, the very exercise of thinking through various possibilities highlights the complexity of trying to fathom the esoteric dimensions of kabbalistic texts. Even after the secret ideas of the text are uncovered, it can remain unclear as to how these ideas function in relation to the exoteric ones.

Asher Versus Isaac and Ezra

My analysis has demonstrated that in the face of attacks against Kabbalah, Asher felt compelled to compose an extended kabbalistic work. Yet by employing techniques of esoteric writing, he was able to preserve his uncle's commitment to esotericism. If Isaac's approach was to limit kabbalistic writing to short dense texts that only an adept would understand, Asher chose to write a rather lengthy text whose exoteric meaning would be readily understandable to most educated readers but whose esoteric meaning would be grasped only by a select few. In this manner, his approach also differed from that of Ezra. As I argued in Chapter 5, Ezra seemed satisfied with making the common reader aware of the existence of Kabbalah while writing in an opaque manner that the common reader would not understand. Ezra's approach was driven by his dual need to make clear that an alternative to Maimonideanism exists while still preserving the secrecy of kabbalistic traditions. Asher's approach was driven by a different imperative. His goal was not to polemicize against another approach but to defend the kabbalistic one, which had come under attack. To do so, he had no choice but to exoterically engage kabbalistic thought. He, however, offered his esoteric traditions between the lines of his exoteric presentation.

Conclusion

The rhetoric of secrecy envelops kabbalistic literature. The word "secret" occurs so frequently in kabbalistic literature that, at times, it appears to be a mere "filler" word rather than one with semantic content. Indeed, in many cases, the rhetoric of secrecy serves to create an atmosphere of mysteriousness in which no actual secrets are concealed. This "secretism" of kabbalistic literature may have led scholars to neglect the phenomenon of actual secrecy, which also pervades kabbalistic writing. If all of Kabbalah is a "secret," the general study of Kabbalah seems tantamount to the study of kabbalistic secrecy, and there appears to be no need to subject secrecy to separate investigation. In fact, as I have highlighted in this book, in addition to "secretism," there is much real secrecy in Kabbalah that requires particular study. Accordingly, I have turned my attention to the practice of secrecy in kabbalistic literature, with particular attention to the manner in which Kabbalists employ techniques of esoteric writing.

In Chapter 1, I contrasted the model of secrecy operative in "defensive" and "protective" esotericism to that operative in the model of secrecy described by Hugh Urban and others. According to this latter model, the contents of secrets are less important than the social function of secrecy, which often includes endowing one who possesses the secret with "symbolic capital." A different type of analysis applies in cases of defensive and protective esotericism, in which, I have argued, the content of the secret drives its social function. In defensive esotericism, heterodox ideas or practices are kept secret from those in authority, who might feel challenged by them and who might persecute those who adhere to them. Here the social function of secrecy is intertwined with the content of the secrets, since it is the content that triggers the social function of secrecy as a defense mechanism. Similarly, in the case of protective esotericism, in which certain ideas are kept secret to prevent them from undermining the social order, the content of the secrets dictates the social function of secrecy—to protect the public from dangerous ideas. I proceeded to contrast Urban's model to the model of secrecy entailed in esoteric writing. Those who write esoterically either choose to hide their secret knowledge by not admitting that their texts contain esoteric ideas, as was the case with Rabad, or they publicize that they wrote their works in an esoteric style by using phrases like "the knowledgeable will understand," as was the case with Asher. In the former scenario, it is obvious that no social capital accrues to the author by writing esoterically. In the latter scenario, any social capital that might accrue is counterbalanced by the potentially deleterious effects that might result, should the secrets be deciphered (accurately or not) by an adversary.

In Chapter 2, I turned my attention to the manner in which Kabbalists have kept secrets throughout Kabbalah's long literary history. In addition to keeping kabbalistic ideas out of circulation by transmitting them only orally or by sequestering kabbalistic manuscripts, Kabbalists also adopted various techniques of esoteric writing. These include ciphers, dispersion of knowledge, intentional contradictions, Zoharic symbolic code, and allusive writing. I presented numerous examples of the use of these techniques in kabbalistic texts of different genres and from different periods.

My analysis in the subsequent chapters shows that many of the esoteric techniques that would be used in the later history of Kabbalah were already in place in the earliest kabbalistic writings. Various social and historical circumstances led the first kabbalistic authors to take different approaches to preserving the secrecy of kabbalistic knowledge. Rabad, who lived before the existence of Kabbalah was publicly known, never composed an outward-facing kabbalistic text but restricted his explicit kabbalistic writing, insofar as it existed, to brief passages intended for limited circulation. Yet he also seeded his halakhic works with clues that point to his esoteric views. His son, Isaac, similarly chose not to write public-facing kabbalistic texts and, indeed, criticized other Kabbalists who did so. His written legacy is limited to brief passages intended only for fellow Kabbalists, which he composed in a highly allusive fashion. Unlike his father, he did not compose any exoteric works. Ezra's *Song Commentary* is likely the first kabbalistic text that was made openly available. He was motivated to direct this work toward a wide audience by his concern that Maimonides and his followers had usurped ancient Jewish esotericism. This did not mean that Ezra had any intention of revealing his kabbalistic teachings to a broad audience. Thus, on the one hand, he wrote the first part of the introduction of the work, in which he attacks Maimonideans and proclaims the existence of Kabbalah as an alternative to Maimonidean thought, in an accessible style. On the other hand, he composed the remainder of the work in a style that is impenetrable to those without significant kabbalistic background. He adopted a similarly impenetrable style in *Aggadot Commentary*. Nevertheless, works like Azriel's *Sha'ar ha-sho'el* provided a kind of key that would help the uninitiated decipher works like Ezra's. Accordingly, by the time Asher composed *Sefer ha-yiḥud*, there was some public knowledge of kabbalistic doctrines, which led to attacks on Kabbalah. In *Sefer ha-yiḥud*, Asher therefore chose to defend Kabbalah in an exoteric style. Yet he concealed the doctrine of the sexual union of the sefirot by employing elaborate techniques of esoteric writing.

In the remainder of this conclusion, let me highlight some of the ramifications of my work, as well as offer suggestions for future study:

1. Scholars of the medieval Jewish philosophic tradition—particularly those who study Maimonides under the influence of Leo Strauss—are well aware of the centrality of esoteric writing in the works that they study. Numerous studies have been dedicated to examining Maimonides's techniques of esoteric writing and the esoteric dimension of his thought. Yet there has been a relative dearth of similar studies in the case of avowedly secretive kabbalistic literature. This is the first book-length study to attempt to redress this imbalance, and I hope that it will spur additional studies.
2. Scholars should not assume that Kabbalists explicitly recorded all their kabbalistic knowledge. All authors need to choose what to include and what to exclude in their texts. In the case of a secret tradition like Kabbalah, there is the added burden of deciding which secrets can be written about and which must remain oral. Moreover, a decision must be made about how to record ideas that are considered properly secret. Already at the earliest stages of kabbalistic literary history, and certainly at later stages, many Kabbalists abandoned esotericism, but many others did not. Thus, an important component in evaluating a kabbalistic text is determining both the nature of its author's commitment to esotericism and how that commitment might have guided the manner in which he composed his text. In some cases, such as in Asher's *Sefer ha-yiḥud*, it is appropriate to approach kabbalistic literature with what I would term a

"hermeneutic of suspicion," wherein the extent to which the external meaning of a text captures its full meaning must be questioned. It is possible that applying such a hermeneutic to various other texts will allow us to arrive at a richer history of kabbalistic thought and practice.

3. Scholars have come to understand the emergence of kabbalistic literature, at least in part, as a move from an oral to a written tradition. In this account, Kabbalists first recorded their oral traditions in publicly available works in the first half of the thirteenth century. My analysis of Rabad's work introduces an intermediary stage in which, already in the second half of the twelfth century, Rabad esoterically alluded to kabbalistic ideas in his exoteric halakhic works.

4. A corollary of this finding is that if Rabad embedded his kabbalistic ideas in his exoteric work, he must have believed that there was an audience who could decipher them. I thus provide further evidence for the position, articulated by Idel,[1] that knowledge of Jewish esoteric material was more widely diffused earlier than scholars have typically assumed. Future scholarship should continue to search for evidence of this diffusion. In keeping with a research agenda set by Idel, a promising area of focus is on the differences in opinion between the first kabbalistic authors, insofar as these differences might point to existence of earlier discrete, yet closely aligned, traditions that may have spanned various locales. Further research into the esoteric doctrines of northern French and German Jews will also help provide a fuller picture.

5. Building on the recent work of Avishai Bar-Asher ("Illusion"), I have shown that scholars have considerably overestimated the literary output of Isaac the Blind. In fact, this output was limited to brief passages that he composed in an allusive style. Much of what has been attributed to him is really the work of later authors. This research should lead to a fuller reassessment of Isaac's place in the early history of Kabbalah, a reassessment that Bar-Asher has already begun to undertake. Isaac has commonly been presented in scholarship as the central figure in the early development of Kabbalah. It seems clear that Isaac still had a significant role in this development, but in light of

Bar-Asher's and my research, it is difficult to assess just how significant. First, we must realize that this role was primarily limited to his activities as a teacher of Kabbalah rather than as an author. Second, without any confidence in the veracity of the attributions to him of various extended passages, such as those found in *Explanation*, we lack sufficient information to fully reconstruct his thought. This means that it is very difficult to assess the extent to which the ideas found in the first generation of kabbalistic texts derive from him. Certainly, on some matters, such as the notion that sexual union between the sefirot marks divine unity, we can draw a straight line between his thought and what we find in the work of the first kabbalistic authors. This does not necessarily imply that this is the case in all matters. Future research should continue to track the numerous ideas attributed to Isaac in later kabbalistic works with the aim of assessing the veracity of these attributions.

6. In contrast to the prevailing assumption that Ezra and Asher rejected Rabad's and Isaac's commitment to esotericism, I show that they remained committed to the secrecy of kabbalistic ideas. Unlike Rabad and Isaac, they felt compelled, because of various communal pressures, to compose more widely available kabbalistic texts. Thus, rather than concealing the very existence of Kabbalah, they wrote openly about Kabbalah even while adopting esoteric strategies of writing.

7. Asher distinguished between esoteric and exoteric Kabbalah. Thus, even the exoteric content of *Sefer ha-yiḥud* is kabbalistic insofar as it deals with some of the basics of kabbalistic thought, such as the sefirot. In contrast, Rabad seems to have regarded all of Kabbalah as esoteric and therefore did not make any of his kabbalistic knowledge publicly available. Ezra and even Isaac are intermediate cases. Ezra, for the most part, treated all his kabbalistic teachings as equally esoteric by recording them all in an allusive form that would be inaccessible to novices. Yet in one of his letters to Abraham, he mentions an idea that he can convey only orally. Moreover, in *Aggadot Commentary* he employed the additional technique of dispersion to provide certain matters with an additional layer of protection. Ezra, therefore, had some sense of a hierarchy of kabbalistic secrets. The evidence is far

scanter in the case of Isaac, but we did see that in his letter to Nahmanides and R. Jonah, amid his already esoteric interpretation of Psalm 150, he makes note of a particular matter that he cannot reveal.

Future scholarship would be well served by being attentive to the distinction between esoteric and exoteric Kabbalah. Thus, Kabbalah scholars should question which ideas a particular Kabbalist views as exoteric and which he views as esoteric. Scholars should further consider the relationship between the exoteric and esoteric Kabbalah of various Kabbalists. Are the esoteric ideas fuller and more sophisticated versions of the exoteric ones? Are they additional ideas not reflected in the exoteric layer of the text? Do the esoteric and exoteric ideas conflict, such that the exoteric ones may be screens to hide the esoteric ones? Answering these and related questions will offer a window into the manner in which Kabbalists attempted to mold their public personae even while revealing their private personae to the select few.

Appendix 1

See Chapter 4, note 28 for related text. Due to space considerations, I will cite only some of the overlapping material within the larger texts. The shared language is in bold font.

"Commentary on Sacrifice" in Explanation (*MS Parma 2704, 27b*, with variants from the printed edition, *Bei'ur 23c*)	Aggadot Commentary (*MS Vat. 441, 27b*)	*"Excursus on the Commandments,"* in Travis *25–27*, Hebr. sec.
וידעת כי כהנים לויים וישראלי' מעכבין הקרבן ומזהירי' [דפוס: ומוזהרים] **כהנים כלויים שלא יתעסקו** זה במלאכת זה כי הם **דוגמא שני דברי' הפכים. הכהני' ממוני' על הקרבן** והלויים על השיר ושניהם מעכבין **השחיטה כשירה בזר והכהני' היו נמנעי' מלשחוט והלוים על השיר**, ולא אחר משער' במשפט [דפוס: ומורין במשפט כמה שני'], (יחזקאל מד, כ) ועל ריב המה יעמדו למשפט ולזה (חולין כד ע"א) **כהני' במומין פסולי' בשני' כשרי' ולויים בהפך** וזהו ענין תורים ובני יונה והכהן היה שלם בעבודתו וזריז בהמשכתו ובכונתו [דפוס: וזריז בכוונתו] להמשיך בעת העבודה הרצון ע"י השיר [דפוס: להמשיך הרצון בענין העבודה על ידי השיר] וע"י כונת הכהני' והלויים והישראלי' המעכבין הקרבן לבא העניין בכיון ועל דרך המיצוע כמו ששלשתן רומזי' והיה מתרבה השפע **על כל בעלי חיים ואף הצמחי' הצריכי' לכחות עליוני' להצמיחם** [דפוס: **להגדילם ולהצמיחם**] כדכתיב (בראשית ב, טו) לעבדה ולשמרה. וארז"ל (בראשית רבה פ' טז) אלו הקרבנות **וסוף הכל לשוב** לכחות העליוני' אשר שם שרשם.	**כי הצמחים וכל בעלי החיים צריכין לכוחות הראשונים להגדילם ולהצמיחם וסופם לשוב אליהם.**	**וממצות לא תעש' שלא יתעסקו הכהנים בעבודת הלוים ולא הלוים בעבודת הכהנים שכל א' וא' הוא דוגמא שני דברים הפכים** לכך לא יתכן להם להכנס בתחום שאינו שלו. **הכהנים ממונים על קרבן** וכפרה [ו]לברך את העם. ואמ' חכמים (זבחים לב ע"א): מקבלה ואיליך מצות כהונה, **שהשחיטה כשרה בזר.** ובכל מקום תראה 'וסמך' 'ושחט' לפי שהיו **הכהנים נמנעים מלשחות** (לעיל) **אך הלויים היו ממונים על השיר** ודנים ומורי' **במשפט.** וכל זה דוגמא. ועל זה אמ' רז"ל בחולין (כד ע"א), ת"ר: **כהנים במומין פסולין בשנים כשרים. ולוים במומין כשרים בשנים פסולין,** נמצא הכשר בכהנים פסול בלוים, כשר בלוים פסול בכהנים. [. . .] וזה מבאר **כי הצמחים [ו]כל בעלי חיים צריכין לכוחות הראשונים להגדילם ולהצמיחם, וסופם לשוב אליהם.** והכהן היה שלם בידיעתו וזריז <וזהיר> בכוונתו להמשיך הרצון בעת העבודה על ידי שיר הפה והכלי, שהנשמה נהנית ומתקרבת <ומתפשטת> בהם ועל ידי כוונת כהנים ולוים וישראלים שהיו על הקרבן, כמו שאמ' חכמים בתענית (כז ע"א): כהנים לוים וישראלים מעכבין את הקרבן.

Appendix 2

See Chapter 4, note 29 for related text. The shared language is in bold font.

"Commentary on Sacrifice" in Explanation *(MS Parma 2704, 27b, with variants from the printed edition,* Bei'ur *23c)*	Text on sacrifice attributed to Azriel *(Porat, Kabbalistic 164–65)*
(ספרא ויקרא פרק א:ט, פינקלשטין ב, 48): אשה לשם אשה:שהמזבח מקבל [דפוס: תחלה] **ומתערב** [דפוס: ומתעכב] **עם האש** הגדולה ועולה לריח ולרוח וזהו כליל לאישים לשום נחת רוח שמשם יתברכו כלם ומתייחד המלך בכסאו ומברך פועליו ועושי רצונו וזהו מאמרם הריח הריח והניח הניחוח שהוא כלל הרוח והריח והכלל כי כאשר ישרף הבשר או האימורים כפי מלאכתן יערב עשן ואש [בשולים ובדפוס: המזבח] במזבח ובאש הגדולה וזהו שתמצא כתו' המזבחה במקומות בשני ההי"ן להורות על זה **כשתתבטל האש** חוזרת **להיות רוח ומתייחד רוח ברוח** ובריח עד [ש]האומן שממנו כל אמן מתברך.	בתחלה העשן עולה עד המעלה הראשונה ונקראת רצון שהיא מתקרבת לעלותו משם ולהלן. ואחרי הפסק עלית העשן יהפך הבשר לאש ונקרא אשה. **ואותה האש מתערבת באש** אוכלת אש הנקרא אש ושניהם נקראים אשים והינו הפחד. **ואחרי התבטל האש וניצוציו לגמרי ישובו להיות רוח. ויתעלה ויתקרב אותו רוח להתערב ברוח העליון** כדכתי' (יחזקאל כ, מא) בריח ניחח ארצה אתכם.

Appendix 3

See Chapter 4, note 30 for related text. The shared language is in bold font.

"Commentary on Sacrifice" in Explanation (MS Parma 2704, 27b, with variants from the printed edition, Bei'ur 14c)	*Extended discussion of sacrifice* (Porat, Kabbalistic 168)
(ספרא ויקרא פרק א:ט, פינקלשטין ב, 48): אשה לשם אשה:שהמזבח מקבל [דפוס: תחלה] **ומתערב** [דפוס: ומתעכב] **עם האש** הגדולה ועולה לריח ולרוח וזהו כליל לאישים לשום נחת רוח שמשמש יתברכו כלם ומתיחד המלך בכסאו ומברך פועליו ועושי רצונו וזהו מאמרם הריח הריח והנה הניחוח שהוא כלל הרוח והריח והכלל כי כאשר ישרף בבשר או האימורים כפי מלאכתן יערב עשן ואש [בשולים ובדפוס: **כתי' המזבחה במקומות בשני ההי"ן** להורות על זה כשתתבטל האש חוזרת להיות רוח ומתיחד רוח **ברוח ובריח עד** [ש]האומן ששממנו כל אמון מתברך. **ויורד י"י לי"י** מתברכים עליוני **ותחתוני** ונפשו' המקריבים.	אמרו חכמים: (ספרא ויקרא פרק א:ט, פינקלשטין ב, 48) עולה לשם עולה, אשה לשם אישים, ריח לשם ריח, ניחוח לשום נחת רוח, ליי' למי שאמר והיה העולם. ופירוש הפסוק. **כתב המזבחה בה"א כי בה"א** האחרונה מן השם יתחיל ההמשכה עד למעלה במחשבה מעילוי לעילוי. עלה: שעולה רצון התחתון שהוא כח הרבוי עד הרצון שהוא המזבח. אשה: שמתיחד עם אש אוכלת אש **המתערבת עמו** לעלות גם כן למעלה. ריח: אחרי **התבטל האש** וניצוציו **חוזר להיות רוח ומתיחד הרוח ברוח ובריח עד** המחשבה. ניחוח: שמתיחד רום מעלה עם ריח ורוח. ליי': שיורד יי' לרחמים ומתיחד עם **התחתונים** ברחמים. והיינו למי שברא העולם.

Notes

INTRODUCTION

1. In addition to the sources already referenced, see, e.g., Wolfson, "Circumcision, Secrecy"; *Language* 128–41; "Murmuring Secrets"; *Open Secret*; *Giving* 154–200.

2. See, e.g., Idel, *Absorbing* 1–12, 200–220; "From R. Isaac." See also n. 8 below.

3. The most comprehensive overview, to date, of esoteric writing in general philosophical literature is by Arthur Melzer. The most comprehensive overviews dealing specifically with Jewish philosophical sources are Schwartz, *Contradiction*; and Halbertal, *Concealment*, which treats kabbalistic texts in addition to philosophic ones. These works are written in critical engagement with Strauss, even if they do not necessarily agree with his positions.

4. Strauss's writings on Maimonides were collected by Kenneth Green, in *Leo Strauss on Maimonides*. Strauss's most influential essays relating to Maimonides's esotericism are "The Literary Character of *The Guide of the Perplexed*" (341–98) and "How to Begin to Study *The Guide of the Perplexed*" (491–549). The first of these essays was originally published in Strauss, *Persecution*, which also includes studies on Judah ha-Levi and Spinoza. These studies, too, contributed to the discussion of esoteric writing in Jewish philosophy.

5. See Smith 6: "Straussianism is characterized above all by what its practitioners often call the art of 'careful reading.' When asked what he taught, it is said, Strauss often replied 'old books.'"

6. For an analysis of the relationship of Strauss's rediscovery of esoteric writing to his rejection of historicism, see Meier 55–73; Melzer 325–66.

7. See the studies cited in n. 1 above.

8. In this context, I will not provide a comprehensive bibliography. Rather, I will highlight some salient examples. Some of this work has focused on the writing of the German Pietists, who were roughly contemporary with the first Kabbalists and whose ideas share various points of contact. See, e.g., Abrams, "Literary Emergence" and "Shekhinah Prays"; Wolfson, "Image." In the case of Kabbalah, see, e.g., Idel, "The Image of Man Above the Sefirot: R. David"; "Kabbalistic Interpretation"; "Commentaries"; *Abraham Abulafia's Esotericism* 107–256; Garb, "Kabbalah of Rabbi Joseph" 260–61. See also n. 9 below.

9. One partial exception is Pedaya, *Name*, which I will have occasion to discuss below. Another exception is Laura, who discusses the technique of dispersion in the work of the late fourteenth-century Kabbalist Menaḥem Tsiyyoni.

10. The fullest general account of these figures may be found in Scholem, *Origins* 205–475. For other general surveys, see Tishby, *Studies* 3–35; Pedaya, *Name* 36–69. On Azriel's relationship with Isaac and Ezra, see Chap. 5 below.

CHAPTER 1. SECRETS AND SECRETISM

1. The essay was originally written in German but appeared in English in 1906 before it appeared in German. The German version subsequently appeared in 1908 in Simmel, *Soziologie* 307–402.
2. Cf. Chilson 8, who refers to a similar concept as "secretizing."
3. On Blavatsky's own ambiguous attitude toward Kabbalah, see Pasi.
4. Cf. von Stuckrad, "Secrecy."
5. Cf. Urban, "Fair Game" 359; "Adornment" 8; *Economics* 23–27.
6. See Strauss's early articles: "Some Remarks" 20–24; "On Abravanel's Philosophical Tendency." Cf. Strauss, "Farabi's Plato." See also, more broadly, Strauss, *Persecution* 35–37; "On a Forgotten Kind of Writing" 64–65.
7. For a few further examples, see Nahmanides, *Perushei ha-torah* II on Gen. 1:1; "Anonymous Commentary on the Song of Unity" (MS Vat. ebr. 274, 175a–b; cited in Chap. 2 below); Moses Basola's ban on printing the Zohar, cited in Tishby, *Studies* 108 (on Basola, see Chap. 2 below); Luria 234, sec. 98.
8. See, e.g., *Otsar* II, 29, 47.
9. Cf. Yosef Ḥayyim 1:81c–82d, *Yoreh de'ah* 56.
10. See Campany 294.
11. Cf. the comments by Catholic theologian Ernest Fortin, who was influenced by Strauss: "By shrouding the truth in mystery and erecting barriers between himself and his reader, the writer was actually making the truth more attractive psychologically and spurring the reader on to greater efforts" (21).
12. Melzer (205–34) extensively discusses what he refers to as "pedagogical esotericism." He focuses on the fact that writing obscurely is itself a teaching tool insofar as it forces the reader to move slowly and carefully consider the secret teaching. My focus, here, in contrast, is not on the pedagogical merits of esoteric writing as an effective way to teach but on its usefulness in spreading secret teachings to those who are worthy.

CHAPTER 2. A TYPOLOGY OF ESOTERIC WRITING IN KABBALISTIC LITERATURE

1. Many studies have discussed Nahmanides's esotericism. See, e.g., Wolfson, "By Way"; Idel, "We Have"; "Nahmanides" and "Leadership" 12–15; Halbertal, *By Way* 297–333 and *Concealment* 69–92, 93–104; Yisraeli, "Early" and *R. Moses* 224–35; Pedaya, *Nahmanides* 47–85; Lorberbaum, "Did Nahmanides." Relatively less has been written about the place of secrecy in Nahmanides's wider school. See, e.g., Halbertal, *Concealment* 93–104; Abrams, *Kabbalistic Manuscripts* 199–223; Idel, "'In a Whisper'" 501–11; Mottolese; Pedaya, *Nahmanides* 98–119; Lorberbaum, "Did Nahmanides" 340–53.
2. Idel ("Anonymous Kabbalistic Commentary" 146) concludes, in response to the possibility that expressions of oral transmission in kabbalistic texts should not be taken seriously, that he is "inclined to doubt such attempts to attenuate in principle the oral nature of the traditions transmitted in certain Kabbalistic schools." I fully concur with Idel's assessment.
3. This passage has been the subject of scholarly attention. See the studies cited by Bar-Asher, *Mishkan* 49n264 (introduction). Cf. the similar passages elsewhere in *Mishkan* 133, 148–49.

4. See *Moreh ha-nevukhim* 5, introduction.

5. See also the discussion of this passage in Bar-Asher, *Mishkan* 69 (introduction) and the similar passages in *Mishkan* 131, 165, as well as the discussion in Bar-Asher, *Journeys* 350–53.

6. Cf. Bar-Asher's comments in *Mishkan* 48.

7. The letter has survived in a number of versions. The passage that I cite here is missing in one of the versions. According to Moshe Rosman, the version in which it is missing is the only authentic one. The other versions, in Rosman's view, contain additions from a later hand, including this passage. Other scholars, such as Yehoshua Mondshine, Immanuel Etkes, Haviva Pedaya, and Moseson, have disagreed and have argued that at least one of the versions that contains this passage is from the Baal Shem Tov's hand. For a full discussion and specific citations, see Dauber, "Baal Shem Tov"; Moseson 35–117.

8. Also printed in Idel, "Image of Man" 42.

9. On David's esoteric ideas, see Idel, "The Image of Man Above the Sefirot: R. David."

10. On this figure, see Idel, *Kabbalah in Italy* 222–26 and the studies cited there.

11. On this passage and for another example, see Altmann 70.

12. For a summary of this debate and for a critical evaluation of relevant scholarship, see Huss 190–201.

13. See also Tishby, *Studies* 139. Finzi wrote this text after some of the Zohar had already been published. See Assaf 240.

14. A slightly different version is printed in Rabinowitsch 171.

15. For a full account of the practice of Luria's students to sequester their manuscripts, see Avivi 37–40, 52–56.

16. See J. G. Weiss 215–43. On esotericism in Bratslav Hasidism, see Mark 209–45 and the studies cited there, 220n31. See also below.

17. See Bar-Asher, "This Fourth Part"; Magid 210–18. For a discussion of the complexity of publishing esoteric materials, including the fourth section of *Sha'arei kedushah*, see Chajes. It should be noted that Bar-Asher shows that Vital may have only partially completed the fourth section and that more recent attempts by traditional presses to print it are based, at least in part, on material that was not originally part of the work.

18. A similar example is found in a recently published edition of the eighteenth-century scholar and Kabbalist Ḥayyim Josef David Azulai's *Kuntres zahav sagur*, a work that previously had been available only in manuscript. The editor notes that Azulai wrote another book by the same name, also available only in manuscript, that he has chosen not to publish because "it deals entirely with holy names, unifications, and practical Kabbalah, which, in this generation, are not suitable to be published" (10).

19. Lit., "teacher of righteousness" (*moreh tsedek*).

20. In the continuation (4a), he forbids anyone else to print the book without his permission.

21. For further recent examples, see Abrams, *Kabbalistic Manuscripts* 655–56.

22. See http://www.dafyomireview.com/shaarei_kedusha.php (accessed Oct. 18, 2021).

23. See http://www.dafyomireview.com/shaarei_kedusha.php (accessed Oct. 18, 2021).

24. No information is provided regarding the edition that served as the basis for the translation.

25. See http://www.dafyomireview.com/shaarei_kedusha.php#p4g1 (accessed on Oct. 18, 2021). A fuller critical translation of the text was prepared by Magid 234–64.

26. "Master" (*adon*) follows Tzahi Weiss's reading of the manuscript that contains Isaac's remarks, MS Vat. ebr. 202, 59a-60a. See his defense of this reading in "Letter" 33n13. Idel ("From R. Isaac" 7) also defends this reading. In contrast, Scholem ("Te'udah" 9) reads "closet" (*aron*), a reading supported by Abrams (*Kabbalistic Manuscripts* 92n271). See also the additional scholarship cited by Abrams.

27. These remarks are not included in all versions of *Keter Shem Tov*. See below. They are printed in the modern version included in *'Ammudei ha-kabbalah* 2. This version does not list which manuscripts it is based on. It is not included in the version printed in Coriat 25a–117b.

28. E. Fishbane (*As Light* 56n14) translates *birmazim metsorafim* as "in permutated hints." In the language of the ecstatic Kabbalist Abraham Abulafia, *tserufei otiyyot* ("combining letters") refers to a practice of combining or permuting letters to induce mystical ecstasy. In Ibn Gaon's later work, *Badei ha-aron u-migdal Ḥananel*, he uses the term in this sense, apparently under the influence of Abulafian ideas. See Idel, *Studies* 121. As Idel notes (121–22), there is no evidence of Abulafian influence in Ibn Gaon's earlier *Keter Shem Tov*. Moreover, in the earlier work, he speaks of combining "hints" rather than "letters," and he refers to a praxis of esoteric writing rather than one intended to lead to ecstasy. *Birmazim metsorafim* perhaps refers to the technique of dispersion, which I will describe below, whereby the author leaves scattered partial hints across his work. The reader must assemble or combine these hints in order to understand the full concept.

29. These are both known methods of encrypting alchemical and scientific information. For example, letter substitution, in which one letter is substituted for another, is used in a fourteenth-century manuscript of *De Separatione Elementorum*, attributed to Roger Bacon (Rec 3). An example of anagrams can be found in the work of Galileo, who employed them in documenting certain discoveries (Láng, "Ciphers in Magic" 129–30; *Ciphers and Secrecy* 161–62).

30. Cf. Scholem, "Sefer shevilei" 12n2.

31. Cf. Levinger 31.

32. For a full account of the use of "chapter headings" and the general tension between exotericism and esotericism in *Keter Shem Tov*, see Mottolese. See also Halbertal, *Concealment* 93–104; Lorberbaum, "Did Nahmanides" 347–53. As Lorberbaum points out (352–53), in Ibn Gaon's much later work, *Baddei ha-aron u-migdal Ḥananel*, he no longer writes in an esoteric style.

33. It is even possible that the first passage that I cited was originally attached to the now-lost *Secrets of Secrets* and was appended by a later scribe to *Keter Shem Tov*. Support for this possibility comes from the fact that this passage describes a work written in a deeply esoteric style. It does not seem to fit the relatively more exoteric *Keter Shem Tov*. It also may be supported by the manuscript evidence. Some manuscripts of *Keter Shem Tov*—such as MS Paris hebr. 774, 73a–115a; MS Columbia University X 893 G 15, 1a–47a; and MS Vat. Barb. Or. 110, 91a–137b—include the poetic introduction but lack the introductory remarks where the first passage appears. This may suggest that this passage (and the surrounding material) was not always an organic part of the completed *Keter Shem Tov* (I would note, parenthetically, that various manuscripts of *Keter Shem Tov*—such as MS Vat. ebr. 214, 93b–163b; and MS Bavarian State Library, Cod. hebr. 341, 2a–55b—lack both the introductory remarks in which this passage appears, as well as the poetic introduction).

34. On the possible identity of this figure, see Idel, "Commentaries" (72) 48–49.

35. Idel ("Commentaries" [72] 47n59) suspects that it is not the same technique.

Notes to Pages 36–39   223

36. I have examined the text in MS JTS 2325, 113–15. For other manuscripts in which the text is found, see Idel, "Commentaries" 48n67. A brief example concerning divine unity, found in MS JTS 2325, 113, will provide a sense of the nature of the text:
אמרו תסקפא שלימה מלכות שמים שלימה במילת לרמוז תכלית כל התשובות כי אין בביפא
הבורא יתברך בי מיוחד לגמרי בלתי כלילות שאר כל הביכא.

The words, which I have underlined, are marked in the manuscript with little dots above them to indicate that they are encoded words. (Later in the text, some encoded words are marked with a line above the word.) When decoded, this line reads as follows:
אמרו אחדות שלימה מלכות שמים שלימה במילת לרמוז תכלית כל התשובות כי אין בשמות
הבורא יתברך שם מיוחד לגמרי בלתי כלילות שאר כל השמות.

"They said that [when God's] <u>unity</u> is perfect [then] the kingship of heaven is perfect. [They said this] to hint in the word 'perfect' the aim of all of the answers [that the text will provide], for there is not among the <u>names</u> of the Creator, may He be blessed, a completely unified <u>name</u> that does not include all the other <u>names</u>."

37. Cf. Scholem, *Kitvei* 162.

38. The technique of placing dots above the letters is also employed in the responsa to Isaac ben Todros, described above (n. 36), as it is found in MS JTS 2325.

39. Note that this term is similar to the one employed by Ibn Gaon, "substituted letters" (*ve-otiyyot meḥullafot*), as seen above.

40. See the studies cited above in Introduction, n. 8.

41. The seventeenth-century text is found in MS Jerusalem, National Library, 8°330, 248a–249a. According to Scholem (*Kitvei* 75), this feature is not found in the earlier versions that he consulted, which include MS London, British Library, Add. 27187, 66a–67a; MS Cambridge, Cambridge University Library, MS Add. 647, 18a–19a; MS London, British Library, Add. 15299, 85a–90b. It is also not found in the following manuscripts, which I consulted: MS Florence, Laurentian Library, Plut.44.16, 4a–5a; MS Jerusalem, National Library, 38°1073, 89b–90b; MS Florence, Laurentian Library, Plut.44.13, 215a–216a. The following example from MS Jerusalem, National Library, 8°330, 248a should give a sense of the nature of the anagrams employed by the text. Toward the beginning of the text, we read, כשתרצה בלארתו שמו רבהי. This apparently can be decoded as כשתרצה לבראתו שום בריה ("when you want to create any creature"). For another example, see Scholem, *Kitvei* 75.

42. See also Melzer 316–17.

43. A secondary influence is Eleazar of Worms, the leading exponent of German Pietism, who was active in the twelfth and the beginning of the thirteenth centuries. On the use of this technique in Eleazar's work, see Abrams, "Shekhinah Prays" 522–25, 529–30. Laura argues that the late fourteenth-century Kabbalist Menaḥem Tsiyyoni employed this technique under Eleazar's influence.

44. This passage is cited in Scholem, *Major Trends* 127, but I have used my own translation.

45. On Todros Abulafia's esoteric style, see Kushnir-Oron's brief comments in *Sha'ar ha-razim* 16, 25. Abulafia also assumes that rabbinic literature employs the technique of dispersion. See, e.g., T. Abulafia, *Otsar* (Warsaw), 13.

46. See Kraus 1:xxvii–xxxi, 6–7; Haq 6–7, 12–14; Principe 44.

47. See Bar-Asher, "Samael" 539n2.

48. On this text, see Idel, "Anonymous Kabbalistic Commentary." As Idel notes (145–46), on numerous occasions the author indicates that various secrets can be transmitted only orally.

49. After "to reveal" (לגלות), the ms. has the word לפ"י, which I did not translate. This may be a scribal error and is not found in all the mss. E.g., it is missing in MS Columbia University X 893 G 15, 4b; and MS Vat. Barb. Or. 110, 95b.

50. The material from *Even ha-shoham* that I have cited here is also partially cited in Scholem, *Kitvei* 90 from a different manuscript. For further discussion of Ibn Sayyah's esoteric style of writing, see Garb, "Kabbalah of Rabbi Joseph" and "Trance Techniques" 58–60.

51. Earlier in his comments (Shar'abi 140), he mentions the importance of studying only the direct teachings of Isaac Luria and those of Luria's student Ḥayyim Vital, to the exclusion of works by other students of Luria. See Giller, *Shalom Shar'abi* 98–100.

52. On this practice, see Strauss, *Persecution* 67–74; Melzer 309–16. The fullest account of the use of this practice by Jewish philosophers is Schwartz, *Contradiction*.

53. As Maimonides explains: "In speaking about very obscure matters it is necessary to conceal some parts and to disclose others. Sometimes in the case of certain dicta this necessity requires that the discussion proceed on the basis of a certain premise, whereas in another place necessity requires that the discussion proceed on the basis of another premise contradicting the first one. In such cases the vulgar must in no way be aware of the contradiction; the author accordingly uses some device to conceal it by all means" (Maimonides, *Guide* 18, introduction).

54. As indicated, in Strauss's view, Maimonides deliberately included contradictory ideas. Only one side of the contradiction, however, is true. Maimonides's seventh contradiction assumes that most "vulgar" readers will not even discern the existence of the contradiction, which might be quite subtle. Yet even a reader who does become aware of the contradiction will be forced to choose which side reflects Maimonides's true view (*Persecution* 67–74). Other scholars have understood Maimonides's use of contradictions differently, even if there is basic agreement that the use of contradictions is related in some way to keeping knowledge out of the hands of the masses. See, e.g., Lorberbaum, "On Contradictions"; Davies.

55. On his drive to popularize Kabbalah, in addition to his comments in *Ḥesed le-Avraham*, which I will cite below, see his comments in *Or ha-ḥammah* 2c–d.

56. Beyond the material that I will discuss, there is other evidence that he occasionally concealed certain ideas. On three occasions in *Ḥesed le-Avraham*, Azulai indicates that he cannot fully divulge certain details regarding appropriate mystical intentions during prayer. Instead, employing a version of the technique of dispersion, he directs the reader to one of his other books that deals with these matters—either *Ma'aseh ḥoshev* or *Kenaf renanim*. To cite one of these occasions, "This exposition is sufficient for this book for we do not have permission to reveal more. We have already spoken at length about the deepest meaning of this matter in the book *Ma'aseh ḥoshev*, with God's help" (*Ḥesed le-Avraham* 310; cf. 82, 286). See also the comments of the editor Yitsḥak Mosheh Erlanger (3).

57. Brackets in the original.

58. Lit., "he should not jump to respond to his words" (*she-lo' yikpots lehashiv 'al devarav*). Here Azulai is borrowing Maimonides's language in the introduction to the *Guide* as rendered into Hebrew by Samuel Ibn Tibbon: "He should not destructively hasten to refute my words (*ve-lo' yaharos ve-yikpots 'atsmo lehashiv 'al devarai*), since it is possible that what he understood of my words is the opposite of what I intended" (*Moreh ha-nevukhim* 14).

59. De la Rosa (160a) also suggests that Sharabi believed that Isaac Luria employed intentional contradictions. These sources and other similar ones are collected in *Yira'ukha* 48–49. See also the sources collected in Hillel 346–48.

60. For a recent summary of the relevant research including that of Yehuda Liebes, Ronit Meroz, Boaz Huss, and Daniel Abrams, see E. Fishbane, *Art* 38–42.

61. This is the view of Abrams, *Kabbalistic Manuscripts* 224–438.

62. E. Fishbane (*Art* 45–46) refers to Wolfson's remarks. Later in the essay, Wolfson ("Zoharic Literature" 324) writes that it is viable "to speak of a homogeneous vision underlying the various strata of the Zohar."

63. Cf. Liebes, "Zohar as Renaissance" 2.

64. For a list of such lexicons, see Giller, *Reading* 178–79. See also Gondos 131–51.

65. The text is partially cited in Huss 172. The translation is my own.

66. Based on Isa. 35:6.

67. See the discussion in Huss 197. Cf. 208–10, 217–18. Notably, Basola later changed his mind and argued against publication of the Zohar. See Tishby, *Studies* 159–63.

68. In the Talmudic exegesis of the mishnah (B. Ḥagigah 13a), there is a discussion regarding precisely which parts of Ezekiel 1 are part of the "account of the chariot."

69. See also Gruenwald 114n15.

70. On Ibn Ezra's esotericism, see Halbertal, *Concealment* 34–43.

71. For further analysis of the use of such expressions, see Wolfson, "Anonymity" 77–80.

72. Based on Gen. 33:14.

73. See also Green, "Rabbi Isaac" 450.

74. That this is the result of intentional esotericism was clear to various Kabbalists. Thus, Isaac ha-Kohen characterizes it as a work that "reveals in concealed and hidden hints" (Scholem, *Re'shit* 18), and Todros Abulafia describes one passage in the *Bahir* as "only comprehensible to one to whom the keys of wisdom have been transmitted" (*Otsar*, Warsaw 9).

75. Wolfson ("Anonymous Chapters" 166) discusses this passage. See also the analysis of this passage and related examples in Wolfson, "Beyond" 183–84.

76. For a concise summary of the debate, see Wolfson, "Murmuring Secrets" 77–78n50.

77. Wolfson ("Murmuring Secrets" 77–84) offers an analysis of its esoteric motifs. He cites Scholem's statement on 78–79.

78. Wolfson's fuller discussion of Abulafia's esotericism contains an important discussion of Abulafia's dual desires to spread and conceal his Kabbalah. See *Abraham Abulafia* 52–93.

79. For numerous further examples, see Wolfson, *Abraham Abulafia* 55–56, 68–69, 72–75, 81–86.

80. On his exotericism, see Idel, "From R. Isaac" 12–13; *R. Menahem Recanati* 171. In addition to secrets that Recanati thought were theoretically communicable but chose to withhold, such as in the examples that I will present here, he also thought that certain matters were intrinsically incommunicable due to human limitations (168–71).

81. As well as in another cryptic reference that I did not cite.

82. He also notes (65, 156) that certain matters can only be revealed orally.

83. On Cordovero as a popularizer of Kabbalah, see the helpful analysis in I. Robinson.

84. It is worth noting that in his brief introduction to *Sefer pardes rimmonim* (1b), he advises a prospective reader without sufficient kabbalistic background to avoid the work, since it might lead to more harm than good. Yet for the most part, he does not write in an esoteric style.

85. The phrase "out of consideration for (*laḥus*) God's glory" is based on M. Ḥagigah 2:1, the mishnah that limits public exposition of esoteric matters. The mishnah concludes: "Anyone who does not show consideration (*ḥas*) for the Glory of his maker, it would have been better for him not to have been brought to the world."

86. This work is, in fact, Cordovero's introduction to the portion of his Zohar commentary that deals with the *idrot* sections of the Zohar.

87. The expression "to and fro" originally refers to the motion of the "creatures" as described in Ezek. 1:14 but is used, in this context, to describe the activity of the human intellect.

88. Ben-Shlomo (302–4) suggests that the secret is related to a pantheistic conception. Cf. Cordovero, *Sefer pardes* 29a–b, gate 6, chap. 3; Shmueli 135n68.

89. Schuchat (202–3) presents a drive to conceal kabbalistic ideas as one of the defining features of Lithuanian Kabbalah, in contrast to Hasidism. See also Nadler 29–49.

90. For overviews of the tension between revealing and concealing in Hasidic thought, see Loewenthal 1–28; Haran 533–40.

91. For a recent reflection on the importance of being attentive to the oral and Yiddish basis of written Hasidic homilies, see Mayse and Reiser.

92. At the same time, in the particular case of the collection of Heshel's teachings, *Ohev Yisra'el*, Heshel's grandson, who published the work, indicates in the introduction (1—unpaginated) that his grandfather reviewed the text of his teachings that had been prepared by a disciple and made corrections as he saw fit. Thus, the examples of allusive writing in *Ohev Yisra'el* were likely approved by Heshel himself. On these issues as they pertain to Menachem Mendel Schneerson, see Wolfson, *Open Secret* 15–16.

93. This criticism was part of broader dispute between the two men. For an account of this dispute, see Etkes 317–85 (on the issue of publicizing Kabbalah, see, especially, 319–20).

94. See Haran 535.

95. A more elaborate version of the same teaching is found in a second collection of the Apter's work, *Ohev Yisra'el* 107–8. There, the teaching ends with "the knowledgeable will understand all of this well." This is a less emphatic profession of esotericism, which is in keeping with the more elaborate explanation of the teaching. On the relationship between *Torat emet* and *Ohev Yisra'el*, see Alfasi 99–106.

96. As will be seen in Chap. 3, this verse was already depicted as having a secret meaning in the twelfth century by Abraham ben David.

97. A slightly different version of the same teaching appears in the Apter's *Torat emet* 79–80 (*parashat tissa'*). There, after the analysis of Exod. 33:23, we find: "More should not be spoken about this, and 'It is the Glory of God to conceal a matter' (Prov. 25:2)' for it is a deep secret." For other examples of allusive writing in the Apter's work, see *Ohev Yisra'el*, 147 (*parashat terumah*), 237–38 (*parashat masse'ei*). Beyond the examples of esoteric writing that I have presented here, another sign of his commitment to esotericism may be his objection to the publication of a new edition of the Zohar, of which we learn from a letter to him by Tsvi Hirsch of Zydachov, who was interested in publishing such an edition (see Segal 30). An annotated version of the letter can be found in Heshel, *Letters* 71–76.

98. For the details of his voluminous writings, see Ortner 2:313–84.

99. In *Or ha-Ḥayyim*, Jabez blames the expulsion of Jews from Spain in 1492 on the Jewish embrace of philosophy. In *Ma'ayan ganim*, Tsvi Elimelekh marshals Jabez's criticism of philosophy to criticize the Jewish enlightenment. See Piekarz 87–97.

100. It should be noted that Jabez had philosophical secrets rather than kabbalistic ones in mind. Jabez was keen to limit their study because of what he believed was their corrupting influence. Tsvi Elimelekh, however, responds to Jabez's contention as though it might also apply to Kabbalah.

101. Lit., "lifting of the head."

102. For numerous other examples, see Ortner 1:216–31.

103. Wolfson provides numerous examples throughout *Open Secret*. See, e.g., 35–37.

104. See Steiner 81–84 and the sources cited there.

105. Rashi on Jer. 25:26, 51:1, 51:41.

106. He adds that select examples, in which truly difficult codes are employed, can be interpreted following the rubric of Simmel and others: "Relying on their analyses, I would claim that encryption here is a social practice, expressing and regulating how far certain information is shared, and how far one might belong to a specific community. Secrecy indeed becomes an organizing tool of social hierarchy, fundamentally influencing the mechanisms of exclusion-inclusion, and forming a group of those who grasp the mystery" ("Ciphers in Magic" 137).

107. For the popularizing activities of Ashlag and his various followers, as well as for the opposition to these activities, see Garb, *Chosen* 29–36; Meir, "Revealed."

108. For further examples, see above, Introduction, n. 8.

CHAPTER 3. ABRAHAM BEN DAVID AS AN ESOTERIC WRITER

1. The fullest appraisal of Rabad's life and scholarly contribution remains Isadore Twersky, *Rabad*. For a differing portrait, see Soloveitchik, "Rabad"; "History of Halakhah."

2. For basic discussions of Rabad as a Kabbalist, see Twersky, *Rabad* 286–300; Scholem, *Origins* 205–26; Idel, "Kabbalistic Prayer"; Pedaya, *Name* 42–55.

3. Here, and in the remainder of this book, I have used the edition and translation of the letter provided in T. Weiss ("Letter" 300–35) with some emendations. As Weiss (330n9) explains, his translation is based on the partial translations found in Scholem, *Origins* 394–95 and Bar-Asher, "Isaac" 421–23. T. Weiss ("Letter" 330n9) and Bar-Asher ("Isaac" 441n26) note that Scholem's edition of the letter, published in "Teʿudah" 9–11, contains transcription errors. Bar-Asher ("Isaac" 442–43) also published his own edition.

4. These are described in Scholem *Origins* 205–27.

5. See Scholem, "Teʿudah" 22; *Origins* 206.

6. Scholem (*Origins* 216, 220) suggests that some of the aforementioned brief passages that appear in Rabad's name in works by later Kabbalists or in miscellanies derive from the *Commentary*. One possibility, therefore, is that Ibn Gaon may have referred to such passages. I find this possibility highly unlikely, since these passages tend to be clear statements of theosophic ideas and, as such, would violate the code of esotericism that, as we saw, Isaac testified his father adhered to. Moreover, if these passages did indeed derive from the *Commentary*, we might expect some indication of this fact in the passages themselves. Yet no such indications are found. As I will argue, these passages more likely are based on Rabad's oral teachings, or, if Rabad did, in fact, compose them, they were circulated only to confidants.

7. See Abrams's comments in his introduction to A. Ben David 18.

8. Scholem (*Origins* 212) suggested that this passage derived from Rabad's *Commentary on Tractate Berakhot*. An alternate possibility, suggested by Idel ("'In a Whisper'" 496), is that in the case of the present passage, we are dealing with "a family oral tradition that has been committed to writing by the grandson." It seems to me, however, that Asher's formal introductions to this passage, as well as to a second one, which I will discuss below—"in tractate Berakhot" and "in tractate Ta'anit"—implies that the passages were taken from the *Commentary*. Idel's suggestion is based on the fact that Isaac, as seen, makes clear that Rabad never recorded kabbalistic ideas. As I will explain below, there is nothing (at least on a simple reading) overtly kabbalistic about either of these passages.

9. For background, see Orlov; Idel, *Angelic World* 74–104.

10. *Guide* 1:54.

11. See also Abraham ben David, *Hassagot* 13–16.

12. B. Shabbat 88b.

13. See my discussion in *Knowledge* 128–33.

14. I have omitted the following comment: "A gloss: or perhaps there is one who is above him who emanated from the first cause, and the power of the highest one is in him (*ve-yesh bo kkoaḥ ha-'elyon*). Until here were the words of the gloss." As Daniel Abrams ("From Divine Shape" 55–60) points out, in other versions of this text, this addition is not indicated as a gloss. Scholem, as Abrams notes (57), was unaware that the addition was a later gloss, and his analysis of the passage was thus flawed. See n. 21 below for further details.

15. See Twersky, *Rabad* 7–10.

16. For his knowledge of Barzillai's works, see Twersky, *Rabad* 232.

17. Cf. Harvey 72–73n29. Harvey also suggests that Rabad, in juxtaposing the comment from *Shi'ur komah* literature ("anyone who knows the measurements of the Former of Creation is promised that he will be a member of the world to come") to Gen. 1:26, as he does at the end of the passage cited by Asher, may have drawn on Abraham Ibn Ezra's commentary on Exod. 33:23 (Ibn Ezra's relevant remarks appear in his comments on Exod. 33:21 in the long version of his commentary). As Harvey points out, the likelihood of a connection to Ibn Ezra is enhanced by Rabad's allusion to Exod. 33:23 in the words "has no front and has no back."

18. "Minister of the Countenance" is a standard designation of Metatron in *heikhalot* and rabbinic literature. The idea that his "name is like that of his Master" is also associated with Metatron. See B. Sanhedrin 38b.

19. This is the standard way in which scholars have interpreted Rabad's comments. See, e.g., Idel, "Enoch Is Metatron" 231–32; Green, *Keter* 99–100. I consider another possibility below.

20. Scholem, in criticizing Heinrich Graetz for seeing in this passage "uncertain groping," argues that "he did not take into consideration that the cautious but nevertheless highly suggestive formulation of the passage in the commentary on the Talmud could have been the result of a conscious desire to veil an esoteric position and not of an uncertain groping" (*Origins* 213). As will be pointed out in the following note, Scholem's actual analysis of the passage was marred as a result of the fact that he was unaware that a portion of the passage upon which he based it was an added gloss.

21. Scholem (*Origins* 212–15) offered a related suggestion. For him, the passage speaks not only of Metatron but of something higher than Metatron (or perhaps a higher Metatron following a double-Metatron doctrine found in some mid-thirteenth-century kabbalistic sources), which may be identified as the tenth sefirah and which must be seen against the

background of both the Philonic idea of the logos and Ashkenazic sources regarding the "special cherub." Scholem's analysis is marred by the fact that his analysis depends on the gloss (see n. 14 above) that was added to the passage by a later hand. This gloss implies that there is an entity higher than Metatron that emanated from a still-higher power and that it is this former entity that is the subject of the Talmudic statement that God wears tefillin. Nevertheless, I agree with Scholem that the passage deals with the tenth sefirah. In contrast to Scholem, my contention is that it is Metatron himself, rather than a higher Metatron or a power above Metatron, who is this sefirah.

22. In some Ashkenazic sources, Metatron is identified with the divine presence (*shekhinah*). It is a short leap from this position to one that identifies Metatron as the tenth sefirah, insofar as the divine presence is identified with this sefirah in kabbalistic sources. On the relationship between Metatron and the tenth sefirah in Ashkenazic sources, see Wolfson, "Metatron." Wolfson (64–66) discusses the passage from the *Commentary* but does not make the argument that Metatron and the tenth sefirah should be identified in this passage. See also Abrams, "Boundaries" 298–311.

23. See Scholem, *Origins* 187n214; Abrams, "Boundaries" 311–16, 320–21. Notably, Ezra of Gerona, the student of Rabad's son, Isaac, identifies Metatron and the tenth sefirah. See Azriel of Gerona, *Commentary* 72–73 (this section of Azriel's *Commentary* is by Ezra, as Tishby notes on 18); see also Tishby's comments, ibid. 73n2; Gottlieb, "R. Baḥya ben Asher's Dependence" 228. For further sources, see T. Weiss, *Cutting the Shoots* 25n6.

24. The printed version of B. Ta'anit 2a reads: "There are three keys in the hands of the Holy One, blessed be He that were not put into the hands of a messenger."

25. On the background of the identification of the "Minister of the World" and Metatron, see Scholem, *Jewish Gnosticism* 44–50; *Origins* 214–15n26.

26. Notably, the added gloss to the first passage of the *Commentary*, which was the basis of Scholem's contention, as I described in n. 21 above—that that passage refers to the tenth sefirah—uses similar language: "perhaps there is one who is above him who emanated from the first cause, and the power of the highest one is in him" (*ve-yesh bo koaḥ ha-'elyon*) (A. ben David 141).

27. Notably, in another version of this passage, quoted in the name of Rabad by Jacob ben Solomon Ibn Habib in his *Ein Ya'akov* (on B. Ta'anit 2a), the words "who ruled over the first chariot (*moshel ba-merkavah ha-ri'shonah*) and the power of the highest one is in him (*ve-khoaḥ ha-'elyon bo*)" are replaced by "who ruled over the chariot (*moshel ba-merkavah*) and was emanated from the highest cause (*ne'etsal min ha-sibbah ha-'elyonah*) and the power of the highest one is in him (*ve-kkoaḥ ha-'elyon bo*)." (I would note that the wording here ["emanated . . . is in him"] is almost identical to the wording of the gloss that was added to Rabad's passage from the *Commentary on Tractate Berakhot*, as described in n. 14 above.) Thus, in this version, the fact that Metatron emanated from a higher power is explicit. While this version may reflect a later change in the text, it is possible that this change is in keeping with the intention of the original.

28. On this figure, see Roth 81–93.

29. For a discussion of the possible identity of this figure, see Dinur 420n24; Porat, *Founding* 104–107.

30. See Scholem, "Traces" 65; *Origins* 226–27n58.

31. Ben Zion Dinur (420n44) suggests that Samuel himself was a Kabbalist. This is apparently also the view of Scholem (*Origins* 224–27), who regards the letter as a reliable

witness of Rabad's position. Ben-Shalom ("Kabbalistic Circles" 591–93; *Jews of Provence* 607–8) argues that he was a member of a circle of Kabbalists in Narbonne, whose teachings melded southern French Kabbalah, German Pietism, Maimonidean thought, and Spanish ideas. He also suggests that he was in contact with the Kabbalist Isaac ha-Kohen. In contrast, Roth (83–84) argues—in my view correctly—that he is, in fact, a moderate Maimonidean. I expand upon Roth's argument in "Secrecy." Whatever his precise intellectual orientation, it is not clear that he had any reliable knowledge of Rabad's kabbalistic teachings. Rather, his ideas may be based on hearsay.

32. See Scholem, *Origins* 299.

33. See Tishby's comments in Azriel of Gerona, *Commentary* 27.

34. See the discussion in Chap. 4, pp. 114–15.

35. See above, n. 23.

36. It is usually assumed (Twersky, *Rabad* 125) that Rabad did not compose the glosses on Maimonides's *Mishneh torah* until early in the 1190s, since Maimonides *Mishneh torah* was not available in southern France before then. If I am correct that the passage in the *Commentary on Berakhot* borrows from the *Mishneh torah*, we would have to assume a similarly late date for this composition. I have been unable to find references to his *Commentary on Berakhot* in Rabad's other extant works, which, should they be identified, might be helpful in dating it more precisely.

37. For further discussion of this passage, see below, Chap. 4, p. 118.

38. See my comments, below, Chap. 4, p. 113.

39. On this text and on its various manuscripts, see below, Chap. 5, n. 3.

40. See the discussion below, Chap. 4, p. 114.

41. Cf. MS Vat. 441, 13a. (The writing in this manuscript is damaged and quite difficult to read.) The passage is reproduced, with some changes, in Azriel of Gerona, *Commentary* 119. There, however, there is no mention of the attribution to Isaac.

42. *Explanation of Nahmanides's Torah Commentary* (*Be'ur* 34d), a work that I discuss in Chap. 4, claims to possess a document written by Isaac that includes a more expansive version of the same teaching. I am skeptical that this document was really by Isaac. First, as I will argue in Chap. 4, many of the attributions to Isaac in *Explanation* are unreliable. Second, it is difficult to believe that the author of *Explanation*, who wrote some seventy years after Isaac, had access to a text of Isaac, which neither Ezra nor Jacob, who both studied with Isaac, seem to know of. Most likely, this text reflects a later elaboration of Isaac's tradition. A conceptually similar explanation of the Trisagion is also found in the name of Jacob ben Saul (= Jacob the Nazarite) (Scholem, *Re'shit* 73n2) and in the name of Abraham Ḥazan, the cantor of Gerona (246).

43. For examples of this understanding of the ninth sefirah in early kabbalistic sources, see A. ben David 320; Ben Sheshet, *Sefer meshiv* 190, lines 35–36.

44. On the relationship between the two works, see Tishby's analysis in Azriel of Gerona, *Commentary* 18–25.

45. Cf. Porat, *Kabbalistic* 137, where, among other explanations, Azriel glosses "from His place" as "from the place of His blessing," a reference to the tenth sefirah. As in the case of the kabbalistic interpretation of the Trisagion, this interpretation is also recounted in the name of Jacob ben Saul (Scholem, *Re'shit* 74n2).

46. Apparently, this union is described—and, indeed, theurgically enacted—by the recitation of the final verse of the Sanctus: "The Lord will reign forever; your God, O Zion,

from generation to generation" (Ps. 146:10), a verse that Ezra mentions after the conclusion of the citation of Rabad. This is because the verse describes God's reign, which is successfully established only after the sefirot are united. That this verse functions theurgically to unite the sefirot is, I believe, the force of "thereafter he joins them one to the other," which is mentioned in the body of the citation. I.e., after reciting Isa. 6:3 and Ezek. 3:12, one unites the sefirot mentioned in these verses by reciting Ps. 146:10.

47. An accessible, if somewhat dated, account of this motif can be found in Scholem, *On the Mystical Shape* 140–96.

48. See the discussion below in Chap. 5, pp. 162–64.

49. On this work, see Sed. Sed published an edition and French translation of this work in part 2 of his study of the work. See also Schäfer, "In Heaven"; Dan, *History* 3:1123–47.

50. See Ezra's comments on Song 1:15. I would note that in the highly deficient edition of the *Commentary* published by Chavel (Ben Solomon 489), the "holy of holies" is identified with the tenth sefirah. This reflects a scribal error. In more reliable manuscripts, it is clear that the "holy of holies" is a reference to the bridal canopy. See, e.g., MS Vienna Cod. hebr. 148, 8b; MS Vat. 86, 11a; and Vajda's French translation of the passage in *Le Commentaire* 66, which is based on a number of manuscripts. For more on the various versions of *Commentary on the Song of Songs*, see below, Chap. 5, n. 2. I also discuss this particular passage more fully in Chap. 5, p. 163.

51. See, e.g., B. Rosh ha-Shanah 31a. It must be noted that in classical rabbinic tradition, *shekhinah* was not a technical term for the tenth sefirah. This understanding was a later development. Kabbalists, however, read classical rabbinic tradition anachronistically in light of their own theosophy.

52. Scholem (*Origins* 206–7) gives more mystical significance to Rabad's use of the term *sod*.

53. Scholars have debated whether Rabad's use of language of this sort refers to an actual divine revelation. See the discussion in Twersky, *Rabad* 291–96.

54. Twersky (*Rabad* 29) cites the gloss without any mention that it may conceal a secret teaching.

55. See Kellner 209–11.

56. See also Kellner 211.

57. See, e.g., Scholem, "Kabbalah and Myth" 100–109; *Kabbalah* 104; Tirosh-Samuelson, "Philosophy" 220–21, 227–29.

58. B. Berakhot 61a; see also B. 'Eruvin 18a.

59. See, e.g., Scholem, *Re'shit* 79–90; *Origins* 216–18; Idel, *Kabbalah: New Perspectives* 128–29; *Kabbalah and Eros* 59–73; Pedaya, *Name* 104–5; Mopsik, *Sex* 75–114; Ḥadad; Abrams, *Female Body* 476–96; Wolfson, "Woman" 173–75; *Language* 161–71; Grossman 150–51.

60. See n. 65 below.

61. See the discussion in Chap. 4, p. 109.

62. See Scholem, *Origins* 78. See further below, p. 92.

63. Cf. Idel, *Kabbalah and Eros* 65, 67. Both Scholem and Idel note that in later kabbalistic literature, the rabbinic term *du partsufin* ("two-faced") is employed as a reference to the sixth and tenth sefirot and not to mercy and judgment, as it is in Rabad's text.

64. As is assumed in Idel, *Kabbalah and Eros* 61; and Wolfson, *Language* 167.

65. Scholem published the text on the basis of two sixteenth-century manuscripts: MS British Library Add. 27003, 14a; and MS Oxford Mich. 236, 7a (Neubauer 1956). As Idel

(*Kabbalah and Eros* 271–72n30) notes, a third copy is found in MS Manchester Gaster Add. 11, 39b–40a.

66. 'הנהיר ה (YHVH shined) which Scholem corrects as 'המטיר ה (YHVH rained down). MS Manchester Gaster Add. 11, 40a reads instead of הנהיר ה (YHVH shined), 'וזהו הנה יד ה (this is also the case with "behold the hand of YHVH"). "Behold the hand of YHVH" is the beginning of Exod. 9:3, which reads in full "Behold the hand of YHVH is upon your cattle, which are in the field, on the horses, on the asses, on the camels, on the herds, and on the flocks; there will be a very severe pestilence." This verse serves as another example in which YHVH is used when describing a divine act of judgment rather than of mercy.

67. I translated this part of the text in consultation with the translation that appears in Scholem, *Origins* 217.

68. Idel (*Kabbalah and Eros* 63) raises the possibility that "perhaps in the case of this early stage of kabbalistic theosophy an attempt to pinpoint one specific sefirah may be an anachronistic enterprise" (Cf. Scholem, *Origins* 217). Idel (63), however, ultimately concludes that sefirotic identifications of "complete judgment" and "complete mercy" are appropriate. I concur with this point, since in other traditions attributed to Rabad, he is already working with a fully formed theory of ten sefirot.

69. See *Sifrei* Deuteronomy, sec. 27.

70. See, e.g., *Bere'shit rabba'* 33:3, 73:3 (ed. Theodor-Albeck 308, 847). In an exoteric context, A. ben David (55) attributes to an unnamed rabbinic source the notion that wicked people can change the attribute of mercy into that of judgment. He further explains that this source uses Gen. 19:24—the verse used in Rabad's passage—as a prooftext for this point. I have been unable to locate a rabbinic text that employs the verse in this fashion.

71. For a parallel analysis of Rabad's tradition, see Dauber, "Competing" 82–84.

72. Unsurprisingly, different sefirot are involved in each instance, since, following the logic of early kabbalistic theosophy, the sixth and tenth sefirot—the subject of the comments on the Sanctus—are effectively lower manifestations of the fourth and fifth sefirot—the apparent subject of Rabad's comments on the two-faced original human.

73. *Mekhilta de-Rabbi Yishma'el, parashat be-shalaḥ,* to Exod. 15:3 (ed. Horovitz-Rabin, p. 130).

74. Kafaḥ's edition, which I use here, is based on a manuscript that reflects Rabad's final edition of the work after he made changes on earlier versions. See the analysis in Ta-Shma 129–30. These changes do not affect the argument that I make in this chapter.

75. See, e.g., Twersky, *Rabad* 291n20; Idel, *Kabbalah and Eros* 70–72; Grossman 150–51.

76. In contrast, Ḥadad (479–83, 486–91) argues that the passage in *Ba'alei ha-nefesh* stresses the subservience of the female to the male while the overtly kabbalistic passage stresses the basic equality of the male and the female. I cannot in this context go into the details of Ḥadad's position. Suffice it to say that in my view, while it is true that the wife's subservience is given greater emphasis in *Ba'alei ha-nefesh* than in the kabbalistic passage, this is merely a reflection of rhetorical difference and not of a fundamentally different view. See also the comments of Grossman 151.

77. Cf. Wolfson, *Language* 170.

78. Scholem, "Te'udah" 26; *Be'ur* 4c. As I will show in Chap. 4, it is doubtful that the various texts that the author of *Explanation* attributed to Isaac were actually written by him or were even direct transcriptions of his oral teachings. In this case, though, given that the far more reliable Ezra attributed a similar idea to Isaac, it is likely that the teaching in *Explanation* at least reflects Isaac's view.

79. See Twersky, *Rabad* 277; Scholem, *Origins* 222–23.

80. On these developments, see further below, pp. 98–100.

81. Judah describes these developments in his translator's introduction to the second section of the work, which is printed in Ibn Pakuda 162–65.

82. Note that the main purpose of this chapter is merely to demonstrate that there is only one God. The nature of that oneness, as defined by simplicity, is the subject of Chaps. 4–5. Nevertheless, God's simplicity repeatedly comes up in this chapter, as well.

83. Scholem, *Origins* 36–37; Tishby, *Studies* 8–9; Yisraeli, "Jewish Medieval" 23–31. Yisraeli (29–30) dates the earliest such tradition to the end of the thirteenth century. I would note that some accounts leave out Rabad's father-in-law.

84. Idel has made similar points in a number of studies. See, e.g., Idel, "Nahmanides" 91–93; "Kabbalistic Interpretation" 95–96; "Kabbalah in Byzantium" 661–64.

85. In addition to the more well-known circle of Isaac the Blind in the Posquières and Lunel area, where Isaac's father, Rabad, was also active, Ram Ben-Shalom has documented the existence of kabbalistic circles in both Arles and Narbonne in the first half of the thirteenth century ("Kabbalistic Circles" 579–603; *Jews of Provence* 583–85, 609–10). Ben-Shalom points out in reference to Arles and Narbonne: "According to the traditions of the circles of Kabbalah that were present there, they had local roots already in the twelfth century. But we do not have any new external evidence about this foundational period; we only have these circles' own mythographic traditions that indicate continuity" ("Kabbalistic Circles" 570). These mythographic traditions may at least partially reflect a historical reality.

86. This cultural shift has been well documented. See, e.g., Septimus; Freudenthal, "Sciences" (and the shortened but revised English version of this study: "Science"); J. Robinson; Stern 9–25.

87. His role has been widely discussed; see, e.g., Twersky, "Aspects" 195–202; Benedikt 19–24; Ta-Shma 50–53.

88. I am using the translation found in Freudenthal, "Abraham Ibn Ezra" 68 (brackets were added by Freudenthal).

89. It is printed in a critical edition in Freudenthal, "Causes" 651–72.

90. I am using the translation found in Freudenthal, "Abraham Ibn Ezra" 80.

91. I am using the translation found in ibid. 81.

92. In the early 1160s, Rabad was in Nîmes; see Twersky, *Rabad* 31.

93. This thesis was critiqued in Lasker. Freudenthal responded to this critique in "Philosophy."

94. Freudenthal ("Arabic" 205n20) refers to these passages but does not refer to Rabad.

95. Cf. Shaḥar 483.

96. These events have been described by many scholars; see, e.g., Wakefield 83–86; Cheyette 308–19; Moore, *War* 191–200, 215–19; Kienzle 109–29.

97. Moore's thesis is debated by the contributors to a helpful recent volume, *Cathars in Question*, ed. Sennis.

98. For some relevant scholarship, see Idel, *Kabbalah* 20–22; "Transmission"; Wolfson, "Beyond"; Pedaya, *Name* 10–12; *Nahmanides* 47–85.

99. Cf. the comments of Guy Stroumsa (6), in an unrelated context: "Esotericism is inherently prone to instability: if the secret is disclosed, it is no longer a secret; if it is not divulged, it loses its power and impact, and eventually disappears."

CHAPTER 4. ISAAC THE BLIND'S LITERARY LEGACY

1. See the comments in Bar-Asher, "Isaac" 417–18.

2. Cf. Abrams, *Kabbalistic Manuscripts* 92.

3. It should be noted that Haviva Pedaya, in contrast to most scholarship, states that "it appears that no kabbalistic teachings actually written by Isaac's own hand remain in our hands" (*Name* 55). She does not elaborate on this point. It is unclear whether she means to suggest that Isaac recorded kabbalistic teachings but that they have not survived, or that he never recorded kabbalistic ideas. In the course of her work, she does, however, treat statements in Isaac's name as authentically conveying his views. In any case, her observation provides an important direction for my work. See also the summary of her position in Bar-Asher, "Illusion" 279.

4. Printed in Abramson, *'Inyyanut* 150–55. On this responsum, see also Pedaya, *Name* 148–77, esp. 164–69.

5. Given that Bar-Asher promises a future study on this question, I will offer only a few brief comments here.

6. See Abramson, *'Inyyanut* 151; see also Katz 17–20. At the same time, there is some reason to question whether the Isaac referred to by Jacob ben Sheshet is Isaac the Blind. See n. 60 below.

7. Scholem (*Origins* 254) remarks that the responsum "is in fact full of kabbalistic allusions" but provides no examples. I have not been able to identify any kabbalistic allusions in this text. Perhaps Scholem has in mind the fact that the text makes reference to a work it calls *Shemoneh 'esreh de-Eliyahu ha-navi'* (*Shemoneh 'Esreh* prayer of Elijah the Prophet), which it describes as "making (magical) use of divine names" (*shimmush shemot*) (Abramson, *'Inyyanut* 153; cf. 155). Scholem, in another context, refers to *Shemoneh 'esreh de-Eliyahu ha-navi'* as an "out-of-the way mystical text" (*Origins* 120). As Scholem (*Origins* 255n120) and Abramson (*'Inyyanut* 153n7) note, this is apparently a magical text known elsewhere as *Tselota' de-Eliyahu*. While the text may be magical, it is not a specifically kabbalistic text and, in any case, the responsum uses the text as evidence for the proper version of the liturgy and not for mystical or magical purposes.

8. Here it should be mentioned that Sed-Rajna has published a very brief petitionary prayer ascribed to Isaac, which appears in a 1484 manuscript of a siddur of the Spanish rite. The prayer includes general requests for things such as success and freedom from sin but lacks any kabbalistic content.

9. Scholem collected many teachings attributed to Isaac, to which he, at times, added short notes. This unpublished collection is preserved at Hebrew University, where it is cataloged under the title "R' Yitzhak Sagi Nahor: Excerpts Collected from the Surviving Writing of R' Sagi Nahor." I have made use of Scholem's collection in this chapter. I would note that Scholem's collection is not complete. It remains a desideratum to collect all the teachings attributed to Isaac.

10. The most extensive treatments include Scholem, *Origins* 249–309; Pedaya, *Name*; Sendor.

11. One notable teaching that I will not analyze is the brief passage on the mystical intentions of the *'Amidah* prayer attributed to Isaac. It was published and analyzed in Idel, "On R. Isaac."

12. It was published in the appendix of Scholem, *Kabbalah in Provence*.

13. For a summary of earlier views about the authorship of this text, see Sendor 45–50.

14. As will be seen, the author of *Explanation of Nahmanides's Torah Commentary* records numerous passages that he claims were composed by Isaac. Scholem (*Origins* 258) argues that "the relatively homogenous character" of these passages "leads me to suppose that they derive from a single collection or work." If so, we are dealing with a much larger text. Scholem's assumption is difficult to verify. What he means by the "relatively homogenous character" of these passages is unclear because they treat disparate themes. If he is correct, we are likely dealing with a collection of separate brief commentaries and explanations that were not composed as a continuous narrative. The longest of these would have been "Commentary on Sacrifice." Even if Scholem is correct that the author of *Explanation* draws on a single work, my analysis of the individual passages below will make clear that this work was not composed by Isaac.

15. I will not engage in an extended discussion of a fourth lengthy text that Scholem attributes to Isaac, a portion of a commentary on *Midrash konen*, which is extant only in a single seventeenth-century manuscript: MS JTS 1777, 4b–5b. The text is identified as being בשם הרב הזקן ר' יצחק ז"ל ולא ידעתי מי הוא ("in the name of the aged Rabbi, R. Isaac, and I do not know who he is") (MS JTS 1777, 5b). Scholem (*Origins* 260) identified this aged R. Isaac as Isaac the Blind. It must be noted that Scholem does not regard the text as one actually authored by Isaac. Rather, he indicates that "we are dealing with the notes of a disciple that were based upon a lecture or dictation of Isaac" (*Origins* 260n131). This identification has been roundly rejected by more recent scholarship. See Idel, "Kabbalistic Materials" 170n9; "Nahmanides" 88n168; *Absorbing* 54, 503–4n36; Verman 41n18; Sendor 45; Pedaya, *Name* 77n22. Neither Scholem nor the more recent scholars have provided detailed arguments for their views. Scholem (*Origins* 260) is content with stating that "the terminology and the basic ideas are so close to those of Isaac the Blind in his commentary on the *Yeṣirah* that I am inclined to consider both Isaacs as one and the same person." The view of more recent scholarship is summed up by Sendor 45n5, who writes the following of Idel's rejection of Isaac's authorship: "Idel's assessment was conveyed to me in person, and based on proofs drawn from language and content with which I wholly concur." Unfortunately, in his published works, Idel has yet to provide a detailed assessment other than to note that the use in the text of the term *ketarim* ("crowns") to refer to the sefirot is uncharacteristic of the Kabbalah of the earliest Kabbalists (*Absorbing* 503n38) and to note that the term *ḥavvayot* is missing in the text where we would expect to see it, since it is found in a related context ("Sefer ha-emunah" 409) in a tradition attributed to Isaac by Jacob ben Sheshet (Idel, *Absorbing* 523n24). (As I note below (p. 118), whether this tradition should be seen as a verbatim rendition of Isaac's words is an open question.) I would add that the focus on angels found in the commentary on *Midrash konen* is also not characteristic of the Kabbalah of the first Kabbalists. Additionally, as far as I am aware, the title "the aged Rabbi, R. Isaac" is never used anywhere else in reference to Isaac the Blind. Finally, Bar-Asher's compelling argument that the identification of the author of *Commentary on Sefer Yetsirah* as Isaac is spurious undercuts Scholem's contention.

16. See, e.g., Scholem, "Tikkunim" 252; Idel, "Kabbalistic Interpretation" 101; Ben-Shalom, *Jews of Provence* 571; A. ben David 312–13. In *Kabbalistic Manuscripts* 91, 93, Abrams suggests that Isaac was the actual author. Later in this work (450), however, he is more circumspect: "Another text that he apparently wrote, or whose composition he instigated, is a commentary to the Account of Creation."

17. In MS Vat. 441, in the course of the "Commentary on Creation," an attribution to Isaac, under the name of the "Pious One," appears twice. The first attribution occurs following the explication of Gen. 1:6: "'Let it divide [the waters from the waters]': The form of water from spirit, and fire from water. The words of the Pious One (*leshon he-ḥasid*)" (MS

Vat. 441, 24b). The second attribution follows the explication of Gen. 2:4: "'In the day that the Lord God': The name was not complete until Adam was created in the image of God, and the seal (ḥotam) was complete. The words of the Pious One (leshon he-ḥasid)" (MS Vat. 441, 25a). "Commentary on Creation" then continues into the sixth chapter of Genesis, and there are no further mentions of Isaac. It seems clear, therefore, as Gottlieb (*Studies* 61) already surmised, that most of the commentary is Ezra's own words, and the only material that he intends to attribute to Isaac is what comes immediately before the two times that he writes "the words of the Pious One." Otherwise, Ezra would have indicated that the entire "Commentary on Creation" is by Isaac. Note that when Ezra introduces the "Commentary on Creation" by writing, "Here I briefly explicate the matter of the account of creation" (MS Vat. 441, 24a), he makes no claim that the passage derives from Isaac. On the contrary, Ezra seems to present it as his own teaching.

18. For a review of the discussion of the authorship of *Explanation*, see Galili 83–84. See also Idel, "Kabbalistic Interpretation" 141n345.

19. Vajda (385–90) has provided a French translation of the text with elaborate explanatory notes. It is also partially translated into French in Mopsik, *Grands textes* 135–36.

20. Note that the page is mispaginated as 14b. Cf., e.g., MS Parm. 2704 (De-Rossi 68), 27a; Mantua, Comunità Israelitica, MS ebr. 110, 32b; MS JTS 325, p. 116.

21. ואכתבהו בלשונו אף שאקצרו אבל אכתו' העקר: MS Paris hebr. 798, 122b. Cf. MS Oxford, Opp. Add. Qu. 42, 69a (Neubauer 1644); MS JTS 998, 71a (note that the text in this manuscript is partially unreadable).

22. See the partial French translation in Mopsik, *Grands textes* 136n50.

23. See Goldreich 90–103.

24. See, e.g., MS Christ Church 198, 12b–13b; MS JTS 827, 10a–12b. This version is also published in Porat, *Kabbalistic* 169–71.

25. In this study, I transcribed the text from Zurich Central Library, MS Heid. 27, 122b–124. I also provided variants from the following manuscripts: MS Oxford, Mich. 217, 26a–28b (Neubauer 1945); MS Munich, Bavarian State Library, Cod. hebr. 357, 1a–2b; MS Munich, Bavarian State Library, Cod. hebr. 92, 214b–216a; MS Munich, Bavarian State Library, Cod. hebr. 56, 350a–351b; Jerusalem, Benayahu, Meir, Israel MS K 18, 89a–90a. In addition to the three recensions that I have referred to, mention should be made of MS JTS 1878, 121b–122b, which is mostly identical to the third recension but includes additional material at the end of the text from the end of the second recension.

26. See, e.g., Vajda 385; Tishby, *Wisdom* 3:881; Scholem, *Origins* 306; Gottlieb, *Studies* 562; Pedaya, "Possessed" 587–88. Vajda (387), for his part, suggests that Isaac's remarks end at the words בעולה שהיא עולה כשמה (*Bei'ur* 23c). He admits, however, that the text makes no such formal indication. The remaining remarks are, in Vajda's view, no longer in keeping with Isaac's style but nevertheless reflect the ideas of his students.

27. A critical edition of the excursus was prepared by Yakov M. Travis.

28. For a comparison of these texts, see Appendix 1.

29. The text attributed to Azriel is printed in Porat, *Kabbalistic* 164–65. It is translated in Vajda 400–402. Cf. Mopsik 130. For a comparison of this text to "Commentary on Sacrifice," see Appendix 2.

30. The extended discussion of sacrifice is printed in Porat, *Kabbalistic* 166–68 (Cf. Dan, *History* 8:254–59). The full text is translated in Vajda 395–400. For a comparison of the text to "Commentary on Sacrifice," see Appendix 3.

31. See e.g., Scholem, *Origins* 373n26; Idel, *Kabbalah* 52. Vajda (395) is somewhat more skeptical of the attribution to Azriel.

32. See also Martel Gavrin's comment that compositions on blessings and on sacrifices in Isaac's circle "took on varying literary forms" (107).

33. In the case of Ezra's works for which there are no critical editions—*Commentary on the Song of Songs* (*Song Commentary*) and *Commentary on the Talmudic Aggadot* (*Aggadot Commentary*)—I compared multiple manuscripts to ensure that the language of the attribution was uniform and not merely a matter of scribal proclivity. For *Song Commentary*, I compared the printed version against MS Vat. 86, 2a–53a and MS Vienna 148, 1a–47a. These are the manuscripts that serve as the basis of Travis's critical edition of the excursus on the commandments that Ezra included in *Song Commentary*. For an explanation of Travis's decision to use these manuscripts, see Travis 149. For *Aggadot Commentary*, I consulted MS Vat. 441, 1a–74b; MS Vat. 185, 1a–18b; MS Vat. 294, 28a–48b; MS Parma 1390, 110b–118a. These manuscripts are described by Tishby in Azriel of Gerona, *Commentary* 25–27.

34. Indeed, some of Wolfson's examples include citations of Isaac by Ezra and Jacob ben Sheshet. See "Beyond" 199–201.

35. See n. 42 below.

36. Ibid.

37. A second passage in the "Excursus" (Travis 5, Hebr. sec.) reads: "And the Pious one (*he-ḥasid*) said to his students, 'When you are praying, know before Whom you are standing' (B. Berakhot 28b)." Here the Pious One may again be a reference to Isaac, but it may also be a reference to R. Eliezer, in whose name the statement from B. Berakhot is cited. See my discussion in *Knowledge* 174–75.

38. The passage in *Bere'shit rabba'* under discussion appears in 25:5 (ed. Theodor-Albeck 237). The attribution to Isaac is missing in MS Vat. 294, 44a. On this manuscript, see n. 41 below.

39. The attribution is missing in MS Vat. 294, 45b. On this manuscript, see n. 41 below.

40. Tishby (Azriel of Gerona, *Commentary* 27) suggests that the text should be amended to "our Rabbi."

41. Here is a list of the locations in *Aggadot Commentary* in which Ezra refers to the "the words of the Pious One":

1. MS Vat. 441, 8a (02); MS Vat. 185, 6a; MS Parma 2784, 113b.
2. MS Vat. 441, 17b; MS Vat. 185, 15a; MS Vat. 294, 32a.
3. MS Vat. 441, 19a; MS Vat. 185, 16a. Cf. Azriel of Gerona, *Commentary* 172–73. The attribution is missing in MS Vat. 294, 33b.
4. MS Vat. 441, 20a; MS Vat. 185, 17a. The attribution is missing in MS Vat. 294, 34b.
5. MS Vat. 441, 22a. A page is apparently missing in MS Vat. 294, where the attribution to Isaac should have appeared. See Tishby's comment in Azriel of Gerona, *Commentary* 27.
6. MS Vat. 441, 24b. The attribution is missing in MS Vat. 294, 37b. The passage is printed from this MS by Abrams in A. ben David 311. This is part of the "Commentary on Creation" discussed above.
7. MS Vat. 441, 25a. The attribution is missing in MS Vat. 294, 37b. The passage is printed from this MS by Abrams in A. Ben David 311. This is part of the "Commentary on Creation" discussed above.

8. MS Vat. 441, 30b. The attribution is missing in MS Vat. 294, 43a.

9. MS Vat. 441, 35a. The attribution is missing in MS Vat. 294, 47a.

It should be noted that, as Tishby (Azriel of Gerona, *Commentary* 27) has pointed out, MS Vat. 294, which contains only the section of *Aggadot Commentary* on the second chapter of tractate Ḥagigah, is full of anomalies. These include missing rabbinic passages, missing mentions of the names of sources, and missing phrases that are characteristic of Ezra's style. Accordingly, the fact that it is missing attributions to Isaac should not be given weight.

42. Some evidence for my assumption that the phrase "the words of the Pious One" (*leshon he-ḥasid*) suggests a verbatim transcription of Isaac's words can perhaps be gleaned from the fact that, in a number of instances, material parallel to the passages marked as "the words of the Pious One" appears elsewhere in Ezra's work without the attribution to Isaac. In these cases, the wording or context is somewhat different, suggesting that Ezra notes only that the source is Isaac's words when he cites these words verbatim. Consider the following example: in *Aggadot Commentary*, Ezra first cites a passage from *Bere'shit rabba'* 78:27 (ed. Theodor-Albeck 916): "Rabbi Ḥelbo said, On each and every day, the Holy One, blessed be He, creates a new group of angels. They sing their song and depart." He then cites Isaac's comments: "Their cause is external [*sibbatam hi' ḥitsonah*—or perhaps 'their causes, *sibbotam*, are external' in keeping with the text from *Song Commentary* that is discussed immediately below], and their strength weakened, and their ability to stand before their Creator is nullified like a spark upon a coal is nullified. The words (*leshon*) of the Pious One, may God protect him" (MS Vat. 441, 35a). There is a parallel passage in *Song Commentary*. Referring to angels that were created on the fifth day of creation, Ezra writes: "They became nullified like a spark upon a coal is nullified after they sing their song, for their causes are external (*sibbotam hi' ḥitsonah*) and their strength weakened, and their ability to stand before their Creator is nullified. And they return at a different time, and they sing their song and depart" (*Song Commentary* 510; the text was published by Abrams in A. ben David 323, from MS Vat. 86).

Ezra, here, takes the language of the passage from *Bere'shit rabba'* ("they sing their song and depart") upon which Isaac's statement, as cited in *Aggadot Commentary*, is based, and weaves in Isaac's words. It seems possible that in *Song Commentary*, Ezra does not feel compelled to mention Isaac because he has rearranged Isaac's words, while in *Aggadot Commentary* he does directly cite Isaac because he is conveying Isaac's teaching verbatim. [It is worth noting that Todros Abulafia, the mid-thirteenth century Castilian Kabbalist and communal leader, complicates matters even further when he cites Isaac's teaching in his own commentary on the aggadot, *Otsar ha-kavod*. In some manuscripts of this work, he is recorded as citing this teaching as, "I have seen it recorded in the book (*be-sefer*) of the Pious One, Rabbi Isaac, the memory of the righteous should be for a blessing, and these are his words (*leshono*)" (see, e.g., MS Vat. 185, 114b; MS Vat. 229, 225a; MS Hamburg Cod. hebr. 92, 188b). In other manuscripts and in printed editions, in contrast, he is recorded as citing the teaching as, "I have seen it written in the name (*be-shem*) of the Pious One, Rabbi Isaac, of blessed memory, and these are his words (*leshono*)" (see, e.g., MS JTS 997, 180b; *Otsar* (Navidvar), 31b; *Otsar* (Warsaw), 46; *Otsar* (Satmar), 40b). According to the first version, Todros had access to a work of Isaac's teachings. Yet if Todros had such a book, we might expect him to also cite it elsewhere, which, as far as I know, he does not. I suspect, therefore, that the second version, according to which Todros saw a teaching recorded in Isaac's name in another source not written by Isaac himself, is correct. In all likelihood, this source is Ezra's *Aggadot Commentary*. Cf. Scholem, *Origins* 258n127.

For other unattributed passages that are parallel to passages attributed to "the words of the Pious One" in *Aggadot Commentary* but that include various differences, cf. *Aggadot Commentary* MS Vat. 441, 8a (02) (= MS Vat. 185, 6a; MS Parma 2784, 113b) to *Song Commentary* 493 and to Ezra's letter to Abraham in Scholem, "Te'udah" 29; cf. *Aggadot Commentary* MS Vat. 441, 19a (= MS Vat. 185, 16a) to *Song Commentary* 493; cf. *Aggadot Commentary* (MS Vat. 441, 30b) to Travis 61 (Hebr. sec.).

A similar line of reasoning may allow us to assume that another passage not identified as "the words of Pious One" but as "the Pious One explicated" (*peiresh*) (*Song Commentary* 499—the passage regarding sacrifice discussed above) is also a verbatim transcription of Isaac's words. A similar passage appears in Ezra's letter to Abraham (Scholem, "Te'udah" 30), without the attribution to Isaac. Yet the wording in the latter passage is somewhat different. Finally, the same line of reasoning may also be applied to a passage from Ezra's letter to Abraham (26) introduced as "The Pious One hinted" (see above) when it is compared with an unattributed passage in *Song Commentary* 481–82.

43. Cf. Idel, "Kabbalistic Interpretation" 101.

44. This is the passage in the letter to Abraham found in Scholem, "Te'udah" 26.

45. Here, Ezra skips some intervening text that appears in the original midrash.

46. Again, a few intervening words are missing. They are, however, supplied in the version of the passage found in MS Vat. 294, 34b.

47. See *Bere'shit rabba'* 4:3 (ed. Theodor-Albeck 26–27).

48. In MS Vat. 294, 34b, the passage appears without the attribution to Isaac.

49. The first is found in "Commentary on Creation" in *Aggadot Commentary*, which, as noted above, has been erroneously attributed to Isaac. See A. ben David 311. The second is found in Azriel of Gerona, *Commentary* 93–94.

50. The term "lower waters" is not used here but is used in other places in rabbinic literature (for an example, see the next note), and it is clear that the passage means to explain that the firmament is between the upper and lower waters.

51. Indeed, in the continuation (MS Vat. 185, 17a; MS Vat. 294, 34b; MS Vat. 441, 20b), Ezra cites, without explanation, a text from *Bere'shit rabba'* 13:13 (ed. Theodor-Albeck 122–23) according to which "the upper waters are male and the lower ones are female."

52. In the case of "Sefer ha-emunah veha-bittaḥon," for which no critical edition exists, I checked the edition printed in Chavel (*Kitvei Ramban* 2:353–448) against a number of early manuscripts, including MS Vat. 277, 120b–177a; MS Parma 2982, 45a–80a; MS JTS 1641, 54a–113b. I have cited these manuscripts only when there is a significant difference between them and the printed text.

53. For the source from *Aggadot Commentary*, see MS Vat. 441, 17b.

54. See the comments in Pedaya, *Name* 56n229, 68–69. In another passage in "Sefer ha-emunah" 380, he writes: "So I have received from the mouth of the sage Isaac the Frenchman, of blessed memory." Isaac the Frenchman is not, however, a reference to Isaac the Blind. In some manuscripts, he is identified as Isaac ben Menaḥem. See MS Vat. 277, 135a; MS Parma 2982, 60b; MS JTS 1641, 75a–b. Cf. Scholem, *Origins* 251–52n110.

55. See Wolfson, "Beyond" 197.

56. "Sefer ha-emunah" 362, 409; *Sefer meshiv* 151, lines 58–59. In "Sefer ha-emunah" 411, he writes: "So I have heard in the name of the sage, R. Isaac the Frenchman, of blessed memory." As seen in n. 54 above, Isaac the Frenchman is not a reference to Isaac the Blind. Here, again, some manuscripts read "Isaac ben Menaḥem." See, e.g., MS Vat. 277, 154b; MS Parma 2982, 70a; MS JTS 1641, 101b.

57. Corrected on the basis of MS Vat. 277, 125a. Cf. MS Parma 2982, 55b; MS JTS 1641, 60b.

58. Indeed, Bar-Asher ("Illusion" 370–72) shows that an interpretation similar to that of the letter is also found in *Sefer ha-yiḥud* by Isaac's nephew Asher ben David, even if it is not cited in Isaac's name.

59. See the analysis of Bar-Asher, "Illusion" 374–75.

60. Note that the printed version of the text reads "the sage R. Isaac, of blessed memory," instead of "the Pious One, R. Isaac, of blessed memory." All the manuscripts that I have been able to check follow this latter version. See MS Vat. 277, 145a; MS Parma 2982, 65b; MS JTS 1641, 87b; MS Vat. 236, 245b; MS Paris 84, 88a; MS Vat. 505, 172a; MS JTS 2419, 32b. Still, the matter requires closer examination, for if the reading in the printed version is correct, the Isaac referred to might not be Isaac the Blind but Isaac ben Menaḥem, who is referred to elsewhere in ben Sheshet's work, as noted earlier (see nn. 54 and 56 above). In all other citations of Isaac the Blind in ben Sheshet's work, he is referred to as "the Pious One," whereas Isaac ben Menaḥem is referred to as "the Sage." Even if the reading of "the Pious One" is accurate, the attribution to Isaac the Blind remains suspect because all of ben Sheshet's other citations of Isaac mention his father's name, while this one does not.

61. Both Ezra and Azriel allude to this practice without mentioning Isaac. See Azriel of Gerona, *Commentary* 83 and the material cited there, n. 5.

62. See *Bere'shit rabba'* 1:1 (ed. Theodor-Albeck 2).

63. I have adopted the translation of Wolfson, "Wings" 225. See Wolfson's discussion there and the sources cited there, 225n63. See also Idel, "Jewish Kabbalah" 319–22, 325–31; "Maimonides's Guide" 199–201.

64. *Bei'ur* 3a, 3d, 4c, 5b, 15c, 17a, 19d, 23b, 24b, 24b, 25c, 26a, 29b, 31a, 32d, 34a, 34d. I have checked the language of the attributions found in the printed version of *Explanation* against a number of manuscripts. In all cases, I consulted MS Parma 2704 (= De-Rossi 68), 2a–42b; MS Vat. 202, 92a–106b, 118a–199b, 219a–223b, 224a–226b (note that this manuscript does not contain a complete version of the text); MS Oxford, Opp. Add. Qu. 42 (= Neubauer 1644), 1a–108a; MS Paris hebr. 798, 54a–174a. I have occasionally also checked additional manuscripts, as needed. I will indicate significant differences in the way that passages are ascribed to Isaac in my discussion of the individual passages, as warranted.

65. In its current form, this passage is about 250 words long, but the author indicates that he is merely paraphrasing a longer passage. He opens the passage by stating: "The Pious One, of blessed memory, already wrote something wondrous about this matter. I will write some of his words regarding this matter in an abbreviated fashion even if I do not employ his language." He concludes the passage by noting: "Until here [I have recorded] the essence of his words, even if he wrote at length about it." In the version of the text in MS Parma 2704, 4b–5a, there is no indication that the text is a paraphrase. There, the introduction reads: "The Pious One, of blessed memory, wrote something wondrous about this matter, and I will write his words in an abbreviated fashion." Other manuscripts agree with the printed version. See, e.g., MS Mantua, Comunità Israelitica, ebr. 110, 2b; MS Opp. Add. Qu. 42, 4b–5a; MS Vat. 202, 122a–122b.

66. As I discuss below, it is unclear where the passage ends, so it may continue for about thirty more words.

67. Note that MS Paris hebr. 798, 95b does not mention the Pious One and instead reads: "I heard (*ve-shama'ti*) that the Rabbi would make sure that a person should only write [the divine name in the form of three *yods*] one next to the other." Generally, in *Explanation*,

the Rabbi is a reference to Nahmanides. Other manuscripts agree with the printed version. See, e.g., MS Parma 2704, 18a; MS Vat. 202, 155b; MS Opp. Add. Qu. 42, 44b.

68. The printed version (*Bei'ur* 31a) reads: ושמעתי כי סברת החכם בענין האישים בשם החסיד ז"ל הוא ("I have heard, in the name of the Pious One, of blessed memory, that the view of the Sage regarding the fire offerings is"). The syntax of the Hebrew here is not particularly smooth. Moreover, it is unclear who the "Sage" is. The version in MS Parma 2704, 37a, which I employed, reads ושמעתי כי החסיד דעתו בענין האישים הוא ("I have heard that the opinion of the Pious One regarding fire offerings is"). The syntax of the Hebrew is clearer in this version, and the "Sage" is not mentioned. Other manuscripts agree with the printed text.

69. See Tishby, *Studies* 8–9. See also Idel, "We Have" 56–60, 67–68; "Nahmanides"; Yisraeli, *R. Moses* 191–97.

70. On the authorship of this work, see Galili.

71. See Scholem, *Origins* 256n121.

72. *Bei'ur* 3d, 4c, 5b, 23b ("Commentary on Sacrifice"—), 24b (second mention of Isaac on the page), 26a, 34d.

73. *Bei'ur* 3a (on Gen. 1:1); 17a (on Exod. 17:16); 24b (on Exod. 10:2—the first mention of Isaac on the page).

74. He first offers an explanation of Exod. 17:16 as something that Isaac explicated. He then continues, "he additionally wrote" and proceeds to provide a further explication of the Israelites' encounter with Amalek, the narrative of which Exod. 17:16 is a part.

75. In the version of the *Keter Shem Tov* printed in Coriat 43a, the text about the prohibition of incestuous relationships is attributed to Nahmanides and indirectly to Isaac himself: "I have found in a scroll of secrets from the Rabbi (= Nahmanides) who received from the Pious One the explanation of forbidden incestuous relationships." Yet, as Idel, "Kabbalistic Interpretation" (141), notes, this attribution is not found in a number of the best manuscripts and was apparently added to the text at a later time.

76. See Idel, "Kabbalistic Interpretation" 141–43, 196–99; "An Anonymous Commentary" 11–14.

77. Idel suggests that the unnamed addressee may have been Nahmanides himself. He further suggests that Meshullam might be Meshullam ben Moses, a southern French figure who was active in the first half of the thirteenth century. Rather than a Kabbalist, he was an antagonist of Kabbalah, as is clear from the fact that he was a signatory on Meir ben Simeon of Narbonne's critique of Kabbalah, which I describe in Chap. 6, pp. 175, 202. According to Idel, a close reading of the "scroll of secrets" shows that it was not a kabbalistic text at all. Instead, it was intended as a philosophic critique of a kabbalistic position.

78. See n. 87 below.

79. Regarding Ezra's *Commentary on Sefer Yetsirah*, see Chap. 5n5.

80. As far as I am aware, the only scholarly study dedicated to this work is Idel, "An Anonymous Commentary." So far, only the volumes on Genesis (Z. Holzer) and Exodus (D. Holzer) have been published. The full text is extant in two manuscripts: MS Estense University Library, Modena, Italy O.7.26; and MS Munich, Cod. hebr. 26. According to Z. Holzer (36), the editor of the volume on Genesis, the latter manuscript is a copy of the former. Z. Holzer (3–8) argues that the author of *Anonymous Commentary* is Isaac ben Josef, also known as Isaac Dapira.

81. The passage in *Anonymous Commentary* concludes with the abbreviation (עד כאן = ע"כ) "until here." This, as Z. Holzer notes (319), may imply that *Anonymous Commentary* is bor-

rowing from an outside source. If so, the words "in my opinion" could have appeared in the outside source, and, conceivably, the outside source was a text by Ezra. This possibility can be rejected. While I cannot conclusively prove that *Anonymous Commentary* did not take the entire passage from an outside source, it is unlikely because it would be odd for the author to cite an outside source that has the words "in my opinion" without indicating whose opinion it is. It is possible, therefore, that the passage includes an outside source into which the author of *Anonymous Commentary* threaded his own opinions. This explains why he writes "in my opinion" three times over the course of the passage rather than only once at the beginning. Following this theory, it is somewhat difficult to be sure how much of the text that follows the three mentions of "in my opinion" is by the author. Even on a conservative estimate, material labeled as "in my opinion" makes up a good portion of the remarks, and, as I indicate, even the text so labeled appears in *Explanation* as a citation of Ezra. Nor could the material not obviously attached to "in my opinion" derive from Ezra because this material includes a citation from Rashi. As Z. Holzer (320) notes—and, to the best of my knowledge, he is correct—nowhere in Ezra's extant writings does he cite Rashi.

82. It is also missing in one manuscript of *Explanation*: MS Paris hebr. 798, 113b–114a. This manuscript also lacks the attribution to Ezra.

83. The same variant of the passage in *Sefer Yetsirah* is ascribed to Isaac in the commentary on *Sefer Yetsirah* attributed to Nahmanides. See Scholem, "Perusho ha-'amitti" 92. In keeping with Bar-Asher's view regarding the spurious nature of the attribution to Isaac of *Commentary on Sefer Yetsirah*, there is no evidence of this particular variant in the latter. See Bar-Asher, "Illusion" 373–74.

84. In addition to Travis's edition, I checked the text as it appears in MS State Library of Berlin, Or. Phillip 1392, 175a; MS Paris hebr. 225, 55a. These manuscripts also lack any attribution to Isaac.

85. See, e.g., MS Paris hebr. 798, 126b; MS Mantua, Comunità Israelitica, ebr. 110, 34b; MS JTS 998, 78a; MS Oxford, Opp. Add. Qu. 42, 73a (Neubauer 1644). In MS Vat. 202, 177a, there is a somewhat different version: "I have received (*ve-kibbalti*) that the Rabbi, the Pious One, of blessed memory, wrote the explanation of these [impure female] bloods. And so also the sage Ezra, of blessed memory, in the [*Commentary on*] *the Song of Songs*" (the text of the explanation follows). In this version, it is less obvious that the line about Ezra is an interpolation. Still, the text reads smoothly without this line, so I do not think this version challenges my conclusion.

86. MS Parma 2704 (De-Rossi 68), 28b: "I have received that the Rabbi, the Pious One states that the meaning."

87. Tishby (Azriel of Gerona, *Commentary* 50–51) has already provided a list of passages in *Explanation* attributed to Ezra that can be traced to *Aggadot Commentary*, together with cross-references to *Aggadot Commentary*. I will not reproduce his list here but will supplement it with a list of places in which *Explanation* refers to *Song Commentary*: *Bei'ur* 3b = *Song Commentary* 506; *Bei'ur* 3b (both *Aggadot Commentary* and *Song Commentary* are mentioned) = A. ben David 310–12 (commentary on creation in *Aggadot Commentary*) and A. ben David 318–24 (commentary on creation in *Song Commentary*); *Bei'ur* 20a: Ezra is described as believing that the direction north refers to the sefirah of judgment. While this idea does occur in the excursus (Travis 30–31), it also occurs in the main section of *Song Commentary* (489, 498). I would add that while the kabbalistic explanation of tefillin that *Bei'ur* 15d attributes to Ezra is found in both *Aggadot Commentary* (see Azriel of Gerona, *Commentary* 66–67) and the

"Excursus" (Travis 13–13), a comparison of the precise language makes it apparent that *Explanation*'s source is *Aggadot Commentary*.

88. There is no strong manuscript evidence to support this possibility. Almost all the extant manuscripts of *Song Commentary* include the excursus. The only exceptions are two sixteenth-century manuscripts. See Travis 147.

89. מה שכתב הרב החסיד ז"ל בעניין המולך באותן עזי פנים שבדור והזכיר מדרש רבותינו ז"ל שאמרו עמד ושתלן בכל דור ודור כוונתו לרמוז לדור אנוש שהיו עזי פנים ובאין וחוזרין בכל דור ודור.

90. While Idel makes note of MS Vat. 202, from which I cite the passage, he cites it from MS Cambridge 8,671, 125a. I have not been able to check the manuscript, but in his transcription, it reads מה שכתב הרב החסיד ז"ל בעניין המולך באותן עזי פנים שבדור הזכיר המדרש ז"ל שעמד ושתלן בכל דור ודור כוונתי לדור אנוש שהיו עזי פנים ובאין בכל דור ודור. ("[Regarding] that which the Rabbi, the Pious One, of blessed memory, wrote about the matter of Moloch, in reference to those insolent ones in the generation. He, of blessed memory, mentioned the midrash that He stood and planted them in each and every generation. My intention is to hint at the generation of Enoch, who were insolent, and they come in each and every generation"). See Idel, "Commentaries" 28n90. The words "my intention," in the version that Idel cites, may give the impression that it is Isaac who is writing. Yet the fact that earlier in the statement, the author specified that "he, of blessed memory, mentioned the midrash" makes clear that, even in this version, the author is writing about Isaac's statement rather than citing it verbatim.

91. See also Abrams, *Sefer ha-bahir* 81.

92. This is the thrust of his argument in "Commentaries." Idel (28n90) marshals this point in the course of casting doubt on the authenticity of the passage in *Explanation*, which, to repeat, he regards as an adaptation of the original text.

93. See the remarks in Z. Holzer 323.

94. Here I would note that yet another passage in *Explanation*, allegedly composed by Isaac (*Bei'ur* 26a), appears in *Anonymous Commentary* without attribution. See MS Estense University Library, O.7.26, 120b–121a; MS Munich 26, 277b. As Z. Holzer (323–24) notes, the passage in *Anonymous Commentary* seems to continue for an extra line beyond that in *Explanation*. This seems to show that *Anonymous Commentary* did not take the passage from *Explanation*. Either *Explanation* drew on *Anonymous Commentary*, or they both borrowed from a third source.

95. For discussions of the letter, see, e.g., Scholem, *Origins* 393–403; Dan, *Early Kabbalah* 34–35; *Jewish Mysticism* 36–39; Idel, "Nahmanides" 28–36; Pedaya, *Name* 57–66; Halbertal, *By Way* 299–305 and *Concealment* 67–76; Abrams, *Kabbalistic Manuscripts* 91–92, 450–52; Ben-Shalom, *Jews of Provence* 568–70; Bar-Asher, "Isaac."

96. Recently, Tzahi Weiss ("Letter") has challenged the typical scholarly interpretation (as reflected in the scholarship cited in the previous note) of this part of the letter. In his view, this part of the letter has no connection to kabbalistic secrets. Rather, it pertains to the accusation leveled at Jonah Gerondi, by members of the Jewish community in Béziers, that there was the taint of impurity in his family connected in some way to a missing or defective marriage contract. Since Nahmanides was a relative of Jonah, this accusation also pertains to him and his family. In ways that are not totally clear, this controversy was connected to the concurrent controversies over the writings of Maimonides and over the leadership of Barcelona. In response, Nahmanides wrote letters to southern-French Rabbis defending Jonah and asking for their support in refuting the false accusations. In Weiss's

(337–42) view, when Isaac says that he "saw sages, wise men, and pious men" who wrote "great and sublime matters (*gedolot ve-nora'ot*) in their books and letters," he is not referring to kabbalistic secrets but to missives circulated in the context of the aforementioned controversies. Indeed, in keeping with his thesis, Weiss (333n12) translates *"ve-nora'ot"* as "horrible" instead of "sublime." Weiss's thesis is highly interesting and provocative and deserves careful consideration. In my view, the standard reading remains correct. A point-by point refutation is not possible in this context. Briefly, it seems to me that, on Weiss's reading, the letter becomes quite disjointed. I offer one illustration of this point. In the next part of the letter, as Weiss (342) freely admits, Isaac notes that he warned certain unnamed acquaintances not to disseminate kabbalistic teachings—"As long as I was actually with them, I often warned them" (331)—and he praises his fathers' discretion with kabbalistic wisdom and states that he emulated them (331). For Weiss, this portion of the letter has, therefore, turned to an entirely different matter. Yet, this creates a disjointedness that is hard to account for. Indeed, his analysis accentuates this disjointedness. He claims (335–36), for instance, that the "sages, wise men, and pious men" are not the same people as the acquaintances Isaac subsequently refers to. The sages, Weiss argues are "unknown" people while the acquaintances are "known people he has actually met" (336). This strikes me as a difficult reading. The sages are not "unknown." On the contrary, Isaac writes that he "saw" them. Moreover, the fact that Isaac does not identify the acquaintances but simply refers to them as "them" suggests that he is referring back to the aforementioned sages. Weiss's comment that "this formulation of Isaac's could derive from the letters that he received from Nahmanides and Jonah" (335n36)— i.e., letters that Isaac refers to at the beginning of his letter—does not strike me as persuasive. It is more compelling to read the two portions of the letter as a continuous narrative about the same subject than as one that changes topics with no warning.

97. Cf. Bar-Asher, "Isaac" 425: "This self-imposed silence will not permit more than a string of terse allusions."

98. For the passage from *Aggadot Commentary* that he cites, see MS Vat. 441, 35a; see discussion in n. 42 above.

99. See, e.g., *Moreh ha-nevukhim* 7 (1:introduction).

CHAPTER 5. EZRA BEN SOLOMON OF GERONA AS AN ESOTERIC WRITER

1. We have virtually no details of Ezra's personal life. The fullest scholarly treatment of Ezra and his works can be found in Tishby, *Studies* 3–35.

2. There is no critical edition of *Song Commentary*. Scholarly analyses of *Song Commentary* have typically relied on the deficient version found in *Kitvei Ramban*, ed. Chavel 2:473–548. In-text references to *Song Commentary* refer to Chavel's edition, unless otherwise noted. The work has been translated into English by Seth S. Brody, based on MS JTS 1189, 1a–44a; and into French, based on six manuscripts by Vajda. For the purposes of this study, I have checked Chavel's version against Brody's and Vajda's translations and against MS Vienna 148, 1a–47a and MS Vat. 86, 2a–53a. These are the two manuscripts that Yakov Travis used in his critical edition of the excursus on the meaning of the commandments that Ezra appended to *Song Commentary*. For a discussion of why he chose these manuscripts, see Travis 147–55. My translations are based on those of Brody, with liberal emendations, as needed.

3. *Aggadot Commentary* has only been partially published in Almalikh 1a–20b. It is preserved most fully in MS Vat. 441, 1a–69b and much more partially in a number of other manuscripts, including MS Vat. 185, 1b–18a; MS Parma 2784 (De-Rossi 1390), 110a–118b; MS Vat. ebr. 294, 28a–48b. Additionally, as Tishby notes (Azriel of Gerona, *Commentary* 18), the beginning of MS Jerusalem, 8°91, the lone manuscript of Azriel's own commentary on the aggadot upon which Tishby's edition is based, is, in fact, taken from Ezra's *Aggadot Commentary*. Apparently, the copyist of this manuscript was missing the opening pages of Azriel's commentary and therefore replaced them with *Aggadot Commentary*. These manuscripts are described by Tishby in Azriel of Gerona, *Commentary* 25–27. In citing *Aggadot Commentary*, I have consulted all these versions and indicated variants, as necessary.

4. Tishby (*Studies* 12–15) suggests that Ezra composed *Aggadot Commentary* first. Vajda (17–18n2) casts doubt on this view, and Pedaya ("Possessed" 568–69n2) argues that he wrote *Song Commentary* first. For a fuller discussion of the chronology of his works, see Travis 13–15, esp. nn. 25 and 27.

5. Abraham Abulafia writes that Ezra was the author of a *Commentary on Sefer Yetsirah*, which he characterizes as containing "correct but few" traditions. See Idel, "'Sefer Yetzirah'" 482.

6. They were published in Scholem, "Te'udah" 25–34.

7. See Scholem, *On the Mystical Shape* 65–68; *Ha-kabbalah* 374–76.

8. Many tractates, however, are skipped.

9. Cf. Idel, "Nahmanides" 21–22, 37, 76, 89; Yisraeli, "Early" 502 and *R. Moses* 230, 246–47; Ben-Shalom, *Jews of Provence* 520.

10. Vajda (17–18) suggests that Ezra composed the work between 1225 and 1230.

11. There have been numerous discussions of the controversy; see, e.g., Silver; Shoḥat; Septimus; Berger 85–100; Drews.

12. His critique of Maimonides's followers here is of a piece with other anti-Maimonidean comments that Ezra makes elsewhere in his oeuvre. For other examples, see Dauber, "Ezra."

13. See also Idel, *Kabbalah* 250–53; *Absorbing* 280–89.

14. For examples of this theme in the literature of the Maimonidean controversy, see Halberstam 6, 51–52.

15. For examples of this claim, see Septimus 93–95; see also Matt, "Mystic" 370–82; Travis 46–48.

16. See Dauber, *Knowledge* 149; Idel, "Maimonides" 43–50; Travis 32–48.

17. I follow the reading in MS Vienna 148, 3a; and MS Vat. 86, 4b. Chavel's edition reads *she-ne'emar aḥat mi-shenat ḥayyim* ("as it is said, one of the years of life"). Brody leaves this phrase out in his translation. Vajda (44) translates "et unième année de ma vie." The meaning of the entire statement ("until I reached my fifth rung—one year of the years of my life") is unclear. For different possible interpretations, see Travis 13–14n25.

18. Hebr., *me-rabbotai*. This reading follows MS Vienna 148, 3b; MS Vat. 86, 5a. It is also the reading adopted by Vajda (44), who translates "de mes maîtres." Chavel's edition reads *me-rabboteinu* ("from our teachers"). Similarly, Brody translates "from our Rabbis," which might be taken to imply "from our classical rabbinic sages." In actuality, Ezra means to say that he will interpret the Song of Songs based on the teachings of his own personal kabbalistic teachers.

19. Oded Yisraeli argues, in his excellent recent intellectual biography of Ezra's younger contemporary and fellow resident of Gerona, Nahmanides, that the latter "was born into an

intellectual atmosphere in which the religious and cultural discussion was saturated with the language of Kabbalah and not only among the kabbalistic elite" (*R. Moses* 201). On the basis of this point, he disputes the idea that Nahmanides had a specific teacher who taught him Kabbalah, as some kabbalistic traditions imply. Rather, Kabbalah was something he could absorb organically from his surroundings (190–202). If Yisraeli is correct, Ezra's *Song Commentary* would perhaps have been understandable to a wider audience than I will suggest. I agree that Nahmanides might have absorbed Kabbalah from several sources, rather than from one teacher. As I have already argued in Chap. 3, there was a greater audience for Kabbalah at the end of the twelfth century, when Nahmanides was born, than has often been realized. He thus could have had access to various teachers. Nevertheless, I do not find evidence that kabbalistic knowledge was widely diffused in Catalonia when Ezra wrote his works. Rather, it remained the knowledge of a relatively small elite. The force of Isaac's letter, considered in Chap. 4, is that the spread of Kabbalah was a new and unfortunate reality that breaks with earlier practice. Yisraeli marshals the kabbalistic references in Nahmanides's early works to show that "already in his youth and in his early writings, Nahmanides made use of kabbalistic language as though it was common knowledge familiar to readers" (200). Yet while Nahmanides certainly believed that there were readers who could understand his kabbalistic ideas, his early writings do not show that Kabbalah was common knowledge. On the contrary, Nahmanides presents Kabbalah as esoteric knowledge. Thus, the lone two kabbalistic references in his Talmudic novella (*Hiddushei ha-Ramban* 4:185–86 [on Yevamot 49b], 3:131 [on Shevu'ot 29a]), which he composed early in his career, are written in an obscure cryptic style, and he specifically refers to the second of them as a "secret," a point that he emphasizes by stating: "The Lord of all, in Whose hands is all, will inform us of wisdom in the concealed place (based on Ps. 51:8)." Similarly, the kabbalistic hints in the poems with which he prefaced two early halakhic works, *Sefer ha-milhamot* (published in Goldreich 221; see Yisraeli, *R. Moses* 200n70) and *Hilkhot nedarim u-piskei bekhorot* (Chavel 1:403–6) are just that: hints. Indeed, in one, he underscores the secrecy of his remarks: "I will hint about its foundation with riddles, and it is a concealed and sealed secret" (Goldreich 221). His "Sermon for a Wedding" (Chavel 1:131–38), another early work, which might be viewed as reflecting a public discourse in which Nahmanides spoke openly of kabbalistic ideas, may not have been kabbalistic at all. Yisraeli writes elsewhere, regarding a passage in this work: "It is difficult to determine whether under discussion is, indeed, already the kabbalistic doctrine of the sefirot or the pre-kabbalistic doctrine of cosmic sefirot" ("Initial Ideas" 92). Finally, Bar-Asher ("Illusion" 327n271) has raised doubts and promised a future study about whether another ostensibly early and fairly open kabbalistic work by Nahmanides, a commentary on *Sefer Yetsirah*, was, in fact, by him. Thus, while Nahmanides may have gained knowledge of Kabbalah from many sources, his own early works reflect the elite and esoteric nature of Kabbalah. Of course, in the decades following Ezra, Kabbalah did become more and more available to a wider audience, and works were published with the goal of spreading Kabbalah (see ch. 5, 165–72.). This was a process that caused Nahmanides to stress the esotericism of Kabbalah that much more strongly in his later works.

20. The midrash on Prov. 10:6 appears in *Midrash tehillim* on Ps. 19:3 (ed. Buber 74) and again on Ps. 88:5 (ed. Buber 380). This midrash is cited once in *Song Commentary* 495 and twice in *Aggadot Commentary* (MS Vat. 441, 34b, 46a). On the basis of the first citation from *Aggadot Commentary*, it seems that Ezra identified the angel who forms the crown on God's head with Sandalphon. There, immediately before citing the midrash on Prov. 10:6, he cites

B. Ḥagigah 13a, according to which Sandalphon ties crowns on God's head. The midrash on Deut. 4:7 appears in Y. Berakhot 9:1 (62b–63a). There, the text highlights the distance between God and human beings. Specifically, the text recounts that the distance from the Earth to the firmament would take 500 years to traverse. The next firmament is the same distance from the first one, and so on and so forth, until God is reached. Despite this distance, "A person enters the synagogue and stands behind the lectern, prays in a whisper, and God hears his prayer." The number 500 might be significant. According to B. Ḥagigah 13a, the text that Ezra cites in *Aggadot Commentary* prior to citing the midrash on Prov. 10:6, Sandalphon is taller than other angels by a difference of 500 years. Thus in Ezra's view, the two midrashic passages may have been connected, which might have heightened the contradiction, in his eyes. According to the latter passage, prayer goes directly to God despite the fact that there are many firmaments at distances of 500 years from one another between the Earth and God; according to the former, an angel, who himself is 500 years taller than other angels, has to transport the prayers to God. It is also worth noting that earlier in the letter (Scholem, "Teʿudah" 32), Ezra cites a passage from *Bereʾshit rabba'* 15:6 (ed. Theodor-Albeck 138) according to which the Tree of Life is a length that would take 500 years to traverse, although the precise function of this citation is unclear.

21. See Lieberman 87–88, 204–5; Sussman 216–17n26.

22. See the examples cited in Abramson, *Rav Nisim* 36–37; Sussman 216–17n16. See also Rashi on B. Shabbat 6b, Bava metsia 92a, and Abramson's additional notes in *ʿInyyanut* 268–69.

23. Cf. the comments in Pedaya, "Spiritual" 248.

24. Another reference to the secretive nature of the explanation of circumcision, which I will not deal with here, appears elsewhere in *Aggadot Commentary*. See MS Vat. 441, 50a; Almalikh 13b.

25. For various places in rabbinic literature in which this motif occurs, see Henshke 139–40nn90–91.

26. See, e.g., Wolfson, *Circle* 29–48; "Circumcision and the Divine"; "Occultation" 135–48; "Circumcision, Secrecy"; *Language* 128–41; *Giving* 154–200.

27. See the studies cited in the previous note.

28. The two passages are related because, as Theodor points out in his notes to the passage in chap. 26 (ed. Theodor-Albeck 246), from a midrashic perspective Shem and Melchizedek are one and the same character. Indeed, this identification occurs in the passage from *Avot de-Rabbi Natan*, cited above. This identification is also reflected in *Bereʾshit rabba'* 56:10 (ed. Theodor-Albeck 608) and elsewhere.

29. As Theodor points out in his notes on this passage, this is apparently based on Gen. 9:26: "Blessed be the LORD, the God of Shem."

30. For a complete discussion of the relevant sources, see Wolfson, "Circumcision and the Divine."

31. My citation follows MS Vat. 294, 42b, which contains a fuller quotation of the rabbinic passage. In MS Vat. 441, 30a, it is presented in a more abbreviated fashion. The passage is from *Midrash tanḥuma, parashat lekh lekha* 23 (Buber 1:79–80).

32. See the studies cited in n. 26 above.

33. The passage is taken from *Midrash tanḥuma, parashat Noaḥ* 5. Ezra cites it in an abbreviated fashion (this passage does not appear in the version of *Midrash tanḥuma* edited by Buber).

34. MS Vat. 441a, 30a reads "seven," instead of "offering," which is in keeping with the original midrash as published by Buber.

35. MS Vat. 441a, 30a adds here, in keeping with the original midrash as published by Buber: "The law regarding a person is like the law regarding the animal."

36. Based on *Midrash tanḥuma, parashat emor* 17 (Buber 2:94).

37. See, e.g., Abrams, *Sefer ha-Bahir* 119, sec. 3.

38. The key to understanding Ezra's view lies in two highly obscure passages about the "measure" (*shi'ur*) of the sefirot that appear, respectively, in his two letters to Abraham (Scholem, "Te'udah" 31, 33). Cf. Porat, *Kabbalistic* 21, question 7. See also the analysis in Wolfson, *Language* 198–200.

39. E.g., David Kimḥi criticized anti-Maimonideans for corporealizing God in his letter published in Lichtenberg 3c. See also Fraenkel.

40. Nahmanides, e.g., reported that northern French Rabbis criticized Maimonides's *Sefer ha-madda'* because it affirmed the incorporeality of God. Nahmanides's comments are published in Perles 190–91; Chavel 1:345. See also the sources cited in Kanarfogel 138–39nn1–2.

41. For other examples, see Travis 100–101.

42. See the comments in Scholem, *Origins* 409; Idel, "'In a Whisper'" 495–98.

43. Cf. Idel, "'In a Whisper'" 497.

44. Cf. *Song Commentary* 513 on Song 7:2.

45. In one example, Ezra writes "In *Perek ha-Ḥelek*, the matter of Jeroboam will be explained well" (Azriel of Gerona, *Commentary* 80; MS Parma 2784, 12b; MS Vat. 441, 6b). In a second example, he writes, regarding the secret meaning of blessings: "In the discussion of the subject of vows, you will understand the main point of the matter" (MS Vat. 441, 59b). In a third example, regarding the statement in B. Ta'anit 5b that the patriarch Jacob never died, Ezra writes: "In tractate Megillah, I will inform you of the secret" (MS Parma 2784, 14a; MS Vat. 185, 7a; Almalikh 6b; MS Vat. 441, 10a).

46. I am translating this verse in accordance with the way it is understood by the Talmud. A more literal translation would read "no eye has seen a God other than You."

47. As Tishby (Azriel of Gerona, *Commentary* 78n7) suggests, it is possible that the hint in Berakhot, to which Ezra refers, is found in the words of the passage cited above that I have italicized here: "I will not be able to offer you a hint here (*lirmoz lekha be-khan*) regarding this secret, but, with the help of God, in the chapter titled 'one who hires a workers,' *you will understand (tavin) the fear of the Lord and will find the knowledge of the holy ones.*"

That is, the very passage in which Ezra signals that he will not reveal the secret until later, even in the form of a hint, already contains a hint to the secret! Tishby suggests that "understand the fear" refers to the tenth sefirah, while "knowledge of the holy ones" refers to the sixth sefirah. In turn, he suggests that the "wine preserved in its grapes" refers to the tenth sefirah and "Eden" to the sixth sefirah. I interpret the hints differently. In *Song Commentary* 497–98 (on v. 4:12), "Eden" is interpreted as a reference to the second sefirah, *ḥokhmah* (see also Bar-Asher, *Journeys* 66), and, as Vajda (262n41) already pointed out, Ezra, elsewhere in his comments on this same verse, interprets the "wine preserved in its grapes" as the emanative light that is found in the second sefirah. The "wine" or the emanative light may perhaps also specifically refer to the third sefirah, *binah* (understanding) because this is the sefirah in which the emanative light begins to emerge and become manifest. This symbolism is also apparent in an interpretive remark that appears in *Aggadot Commentary*, after the citation of the view of Rabbi Shim'on ben Lakish that Isa. 64:3 refers to "Eden," in the version found MS Vat. 294, 27a: "This refers to the bright light that emerges from wisdom, [the second sefirah], and is concealed in splendor, [the sixth sefirah], which is the speculum than shines." According to this comment, then, Eden, is the second sefirah out of which a bright light—the emanative flow—emerges. (The same remark is also included in a marginal note in MS Vat. 442, 6a.) While this interpretive remark may be a later interpolation, it is in keeping with the explanation that I have proposed here.

I would suggest that the italicized words may hint at these two sefirot—"wisdom" (*ḥokhmah*) and "understanding" (*binah*). "*You will understand (tavin) the fear of the Lord and will find the knowledge of the holy ones*" is apparently a misquotation of Prov. 2:5: "Then you will understand the fear of the Lord and will find knowledge of God." This misquotation seems to be based on a conflation of Prov. 2:5 with Prov. 9:10: "The beginning of wisdom (*ḥokhmah*) is fear of the Lord and knowledge of the holy ones is understanding (*binah*)." We must wonder, though, whether the misquotation is a simple mistake based on the conflation of two verses, which Ezra may have recorded from memory, or if the misquotation is itself a strategy of esoteric writing. Perhaps, that is, Ezra subtly wants to direct the reader to Prov. 9:10, which refers to wisdom and understanding, the names for the second and third sefirot. If so, in Ezra's original statement, perhaps "understand (*tavin*) the fear of the Lord" would be a reference to the sefirah of "wisdom" (in keeping with Prov. 9:10, "The beginning of wisdom is fear of the Lord) while "find knowledge of God" would be a reference to the sefirah of "understanding" (in keeping with Prov. 9:10, "knowledge of the holy ones is understanding"). Admittedly, one difficulty with this interpretation is that we might expect "understand (*tavin*) fear of the Lord" to refer to "understanding" (*binah*) since "understand" (*tavin*) comes from the same root. Still, adding to the likelihood that Ezra intended to allude to these sefirot is the fact that Prov. 2:2, 2:3, and 2:6 also refer to wisdom (*ḥokhmah*), understanding (*binah*), and discernment (*tevunah*). (*Tevunah* has the same root as *binah*.) Moreover, a passage from *Midrash Proverbs* (Visotzky 159) that immediately follows our passage in some versions of *Aggadot Commentary* (MS Vat. 441, 6a; MS Vat. 294, 27a) also refers to "wisdom" and "understanding."

We find the same misquotation of Prov. 2:5 elsewhere in *Aggadot Commentary*. After citing a series of midrashic statements without providing any explanation, Ezra writes: "You must arouse yourself and inquire regarding these matters and topics as though they were silver and hidden treasures. Then you will understand the fear of the Lord and will find the knowledge of the holy ones" (MS Vat. 441, 48b). (The reference to silver and hidden treasures comes from Prov. 2:4.) Two of the midrashic statements deal with God creating the world through the attributes of "wisdom" (*ḥokhmah*), "knowledge" (*daʿat*), and "discernment" (*tevunah*). They are found in *Midrash tehillim* (Buber 279 on Ps. 50) and in *Pirkei de-rabbi Eliʿezer* (ed. Higger, chap. 3, p. 90). Plausibly, therefore, in this case as well, Ezra means to allude to the second and third sefirot.

48. The version that appears in MS Vat. 441, 73b is almost impossible to read because the letters are smudged. It is not extant in the other versions.

49. See n. 47 above.

50. The full details of Ezra's eschatological views are not sufficiently clear, hidden as they are in his cryptic allusions. Ezra seems to have believed that the ultimate source to which the soul returns is the second sefirah. See my "An Early Kabbalistic Explanation." It is also clear that the third sefirah has a key role in his eschatological vision. Thus, e.g., in a passage in the excursus on the commandments in *Song Commentary* (Travis 19, Hebr. sec.), he describes the soul after death as existing within "the upper and inner place of the Glory,

of the Holy One, blessed be." While Travis (132) suggests that "the upper and inner place of the Glory" refers to the second sefirah, it is more likely a reference to the third sefirah. This is clear from a comparison to a non-eschatological passage in his first letter to Abraham, where Ezra describes all the souls as "bound" in "the Glory of God's name" (Scholem, "Te'udah" 27). As Scholem remarks (27n71), the reference there is clearly to the third sefirah. The passage in the excursus on the commandments is discussed extensively in Idel, "Be-or." See also Idel, "Nishmat" 361.

51. Wolfson refers to this source in *Circle* 62–63. Cf. the statement that Ezra attributes to Isaac in MS Vat. 441, 8a; MS Parma 2784, 13b.

52. See, e.g., Wolfson, *Language* 327–32, 366–71.

53. Examples of these varying positions, including that of Abulafia, are discussed in Septimus 82. See also Schwartz, *Messianism* 86, 96.

54. See also my discussion in *Knowledge* 50–52. Cf., e.g., Maimonides's comments in the introduction to the *Guide*, as rendered by Judah Alḥarizi—Ezra's preferred translation—according to which the Sages, "when they aimed at teaching something of this subject matter (i.e., "the account of creation" and "the account of the chariot"), spoke of it only in parables and riddles. . . . Sometimes the subject intended to be taught to him who was to be instructed was scattered and divided (*mefuzzar u-meforad*)—although it was one and the same subject—among parables remote from one another" (Scheyer and Munk 30).

55. See, e.g., my comments in *Knowledge* 53–55.

56. Cf. Strauss, *Persecution* 60–61.

57. That Adam engaged in sacrifice is based on a midrashic source that Ezra cites prior to making this statement. See MS Vat. 441, 26b, where he cites *Bere'shit rabba'* 16:5 (ed. Theodor-Albeck 148–49). Cf. Travis 27 (Hebr. sec.). As Tishby (*Wisdom* 3:880) suggests, Ezra's emphasis on the fact that Adam engaged in sacrificial worship even though idolatry did not yet exist is likely polemically directed at Maimonides, who, in *Guide* III, 32, presented sacrificial worship as merely a concession to the idolatrous impulses of the ancient Israelites who were accustomed to a sacrificial cult. Rather than prohibiting sacrifice, which, given the religious environment, would have been untenable, God redirected the sacrificial cult to Himself. Yet, as Ezra seems to suggest, Maimonides's argument is called into question by the fact that Adam engaged in sacrifice despite the fact that idolatry did not yet exist. Nahmanides presses a similar critique of Maimonides's view in his commentary on Lev. 1:9.

58. See Tishby, *Studies* 31.

59. My translation follows the variant supplied by Scholem in "Te'udah" 26n61.

60. Cf. Wolfson, "Beyond" 180–81.

61. In addition to the example that I will discuss here, see Azriel of Gerona, *Commentary* 66; MS Vat. 441, 69b.

62. In the version that appears in MS Vat. 441, 61a, Ezra cites the rabbinic passage in an abbreviated form, mentioning only the opening statement and the example of behemoth. He then writes: יש לך לדעת כי כל החי מרגיש לבדו זכר ונקבה וזה אמת מדרך הקבלה הנכונה ואין להאריך. The first four words translate as: "You should know that." The next six words are difficult to translate and seem corrupt. A possible, albeit speculative, translation is: "that each sentient creature in and of itself is male and female." Ezra's comment ends: "And this is the truth according to the path of Kabbalah, but it should not be stated at length." Taken together, Ezra might be saying that each individual creature has male and female aspects and that in this notion is some sort of kabbalistic secret, which may not be expanded upon. The other version, extant in Almalikh 17b, cites the rabbinic passage in a fuller form and then adds: כי

החי שאינו מרגיש כמו זכר ונקבה בראם וזה נימא מדרך הקבלה ואין להאריך. Again, the text seems corrupt, and the translation here is only speculative: "Regarding the creature that is not sentient, like a male and female He created them. And this was stated according to the path of Kabbalah, but it should not be stated at length." According to this version, then, it is nonsentient creatures, i.e., plants, that were created as male and female. The bisexual nature of date palms was already a topic of theosophic speculation in *Sefer ha-bahir* (Abrams, 201, sec. 117; 223, sec. 139), and it is possible that Ezra's comment has some connection to this point. Note that the underlying rabbinic passage was frequently commented on by other Kabbalists. See Idel, "Leviathan." In *Song Commentary* 510, Ezra regards Leviathan as referring to the angels associated with the lowest sefirah but does not mention the question of gender. On the passage in *Song Commentary*, see Idel, "Leviathan" 163; M. Fishbane, *Biblical Myth* 273–74.

63. Cf. Scholem, *Ha-kabbalah* 39–40.

64. See Tishby's comment in Azriel of Gerona, *Commentary* 41.

65. Tishby (Azriel of Gerona, *Commentary* 43) also notes that a few passages in *Aggadot Commentary* are longer and explain matters more clearly. He argues that these are apparently instances where Ezra felt a need for greater explicitness and that he was not bothered by a need for secrecy. Tishby does not explain which passages he has in mind. Earlier, he contends that "in almost all" the longer explanations in *Aggadot Commentary*, "the concealed is greater than the revealed" (41). Apparently, he must have had in mind a very limited number of passages that he viewed as exceptional. Rather than using these exceptions as evidence of Ezra's general approach, it might be more profitable to examine whether there is something about the themes of these particular passages that allows Ezra to abandon his esoteric stance.

66. Based on MS Vienna 148, 3b; and MS Vat. 86, 5a. *Song Commentary* 480 reads "my explanation."

67. Cf. Dan (*History* 8:118), who writes, regarding the phrase "reveal my explanation [of Song of Songs] in hints" (note that Dan uses the version of the text edited by Chavel—see the previous note): "It is possible to conclude from here that there are matters that the author chose to continue keeping secret."

68. See the overview of various current conceptions of the sefirot in Sendor 61–72. See also Tirosh-Samuelson, "Kabbalah" 483–85.

69. It does mention (*Song Commentary* 480; Brody 28) that the Canticle describes the details of the divine throne, without, in this context, mentioning the details. Thus the uninitiated reader will be able to understand that the text describes this matter but will not know how it does so. Ezra also alludes to the kabbalistic doctrine of the *shemittot* (ibid.)— the seven cosmic cycles of the world. This allusion would likely not be understood by the uninitiated reader.

70. While, in the first principle, Ezra does not explicitly mention the interpretation according to which Song of Songs is an account of the relationship between God and Israel, he does explicitly refer to it a little earlier in the introduction. See *Song Commentary* 480; Brody 25–26.

71. "Words that have no parallels that would explain their meaning" translates, מלות אשר אין להם חבר להורות [כ״י וטיקן 86, 6א: להורותך] הענין (corrected on the basis of MS Vienna 148, 4a; MS Vat. 86, 6a). Cf. Vajda (47), "qu'aucune autre attestation scripturaire." Chavel (481) reads: מלות אשר אין להם ספר להורות הענין ("words which would have no book that would explain their meaning"). Similarly, Brody (30) reads: "Words whose meaning is not revealed by any book."

72. The simple translation of the original verse is "the beginning of wisdom," but Ezra intends that the "beginning" is identified with the sefirah of "wisdom."

73. The notion that God dons tefillin is derived from B. Berakhot 6a, which Ezra cites immediately before this passage. See ch. 3, pp. 67–8.

74. Travis (14n68, Hebr. sec.) notes that this sentence is not found in all the mss.

75. My translation follows that of Travis (197, Eng. sec.), with only slight emendations. The passage has a partial parallel in *Aggadot Commentary* MS Vat. 441, 2b; Azriel, *Commentary* 66. The fact that Ezra included a parallel of a passage found in *Aggadot Commentary*—a work that surely was not intended for a novice—in *Song Commentary* demonstrates my thesis that *Song Commentary* should itself be regarded as an esoteric work.

76. In contrast to my reading, Dan argues that Ezra removes any erotic elements from his exegesis of the Canticle. He debates whether this is the result of intentional esotericism or simply a function of the fact that Ezra was not intellectually inclined to such exegesis. He concludes that, while there is no decisive evidence one way or the other, the latter possibility is more likely. This is because, according to Dan, we find a similar state of affairs in the other works of Ezra and Azriel. Needless to say, in light of all the evidence that I have collected in this book thus far (and will continue to collect in the remaining pages), in my view the first possibility is correct. It was standard practice in Isaac's circle to conceal such elements. Ezra's mode of concealing, to repeat, involves talking in terms that would be familiar only to those with access to the symbolism of his circle.

From Dan's perspective, according to either possibility, Ezra omitted erotic elements from the work. In my view, it is not that he omitted them but that he recorded them in an esoteric style. Dan concedes that it is possible to find such elements "with great difficulty" (*be-doḥak*) in select verses. One of these verses is Song 4:9, which I will discuss below. I disagree with Dan's assessment that there is difficulty (presuming knowledge of kabbalistic symbolism) in finding such elements in this verse or in other verses that I will discuss. Other scholars have also taken it as apparent (again, with the benefit of knowledge of early kabbalistic symbolism) that this theme is an important aspect of the work. See, e.g., Vajda 320–28; M. Fishbane, *JPS Bible Commentary* 294–95.

77. See Green, "Intradivine."

78. Ibid. 217–18.

79. See *Midrash tanḥuma, parashat naso'* 26 (Buber 2:28).

80. Slight corrections were made on the basis of MS Vienna 148 8b; and MS Vat. 86, 11a.

81. See Scholem, *On the Mystical Shape* 154–55; Urbach 31–32.

82. הדור. Here I am following the version in MS Vat. 86, 15b. This is the reading followed by Vajda 84. MS Vienna 148, 13a reads הסוד ("the secret"), and Chavel 495 reads ההוד ("the splendor"). These latter two versions make little sense.

83. Despite Lorberbaum's significant disagreements with Idel's interpretation of Nahmanides's kabbalistic stance, he does agree with him on this score. See Lorberbaum, "Did Nahmanides" 330.

84. Idel has made this case in numerous studies. In addition to "Nahmanides," see "Commentaries" and the studies listed there, 7n4.

85. See the discussions in Lorberbaum, "Did Nahmanides" 337–39; Ju. Weiss; Yisraeli, *R. Moses* 191–97, 236–47.

86. Idel presents a comment of the poet Meshullam da Piera as backing up his claim: "We have the son of Nahman as a strong tower [*migdal 'oz*]/ Even if his horses do not neigh or gallop/ Ezra and Azriel and my other friends/ Exposed [some] views [*de'ot*] to me and did not lie" (H. Brody 104, lines 85–86, following the translation of Idel "Nahmanides" 22 with slight emendations).

Idel writes, with regard to these remarks, that "the difference between the reticence of Nahmanides and the readiness of the two other kabbalists to teach their views to the poet is obvious. . . . Though he is a stronghold, Nahmanides is a silent, perhaps also a solitary figure. As a group, the others are more open to imparting their knowledge to others" (22). Yet it is not clear that there are any broad implications, in Meshullam's remarks, concerning the respective views of these Kabbalists vis-à-vis the secrecy of kabbalistic doctrines. Meshullam may be making only the limited observation that Ezra and Azriel were willing to teach him Kabbalah while Nahmanides was not. Indeed, in the continuation of the poem, he makes it quite clear that Ezra and Azriel and, indeed, he himself, were very reluctant to reveal kabbalistic ideas. As partially cited above, (150–51) he says of Ezra and Azriel: "They were cautious about explicating that which is precious/ They know the measure of their Creator (*shi'ur yotseram*)/ But they held back their words for fear of heretics/ And I Meshullam ben Solomon will desist from words/ And my hands will be guarded from writing" (Brody 104, lines 85–89; 105, line 90). As I will argue in the next section, however, when Azriel's extant writings are taken into account, he emerges as a considerably more exoteric figure than Nahmanides or Ezra.

87. See also the brief comments in Halbertal, *Concealment* 77–78.

88. The conclusion that Azriel studied with Isaac is based partly on the testimonies of late thirteenth- and fourteenth-century Kabbalists. See Tishby *Studies* 5–6; Yisraeli, "Jewish Medieval" 23–31. The lateness of these testimonies, however, makes them suspect. Tishby (*Studies* 6–7) seeks to illustrate the indebtedness of Azriel's *Commentary on the Talmudic Aggadoth* to Isaac's terminology. Most of the evidence for the alleged indebtedness is based on a comparison to *Commentary on Sefer Yetsirah*, attributed to Isaac the Blind. Since, however, as seen in Chap. 4, Bar-Asher has shown that *Commentary on Sefer Yetsirah* is misattributed, most of the evidence can be dismissed.

89. Tishby (Azriel, *Commentary* 15–25) meticulously documents the manner in which Azriel reworked Ezra's *Aggadot Commentary*.

90. With the exception of his *Commentary on the Talmudic Aggadoth*, the extant works of Azriel have recently been published in a critical edition by Porat. For details on earlier publications of many of his works, see Porat, *Kabbalistic* 6–7.

91. Cf. Scholem, *Origins* 376.

92. The manuscript version of the text that underlies Porat's edition adds here *dateinu ve-emunat*, such that the text reads: "By this we guard the belief of our faith and the belief of our heart but not the statement of our mouth." This addition is not found in any of the other manuscripts that Porat (*Kabbalistic* 183) includes in his critical apparatus. As Porat (17) notes, the manuscript that underlies his main edition was written by a scribe who made additions to the text before him. The addition here is apparently an example of this phenomenon.

93. Brackets in the original.

94. Somewhat uncharacteristically, this detail is already revealed by Ezra in a partially parallel passage that appears in *Aggadot Commentary* (MS Vat. 441, 2b): "The fourth [chamber of the tefillin, containing] "And it shall be" (Deut. 11:13–21), [pertains to] the attribute of hard judgment (*din ha-kasheh*). [This is] the fifth sefirah, which is called 'strength' (*'oz*), and it is the left hand of the Holy One, blessed be He." Still, without the help of a text such as Azriel's, the reader of *Aggadot Commentary* would be unable to grasp the meaning of the passage.

95. See, esp., Porat, *Kabbalistic* 21–22 (question 5).

96. Each of these texts is a poetic description of the sefirot that presents various symbolic terms associated with each sefirah. The latter text covers only the first five sefirot, but this may be because the entire text is not preserved (see Bos and Pellow 368). Neither text is

as clear as that of Azriel's, although this may partly be a result of the poetic style. Nevertheless, the text by Barzillai is considerably clearer than the one by Jacob. Moreover, both texts systematically describe each sefirah such that even a novice reader could make significant headway. Another anonymous Geronese commentary on the sefirot, probably from the same period (T. Weiss and Ben-Shachar), is similar to Barzillai's work in terms of its level of clarity, and it, too, would be useful to a novice reader.

97. On these guides, see T. Weiss and Ben-Shachar and the studies listed there, 159nn1–2.

CHAPTER 6. ESOTERICISM AND DIVINE UNITY IN ASHER BEN DAVID

1. Scholem, *Origins* 401; A. ben David 23–25; Idel, "Nahmanides" 34, 37; Halbertal, *By Way* 302–5 and *Concealment* 72–76, 153–54.

2. As Idel ("Nahmanides" 30–32) notes, there is no evidence that Asher ever traveled to Gerona to deal with the illicit dissemination of kabbalistic secrets, so his mission may never have come to fruition.

3. All references to *Sefer ha-yiḥud* are to the edition prepared by Abrams.

4. At the end of the manuscript of *Sefer ha-yiḥud*, used by Abrams in his critical edition, there is additional material, which Abrams (A. ben David 18) suggests may also have been composed by Asher. Additionally, there is a short commentary on the opening of Genesis in Asher's name published by Abrams (325–29). D. Schwartz, "Perush ha-amitti" 49–50 and Bar-Asher, *Journeys* 59–62, argue for the authenticity of this attribution.

5. I.e., "the knowledgeable will understand." As detailed in Chap. 2, this formula is used to express that a particular idea is being composed in an esoteric style.

6. In "Te'udah" 14, Scholem suggests that the anti-kabbalistic letter was composed before 1240. In his later *Origins* (397), however, he suggests that the letter was written between 1235 and 1245. The first view seems to be correct. Meir states that he wrote the letter with the approbation of Meshullam ben Moses, of whom he says, "May God protect him." As T. Weiss notes in an article in which he provides an edition of Meir's letter ("Their Heart" 308), since Meshullam died around 1240, the letter must have been composed before this date (for the portion of the text mentioning Meshullam, see 336).

7. T. Weiss ("Their Heart" 307–19) argues that previous scholarship has been misguided in its perception that Meir's missive was directed at the works of the first Kabbalists. Rather, he argues, Meir's true targets were unknown figures who espoused binitarian views, to which the first Kabbalists themselves also objected. Indeed, he suggests that Meir had only heard of the works of the first kabbalists but had not actually read them. Weiss's provocative argument requires a lengthy response, which is not possible here. Suffice it to say that he makes a compelling case that Meir was responding to views rejected by the Kabbalists. Nevertheless, in contrast to his view, it is clear that Meir was *also* referring to the works of the first Kabbalists, even if he did not distinguish, as the Kabbalists themselves would have, between these works and the works of the unknown figures. Meir (336) names a number of works that came into his hands, including a commentary on the Song of Songs, which apparently refers to Ezra's work. Weiss (310) argues that Meir's wording suggests that he had only heard of these works and had not actually seen them. Accordingly, Meir writes: "We have also *heard* that additionally [the following works] were written for them: *Commentary on*

the Song of Songs" (336). Yet from the continuation of the very same passage, it is clear that these works were indeed in Meir's possession, as he concludes: "Inquire and investigate carefully, and if these books are in your midst, burn them . . . just as we have burned these books that are found in our midst" (336). Meir, then, states explicitly that he burned the works of the first Kabbalists, which, of course, means that they were in his possession. See also n. 12 below.

8. If Asher is, indeed, responding to Meir's critique, it would date the composition of *Sefer ha-yiḥud* to about 1240, or, in more precise terms, it would date Asher's final edition of the work to this time. Indeed, any attempt to date *Sefer ha-yiḥud* needs to take into account its complex and not fully clear redactional history. As Abrams (A. ben Asher 14–18) meticulously documents, in MS Moscow, Guenzburg 321, *Sefer ha-yiḥud* includes the following four sections: "Commentary on the Thirteen Attributes," "Commentary on Vows," "Commentary on the Divine Name," and a conclusion and summary. It is in the conclusion and summary that he explains that he wrote the work to respond to Kabbalah's critics. Yet in numerous other manuscripts, individual sections of the text appear independently. In his critical edition of the text (16), Abrams suggests that Asher originally composed the entire text, as it is found in MS Moscow, Guenzburg 321, and later copyists separated the work into individual sections, giving the impression that they are individual freestanding works. In a later study, however, Abrams (*Kabbalistic Manuscripts* 538) revises his view and suggests that Asher himself may have originally composed separate works, which he assembled into the larger *Sefer ha-yiḥud* at a later date. Thus, if Abrams is correct, we should assign different dates to each individual component of the text, as well as to the reissued composite text. In this scenario, it is reasonable to assume that the "conclusion and summary" section of the work, in which Asher mentions the various sections of *Sefer ha-yiḥud* and summarizes the work's content, was added by Asher when he assembled the composite text. It is possible that it was the attacks against Kabbalah that led him to reissue the work as a way of defending Kabbalists. As I will suggest in subsequent notes, some of Asher's emphatic exoteric statements in favor of divine simplicity, as well as some of his esoteric allusions to a seeming counterview, appear only in the final version of the text.

9. Following the variant that appears in MS London 756, 131a. See Abrams's critical apparatus in A. Ben Asher 120n92.

10. Cf. Ben-Shalom, *Jews of Provence* 604.

11. Cf. Bar-Asher, "Isaac" 418.

12. As Scholem (*Ha-kabbalah be-gerona* 47) points out, Meir ben Simeon of Narbonne, in his aforementioned anti-kabbalistic missive, seems to single out the works of Ezra and Azriel as works that he burned because of their heretical contents. Thus Meir mentions that he burned "*Commentary on Song of Songs, Sefer Yetsirah*, and *heikhalot*" (T. Weiss, "Their Heart" 336). *Commentary on Song of Songs*, as noted above, is likely the work by Ezra. The word "Commentary" might refer not only to the Song of Songs but also to *Sefer Yetsirah*, such that the reference to the latter might not mean the work itself but a commentary on it. If so, this could refer to the no longer extant commentary on *Sefer Yetsirah* apparently composed by Ezra or to Azriel's commentary on the work.

13. The esoteric passages appear on the following pages: 57, 62, 63, 65, 85, 88, 90, 101, 105 (twice), 107, 111, 113, 114, 115, and 116 (twice).

14. Pedaya (*Name* 129) argues that Asher employs this technique to conceal a secret idea concerning a rupture in God in which the lowest sefirah is cut off from the emanative flow of the upper sefirot. I will not discuss this secret here.

15. Wolfson ("Wings" 212–21) has pointed out that some of the early Kabbalists accepted Maimonides's position that the Bible and rabbinic literature were written in an esoteric style. It seems that Asher also accepted this position.

16. He may very well be referring to a tradition that derives from Jacob ben Saul (= Jacob the Nazarite), a contemporary of Rabad. A teaching that is preserved in a number of manuscripts in the name of Jacob similarly states that this *vav* is a reference to "the six extremities." See Scholem, *Re'shit* 73n2. The phrase "six extremities" derives from *Sefer Yetsirah* (Hayman 89 § 15 = 1:13, 130 § 38 = 4:3).

17. Such an interpretation was also offered in an anonymous text published by Idel ("Kabbalistic Prayer" 285), which he attributes to Jacob ben Saul (274, 286), the figure whom I mentioned in n. 16 above.

18. While Asher understands the term "might," as it is employed in 1 Chron. 29:11, as a reference to the fifth sefirah, known as the sefirah of "upper judgment," here Asher seems to have the tenth sefirah, which is also known as "lower judgment," in mind. This is the wording in the manuscript that is the base text of Abrams's edition, MS Moscow, Guenzburg 321. It is also possible that the text is corrupt. In alternative versions of the text provided by Abrams in (A. ben David 224) from MS JTS 1069 and MS Munich 11, the text reads: "'Yes, all' is an attribute and sefirah that completes each and every activity below and above." In these versions, the term "sefirah" replaces the term "might" (*gevurah*). According to either reading, the reference is to the tenth sefirah.

19. Once again, Asher's understanding, here, of "yes, all" is in keeping with that found in the anonymous text, mentioned in n. 17 above, which Idel ascribed to Jacob ben Saul. See Idel, "Kabbalistic Prayer" 285.

20. Like "six extremities," the phrase "seven extremities" derives from *Sefer Yetsirah* (Hayman 130 § 38 = 4:3).

21. Earlier in *Sefer ha-yiḥud*, the seventh extremity is referred to as the "cause of causes" (65). Later, the "cause of causes" is explicitly identified with the first sefirah (101). Elsewhere in *Sefer ha-yiḥud*, the seventh extremity is referred to generically as the "Holy One, blessed be He" (see, e.g., 84, 87). It seems, however, that in these passages, too, the first sefirah is implied. This is clear on p. 84, where the action of the Holy One, blessed be He (the seventh extremity), which He carries out through the lower six extremities, is presented as the activity of "His glory and will." "Will" is a reference to the first sefirah (see n. 43 below).

22. This is implied in a parallel passage earlier in *Sefer ha-yiḥud* (68). There he writes that the "seven attributes that are in the seven extremities" "are connected to *Ein Sof*." He then explains that "these seven are alluded to in the candelabra made by Betsalel, which was made without being composed from an extraneous place, and all its vessels were made from one block." It seems that "one block" is parallel to *Ein Sof*.

23. Cf. 107, 118. Elsewhere in this study, I render *middah* as "attribute." Here, I render it as "dimension" because, in this description of the sefirot, Asher's focus is on their dimensionality.

24. See also Sendor 307; A. ben David 25–27; Valabregue-Perry 128–32, 144–48; and see Gottlieb, *Studies* 315.

25. Asher (101) cites this verse immediately after the esoteric passage.

26. This passage occurs shortly before another esoteric passage cited below.

27. Thus, as I pointed out (see n. 18 above), Asher refers to both the fifth and the tenth sefirot as judgment. This is common in kabbalistic sources.

28. Asher also identifies "all" with the ninth sefirah in the poem with which he introduces *Sefer ha-yiḥud* (50).

29. Wolfson ("Images" 164–68) has observed that, in kabbalistic literature, "feet" often functions as a euphemism for the phallic ninth sefirah. It is quite possible that Asher shared this understanding. Thus, he may have understood "under his feet" as a reference to the sefirah beneath the ninth sefirah, i.e., the tenth sefirah.

30. I would add that while this passage is found in MS Moscow, Guenzburg 321, the manuscript that underlies Abrams's edition, it is missing in MS JTS 1609. In MS Paris hebr. 763, it appears in a slightly different form without the words "the knowledgeable will understand." See A. ben David 251. If Abrams is correct that MS Moscow, Guenzburg 321 is Asher's final draft of the work (see n. 8 above), then he only explicitly identified the esoteric hint at a later date.

31. Cf. 86, 104.

32. That "judgment" here refers to the fifth sefirah is clear from the context, where he also refers to "lovingkindness" and "mercy"—the fourth and sixth sefirot. As we will see, however, in the esoteric hint, "judgment" refers to the tenth sefirah.

33. For the rabbinic source, see Mann 1:271; Wertheimer and Wertheimer 1:141.

34. See, e.g., *Sifrei Deuteronomy*, sec. 27.

35. Note that this passage is found only in MS Moscow, Guenzburg 321, the manuscript that underlies Abrams's critical editions and not in the other versions of the text that Abrams supplies. See A. ben David 178. Following Abrams's theory (see n. 8 above) that the version in MS Moscow, Guenzburg 321 reflects Asher's final draft, Asher added this passage at a later date.

36. In this chap., I use the version found in MS Vat. 294, published by Abrams (A. ben David 310–12). The relevant passage appears on 311.

37. The relationship of the passage in Azriel's *Commentary on the Talmudic Aggadoth* to the first passage was noted by Tishby in Azriel, *Commentary* 94n1 and in *Studies* 6–7.

38. Azriel (*Commentary* 93–94) comments on Isa. 45:8, "Shower down, O heavens, from above and let the skies pour down righteousness; let the earth open and be fruitful. Let salvation and righteousness spring up together; I the Lord have created it." According to Azriel, "Shower down, O heavens from above" (Isa. 45:8) describes the manner in which the heavens pour down efflux (= rain), which originates in the skies mentioned in the continuation of the verse ("and let the skies pour down righteousness"). In this reading, "heavens" and "skies" are not synonymous, as a simple reading of the verse implies. Rather, the skies are at a higher station than the heavens. In particular, Azriel identifies the "skies" with the "simple elements," a reference to the second, third, fourth, and fifth sefirot (see Tishby's note in Azriel, *Commentary* 93n12). The "heavens" that receive from the "skies" are therefore a reference to the following sefirah—i.e., the sixth sefirah. In the continuation of his account, he explains that the rain/efflux will ultimately make its way to the tenth sefirah, from where it will flow into our world: "For the rains fall by means of judgment and by means of righteousness, which is the attribute of judgment of the world" (94). As Tishby explains (94n1), the reference here is to the lower divine judgment, otherwise known as the tenth sefirah. In the immediate continuation, it is clear that the term "earth" in the continuation of Isa. 45:8 ("Let the earth open") is a reference to the lower divine judgement, or tenth sefirah. Thus, in reference to this part of the verse, Azriel adds: "Like this female who is open to a male, and she receives those fluids, and they are both fruitful together. For the earth also emits

fluids from beneath her, and they couple one with the other, and both are fruitful together" (94). The earth therefore is the feminine tenth sefirah, which receives the efflux from the male sixth sefirah. This union triggers the emission of efflux below.

39. The opening of the passage in "Commentary on Creation" reads: "'[In the day that the Lord God made] earth and heaven' (Gen. 2:4): This refers to heaven and earth, which were created together like a pot and its lid [based on *Bere'shit rabba'* 1:15 (ed. Theodor-Albeck 13–14)]. And their beginning was from a center point, which is Zion. And it spread out to here and to there" (A. ben David 311).

There is some support for identifying heaven and earth with the fourth and fifth sefirot, respectively, rather than with the sixth and tenth sefirot. This support comes from a parallel passage, earlier in the "Commentary on Creation," in which the words "heaven" and "earth," from Gen 1:1, are identified, using language taken from *Sefer Yetsirah* (Hayman 76–77, sec. 7 = 1:4), as the "dimension of good" and the "dimension of evil." After this identification is presented, the following gloss is added: "With a united thing that was divided into two" (A. ben David 310). In other words, two sefirot, known as heaven and earth, were originally joined together in a third sefirah and were subsequently split into two distinct sefirot. This is the same basic idea as that found in our passage according to which heaven and earth spread out from a center point known as "Zion." Identifying the sefirotic referents of "dimension of good" and "dimension of evil" would thus help identify the sefirotic referents in both passages. In Azriel's *Commentary on Sefer Yetsirah* (Porat, *Kabbalistic* 152), the terms "dimension of good" and "dimension of evil" are interpreted as references to the fourth and fifth sefirot. Furthermore, it seems that Zion, the point from which heaven and earth spread out, is a reference to the third sefirah. This accords well with the notion that heaven and earth are the fourth and fifth sefirot that emerge from it. Other evidence, however, outweighs these considerations and makes an identification of heaven and earth, in the original passage, with the sixth and tenth sefirot more likely. First, earth is explicitly identified with the tenth sefirah ("it is the end of all [*sof hakol*]") elsewhere in the "Commentary on Creation" (A. ben David 310). Second, later in our passage, Ezra speaks of "clouds of glory" emerging from the earth. These "clouds of glory" are related to the tenth sefirah, as is corroborated in Ben Sheshet, *Sefer meshiv* 74–75, lines 10–17; see also 86, lines 204–16. This is yet another confirmation, therefore, that "earth" refers to the tenth sefirah. Third, heaven and earth are identified with the sixth and tenth sefirot in the related passage in Azriel's *Commentary on the Talmudic Aggadoth* (as seen in the previous note). If this understanding of heaven and earth is correct, we must assume that the dimension of good and the dimension of evil should be identified with the sixth and tenth sefirot. This is certainly plausible insofar as in early kabbalistic sources, the sixth sefirah is typically referred to as mercy, the source of good, and the tenth sefirah is often referred to as (lower) judgment, the source of evil. By the same token, it is also plausible, given the theosophic views of the first Kabbalists, to view the sixth and tenth sefirot as divided forms of the third sefirah. The sixth and tenth sefirot are, after all, following the logic of early kabbalistic theosophy, effectively lower versions of the fourth and fifth sefirot such that they, too, can be perceived as a split form of the third sefirah.

40. Regarding the verse, the opening of the passage, basing itself on *Bere'shit rabba'* 1:15 (ed. Theodor-Albeck 13–14), states: "This refers to heaven and earth, which were created together like a pot and its lid" (A. ben David 311). The coming together of the pot and the lid should be understood as signifying the union of heaven (the sixth sefirah) and earth (the tenth sefirah). In the continuation of the passage, it becomes clear that the "full name" (*shem*

male'), i.e., YHVH *Elohim*, as it is used elsewhere in Genesis 2, reflects the unity of the sixth and tenth sefirot. Presumably, therefore, it has the same meaning in Gen. 2:4.

41. I would note that in material appended to MS Moscow, Guenzburg 321, the manuscript used by Abrams as the base text for his edition of *Sefer ha-yiḥud*, there is a discussion of human sexuality that deals with the use of YHVH *Elohim* in a different verse, Gen. 2:19. This discussion may also hint at the sexual union of the sixth and tenth sefirot. The discussion is printed in A. ben David 129. Abrams (18) suggests that this appended material may also be by Asher.

42. I have shown in n. 38 above that the passage in Azriel's *Commentary on the Talmudic Aggadoth* teaches that the efflux/rain falls as a result of the unity of the sixth and tenth sefirot. We find the same idea in the passage in "Commentary on Creation." Gen. 2:5 states: "For the LORD God had not caused it to rain upon the earth, and there was not a man to till the ground." According to Ezra (A. ben David 311), it has not yet rained because man had not yet been created and because God's name was not yet full (despite the fact that the verse employs the full name, a point I will return to below). To understand the nature of this causality, we must first consider Ezra's remarks immediately before this passage. There, he explains that "there was not yet a full name until man was created in the image of God" (ibid.). The "full name," as seen in n. 40, is a reference to the joint divine name Lord God (YHVH *Elohim*), and Ezra implies that it was during the creation of man that the union of the names Lord and God was completed. (Hence, when Gen. 2:7 describes the creation of man, it uses the full name.) Understood sefirotically, YHVH is the sixth sefirah, and *Elohim* is the tenth sefirah. The two names combined are thus a reference to the proper unity of these two sefirot. If we now return to the original passage, we realize that Ezra's point is that efflux/rain could fall only after there is a full name. Yet insofar as man had not yet been created, there was not yet a full name; hence, the rain could not fall. Why, then, does Gen. 2:5 employ the full name? Apparently, if I might paraphrase Ezra's understanding of Gen. 2:5, "YHVH *Elohim* had not caused it to rain" because, effectively, there was no "YHVH *Elohim*" yet, since man had not yet been created. Ezra, however, is not referring to actual rain but to "spiritual rain," or, in other terms, to the divine efflux that will flow as a result of the union of the two sefirot.

43. This understanding of "a time of will" is also found in the writings of other early Kabbalists. E.g., it is implied in Ezra's *Song Commentary* 514 (on v. 8:4) and perhaps in Ben Sheshet, "Sefer ha-emunah" 434. At the same time, it must be noted that for some early Kabbalists, "divine will" is a reference to the first sefirah. For example, this is the case according to Azriel (see, e.g., *Commentary* 146, 178) and even according to Asher in exoteric passages in *Sefer ha-yiḥud* (see, e.g., 106). In one exoteric context, Asher actually uses the phrase "in the time of His will" (*be-'et retsono*) in connection with the emanative flow that emerges from the first sefirah and moves through the lower sefirot: "All of their (i.e., the sefirot's) activity is dependent on the will (i.e., the first sefirah) that spreads through them in the time of His will" (67). It is possible that this is another instance of contradictory exoteric and esoteric positions, but it may also be the case that the two understandings are not mutually exclusive. From Asher's point of view, the union of the sixth and tenth sefirot may ultimately lead to the drawing down of efflux from the first sefirah. In fact, the union of the sixth and tenth sefirot might, in part, be called a "time of will" precisely because this is the moment that causes the efflux of "divine will," i.e., of the first sefirah, to spread through the lower sefirot.

44. Building on a passage in *Bere'shit rabba'* 13:13 (ed. Theodor-Albeck 122–23), Azriel describes the relationship between the tenth sefirah and the sixth sefirah as that of "a female who is open to a male, and she receives those fluids, and they are both fruitful together" (*Commentary* 94).

45. Note that this passage is part of the conclusion of the text that Asher may have added when he assembled the component parts that he had written earlier (see n. 8 above). If, as I suggested earlier, Asher issued the full text to defend against attacks on Kabbalists for not upholding divine unity, we can understand why Asher would have added this particularly emphatic presentation of divine simplicity to the final draft of the text. This state of affairs makes the esoteric hints found in this passage all the more interesting.

46. *Maskil*. Here the term *maskil* simply seems to mean an "educated one"—in philosophical texts, philosophers also refer to their readers as *maskilim* ("knowledgeable ones")—and not to those initiated into kabbalistic secrets.

47. See, e.g., Ibn Pakuda, chap. 1:10, esp. p. 121; *Guide* 1:51–53. This corresponds to 1:52–54 in Alḥarizi's translation (Scheyer and Munk 187–208). Note that this translation was preferred by the first Kabbalists. We saw earlier that both Ezra and Azriel employ this translation.

48. See, e.g., *Mishneh torah, Hilkhot yesodei ha-torah* 2:10; Scheyer and Munk 195 (*Guide* 1:51, following Alḥarizi's division of chapters, which corresponds to chap. 1:52 in the standard division). In this passage in the *Guide*, the phrase "one from every side" is used immediately following a discussion of attributes of action.

49. Here I have amended the text. The original reads *aḥerim harbeh* ("many other parts"). It seems that this is a corruption; instead, the text should read *aḥadim harbeh* ("many individual parts"), in keeping with the earlier usage of the term *aḥadim* in the same passage.

50. It should be noted that starting from "And even though we have found many things," this passage is found only in the version of text reflected in MS Moscow, Guenzburg 321, the base text for Abrams's edition. It is missing in the other versions that Abrams supplies. See A. ben David 173. If, as Abrams argues (see n. 8 above), the text in MS Moscow, Guenzburg 321 represents Asher's final draft of the work in which he assembled the component parts that he had written earlier and added the conclusion, he may have added this passage at a late stage. Here, again, I would suggest that if Asher issued the full text to defend against attacks on Kabbalists for not upholding divine unity, we can understand why Asher would have added this striking account of divine simplicity to the final draft of the text. Again, this state of affairs makes the esoteric hints found in this passage all the more striking. See also n. 45 above, where I make a similar observation about another passage in *Sefer ha-yiḥud*, which argues for divine simplicity.

51. Similar wording was also employed by Ibn Pakuda as seen in chapter 3 p. 94. This wording has an older history in philosophic sources as a way of describing divine simplicity. See Davidson, *Maimonides* 38–39.

52. As is true of the exoteric passage, the esoteric hint is also found only in the version of the text in MS Moscow, Guenzburg 321. See A. ben David 174.

53. I would note that, in this case, Asher's understanding of the names YHVH, *Elohenu*, YHVH, as they are employed in Deut. 6:4, only partially parallels the manner in which he understands the names YHVH and *Elohim* in the other esoteric passages. In those passages, as we saw, YHVH is a reference to the sixth sefirah, and *Elohim* is a reference to the tenth sefirah. His understanding here of the second YHVH in Deut. 6:4, as the sixth sefirah, is the same as his understanding of this divine name in the other esoteric passages.

His understanding, however, of the first YHVH (= fourth sefirah) and *Elohenu* (= fifth sefirah) differs from his understanding of YHVH and *Elohim* in the other esoteric passages. Such fluidity is quite common in kabbalistic literature.

54. See Hershkovits 80, 87; Ben Simeon 151; Herskowitz 17, 72–73, 121–22.

55. For a useful overview, see Chazan, *Daggers* 25–48.

56. For a recent overview of the event with an updated bibliography, see Capelli.

57. On this event, see Chazan, "Confrontation." For further discussion of the forced sermon and Meir's polemical exchanges with Christian clerics, see Chazan, *Fashioning* 105–14; Trautner-Kromann 73–84.

58. See the discussion in Goshen-Gottstein 189–95, esp. 190–91n76.

59. Cf. Shaḥar 483; Ben-Shalom, *Jews of Provence* 603.

60. Cf. Seeskin (99), who develops Davidson's point as part of a critique of Strauss.

61. For a statement of this viewpoint with regard to the emergence of "sexual polarities" in Kabbalah—the issue that concerns us here—see Idel, *Kabbalah and Eros* 49–52. For another articulation of this point of view, see idem, "'In a Whisper'" 443–88, esp. 443–55.

62. See also Mopsik, *Sex* 82–85.

63. See Hyman for a brief overview of the "naturalistic interpretation" of Maimonides, along Straussian lines, versus the "harmonistic interpretation."

CONCLUSION

1. See, e.g., Idel, "Commentaries" 5–8; "Nahmanides" 91–93; "Kabbalistic Interpretation" 95–96; "Kabbalah in Byzantium" 661–64.

Bibliography

MANUSCRIPT SOURCES

Berlin, State Library

MS Or. Phillip 1392

Florence, Laurentian Library

MS Plut.II.20
MS Plut.44.13
MS Plut.44.16

Hamburg, Hamburg State and University Library Carl von Ossietzky

MS Cod. hebr. 92

Jerusalem, National Library

MS 8°330
MS 38°1073

London, British Library

MS Add. 27003

Manchester, University of Manchester Library

MS Gaster Add. 11

Mantua, Comunità Israelitica

MS ebr. 110

Modena, Estense University Library

MS O.7.26

Munich, Bavarian State Library

MS Cod. hebr. 26
MS Cod. hebr. 341

New York, Columbia University

MS X 893 G 15

New York, Jewish Theological Seminary

MS 325
MS 827
MS 997
MS 998
MS 1641
MS 2325
MS 2419

Oxford, Bodleian Library

MS Mich. 236 (Neubauer 1956)
MS Opp. Add. Qu. 42 (Neubauer 1644)

Oxford, Christ Church Library

MS 198

Paris, National Library

MS hebr. 84

MS hebr. 774
MS hebr. 798

Parma, Palatina Library

MS Parm. 2704 (De-Rossi 68)
MS Parm. 2784 (De-Rossi 1390)
MS Parm. 2982 (De-Rossi 1072)

Ramat Gan, Israel, Bar-Ilan University

MS 598

Vatican, Apostolic Library

MS ebr. 86
MS ebr. 185
MS ebr. 202
MS ebr. 214
MS ebr. 229
MS ebr. 236
MS ebr. 274
MS ebr. 277
MS ebr. 294
MS ebr. 441
MS ebr. 505
MS Barb. Or. 110

Vienna, Austrian National Library

MS Cod. hebr. 148

PRIMARY SOURCES

Abrams, Daniel, ed. *Sefer ha-bahir*. Los Angeles: Cherub Press, 1994. Los Angeles: Cherub, 1994.
Abulafia, Abraham. *Gan na'ul*. Edited by Amnon Gross. Jerusalem: Aharon Barzani u-veno, 1999.
———. *Ner elohim; get ha-shemot*. Edited by Amnon Gross. Jerusalem: Aharon Barzani u-veno, 2002.
Abulafia, Todros. *Otsar ha-kavod*. Navidvar, 1808.

———. *Otsar ha-kavod*. Satmar: M.L. Hirsh, 1926.
———. *Otsar ha-kavod ha-shalem*. Edited by Ya'akov Shapira. Warsaw, 1879.
———. *Sha'ar ha-razim*. Edited by Michal Kushnir-Oron. Jerusalem: Bialik Institute, 1989.
Almalikh, Abraham ben Judah, ed. *Likkutei shikheḥah u-fe'ah*. Ferar: Be-vet Avraham n. Ushki, 1556.
Avot de-Rabbi Natan. Edited by Solomon Schechter. New York: Feldheim, 1945.
Azriel of Gerona. *Commentary on the Talmudic Aggadoth*. Edited by Isaiah Tishby. Jerusalem: Magnes, 1982 [Hebrew].
Azulai, Abraham. *Ḥesed le-Avraham*. Edited by Yitsḥak Mosheh Erlanger. Jerusalem: Makhon sha'arei ziv, 1995.
———. *Or ha-ḥammah*. Jerusalem: Yo'el Mosheh Solomon, 1879.
Azulai, Ḥayyim Josef David. *Kunteres zahav sagur*. Edited by Yuval Ivagi. Bnei Brak, 2014.
Barnay, Ya'akov. *Hasidic Letters from Eretz-Israel*. Jerusalem: Yad Yitsḥak ben-Tsevi, 1980 [Hebrew].
Barzillai, Judah. *Perush sefer yetsirah*. Edited by Amnon Gross. Tel Aviv: Aharon Barzani u-veno, 2007.
Bei'ur le-ferush ha-Ramba"n z"l 'al ha-torah. Warsaw: Y. Lebenzohn, 1875.
ben David, Abraham. *Ba'alei ha-nefesh*. Edited by Yosef Kafaḥ. Jerusalem: Mossad Harav Kook, 1964.
———. *Commentary on the Treatise of Abodah Zarah*. Edited by Abraham Schreiber. New York, 1960 [Hebrew].
———. *Hassagot ha-Rabad le-Mishneh Torah . . . Corrected According to Ten Different Manuscripts*. Edited by Bezalel Na'or. Jerusalem: B. Na'or, 1983 [Hebrew].
ben David, Asher. *R. Asher ben David: His Complete Works and Studies in His Kabbalistic Thought*. Edited by Daniel Abrams. Los Angeles: Cherub, 1996 [Hebrew].
ben Isaac of Narbonne, Abraham. *Sefer ha-eshkol*. Edited by Shalom Albeck and Chanoch Albeck. Jerusalem: Mekize Nirdamim, 1937.
ben Jacob of Kiev, Moses. *Sefer shoshan sodot*. Petah Tikva, Israel: Or ha-ganuz, 1995.
ben Joseph, Saadia. *The Book of Beliefs and Opinions*. Translated by Samuel Rosenblatt. New Haven, CT: Yale University Press, 1976.
ben Ruben, Jacob. *Milḥamot ha-shem*. Edited by Judah Rosenthal. Jerusalem: Mossad Harav Kook, 1963.
ben Sheshet, Jacob. "Sefer ha-emunah veha-bittaḥon." In *Kitvei Ramban*, edited by Charles Ber Chavel, 2:341–448. Jerusalem: Mossad Harav Kook, 1967.
———. *Sefer meshiv devarim nekhoḥim*. Edited by Georges Vajda. Jerusalem: Ha-akademyah ha-le'ummit ha-yisra'elit le-mada'im, 1968.
———. "Sha'ar ha-shamayim." Edited by Mordechai Mortara. *Ozar Neḥmad* 3 (1860): 153–65.
ben Simeon, Meir. *Commentary on the Hoshanot, Sefer ha-Mikhtam*. Edited by Abraham Sofer. New York: Defus hadar, 1959 [Hebrew].
ben Solomon, Ezra. "Commentary on the Song of Songs" ("Perush shir ha-shirim"). In *Kitvei Ramban*, edited by Charles Ber Chavel, 2:473–548. Jerusalem: Mossad Harav Kook, 1967
Blavatsky, Helena Petrovna *The Secret Doctrine: The Synthesis of Science, Religion, and Philosophy*. Vol. 1. 1888. Reprint, Pasadena, CA: Theosophical University Press, 2014. https://www.theosociety.org/pasadena/sd-pdf/SecretDoctrineVol1_eBook.pdf.
Bos, Gerrit, and Eric Pellow. "Ma'amar Rabbi Barzillai: A Commentary on the Ten 'Sefirot' by Rabbi Barzillai of Gerona." *Sefunot* 7 (1999): 367–77 [Hebrew].

Brody, H. "Poems of Mešullām ben Šelōmō da Piera." *Studies of the Research Institute for Hebrew Poetry in Jerusalem* 4 (1938): 3–117 [Hebrew].
Brody, Seth, trans. *Commentary on the Song of Songs*. By Ezra ben Solomon of Gerona. Kalamazoo, MI: Medieval Institute Publications, 1999.
Chavel, Charles Ber, ed. *Kitvei Ramban*. Vol. 2. Jerusalem: Mossad Harav Kook, 1967.
Cordovero, Moshe. *Sefer ha-zohar 'im perush or yaker*. Vol. 21. Jerusalem: Aḥuzzat yisra'el, 1990.
———. *Sefer pardes rimmonim*. Munkács: Kahn and Fried, 1906.
Coriat, Judah. *Ma'or va-shemesh*. Livorno: A. M. Oyolingi, 1839.
de la Rosa, Ḥayyim. *Sefer torat ḥakham*. Jerusalem: Mif'al torat ḥakham, 2005.
de León, Moses. *Sefer mishkan ha-'edut*. Edited by Avishai Bar-Asher. Los Angeles: Cherub, 2013.
Gavrin, Martel. "*Perush ha-tefillah*, by Azriel of Gerona." Master's thesis, Harvard University, 1984.
Gikatilla, Joseph. *Sha'arei orah*. Edited by Yosef Ben-Shlomo. Jerusalem: Bialik Institute, 1970.
Goldreich, Amos. "Sefer me'irat 'einayim le-R. Yitsḥak de-Min 'Akko." Ph.D. diss., Hebrew University, 1981.
Hai Ricchi, Raphael Immanuel. *Yosher levav*. Amsterdam, 1742.
Halberstam, S. J., ed. *Kevutsat mikhtavim be-'inyenei ha-maḥloket 'al devar sefer ha-moreh vehamada'*. Bamberg: Max G. Schmidt'schen Officin, 1875.
Hayman, A. Peter, ed. *Sefer Yeṣirah: Edition, Translation and Text-Critical Commentary*. Tübingen: Mohr Siebeck, 2004.
Hershkovits, Yehudah. "Ma'amar meshiv nefesh le-R. Meir ben R. Shim'on ha-Me'ili." *Yeshurun* 27 (2012): 60–118.
Heshel, Avraham Yehoshua'. *Letters of the Ohev Yisroel*. Revised ed. Jerusalem: Mekhon siftei tsaddikim, 1999 [Hebrew].
———. *Ohev yisra'el ha-shalem*. Jerusalem: Mekhon siftei tsaddikim, 1988.
———. *Torat emet*. Bnei Berak: Mishor, 1990.
Higger, Michael, ed. "Pirkei de-rabbi Eli'ezer." *Horeb* 8 (1944): 82–119.
Holzer, Dovid, ed. *Mikra'ot gedolot ha-ḥut ha-meshulash*. Jerusalem: 'Al ha-ri'shonim, 2012.
Holzer, Zechariah, ed. *Perush Morenu h"h R. Yitsḥak b. R Yosef z.l.h.h hu' R. Yitsḥak Dapira 'al ha-torah*. Miami Beach, FL: 'Al ha-ri'shonim, 2011.
Ibn Gaon, Shem Tov ben Abraham. "Keter shem tov." In *'Ammudei ha-kabbalah*. Vol. 1. Jerusalem: Nezer Sheraga, 2001.
———. "Sefer baddei ha-aron." In *'Ammudei ha-kabbalah*. Vol. 1. Jerusalem: Nezer Sheraga, 2001.
Ibn Pakuda, Baḥya ben Joseph. *Sefer ḥovot ha-levavot*. Edited by Avraham Tsifroni. Translated by Judah Ibn Tibbon. Tel Aviv: Maḥbarot le-sifrut, 1964.
Jacob Joseph of Polnoye. *Toldot Ya'akov Yosef.* Koretz: Tsevi Hirsh, 1780.
Lichtenberg, Abraham ben Aryeh, ed. "Iggrot kanna'ut." In *Kovets teshuvot ha-Rambam ve-iggrotav*. Leipzig: H. L. Shnuis, 1859.
Luria, Solomon ben Jehiel. *Sefer she'elot u-teshuvot Maharshal*. Jerusalem: Otsar ha-sefarim, 1969.
Maimonides, Moses. *Mishneh torah, Rambam meduyyak*. 14 vols. Edited by Isaac Shailat. Ma'aleh Adumim, Israel: Hotsa'at Shailat, 2004–2021.

———. *Moreh ha-nevukhim*. Edited by Yehuda Even-Shemuel. Translated by Samuel Ibn Tibbon. Jerusalem: Mossad Harav Kook, 2000.

———. *The Guide of the Perplexed*. Translated by Shlomo Pines. Chicago: University of Chicago Press, 1963.

Margaliot, Reuben, ed. "Or ha-ganuz." In *Sefer ha-bahir/tikkunei zohar*. Jerusalem: Mossad Harav Kook, 1977.

Mekhilta de-rabbi Yishma'el. Jerusalem: Bamberger and Wahrman, 1960.

Midrash tehillim. Edited by Salomon Buber. Vilna: Romm, 1891.

Midrash tanhuma ha-kadum veha-yashan. Edited by Salomon Buber. 2 vols. Vilna: Romm, 1885.

Mondshine, Yehoshua, ed. *Shivhe ha-Ba'al Shem Tov: A Facsimile of a Unique Manuscript, Variant Versions and Appendices*. Jerusalem: Hanahal, 1982 [Hebrew].

Nahmanides. *Hiddushei ha-Ramban*. Edited by Moshe Hershler. 5 vols. Jerusalem: Mekhon ha-talmud ha-yisre'eli ha-shalem, 1970–95.

———. *Perushei ha-torah le-rabbenu Mosheh ben Nahman*. Edited by Charles Ber Chavel. Vol. 1. Jerusalem: Mossad Harav Kook, 1960.

———. "Torat ha-adam." In *Kitvei Ramban*, edited by Charles Ber Chavel, 2:9-311. Jerusalem: Mossad Harav Kook, 1963.

Porat, Oded. *Kabbalistic Works by R. Azriel of Girona*. Los Angeles: Cherub, 2019 [Hebrew].

Recanati, Menahem ben Benjamin. *Perush 'al ha-torah*. 2 vols. Edited by Amnon Gross. Tel Aviv: Aharon Barzani u-veno, 2003.

Schäfer, Peter, ed. *Synopse zur Hekhalot-Literatur*. Tübingen: J. C. B. Mohr, 1981.

Scheyer, Simon B., and Salomon Munk, eds. *Moreh nevukhim*. Translated by Judah Alharizi. Tel Aviv: Mahbarot le-sifrut, 1964.

Shapira, Tsevi Elimelekh. *Agra' de-kallah*. Bnei Brak: Bnei shileshim, 2008.

———. *Benei Yissakhar*. Bnei Brak: Bnei shileshim, 2008.

———. *Sefer Ma'ayan ganim*. Bnei Brak: Bnei shileshim, 2000.

———. *Sefer ve-heyeh berakhah*. Przemyśl: Knoller, 1875.

Shar'abi, Shalom. *Sefer 'ets hayyim ha-shelishi ha-nikra' nehar shalom*. Jerusalem: Yeshivat kol Yehudah, 1988.

Theodor, J., and Chanoch Albeck, eds. *Midrash bere'shit rabba'*. Jerusalem: Wahrmann Books, 1965.

Tikkunei ha-zohar. Mantua: Me'ir ben Efrayim mi-Padovah ye-Ya'akov ben Naftali, 1557.

Vajda, Georges, trans. *Le commentaire d'Ezra de Gérone sur le cantique des cantiques*. Paris: Aubier-Montaigne, 1969.

Visotzky, Burton, ed. *Midrash Proverbs*. New York: Jewish Theological Seminary, 1990 [Hebrew].

Vital, Hayyim. *Sefer 'ets hayyim*. Vol. 1. Bnei Brak: Tsevi mikhal vidavski, 1985.

———. *Sha'ar ha-ma'amarim*. Jerusalem: Mekhon ahavat shalom, 2017.

———. *Sha'arei kedushah*. Constantinople: Yona ben Ya'akov Ashkenazi, 1734.

Wertheimer, Solomon Aaron, and Abraham Joseph Wertheimer, eds. *Battei midrashot*. Jerusalem: Ketav yad va-sefer, 1989.

Yosef Hayyim of Baghdad. *Sefer rav pe'alim*. 1903. Reprint, Jerusalem: Siah yisra'el, 1993.

Zacuto, Abraham ben Samuel. *Sefer yuhasin ha-shalem*. Edited by Herschell Filipowski. London: Societatis Antiquitatum Hebraicarum, 1857.

The Zohar: Pritzker Edition. Translation and commentary by Daniel C. Matt, translation and commentary on some volumes by Joel Hecker and/or Nathan Wolski. 12 vols. Stanford, CA: Stanford University Press, 2004–17.

SECONDARY SOURCES

Abrams, Daniel. "The Boundaries of Divine Ontology: The Inclusion and Exclusion of Meṭaṭron in the Godhead." *Harvard Theological Review* 87 (1994): 291–321.
———. *Female Body of God in Kabbalistic Literature: Embodied Forms of Love and Sexuality in the Divine Feminine*. Jerusalem: Magnes, 2004 [Hebrew].
———. "From Divine Shape to Angelic Being: The Career of Akatriel in Jewish Literature." *Journal of Religion* 76 (1996): 43–63.
———. *Kabbalistic Manuscripts and Textual Theory: Methodologies of Textual Scholarship and Editorial Practice in the Study of Jewish Mysticism*. 2nd ed. Jerusalem: Magnes, 2013.
———. "Literary Emergence of Esotericism in German Pietism." *Shofar* 12, no. 2 (1994): 67–85.
———. "The Shekhinah Prays Before God: A New Text Concerning the Theosophic Orientation of the German Pietists and Their Method for the Transmission of Esoteric Doctrines." *Tarbiz* 63 (1994): 509–32 [Hebrew].
Abramson, Shraga. *'Inyyanut be-sifrut ha-ge'onim*. Jerusalem: Mossad Harav Kook, 1974.
———. *Rav Nisim Gaon*. Jerusalem: Mekize Nirdamim, 1965 [Hebrew].
Afterman, Adam. "The Phylactery Knot: The History of a Jewish Icon, Myth, Ritual and Mysticism." In *Myth, Ritual and Mysticism: Studies in Honor of Professor Ithamar Gruenwald*, edited by Gideon Bohak et al., 441–80. Tel Aviv: Tel Aviv University Press, 2014 [Hebrew].
Alfasi, Yitsḥak. *Ha-rav me-apṭa, ba'al ohev Yisra'el*. Jerusalem: Mekhon siftei tsaddikim, 1980.
Altmann, Alexander. "Beyond the Realm of Philosophy: R. Elijah Ḥayyim ben Benjamin of Gennazano." *Jerusalem Studies in Jewish Thought* 7 (1988): 61–101 [Hebrew].
Andrade, Nathanael. "The Jewish Tetragrammaton: Secrecy, Community, and Prestige Among Greek-Writing Jews of the Early Roman Empire." *Journal for the Study of Judaism* 46 (2015): 198–223.
Assaf, Simha. "Le-pulmus 'al hadpasat sifrei kabbalah." In *Texts and Studies in Jewish History*, 238–46. Jerusalem: Mossad Harav Kook, 1946 [Hebrew].
Avivi, Yosef. *Kabbalah Luriana*. Vol. 1. Jerusalem: Ben-Zvi Institute, 2008 [Hebrew].
Bagley, Paul J. "On the Practice of Esotericism." *Journal of the History of Ideas* 53 (1992): 231–47.
Bar-Asher, Avishai. "Illusion Versus Reality in the Study of Early Kabbalah: The Commentary on *Sefer Yeṣirah* Attributed to Isaac the Blind and Its History in Kabbalah and Scholarship." *Tarbiz* 86 (2019): 269–384 [Hebrew].
———. "Isaac the Blind's Letter and the History of Early Kabbalah." *Jewish Quarterly Review* 111 (2021): 414–43.
———. *Journeys of the Soul: Concepts and Imageries of Paradise in Medieval Kabbalah*. Jerusalem: Magnes, 2019 [Hebrew].
———. "'Samael and His Female Counterpart': R. Moses de León's Lost Commentary on Ecclesiastes." *Tarbiz* 80 (2012): 539–66 [Hebrew].
———. "'This Fourth Part Has Been Neither Copied nor Printed': On the Identification of the Last Part of 'Sha'are Qedusha.'" *Alei Sefer* 23 (2013): 37–49 [Hebrew].
Benayahu, Meir. "Shitrei ha-hitkashrut shele-mekkubalei tsefat u-mitsrayim." *Assufot* 9 (1955): 129–59.
———. *The Toledoth ha-Ari: The History of the Text and Its Value as a Historical Source*. Jerusalem: Yad Ben-Zvi, 1967 [Hebrew].

Benedikt, Binyamin. *Merkaz ha-torah be-provans*. Jerusalem: Mossad Harav Kook, 1985.
Ben-Shalom, Ram. *The Jews of Provence and Languedoc: Renaissance in the Shadow of the Church*. Raanana, Israel: Open University, 2017 [Hebrew].
———. "Kabbalistic Circles Active in the South of France (Provence) in the Thirteenth Century." *Tarbiz* 82 (2014): 569–605 [Hebrew].
Ben-Shlomo, Yosef. *The Mystical Theology of Moses Cordovero*. Jerusalem: Bialik Institute, 1965 [Hebrew].
Berger, David. "Judaism and General Culture in Medieval and Early Modern Times." In *Judaism's Encounter with Other Cultures: Rejection or Integration?*, edited by Jacob J. Schacter, 57–141. Northvale, NJ: Jason Aronson, 1997.
Blau, Adrian. "Anti-Strauss." *Journal of Politics* 74 (2012): 142–55.
Campany, Robert Ford. "Secrecy and Display in the Quest for Transcendence in China, ca. 220 BCE–350 CE." *History of Religions* 45 (2006): 291–336.
Capelli, Piero. "Nicholas Donin, the Talmud Trial of 1240, and the Struggles Between Church and State in Medieval Europe." In *Entangled Histories: Knowledge, Authority, and Jewish Culture in the Thirteenth Century*, edited by Elisheva Baumgarten et al., 159–78. Philadelphia: University of Pennsylvania Press, 2017.
Chajes, J. H. "'Too Holy to Print': Taboo Anxiety and the Publishing of Practical Hebrew Esoterica." *Jewish History* 26 (2012): 247–62.
Chazan, Robert. "Confrontation in the Synagogue of Narbonne: A Christian Sermon and a Jewish Reply." *Harvard Theological Review* 67 (1974): 437–57.
———. *Daggers of Faith: Thirteenth-Century Christian Missionizing and Jewish Response*. Berkeley: University of California Press, 1989.
———. *Fashioning Jewish Identity in Medieval Western Christendom*. New York: Cambridge University Press, 2004.
Cheyette, Fredric L. *Ermengard of Narbonne and the World of the Troubadours*. Ithaca, NY: Cornell University Press, 2001.
Chilson, Clark. *Secrecy's Power: Covert Shin Buddhists in Japan and Contradictions of Concealment*. Honolulu: University of Hawaii Press, 2014.
Compagni, Vittoria Perrone. "'Dispersa Intentio': Alchemy, Magic and Scepticism in Agrippa." *Early Science and Medicine* 5 (2000): 160–77.
Dan, Joseph. *History of Jewish Mysticism and Esotericism*. 13 vols. Jerusalem: Zalman Shazar Center for Jewish History, 2008–20 [Hebrew].
———. *Jewish Mysticism and Jewish Ethics*. Seattle: University of Washington Press, 1986.
———, ed. *The Early Kabbalah*. Translated by Ronald C. Kiener. New York: Paulist Press, 1986.
Dauber, Jonathan. "The Baal Shem Tov and the Messiah: A Reappraisal of the Baal Shem Tov's Letter to R. Gershon of Kutov." *Jewish Studies Quarterly* 16 (2009): 210–41.
———. "Competing Approaches to Maimonides in Early Kabbalah." In *The Cultures of Maimonideanism: New Approaches to the History of Jewish Thought*, edited by James T. Robinson, 57–88. Leiden: Brill, 2009.
———. "An Early Kabbalistic Explanation of Temple Sacrifice: Text and Study." In *Accounting for the Commandments in Medieval Judaism: Studies in Law, Philosophy, Pietism and Kabbalah*, edited by Jeremy P. Brown and Marc Herman, 58–79. Leiden: Brill, 2021.
———. "Ezra ben Solomon of Gerona and the Sabians." *Journal of Jewish Studies* 70 (2019): 276–97.

———. *Knowledge of God and the Development of Early Kabbalah*. Leiden: Brill, 2012.
Davidson, Herbert A. "Maimonides' Secret Position on Creation." In *Studies in Medieval Jewish History and Literature*, edited by Isadore Twersky, 1:16–40. Cambridge, MA: Harvard University Press, 1979.
———. *Maimonides the Rationalist*. Oxford: Littman, 2011.
———. *Moses Maimonides: The Man and His Works*. Oxford: Oxford University Press, 2005.
Davies, David. *Method and Metaphysics in Maimonides' Guide for the Perplexed*. Oxford: Oxford University Press, 2011.
Dinur, Ben-Zion. *Israel in the Diaspora*. Vol. 2, book 4. Tel Aviv: Dvir, 1969 [Hebrew].
Drews, Wolfram. "Medieval Controversies About Maimonidean Teachings." In *Moses Maimonides (1138–1204): His Religious, Scientific, and Philosophical "Wirkungsgeschichte" in Different Cultural Contexts*, edited by Görge K. Hasselhoff and Otfried Fraisse, 120–28. Würzburg: Ergon, 2004.
Eamon, William. *Science and the Secrets of Nature: Books of Secrets in Medieval and Early Modern Culture*. Princeton, NJ: Princeton University Press, 1994.
Etkes, Immanuel. *Baʻal ha-Tanya: Rabbi Shneur Zalman of Liady and the Origins of Ḥabad Hasidism*. Jerusalem: Zalman Shazar, 2011 [Hebrew].
Fishbane, Eitan P. *As Light Before Dawn: The Inner World of a Medieval Kabbalist*. Stanford, CA: Stanford University Press, 2009.
———. *The Art of Mystical Narrative: A Poetics of the Zohar*. New York: Oxford University Press, 2018.
Fishbane, Michael A. *Biblical Myth and Rabbinic Mythmaking*. Oxford: Oxford University Press, 2003.
———. *The JPS Bible Commentary: Song of Songs*. Philadelphia: Jewish Publication Society, 2015.
Fortin, Ernest L. "The Church Fathers and the Transmission of the Christian Message." In *Ever Ancient, Ever New: Ruminations on the City, the Soul, and the Church*, edited by Michael P. Foley, 13–29. Lanham, MD: Rowman and Littlefield, 2007.
Fraenkel, Carlos. "The Problem of Anthropomorphism in a Hitherto Unknown Passage from Samuel Ibn Tibbon's *Ma'amar Yiqqawu ha-Mayim* and in a Newly Discovered Letter by David ben Saul." *Jewish Studies Quarterly* 11 (2004): 83–126.
Freudenthal, Gad. "Abraham Ibn Ezra and Judah Ibn Tibbon as Cultural Intermediaries: Early Stages in the Introduction of Non-Rabbinic Learning into Provence in the Mid-Twelfth Century." In *Exchange and Transmission Across Cultural Boundaries: Philosophy, Mysticism and Science in the Mediterranean World*, edited by Haggai Ben-Shammai et al., 52–81. Jerusalem: Israel Academy of Sciences and Humanities, 2013.
———. "Arabic into Hebrew: The Emergence of the Translation Movement in Twelfth-Century Provence and Jewish-Christian Polemic." In *Beyond Religious Borders: Interaction and Intellectual Exchange in the Medieval Islamic World*, edited by David M. Freidenreich and Miriam Goldstein, 124–43. Philadelphia: University of Pennsylvania Press, 2012.
———. "Causes and Motivations for the Emergence of the Twelfth-Century Translation Movement in Lunel: Judah Ibn Tibbon and His Patrons R. Meshullam b. Jacob and R. Asher b. Meshullam." In *Ta-Shma: Studies in Judaica in Memory of Israel M. Ta-Shma*, edited by R. Reiner, 2:649–70. Alon Shevut: Tevunot, 2001 [Hebrew].
———. "Philosophy in Religious Polemics: The Case of Jacob ben Reuben (Provence, 1170)." *Medieval Encounters* 22 (2016): 25–71.

———. "Science in the Medieval Jewish Culture of Southern France." *History of Science* 33 (1995): 23–58.

———. "Les sciences dans les communautés juives médiévales de Provence: Leur appropriation, leur role." *Revue des études juives* 152 (1993): 29–136.

Galili, Ze'ev. "On the Question of the Authorship of the Commentary 'Or ha-Ganuz' Attributed to Rabbi Meir ben Solomon Abi Sahula." *Jerusalem Studies in Jewish Thought* 4, no. 1/2 (1984): 83–96 [Hebrew].

Garb, Jonathan. *The Chosen Will Become Herds: Studies in Twentieth-Century Kabbalah*. Translated by Yaffah Berkovits-Murciano. New Haven, CT: Yale University Press, 2009.

———. "The Kabbalah of Rabbi Joseph Ibn Sayyah as a Source for the Understanding of Safedian Kabbalah." *Kabbalah* 4 (1999): 255–313 [Hebrew].

———. "Trance Techniques in the Kabbalistic Tradition of Jerusalem." *Pe'amim* 70 (1997): 46–67 [Hebrew].

Giller, Pinchas. *Reading the Zohar: The Sacred Text of the Kabbalah*. New York: Oxford University Press, 2011.

———. *Shalom Shar'abi and the Kabbalists of Beit El*. Oxford: Oxford University Press, 2008.

Gondos, Andrea. *Kabbalah in Print: The Study and Popularization of Jewish Mysticism in Early Modernity*. Albany: SUNY Press, 2020.

Goshen-Gottstein, Alon. "The Triune and the Decaune God: Christianity and Kabbalah as Objects of Jewish Polemics with Special Reference to Meir ben Simeon of Narbonne's Nfilhemet [*sic*] Mitzva." In *Religious Polemics in Context*, edited by T. L. Hettema and A. van der Kooij, 165–97. Assen: Royal Van Gorcum, 2004.

Gottlieb, Efraim. "R. Bahya ben Asher's Dependence on the Writings of R. Yitzhak Sagi Nahor and His Disciples." *Annual of Bar-Ilan University* 2 (1964): 215–50 [Hebrew].

———. *Studies in the Kabbala Literature*. Tel Aviv: Chaim Rosenberg School for Jewish Studies, 1976 [Hebrew].

Green, Arthur. "Intradivine Romance: The Song of Songs in the Zohar." In *Scrolls of Love: Ruth and the Song of Songs*, edited by Peter S. Hawkins and Lesleigh Cushing Stahlberg, 214–27. New York: Fordham University Press, 2006.

———. *Keter: The Crown of God in Early Jewish Mysticism*. Princeton, NJ: Princeton University Press, 1997.

———. "Rabbi Isaac Ibn Sahola's Commentary on the Song of Songs." *Jerusalem Studies in Jewish Thought* 6 (1987): 393–491 [Hebrew].

Greenup, A. W. "A Kabbalistic Epistle: By Isaac b. Samuel b. Hayyim Sephardi." *Jewish Quarterly Review* 21 (1930): 365–75.

Grossman, Avraham. *He Shall Rule over You? Medieval Jewish Sages on Women*. Jerusalem: Zalman Shazar, 2011 [Hebrew].

Gruenwald, Ithamar. *Apocalyptic and Merkavah Mysticism*. Revised 2nd edition. Leiden: Brill, 2014.

Ḥadad, Eli. "Du-partsufin shel 'ezer kenegdo." In *A Good Eye: Dialogue and Polemic in Jewish Culture, a Jubilee Book in Honor of Tova Ilan*, edited by Naḥem Ilan, 476–96. Tel Aviv: Hakibbutz Hameuchad, 1999 [Hebrew].

Halbertal, Moshe. *By Way of Truth: Nahmanides and the Creation of Tradition*. Jerusalem: Shalom Hartman Institute, 2006 [Hebrew].

———. *Concealment and Revelation: Esotericism in Jewish Thought and Its Philosophical Implications*. Princeton, NJ: Princeton University Press, 2007.

Hallamish, Moshe. *An Introduction to the Kabbalah*. Translated by Ruth Bar-Ilan and Ora Wiskind-Elper. Albany: SUNY Press, 1999.

Haq, Syed Nomanul. *Names, Natures and Things: The Alchemist Jābir Ibn Ḥayyān and His Kitab al-Aḥjār (Book of Stones)*. Dordrecht: Springer Science and Business Media, 1994.

Haran, Ra'aya. "The Doctrine of Abraham of Kalisk." *Tarbiz* 66 (1997): 517–41 [Hebrew].

Harvey, Warren Zev. "The Incorporeality of God in Maimonides, Rabad and Spinoza." In *Studies in Jewish Thought*, edited by S. Heller Wilensky and Moshe Idel, 63–78. Jerusalem: Magnes, 1989 [Hebrew].

Hellner-Eshed, Melila. *A River Flows from Eden: The Language of Mystical Experience in the Zohar*. Translated by Nathan Wolski. Stanford, CA: Stanford University Press, 2009.

Henshke, David. "'In the Image of the Form of His Structure'—Blessing as 'Midrash,' with a Comment on Talmudic Anthropomorphism." *Sidra* 24–25 (2010): 123–45 [Hebrew].

Herskowitz, William K. "Judaeo-Christian Dialogue in Provence as Reflected in 'Milhemet Mitzva' of R. Meir Hameili." Ph.D. diss., Yeshiva University, 1974.

Hillel, Ya'akov Mosheh. *Sefer ahavat shalom*. Jerusalem: Ha-makhon le-hotsa'at sefarim ve-khitvei yad ahavat shalom, 2002.

Huss, Boaz. *The Zohar: Reception and Impact*. Translated by Yudith Nave. Oxford: Littman, 2016.

Hyman, Arthur. "Interpreting Maimonides." In *The Legacy of Maimonides: Religion, Reason and Community*, edited by Yamin Levy and Shalom Carmy, 61–72. Brooklyn, NY: Yashar, 2006.

Idel, Moshe. *Abraham Abulafia's Esotericism: Secrets and Doubts*. Berlin: De Gruyter, 2020.

———. *Absorbing Perfections: Kabbalah and Interpretation*. New Haven, CT: Yale University Press, 2002.

———. *The Angelic World: Apotheosis and Theophany*. Tel Aviv: Yedi'ot aḥaronot, 2008 [Hebrew].

———. "An Anonymous Commentary on the Pentateuch, from the Circle of R. Solomon Ibn Adret." *Michael* 11 (1989): 9–21 [Hebrew].

———. "An Anonymous Kabbalistic Commentary on Shir ha-Yiḥud." In *Mysticism, Magic and Kabbalah in Ashkenazi Judaism*, edited by Karl Erich Grözinger and Joseph Dan, 139–54. Berlin: De Gruyter, 1995.

———. "Be-or ha-ḥayyim: 'Iyyun be-eskhatologeyah kabbalit." In *Sanctity of Life and Martyrdom: Studies in Memory of Amir Yekutiel*, edited by Isaiah M. Gafni and Aviezer Ravitzky, 191–211. Jerusalem: Zalman Shazar, 1992 [Hebrew].

———. "Commentaries on the 'Secret of 'Ibbur' in 13th-Century Kabbalah and Their Significance for the Understanding of the Kabbalah at Its Inception and Its Development." *Daat* 72 (2012): 5–49; and 73 (2012): 5–44 [Hebrew].

———. "Enoch Is Metatron." *Immanuel* 24/25 (1990): 220–40.

———. "From R. Isaac Sagi Nahor and R. Isaac Luria: From Hiding to Printing an Esoteric Lore." *Studia Judaica* 21 (2014): 5–40.

———. "The Image of Man Above the Sefirot." *Daat* 4 (1980): 41–56 [Hebrew].

———. "The Image of Man Above the Sefirot: R. David ben Yehuda he-Hasid's Theosophy of Ten Supernal 'Sahsahot' and Its Reverberations." *Kabbalah* 20 (2009): 181–212.

———. "'In a Whisper': On Transmission of Shi'ur Qomah and Kabbalistic Secrets in Jewish Mysticism." *Rivista di storia e letteratura religiosa* 47 (2011): 477–522.

———. "Jewish Kabbalah and Platonism in the Middle Ages and Renaissance." In *Neoplatonism and Jewish Thought*, edited by Lenn E. Goodman, 319–51. Albany: SUNY Press, 1992.

———. "The Kabbalah in Byzantium: Preliminary Remarks." In *Jews in Byzantium: Dialectics of Minority and Majority Cultures*, edited by Robert Bonfil et al., 659–708. Leiden: Brill, 2011.

———. *Kabbalah and Eros*. New Haven, CT: Yale University Press, 2005.

———. *Kabbalah in Italy, 1280–1510: A Survey*. New Haven, CT: Yale University Press, 2011.

———. *Kabbalah: New Perspectives*. New Haven, CT: Yale University Press, 1988.

———. "The Kabbalistic Interpretation of the Secret of 'Arayot in Early Kabbalah." *Kabbalah* 12 (2004): 89–199 [Hebrew].

———. "Kabbalistic Materials from the School of Rabbi David ben Yehudah he-Ḥasid." *Jerusalem Studies in Jewish Thought* 2 (1983): 169–207 [Hebrew].

———. "Kabbalistic Prayer in Provence." *Tarbiz* 62 (1992–93): 265–86 [Hebrew].

———. "Leadership and Charisma: Maimonides, Nahmanides and Abraham Abulafia." *Journal for the Study of Sephardic and Mizrahi Jewry* 1 (2008): 2–34.

———. "Leviathan and Its Consort: From Talmudic to Kabbalistic Myth." In *Myth in Judaism*, edited by Moshe Idel and Ithamar Gruenwald, 145–86. Jerusalem: Shazar Center, 2004 [Hebrew].

———. "Maimonides and Kabbalah." In *Studies in Maimonides*, edited by Isadore Twersky, 31–81. Cambridge, MA: Harvard University Press, 1990.

———. "Maimonides' Guide of the Perplexed and the Kabbalah." *Jewish History* 18 (2004): 197–226.

———. "Nahmanides: Kabbalah, Halakhah, and Spiritual Leadership." In *Jewish Mystical Leaders and Leadership in the 13th Century*, edited by Moshe Idel and Mortimer Ostow, 15–96. Northvale, NJ: Jason Aronson, 1998.

———. "Nishmat eloha: 'Al elohiyut ha-neshamah etsel ha-Ramba"n veha-askolah shelo." In *Ha-ḥayyim ke-midrash: 'Iyyunim bi-pesikhologeyah yehudit*, edited by S. Arzy et al., 338–80. Tel Aviv: Yedi'ot aḥaronot, 2004.

———. "On R. Isaac Sagi Nahor's Mystical Intention of the Eighteen Benedictions." In *Massu'ot: Studies in Kabbalistic Literature and Jewish Philosophy*, edited by Michal Oron and Amos Goldreich, 25–52. Tel Aviv: Bialik Institute, 1994 [Hebrew].

———. "On the Secrets of the Torah in Abraham Abulafia." In *Religion and Politics in Jewish Thought: Essays in Honor of Aviezer Ravitzky*, edited by Benjamin Brown et al., 1:371–458. Jerusalem: Zalman Shazar, 2012 [Hebrew].

———. *R. Menahem Recanati the Kabbalist*. Tel Aviv: Schocken, 1998 [Hebrew].

———. "'Sefer Yetzirah': Twelve Commentaries on 'Sefer Yetzirah' and the Extant Remnants of R. Isaac of Bedresh's Commentary." *Tarbiz* 79 (2010): 471–556 [Hebrew].

———. *Studies in Ecstatic Kabbalah*. Albany: SUNY Press, 1988.

———. "Transmission in Thirteenth-Century Kabbalah." In *Transmitting Jewish Traditions: Orality, Textuality and Cultural Diffusion*, edited by Yaakov Elman and Israel Gershoni, 138–65. New Haven, CT: Yale University Press, 2000.

———. "We Have No Kabbalistic Tradition on This." In *Rabbi Moses Nahmanides (Ramban): Explorations in His Religious and Literary Virtuosity*, edited by Isadore Twersky, 51–74. Cambridge, MA: Harvard University Press, 1983.

Johnson, Paul. *Secrets, Gossip, and Gods: The Transformation of Brazilian Candomblé*. Oxford: Oxford University Press, 2002.

Jütte, Daniel. *The Age of Secrecy: Jews, Christians, and the Economy of Secrets, 1400–1800*, translated by Jeremiah Riemer. New Haven, CT: Yale University Press, 2015.

Kallus, Menachem. *The Pillar of Prayer: Teachings of Contemplative Guidance in Prayer, Sacred Study, and the Spiritual Life from the Ba'al Shem Tov and His Circle*. Louisville, KY: Fons Vitae, 2011.

Kanarfogel, Ephraim. "Varieties of Belief in Medieval Ashkenaz: The Case of Anthropomorphism." In *Rabbinic Culture and Its Critics: Jewish Authority, Dissent, and Heresy in Medieval and Early Modern Times*, edited by Daniel Frank and Matt Goldish, 117–59. Detroit: Wayne State University Press, 2008.

Katz, Jacob. *Halakhah and Kabbalah: Studies in the History of Jewish Religion, Its Various Faces and Social Relevance*. Jerusalem: Magnes, 1986 [Hebrew].

Kellner, Menachem Marc. *Maimonides' Confrontation with Mysticism*. Oxford: Littman, 2006.

Kienzle, Beverly Mayne. *Cistercians, Heresy, and Crusade in Occitania, 1145–1229: Preaching in the Lord's Vineyard*. Rochester, NY: York Medieval /Boydell, 2001.

Kraus, Paul. *Jābir Ibn Ḥayyān: Contribution à l'histoire des idées scientifiques dans l'islam*. Vol. 1. Hildesheim: Georg Olms, 1944.

Lachter, Hartley. *Kabbalistic Revolution: Reimagining Judaism in Medieval Spain*. New Brunswick, NJ: Rutgers University Press, 2014.

Láng, Benedek. *Ciphers and Secrets in Early Modern Hungary*, translated by Teodóra Király and Benedek Láng. Amsterdam: Atlantis Press B.V., 2015.

———. "Ciphers in Magic: Techniques of Revelation and Concealment." *Magic, Ritual, and Witchcraft* 10 (2015): 125–41.

Lasker, Daniel J. "Controversy and Collegiality: A Look at Provence." *Medieval Encounters* 22 (2016): 13–24.

Laura, Heidi. "Collected Traditions and Scattered Secrets: Eclecticism and Esotericism in the Works of the 14th Century Ashkenazi Kabbalist Menahem Ziyyoni of Cologne." *Nordisk Judaistik* 20 (1999): 19–44.

Lenzi, Alan. "Advertising Secrecy, Creating Power in Ancient Mesopotamia: How Scholars Used Secrecy in Scribal Education to Bolster and Perpetuate Their Social Prestige and Power." *Antiguo Oriente* 11 (2002): 13–42.

Lerner, Ralph. "Dispersal by Design: The Author's Choice." In *Reason, Faith, and Politics: Essays in Honor of Werner J. Dannhauser*, edited by Arthur Melzer and Robert Kraynak, 29–42. Lanham, MD: Lexington, 2008.

———. *Playing the Fool: Subversive Laughter in Troubled Times*. Chicago: University of Chicago Press, 2009.

Levinger, David Shemuel. "Rabbi Shem Tob Abraham ben Ga'on." *Sefunot* 7 (1963): 7–39 [Hebrew].

Lieberman, Saul. *Hellenism in Jewish Palestine: Studies in the Literary Transmission, Beliefs and Manners of Palestine in the I Century B.C.E.–IV Century C.E.* New York: Jewish Theological Seminary, 1950.

Liebes, Yehuda. "Zohar as Renaissance." Accessed June 7, 2021, https://liebes.huji.ac.il/files/rnsns.pdf [Hebrew].

———. "Zohar ve-eros." Accessed June 7, 2021, https://liebes.huji.ac.il/files/zoharveros.pdf.

Loewenthal, Naftali. *Communicating the Infinite: The Emergence of the Habad School*. Chicago: University of Chicago Press, 1990.

Lorberbaum, Yair. "Did Nahmanides Perceive the Kabbalah as 'Closed Knowledge'?" *Zion* 82 (2017): 309–54 [Hebrew].

———. "On Contradictions, Rationality, Dialectics, and Esotericism in Maimonides's 'Guide of the Perplexed.'" *Review of Metaphysics* 55 (2002): 711–50.

Magid, Shaul. "Jewish Kabbalah: Hayyim Vital's *Shaarei Kedusha*." In *Contemplative Literature: A Comparative Sourcebook on Meditation and Contemplative Prayer*, edited by Louis Komjathy, 197–265. Albany: SUNY Press, 2015.

Mann, Jacob. *The Bible as Read and Preached in the Old Synagogue*. New York: Ktav, 1971.

Mark, Zvi. *The Scroll of Secrets: The Hidden Messianic Vision of R. Nachman of Breslav*. Translated by Naftali Moses. Brighton, MA: Academic Studies Press, 2010.

Matt, Daniel. "The Mystic and the Miẓwot." In *Jewish Spirituality From the Bible Through the Middle Ages*, edited by Arthur Green, 1:367–404. New York: Crossroad, 1988.

Mayse, Ariel Evan, and Daniel Reiser. "Territories and Textures: The Hasidic Sermon as the Crossroads of Language and Culture." *Jewish Social Studies* 24 (2018): 127–60.

McCall, Timothy, and Sean Roberts. "Revealing Early Modern Secrecy." In *Visual Cultures of Secrecy in Early Modern Europe*, 2–23. Kirksville, MO: Truman State University, 2013.

Meier, Heinrich. *Leo Strauss and the Theologico-Political Problem*. Cambridge: Cambridge University Press, 2006.

Meir, Jonatan. *Reḥovot ha-Nahar: Kabbalah and Exotericism in Jerusalem*. Jerusalem: Yad Izhak Ben-Zvi, 2011 [Hebrew].

———. "The Revealed and the Revealed within the Concealed: On the Opposition to the 'Followers' of Rabbi Yehuda Ashlag and the Dissemination of Esoteric Literature." *Kabbalah* 16 (2017): 151–258 [Hebrew].

Melzer, Arthur M. *Philosophy Between the Lines: The Lost History of Esoteric Writing*. Chicago: University of Chicago Press, 2014.

Moore, R. I. *The Birth of Popular Heresy: Documents of Medieval History*. London: Edward Arnold, 1975.

———. *The War on Heresy*. Cambridge, MA: Harvard University Press, 2012.

Moseson, Chaim Elly. "From Spoken Work to Discourse of the Academy: Reading the Sources for the Teachings of the Besht." Ph.D. diss., Boston University, 2017.

Mopsik, Charles. *Les grands textes de la cabale*. Lagrasse: Verdier, 1993.

———. *Sex of the Soul: The Vicissitudes of Sexual Difference in Kabbalah*. Edited by Daniel Abrams. Los Angeles: Cherub, 2005.

Mottolese, Maurizio. "'Uno dalla bocca di un altro'?: La trasmissione della qabbalah nell'opera di Shem Tov Ibn Gaon e nella scuola di Nahmanide." *Rivista di Storia e Letteratura Religiosa* 47 (2011): 489–520.

Nadler, Allan. *The Faith of the Mithnagdim: Rabbinic Responses to Hasidic Rapture*. Baltimore: Johns Hopkins University Press, 1997.

Newman, William R. "Alchemical Symbolism and Concealment: The Chemical House of Libavius." In *The Architecture of Science*, edited by Peter Galison and Emily Ann Thompson, 59–77. Cambridge, MA: MIT Press, 1999.

Orlov, Andrei A. *The Enoch-Metatron Tradition*. Tübingen: Mohr Siebeck, 2005.

Ortner, Natan. *Ha-rabbi R. Tsevi Elimelekh mi-Dinov*. 2 vols. Tel Aviv: Mekhon benei Mosheh, 2005.

Pasi, Marco. "Oriental Kabbalah and the Parting of East and West in the Early Theosophical Society." In *Kabbalah and Modernity: Interpretations, Transformations, Adaptations*, edited by Boaz Huss et al., 151–66. Leiden: Brill, 2010.

Pedaya, Haviva. *Nahmanides: Cyclical Time and Holy Text*. Tel Aviv: Am Oved, 2003 [Hebrew].

———. *Name and Sanctuary in the Teaching of R. Isaac the Blind*. Jerusalem: Magnes, 2001 [Hebrew].

———. "'Possessed by Speech': Towards an Understanding of the Prophetic-Ecstatic Pattern Among Early Kabbalists." *Tarbiz* 65 (1996): 565–636 [Hebrew].

———. "The Spiritual vs. the Concrete Land of Israel in the Geronese School of Kabbalah." In *The Land of Israel in Jewish Thought*, edited by Moshe Hallamish and Aviezer Ravitzky, 233–89. Jerusalem: Yad Izhak Ben-Zvi, 1991 [Hebrew].

Perles, Joseph. "Nachträge über R. Moses ben Nachmann." *Monatsschrift für Geschichte und Wissenschaft des Judenthums* 9 (1860): 175–95.

Piekarz, Mendel. "'Why Did the Spanish Exile Perish': As a Forewarning of the Dangers of the Enlightenment." *Daat* 28 (1992): 87–115 [Hebrew].

Porat, Oded. *'Founding the Circle:' Rudiments of Esse and Linguistic Creation in 'The Book of Fountain of Wisdom' and Its Related Treatises*. Los Angeles: Cherub Press, 2019 [Hebrew].

———. *'Who Is a Beautiful Maiden without Eyes' and the Riddle of the Tay'a: A Chapter in the History of Kabbalah in the Second Half of the Thirteenth Century*. Los Angeles: Cherub Press, 2019 [Hebrew].

Principe, Lawrence. *The Secrets of Alchemy*. Chicago: University of Chicago Press, 2013.

Rabinowitsch, Wolf. *Lithuanian Hasidism from Its Beginnings to the Present Day*. Jerusalem: Bialik Institute, 1971 [Hebrew].

Rec, Agnieszka. "Ciphers and Secrecy Among the Alchemists: A Preliminary Report." *Societas Magica Newsletter* 31 (2014): 1–6.

Robinson, Ira. "Moses Cordovero and Kabbalistic Education in the Sixteenth Century." *Judaism* 39 (1990): 155–62.

Robinson, James T. "The Ibn Tibbon Family: A Dynasty of Translators in Medieval 'Provence.'" In *Be'erot Yitzhak: Studies in Memory of Isadore Twersky*, edited by Jay M. Harris, 193–224. Cambridge, MA: Harvard University Press, 2005.

Roth, Pinchas. "Later Provençal Sages: Jewish Law (Halakhah) and Rabbis in Southern France." Ph.D. diss., Hebrew University, 2012 [Hebrew].

Sabine, George. "Review of Persecution and the Art of Writing." *Ethics* 63 (1953): 220–22.

Schäfer, Peter. "In Heaven as It Is in Hell: The Cosmology of Seder Rabbah de-Bereshit." In *Heavenly Realms and Earthly Realities in Late Antique Religions*, edited by Ra'anan S. Boustan and Annette Yoshiko Reed, 233–74. Cambridge: Cambridge University Press, 2004.

Scholem, Gershom. "An Inquiry in the Kabbala of R. Isaac ben Jacob Hacohen. III. R. Moses of Burgos, the Disciple of R. Isaac (Cont.)." *Tarbiz* 3 (1932): 193–206 [Hebrew].

———. *Jewish Gnosticism, Merkabah Mysticism, and Talmudic Tradition*. 1960. Reprint, New York: Jewish Theological Seminary, 1965.

———. *Kabbalah*. New York: Meridian, 1978.

———. "Kabbalah and Myth." In *On the Kabbalah and Its Symbolism*, translated by Ralph Manheim, 87–117. New York: Schocken, 1996.

———. *The Kabbalah in Provence*. Edited by Rivka Schatz. Jerusalem: Academon, 1970 [Hebrew].

———. *Ha-kabbalah be-gerona*. Edited by Yosef ben Shlomo. Jerusalem: Beit ha-hotsa'ah shel histadrut ha-studentim, 1964.

———. *Ha-kabbalah shel sefer ha-temunah ve-shel Avraham Abulafia*. Edited by Yosef Ben-Shlomo. Jerusalem: Academon, 1965.

———. *Kitvei yad ba-kabbalah.* Jerusalem: Hebrew University, 1930.
———. *Major Trends in Jewish Mysticism.* 1946. Reprint, New York: Schocken, 1995.
———. *On the Mystical Shape of the Godhead.* Edited by Jonathan Chipman. Translated by Joachim Neugroschel. New York: Schocken, 1991.
———. *Origins of the Kabbalah.* Edited by R. J. Zwi Werblowsky. Translated by Allan Arkush. Princeton, NJ: Princeton University Press, 1987.
———. "Perusho ha-amitti shel ha-Ramba"n le-Sefer yetsirah ve-divrei kabbalah aḥadim ha-mityaḥasim elav." In *Studies in Kabbalah* 1, edited by Yosef Ben-Shlomo, 67–111. Tel Aviv: Am Oved, 1998 [Hebrew].
———. *Re'shit ha-kabbalah.* Jerusalem: Schocken, 1948.
———. "R' Yitzhak Sagi Nahor: Excerpts Collected from the Surviving Writing of R' Sagi Nahor." Gershom Scholem Archive, Hebrew University [Hebrew].
———. "Sefer shevilei de-yerushalayim ha-meyuḥas le-Yitshak Ḥeilo—mezuyyaf." *Tsiyon* 6 (1933): 1–15.
———. "Te'udah ḥadashah le-toldot re'shit ha-kabbalah." In *Studies in Kabbalah* 1, edited by Yosef Ben-Shlomo, 7–39. Tel Aviv: Am Oved, 1998 [Hebrew].
———. "Tikkunim ve-he'arot lirshimat kitvei ha-yad ha-'ivrim be-paris." *Kiryat Sefer* 24 (1947): 250–57.
———. "Traces of Gabirol on the Kabbalah." In *Studies in Kabbalah* 1, edited by Yosef Ben-Shlomo, 39–66. Tel Aviv: Am Oved, 1998 [Hebrew].
Schuchat, Raphael. "Lithuanian Kabbalah as an Independent Trend of Kabbalistic Literature." *Kabbalah* 10 (2004): 181–206 [Hebrew].
Schwartz, Dov. *Contradiction and Concealment in Medieval Jewish Thought.* Ramat Gan, Israel: Bar-Ilan University Press, 2002 [Hebrew].
———. *Messianism in Medieval Jewish Thought.* Translated by Batya Stein. Boston: Academic Studies Press, 2017.
———. "Perush ha-amitti le-ma'aseh bere'shit ha-meyuḥas le-R' Asher ben David." *Sinai* 109 (1991): 48–55.
Sed, Nicolas. "Une cosmologie juive du haut moyen-âge: La bĕraytā dī ma'aseh bĕrēšīt." *Revue des études juives* 123 (1964): 259–305 and 124 (1965): 23–123.
Sed-Rajna, Gabrielle. "Une 'baqqasah' attribuée à Isaac l'Aveugle." *Revue des études juives* 126 (1967): 265–67.
Seeskin, Kenneth. "Maimonides' Conception of Philosophy." In *Leo Strauss and Judaism: Jerusalem and Athens Critically Revisited*, edited by David Novak, 87–110. Lanham, MD: Rowman and Littlefield, 1996.
Segal, Avraham. *The Path of Worship: Topics in the Hassidic Kabbalah of Rabbi Tzvi Hirsch of Zydachov.* Jerusalem: Rubin Mass, 2011 [Hebrew].
Sendor, Mark Brian. "The Emergence of Provençal Kabbalah: Rabbi Isaac the Blind's Commentary on Sefer Yeẓirah." Ph.D. diss., Harvard University, 1994.
Sennis, Antonio, ed. *Cathars in Question.* Melton, England: York Medieval Press, 2016.
Septimus, Bernard. *Hispano-Jewish Culture in Transition: The Career and Controversies of Ramah.* Cambridge, MA: Harvard University Press, 1982.
Shaḥar, Shulamit. "Catharism and the Beginnings of Kabbalah in Languedoc: Elements Common to the Catharic Scriptures and the Book 'Bahir.'" *Tarbiz* 40 (1971): 483–507 [Hebrew].
Shatzmiller, Joseph. "L'heresie des albigeois vue par les juifs au XIIIe siècle." *Heresis* 35 (2001): 59–81.

Shmueli, Leore Sachs. "The Reception of Traditions of Two Channels of the Divine Masculine in the Kabbalah of R. Moses Cordovero." *Kabbalah* 38 (2017): 117–58 [Hebrew].

Shohat, Azriel. "Concerning the First Maimonidean Controversy on the Writings of Maimonides." *Zion* 36 (1971): 27–60 [Hebrew].

Silver, Daniel Jeremy. *Maimonidean Criticism and the Maimonidean Controversy, 1180–1240*. Leiden: Brill, 1965.

Simmel, Georg. *Soziologie: Untersuchungen über die Formen der Vergesellschaftung*. Leipzig: Duncker and Humblot, 1908.

———. "The Sociology of Secrecy and of Secret Societies." Translated by Albion W. Small. *American Journal of Sociology* 11 (1906): 441–98.

Smith, Steven B. *Reading Leo Strauss: Politics, Philosophy, Judaism*. Chicago: University of Chicago Press, 2006.

Soloveitchik, Haym. "History of Halakhah: Methodological Issues: A Review Essay of I. Twersky's 'Rabad of Posquières.'" *Jewish History* 5 (1991): 75–124.

———. "Rabad of Posquières: A Programmatic Essay." In *Studies in the History of Jewish Society in the Middle Ages and in the Modern Period*, edited by E. Etkes and Y. Salmon, vii–xl. Jerusalem: Magnes, 1980.

Steiner, Richard C. "The Two Sons of Neriah and the Two Editions of Jeremiah in the Light of Two Atbash Code-Words for Babylon." *Vetus Testamentum* 46 (1996): 74–84.

Stern, Gregg. *Philosophy and Rabbinic Culture: Jewish Interpretation and Controversy in Medieval Languedoc*. New York: Routledge, 2009.

Strauss, Leo. "Farabi's Plato." In *Louis Ginzberg Jubilee Volume*, 357–93. New York: American Academy for Jewish Research, 1945.

———. *Leo Strauss on Maimonides: The Complete Writings*. Edited by Kenneth Hart Green. Chicago: University of Chicago Press, 2013.

———. "On a Forgotten Kind of Writing." *Chicago Review* 8, no. 1 (1954): 64–75.

———. "On Abravanel's Philosophical Tendency and Political Teaching." In *Isaac Abravanel*, edited by J. B. Trend and H. H. Ben-Sasson, 196–200. Cambridge: Cambridge University Press, 1937.

———. *Persecution and the Art of Writing*. Glencoe, IL: Free Press, 1952.

———. "Some Remarks on the Political Science of Maimonides and Farabi." Translated by Robert Bartlett. *Interpretation* 18 (1990): 3–30.

Stroumsa, Guy G. *Hidden Wisdom: Esoteric Traditions and the Roots of Christian Mysticism*. Leiden: Brill, 1996.

Sussman, Ya'akov. "Torah she-be'al peh'—peshutah ke-mashma'ah: Koḥo shel kotso shel yod." *Meḥkerei talmud* 3 (2005): 209–384.

Ta-Shma, Israel. *Rabbi Zeraḥyah ha-Levi Ba'al ha-Ma'or u-venei ḥugo*. Jerusalem: Mossad Harav Kook, 1992.

Tirosh-Samuelson, Hava. "Kabbalah and Science in the Middle Ages: Preliminary Remarks." In *Science in Medieval Jewish Cultures*, edited by Gad Freudenthal, 476–510. New York: Cambridge University Press, 2011.

———. "Philosophy and Kabbalah: 1200–1600." In *The Cambridge Companion to Medieval Jewish Philosophy*, edited by Daniel H. Frank and Oliver Leaman, 218–32. Cambridge: Cambridge University Press, 2003.

Tiryakian, Edward A. "Toward the Sociology of Esoteric Culture." *American Journal of Sociology* 78 (1972): 491–512.

Tishby, Isaiah. *Studies in Kabbalah and Its Branches.* Vol. 1. Jerusalem: Magnes, 1982 [Hebrew].

Tishby, Isaiah, and Fischel Lachower, eds. *The Wisdom of the Zohar: An Anthology of Zoharic Texts.* Translated by David Goldstein. 3 vols. London: Littman, 1994.

Trautner-Kromann, Hanne. *Shield and Sword: Jewish Polemics against Christianity and the Christians in France and Spain from 1100–1500.* Translated by James Manley. Tübingen: J. C. B. Mohr (P. Siebeck), 1993.

Travis, Yakov M. "Kabbalistic Foundations of Jewish Spiritual Practice: Rabbi Ezra of Gerona on the Kabbalistic Meaning of the Mizvot." Ph.D. diss., Brandeis University, 2002.

Twersky, Isadore. "Aspects of the Social and Cultural History of Provençal Jewry." In *Jewish Society Through the Ages*, edited by H. H. Ben-Sasson and S. Ettinger, 185–207. New York: Schocken, 1973.

———. *Rabad of Posquières: A Twelfth-Century Talmudist.* 1962. Reprint, Philadelphia: Jewish Publication Society of America, 1980.

Urbach, Ephraim E. *The Sages: Their Concepts and Beliefs.* Jerusalem: Magnes, 1986 [Hebrew].

Urban, Hugh B. "The Adornment of Silence: Secrecy and Symbolic Power in American Freemasonry." *Journal of Religion & Society* 3 (2001): 1–29.

———. *The Economics of Ecstasy: Tantra, Secrecy and Power in Colonial Bengal.* New York: Oxford University Press, 2001.

———. "Fair Game: Secrecy, Security, and the Church of Scientology in Cold War America." *Journal of the American Academy of Religion* 74 (2006): 356–89.

———. "Secrecy and New Religious Movements: Concealment, Surveillance, and Privacy in a New Age of Information." *Religion Compass* 2 (2008): 66–83.

———. "'The Third Wall of Fire': Scientology and the Study of Religious Secrecy." *Nova Religio* 20, no. 4 (2017): 13–36.

———. "The Torment of Secrecy: Ethical and Epistemological Problems in the Study of Esoteric Traditions." *History of Religions* 37 (1998): 209–48.

Valabregue-Perry, Sandra. *Concealed and Revealed: "Ein Sof" in Theosophic Kabbalah.* Los Angeles: Cherub, 2010 [Hebrew].

Verman, Mark. *The Books of Contemplation: Medieval Jewish Mystical Sources.* Albany: SUNY Press, 1992.

Vermeir, Koen. "Openness Versus Secrecy? Historical and Historiographical Remarks." *British Journal for the History of Science* 45 (2012): 165–88.

von Stuckrad, Kocku. *Locations of Knowledge in Medieval and Early Modern Europe: Esoteric Discourse and Western Identities.* Leiden: Brill, 2010.

———. "Secrecy as Social Capital." In *Constructing Tradition: Means and Myths of Transmission in Western Esotericism*, edited by Andreas Kilcher, 239–52. Leiden: Brill, 2010.

Wakefield, Walter L. *Heresy, Crusade and Inquisition in Southern France, 1100–1250.* Berkeley: University of California Press, 1974.

Weiss, Joseph G. *Studies in Braslav Hassidism.* Jerusalem: Bialik Institute, 1974 [Hebrew].

Weiss, Judith. "Kabbalah in Gerona in the Thirteenth Century: Azriel and Nahmanides. A Reevaluation." *Tarbiz* 87 (2019): 67–97 [Hebrew].

Weiss, Tzahi. *Cutting the Shoots: The Worship of the Shekhinah in the World of Early Kabbalistic Literature.* Jerusalem: Magnes, 2015 [Hebrew].

———. "'Their Heart Was Turned Away from the Uppermost': Rethinking the Boundaries of Kabbalistic Literature and the Opposition to Kabbalah in the First Half of the 13th Century." *Daat* 85 (2018): 307–39 [Hebrew].

———. "The Letter of Isaac the Blind to Nahmanides and Jonah Gerondi in Its Historical Context." *Journal of Jewish Studies* 72 (2021): 327–48.

Weiss, Tzahi, and Naʿama Ben-Shachar. "An Anonymous Geronese Commentary on the Ten Sefiroth." *Kabbalah* 38 (2017): 159–70 [Hebrew].

Wolfson, Elliot R. *Abraham Abulafia: Kabbalist and Prophet: Hermeneutics, Theosophy, and Theurgy*. Los Angeles: Cherub, 2000.

———. "Anonymity and the Kabbalistic Ethos: A Fourteenth-Century Supercommentary on the Commentary on the Sefirot." *Kabbalah* 35 (2016): 55–112.

———. "The Anonymous Chapters of the Elderly Master of Secrets: New Evidence for the Early Activity of the Zoharic Circle." *Kabbalah* 19 (2009): 143–278.

———. "Beneath the Wings of the Great Eagle: Maimonides and Thirteenth-Century Kabbalah." In *Moses Maimonides (1138–1204): His Religious, Scientific, and Philosophical "Wirkungsgeschichte" in Different Cultural Contexts*, edited by Görge K. Hasselhoff and Otfried Fraisse, 209–37. Würzburg: Ergon, 2004.

———. "Beyond the Spoken Word: Oral Tradition and Written Transmission in Medieval Jewish Mysticism." In *Transmitting Jewish Traditions: Orality, Textuality and Cultural Diffusion*, edited by Yaakov Elman and Israel Gershoni, 166–224. New Haven, CT: Yale University Press, 2000.

———. "By Way of Truth: Aspects of Naḥmanides' Kabbalistic Hermeneutic." *AJS Review* 14 (1989): 103–78.

———. *Circle in the Square: Studies in the Use of Gender in Kabbalistic Symbolism*. Albany: SUNY Press, 1995.

———. "Circumcision and the Divine Name: A Study in the Transmission of Esoteric Doctrine." *Jewish Quarterly Review* 78 (1987): 77–112.

———. "Circumcision, Secrecy, and the Veiling of the Veil." In *The Covenant of Circumcision: New Perspectives on an Ancient Jewish Rite*, edited by E. W. Mark, 58–70. Hanover, NH: Brandeis University Press, 2003.

———. *Giving Beyond the Gift: Apophasis and Overcoming Theomania*. New York: Fordham University Press, 2014.

———. "The Image of Jacob Engraved upon the Throne: Further Reflection on the Esoteric Doctrine of the German Pietists." In *Along the Path: Studies in Kabbalistic Myth, Symbolism, and Hermeneutics*, 1–63. Albany: SUNY Press, 1995.

———. "Images of God's Feet: Some Observations on the Divine Body in Judaism." In *People of the Body: Jews and Judaism from an Embodied Perspective*, edited by Howard Eilberg-Schwartz, 143–81. Albany: SUNY Press, 1992.

———. *Language, Eros, Being: Kabbalistic Hermeneutics and Poetic Imagination*. New York: Fordham University Press, 2005.

———. "Metatron and Shiʿur Qomah in the Writings of Haside Ashkenaz." In *Mysticism, Magic, and Kabbalah in Ashkenazi Judaism*, edited by Karl-Erich Grözinger and Joseph Dan, 61–92. Berlin: De Gruyter, 1995.

———. "Murmuring Secrets: Eroticism and Esotericism in Medieval Kabbalah." In *Hidden Intercourse: Eros and Sexuality in the History of Western Esotericism*, edited by J. Kripal and W. Hanegraaff, 65–109. Leiden: Brill, 2008.

———. "Negative Theology and Positive Assertion in the Early Kabbalah." *Daat* 32–33 (1994): v–xxii.

———. "Occultation of the Feminine and the Body of Secrecy in Medieval Kabbalah." In *Rending the Veil: Concealment and Secrecy in the History of Religions*, edited by Elliot R. Wolfson, 113–54. New York: Seven Bridges, 1999.

———. "Open Secret in the Rearview Mirror." *AJS Review* 35 (2011): 401–18.

———. *Open Secret: Postmessianic Messianism and the Mystical Revision of Menaḥem Mendel Schneerson*. New York: Columbia University Press, 2009.

———. "Woman—The Feminine As Other in Theosophic Kabbalah: Some Philosophical Observations on the Divine Androgyne." In *The Other in Jewish Thought and History: Constructions of Jewish Culture and Identity*, edited by L. Silberstein and R. Cohn, 166–204. New York: New York University Press, 1994.

———. "Zoharic Literature and Midrashic Temporality." In *Midrash Unbound: Transformations and Innovations*, edited by Michael Fishbane and Joanna Weinberg, 321–43. Oxford: Littman, 2013.

Yira'ukha 'im SHM"SH. Jerusalem: Mekhon yam ha-ḥokhmah, 2011.

Yisraeli, Oded. "Early vs Late in the History of Kabbalistic Ideas in Nahmanides' Torah Commentary." *Zion* 79 (2014): 477–506 [Hebrew].

———. "Initial Ideas of Nahmanides' Kabbalah in His 'Discourse for the Wedding.'" *Pe'amim*, 153 (2017): 87–124 [Hebrew].

———. "Jewish Medieval Traditions Concerning the Origins of the Kabbalah." *Jewish Quarterly Review* 106 (2016): 21–41.

———. *R. Moses b. Nachman (Nachmanides): Intellectual Biography*. Jerusalem: Magnes, 2020 [Hebrew].

Index

Aaron (biblical figure), 186–187
Abraham (biblical figure), 76
Abraham (Rabbi), 113, 140
Abrams, Daniel, 112, 225n60, 228n14
Abramson, Shraga, 143–144
Abulafia, Abraham, 41, 50, 222n28, 225n78
Abulafia, Meir, 154
Abulafia, Todros, 18, 38–39, 132
"account of creation," 136
"account of the chariot," 46–48, 136. *See also* "first chariot"
acronyms, 33, 56
Adam, 144, 147–148, 250n57
Adam and Eve, 84–86, 90–91, 98, 192–193
Afterman, Adam, 68
Aggadot Commentary. See Commentary on the Talmudic Aggadot (Ezra ben Solomon of Gerona)
Agrippa, Heinrich Cornelius, 37
al-Farabi, Abû Nasr, 17
"all" (use of word), 77, 181, 186
allegory, 137
allusive writing, 6, 12, 47–55; in Asher ben David, 50, 179, 185; authorship of, 52; and book of Psalms, 50–51; in Ezra ben Solomon of Gerona, 155–164, 213; Isaac the Blind, 131–132; mentioned, 27; in the Zohar, 44
anagrams, 34–35, 56
anger (divine), 88–89
Anonymous Commentary, 123–124, 128
anthropomorphism, 149–151, 158
Apter Rebbe. *See* Heshel, Avraham Yehoshu'a
Aristotelian philosophy, 25
"as a scourge," 185
ascent of the soul, 30
Ashlag, Yehuda Leib Ha-Levi, 58

ATBaSH (technique), 36, 56
the attribute of hard justice, 162
authorship, 227n6, 228n8; Ezra ben Solomon of Gerona, 135–136; of Hasidic homiletical works, 52; Idel on, 241n77; Isaac the Blind, 106–128 passim; and Rabad, 74–75, 84–85, 230n36; reliability of, 75; Scholem on, 227n6; self-identifications of, 107; and textual record, 211
Avivi, Yosef, 36
'Avodah Zarah (tractate), 152, 154
Avot de-Rabbi Natan (aggadic work), 142, 143–144, 145, 146, 147–148
"a word fitly spoken is like golden apples in silver filigree" (Maimonides), 180
Azriel of Gerona, 3–4, 77, 111, 165–171
Azulai, Abraham, 41–43
Azulai, Hayyim Josef David, 221n18

Ba'alei ha-nefesh (Rabad), 84, 90–92, 93, 95, 98–99
Baal Shem Tov, Israel, 30, 53
Bacon, Roger (attr.), 222n29
Badei ha-aron (Ibn Gaon), 222n28
Bagley, Paul, 22
Bar-Asher, Avishai, 106–107, 108, 119, 130–131, 212
Bar Sheshakh, 153, 154
Barzillai, R., 171–172
Basola, Moses, 46
be'er (well/expound), 35
ben David, Abraham (Rabad). *See* Rabad
ben David, Asher: allusive writing in, 50, 179, 185; biographical details, 173–174; defense of Kabbalah, 175–179; dispersion of knowledge, 179; on divine simplicity, 194–196; and divine unity, 174, 184,

ben David (continued)
195–197, 203–207; exotericism of, 173, 174, 197–198, 213; intentional contradictions in, 179–180; and Maimonides, 206; on mercy/judgment, 187–188; and public aspects of Kabbalah, 15, 173; scholarly reception of, 182; on sefirot, 183–184, 188, 198; on vision of Aaron, 186–187
ben Isaac of Narbonne, Abraham, 62, 68, 96, 97, 129
Ben Ish Hai, 18–20
ben Jacob of Kiev, Moses, 51
ben Jacob, Meshullam, 99–100
ben Judah he-Hasid, David, 30–31
ben Lakish, Shimon, 151–152, 153
ben Mordekhai, Samuel, 71
ben Ruben, Jacob, 100
Ben-Shalom, Ram, 106, 230n31, 233n85
ben Sheshet, Jacob, 74, 77, 107, 117–121, 171–172
Ben-Shlomo, Yosef, 226n88
ben Simeon, Meir, 175, 202–203, 254–255n7, 255n12
ben Todros, Isaac, 29, 34, 35, 123
Bere'shit rabba', 114, 115, 142, 143–145, 147
be-safah berurah (clear language), 36
bikhvod YY le-'olam ("by the glory of God for eternity"), 81–82
binah (third sefirah), 169, 248n47
birmazim metsorafim (with combined hints), 34, 222n28
Blavatsky, Helena Petrovna, 11, 12
"books of secrets," 12
Bourdieu, Pierre, 9
brevity, 11–12, 40–41, 115, 129, 131–133, 139, 156, 173
"The Burnt Book" (Bratslav tradition), 32
"by the glory of God for eternity" *(bikhvod YY le-'olam)*, 81–82

candelabra, 182–183
Catharism, 8, 101, 102, 203
"Cause of causes," 68–69, 256n21
chapter headings, 35, 38, 48, 50, 53, 117
Christian polemics against Judaism, 100, 202–203
ciphers, 6, 27, 33–37, 56
circulation of kabbalistic manuscripts, 30–33
circumcision, 142–150
clear language *(be-safah berurah)*, 36

Clement of Alexandria, 37
codes, 57
"combining" *(tseruf)*, 35
combining letters *(tserufei otiyyot)*, 222n28
"Commentary on Creation" (attr. Isaac the Blind), 109
"Commentary on Sacrifice," (attr. Isaac the Blind), 108–112
Commentary on Sefer Yetsirah (Azriel of Gerona), 166
Commentary on Sefer Yetsirah (Barzillai), 68, 159
Commentary on Sefer Yetsirah (Ezra ben Solomon of Gerona), 124 134, 255n12
Commentary on Sefer Yetsirah (attr. Isaac the Blind), 106, 108, 119, 120
Commentary on Sefer Yetsirah (Togarmi), 38
Commentary on Sefer Yetsirah (Nahmanides), 246n19
Commentary on the Liturgy (Azriel of Gerona), 166
Commentary on the Song of Songs (Ezra of Gerona), 134–135; allusive writing in, 156, 158–164; and Azriel of Gerona, 169–170, 171; circumcision in, 149–150; citations of Isaac the Blind in, 113–114; and Maimonides, 135–138; on rabbinic teachings, 111, 155; readership, 138–140; sefirot in, 78
Commentary on the Talmud (Rabad), 63, 75, 85
Commentary on the Talmudic Aggadot (Ezra ben Solomon of Gerona), 134–135; allusive writing in, 155–158; and ben Sheshet, 117; circumcision in, 149; citations of Isaac the Blind, 74–75, 114–115; creation narrative in, 108; dispersion in, 142–143, 151–153, 213; incommunicability, 140–141; literary legacy, 132, 166; Metatron in, 72; rain passages in, 190–191; and sefirot, 82; transmission of, 84; writing style, 76, 211, 251n65
Commentary on the Talmudic Aggadoth (Azriel of Gerona), 77, 166, 171, 190, 191, 259n42
Commentary on Tractate Berakhot (Rabad), 67–68, 69–70, 73–74
Commentary on Tractate Ta'anit (Rabad), 70, 71–72, 73–74
commodity status, 10, 21–22
complete judgment/complete mercy, 86, 101, 232n68

compound *(mehubbar)*, 93, 94, 195, 197, 198
contradictions, 140–141, 224n54. *See also* intentional contradictions
Cordovero, Moshe, 51–52
corporeality, 111, 149, 154, 177
cosmological speculation, 82
Creator/creature distinction, 93

Dan, Joseph, 111, 252n76
da Piera, Meshullam, 150–151, 252n86
darkness and light, 29
Davidson, Herbert, 204–205
defensive esotericism, 5, 14, 15, 18, 24, 30, 102–103, 129, 149, 151, 201–202, 209
de la Rosa, Hayyim, 43, 224n59
delimited *(mugbal)*, 93–94, 195
Deuteronomy (book of), 140
digital access, 33
Dinur, Ben-Zion, 229n31
discrete, 188, 197–198, 206. *See also* finitude
dispersion of knowledge, 37–41, 57; in Asher ben David, 179, 185; in Ezra ben Solomon of Gerona, 142, 151–155, 178, 213; in Maimonides, 38; in Rabad, 73–74; by Talmudic Rabbis, 155
divine brain, 154
divine love, 162
divine names, 156
"divine presence." *See* shekhinah (God's presence)
divine simplicity, 65, 93–95, 98–100, 150, 174, 183, 184–185, 187, 194–196, 202–203, 204, 206–207. *See also* divine unity.
divine unity: Asher ben David on, 174, 184, 195–197, 203–207; competing views of, 92–96; esoteric/exoteric accounts of, 180–194, 203–207; Meshullam, 100; and names, 223n36; negative definitions of, 199; popularity of concept, 99; Rabad on, 86–87, 92–96; and sexual union, 8, 15, 77–78, 86–87, 180, 184–185, 194, 199, 204, 213
double bind (Urban), 15–16
dualism, 102
du partsufin. See two-faced
Duties of the Heart (Bahya Ibn Pakuda), 93–95, 99, 195, 202

Eamon, William, 12
"earth" *(erets)*, 185, 187, 189
ecstatic Kabbalah, 41. *See also* Abulafia, Abraham

Eden, 29–30, 152, 153, 154
Ein Sof, 169, 182–184
Eleazar of Worms, 223n43
Elohim, 86, 187, 188, 190, 193
emanative rains, 115–116, 189, 190–191
Enoch, 136
eroticism, 87, 154
eschatology, 151–152, 154
esoteric writing, 20–24; decoding, 4, 5; difficulty in deciphering, 55–57; as pedagogical, 23; publication of, 221n17; scholarly work on, 219n3; self-reflexive use of, 61; and Strauss, 3; undisclosed use of, 60; in the Zohar (text), 43–47
"essences of wisdom," 132. *See also* wisdom
'*EtsḤayyim* (Luria/Vital), 11, 12, 19
Even ha-shoham (Ibn Sayyah), 39–40, 43
Exodus (book of), 53, 54, 64–69, 124, 186–187, 199
exotericism, 95–96, 128–133; of Asher ben David, 173, 174, 197–198, 213; of Azriel of Gerona, 165–172
Explanation of Nahmanides' Commentary on the Torah (attr. Ibn Sahula), 84, 108–110, 121–128
Ezekiel (book of), 47–48, 70–71, 76, 77, 78
Ezra (biblical figure), 80
Ezra ben Solomon of Gerona: allusive writing in, 155–164, 213; authorship, 135–136; dispersion of knowledge in, 142, 151–155, 178; eschatology in, 154, 249n50; on Isaac the Blind, 112–117; kabbalistic monographs of, 134–135; kabbalistic symbolism of, 154; literary style of, 210–211; and Maimonidean philosophy, 164–165; as publicizing Kabbalah, 135, 138–140, 160; scholarly reception, 135; and wisdom, 139, 251n72. *See also* circumcision; *Commentary on the Talmudic Aggadot* (Ezra ben Solomon of Gerona)

fear (fifth sefirah), 170
fear of the Lord, 141–142, 146
finitude, 94, 183–184
Finzi, Jacob Israel, 31, 46
"first chariot," 70
Fishbane, Eitan, 44
Fortin, Ernest, 220n11
French Jews, 93, 95, 98–99, 100, 135–136, 202
Freudenthal, Gad, 99, 100

gender, 186, 192–193, 232n76
Genesis (book of), 50–51, 69, 141, 144, 189–190, 199
German Pietism, 36–37, 223n43
Gerondi, Jonah, 62, 96–97, 106, 139, 243n96
Gikatilla, Joseph, 12–13, 29, 45, 159
Giller, Pinchas, 44–45
"glory" *(kavod)*, 64–67, 69, 76–78, 81–82, 163–164, 199–200
God: Adam as image of, 144; anger of, 88; aspects/attributes of, 86, 196; corporeality of, 177; essence of, 182; feet of, 257n29; heretical views of, 18; and Israel, 163; judgment/mercy, 86, 88; knowledge of, 137; names for, 53, 86–87; oneness/unity of, 8, 15, 18, 19, 69–70, 77–79, 82, 87, 89–90, 92–96, 98–101, 102, 115–116, 168, 173–208, 223n36; phylacteries of, 67–68; physical qualities of, 64–65, 68, 72–73, 83–84, 149; and sefirot, 72–73, 196; works of, 92
Gottlieb, Efraim, 109, 118–119
Graetz, Heinrich, 228n20
grapes, 154
Green, Arthur, 49
Guide of the Perplexed (Maimonides), 23–24, 38, 41, 42, 48, 65, 132, 167, 179–180; intentional contradictions, 41; scholarly work on, 204

Hadad, Eli, 88, 232n76
ha-devarim ha-ruḥaniyyim (spiritual entities), 150
Hai Ricchi, Raphael Immanuel, 32
Hakdamat reḥovot ha-nahar (Sharabi), 40–41
Halbertal, Moshe, 1, 167, 174
ha-Levi, Judah, 67
ha-maskil yavin. See "the knowledgeable will understand"
Harvey, Warren Zev, 228n17
Hasidism, 30, 37, 52–55
Hayyim, Yosef, 18–20
heaven and earth, 185, 187, 189, 190, 197, 258n39
Hellner, Melila-Eshed, 44
Henri of Marci, 101, 102
heresy, 15, 18, 101–102
hermeneutic of suspicion, 212
ḥesed (fourth sefirah), 13
Ḥesed le-Avraham (Azulai), 41–42, 224n56
Heshel, Avraham Yehoshu'a, 52, 54, 226n92

heterodox ideas/practices, 14
historicism/historiography, 3, 96
Hiyya (Rabbi), 48
holy of holies, 78, 79, 231n50. *See also* Sanctus prayer
Holzer, Zechariah, 124–125
homoeroticism, 154
House of Hillel/Shammai, 53–54
Huss, Boaz, 45, 46, 47

Ibn Adret, Shlomo ben Abraham, 29, 34
Ibn Ezra, Abraham, 48, 179, 228n17
Ibn Gaon, Shem Tov ben Abraham, 33–35, 39–40, 56, 63
Ibn Pakuda, Baḥya, 93–95, 174, 183, 195, 196–197, 202
Ibn Sahula, Isaac, 49
Ibn Sahula, Meir ben Solomon, 84, 109
Ibn Sayyah, Joseph, 40, 43
Ibn Shuaib, Joshua, 109, 127
Ibn Tibbon, Judah, 93–94, 98, 99
Ibn Tibbon, Samuel, 224n58
Idel, Moshe: on Abraham Abulafia, 41; on Adam and Eve/two-faced human, 86, 91; on Asher ben David, 174; on authorship, 241n77; circulation of Jewish esoteric material, 212; *Explanation*, 126–128; *Explanation* versus *Anonymous Commentary*, 124–125; on Isaac the Blind, 105–106, 126; on Kabbalah, 4–5, 59, 97, 136, 137, 205; on letter substitution, 36; on Nahmanides, 165; on oral transmission, 220n2, 223n48; on philosophical/social implications of secrecy, 1; on sefirot, 232n68
"I have heard" *(shama'ti)*, 113, 118
"I have received" *(ve-kibbalti)*, 113, 118, 126
imitatio dei, 144
infinity, 94, 183. *See also* finitude
intentional contradictions: about, 41–43, 57; in Abulafia, Abraham, 50; in Asher ben David, 179–180, 201; in Isaac Luria, 224n59; and Maimonides, 3, 41–43
Isaac (patriarch), 76
Isaac (Rabbi), 35–36
Isaac Mor Hayyim, 31
Isaac of Acre, 45, 110
Isaac the Blind: about, 105–106; allusive writing, 131–132; authorship, 106–128 passim; brevity in writing, 139; Idel on, 126; in letters, 96–97, 141; literary legacy,

Index 287

7, 106–108, 128, 132, 212; and Nahmanides, 122; on oral aspect of Kabbalah, 28; and Psalms (book of), 132; quoted, 33; rain passages, 116; scholarly work on, 128–129; and Scholem, 105–106; "the language of Isaac," 132. *See also* Sanctus prayer
Isaiah (book of), 76, 77, 151
Israel, 58, 77–78, 79, 136, 160, 162–163. *See also* Jerusalem

Jabez, Joseph ben Hayyim, 226n99, 227n100
Jābir Ibn Ḥayyān, 37
Jacob (patriarch), 76
Jacob Joseph of Polnoye, 53
Japheth (biblical figure), 145
Jeremiah, Book of, 56
Jerusalem, 33, 79, 80, 82, 136, 206
Jewish philosophy: and Asher ben David, 174; and Rabad, 103; scholarly work on, 59, 211, 219n4; secrets in, 25; translation of, 93
Job (book of), 28–29, 35, 185
Johnson, Paul, 10, 23
Joshua (biblical figure), 80
judgment (divine), 76, 78, 86, 87–90, 91, 92, 101, 162, 170–171, 185–186, 187–188, 189, 192–193, 199

KaLAT/KaLOT, 163
Kalisker, Abraham, 53
Kallus, Menachem, 53
katavti leshono, 118
Keter Shem Tov (Ibn Gaon), 29, 33–35, 39–40, 56, 122, 123, 222n33
KHHT, 53
khol ("all"), 181
"the knowledgeable will understand," 158, 181, 186, 200, 201, 210
Kuzari (ha-Levi), 67

Lachter, Hartley, 1, 10–11
Láng, Benedek, 56
Lebanon, 161
León, Moses de, 13, 14, 29–30, 39, 45, 159
letter combination, 34–35, 222n28. *See also* letter substitution
"letter to Nahmanides and Jonah Gerondi" (Isaac the Blind), 62, 96, 105, 106, 111, 112, 119, 128–132, 139, 141, 173, 177, 243–244n96

letter substitution, 34, 35–36, 222n29. *See also* ATBaSH
Leviticus (book of), 51, 126
Liebes, Yehuda, 44
light and darkness, 29
literary decisions and techniques, 1, 59
Lithuanian Kabbalists, 52
lovingkindness (fourth sefirah), 76, 78, 130, 162, 169–171, 185
"lower waters," 239n50
Lubavitcher Rebbe. *See* Schneerson, Menachem Mendel
Luria, Isaac, 11–12, 31–32, 47, 224n51, 224n59

Ma'ayan ganim (Tsvi Elimelekh), 54
Maimonidean controversy, 136–137, 154–155, 166–169
Maimonideans, 136–138, 149–151, 160, 210–211
Maimonides: and Asher ben David, 179–180, 196, 206; in Azriel of Gerona, 167–168; Azulai on, 42; chariot teaching, 47; on concealment, 224n53; and corporeality of God, 149–150; dispersion of knowledge in, 38, 179; esotericism *versus* exotericism of, 23–24, 58; face and back of God, 64–65; influence on Kabbalists, 2, 29, 132, 155, 167–168, 174, 179, 180; intentional contradictions, 3, 41–43, 179; on Israel/Jerusalem, 80; morality in, 17; oral transmission in, 48; Rabad on, 66–68, 73, 80–83; "secret" view of creation, 205; on *shekhinah*, 83; Strauss on, 2, 3, 180, 224n54. *See also* chapter headings; *Guide of the Perplexed*; Maimonideans
Mark, Zvi, 37
marriage, 91, 95
Matt, Daniel, 45
megillat setarim (scroll of concealments), 140, 141
Me'irat 'einayim (Isaac of Acre), 110
Mekhilta de-rabbi Yishma'el, 89
Melchizedek (biblical figure), 144
Melzer, Arthur, 3, 14, 15, 219n3, 220n12
menstruation, 90–91
mercy (divine), 76, 78, 86, 87–90, 91, 92, 101, 131, 185–186, 187–188, 189, 192–193, 199
messianism, 78
Meshullam (Rabbi), 124

Metatron (angel), 63–64, 69, 70–72, 228n21, 229n22. *See also* 'Minister of the Countenance'/'Minister of the World'
metempsychosis, 28–29
Midrash tanhuma, 146, 148
Milḥamot ha-shem (Jacob ben Ruben), 100
Milḥemet Mitsvah (Meir ben Simeon), 203
'Minister of the Countenance'/'Minister of the World,' 70–71. *See also* Metatron
Mishkan ha-'edut (de León), 39
Mishneh torah (code of Jewish law), 64–65, 79
Moloch, 127–128
Moore, R. I., 102
Moses, 64–66, 69, 72–73
mysticism, 1

Nahmanides, 28–29; and Ezra ben Solomon of Gerona, 157; Idel on, 165; and Isaac the Blind, 122, 123, 129, 131, 139; legacy of teachings, 34. *See also* Explanation of Nahmanides' Commentary on the Torah (attr. Ibn Sahula)
Nahman of Bratslav, 32, 37, 56
Nahum (book of), 87
Natan of Nemirov, 37

Ohev Yisra'el (Heshel/the Apter), 54
"one from every side" (Maimonides), 198
open secrets, 12
oral esotericism *versus* written esotericism, 48, 75
oral traditions/transmission: and history of kabbalah, 63–64; Idel on, 220n2, 223n48; and kabbalistic literature, 103, 205, 212; in Maimonides, 48; scholarly work on, 220n2; Simmel on, 21–22; *versus* writing, 28
Or ha-ganuz (anonymous), 122
Or ha-ḥayyim (Jabez), 54

pantheism, 226n88
Papa (Rabbi), 87–88
parables/riddles *(meshalav ve-ḥidotav),* 132
Pardes rimmonim (Cordovero), 51
pedagogical esotericism, 23–24, 220n12
Pedaya, Haviva, 58; on Asher ben David, 177, 179, 255n14; on Azriel of Gerona, 166; on Ezra ben Solomon of Gerona, 79, 135; on Isaac the Blind, 234n3; on Rabad, 81–82

Pentateuch, 165
persecution, 202–203
Persecution and the Art of Writing (Strauss), 103
"perverse ingenuity" (Sabine), 61
philosophical secrets, 227n100
philosophy, 93, 100, 211. *See also* Jewish philosophy
Pietism, 36–37, 223n43
Pious One. *See* Isaac the Blind; Sanctus prayer
prayer books, 33
prayers: and angels, 140; and the anger of God, 88; Asher ben David on, 182; and Isaac the Blind, 234n8; and sefirot, 76; *Shema',* 121; *Shemoneh 'Esreh,* 107
presence: and glory, 78–82; and Jerusalem, 80; Maimonides on, 83; and Rachel (biblical figure), 13. *See also* sefirah (tenth)
protective esotericism, 5, 15, 17–20, 209–210
Proverbs (book of), 54, 140–142
PRSh (Hebrew root), 122
Psalms (book of): and allusive writing, 50–51, 55; and Ezra ben Solomon of Gerona, 146; and Isaac the Blind, 129–132; quoted, 153; and Rabad, 79–80; and Sanctus prayer, 76
public knowledge of Kabbalah, 210, 211, 213; and Asher ben David, 173, 175; and Ezra ben Solomon of Gerona, 135, 138–140, 160; and Isaac the Blind, 105
public knowledge of secrets, 15, 30–32, 58
public/private audiences, 2, 5, 58, 174–175
publishing, 32, 221n17

Rabad: about, 61–62; authorship, 84–85, 230n36; and Christian polemics, 100–101; dispersion of knowledge in, 73–74; on divine names, 86–87, 193–194; divine unity in, 86–87, 92–96, 199; "holy" in, 200; Ibn Gaon on, 63; influences on, 228n17; intellectual milieu of, 98; on Maimonides, 64, 80–81; on Moses, 65–68; Pedaya on, 81–82; readership of, 96–98; on secret knowledge, 62–63, 64, 92; theological discussions, 93; on the two-faced first human, 88–89; word choice, 81. *See also* Sanctus prayer
Rachel (matriarch), 13
rain passages, 115–116, 189, 190–191

the Ramah (Meir Abulafia), 154
ra'shei perakim. See chapter headings
ratson. See will
Rava (Jewish sage), 153
Raymond, Bernard, 102
Raymond de Baimac, 102
readership, 24–25, 96–98, 138–140
Recanati, Menahem, 50–51
repetition, 176
rhyming, 39
Roger II Trencavel, 101
Rosman, Moshe, 221n7

Sabbath, 12
Sabine, George, 61
sacrifice, 12, 108, 123, 127, 250n57. *See also* "Commentary on Sacrifice" (attr. Isaac the Blind)
Saadia Gaon, 163
Sagi Nahor. *See* Isaac the Blind
Sanctus prayer, 75–79, 93, 98, 114, 186, 199–200, 230n46
Sarug, Israel, 36
Schäfer, Peter, 82
Schneerson, Menachem Mendel, 52, 55
Scholem, Gershom: on Adam and Eve, 85; on allusive writing, 49; on Asher ben David, 174, 175, 177; on authorship, 227n6; on Azriel of Gerona, 105, 139, 167, 177–178; criticism of others, 228n20; on earlier manuscripts, 37; on Ezra ben Solomon of Gerona, 105, 135, 139, 177–178; on *Explanation*, 109; and Isaac the Blind, 105–106, 109, 130–131, 132–133; on Metatron, 228n21; on the responsum, 234n7
scroll of concealments. *See megillat setarim*
Scroll of Secrets (Nahman of Bratslav/Natan of Nemirov), 37, 56
secret (term), 12–13, 79, 92, 209
The Secret Doctrine (Helena Petrovna Blavatsky), 11
secretism: and ben David, Asher, 201; definitions/examples of, 10–13, 19, 56, 209; effectiveness of, 22–23; of kabbalistic literature, 209; in late medieval/early modern magical texts, 56; and Rabad, 73–74, 103; *versus* secrecy, 26
Secrets of Secrets, 222n33
Seder rabbah de-bere'shit (haggadah), 78, 82
Sed-Rajna, Gabrielle, 234n8

Sefer ha-bahir, 49
Sefer ha-eshkol (Abraham ben Isaac), 68
Sefer ha-pardes, 39
Sefer ha-temunah (anonymous), 49
Sefer ha-yiḥud (Asher ben David), 173; allusive writing in, 50; divine unity, 194; esoteric vs exoteric divine unity in, 203–207; exoteric style of, 174, 178, 180–181, 185–189; and public knowledge of kabbalah, 211; reasons for writing, 175–176; sexual union/gender in, 191; text appended to, 63
Sefer ha-Zohar. *See* the Zohar (text)
Sefer mishkan ha-'edut (de León), 29
Sefer pardes rimmonim (Cordovero), 225n84
Sefer shi'ur komah (Cordovero), 51–52
Sefer Yetsirah, 40, 50, 120, 124–125, 159
sefirah (first), 171
sefirah (second), 121, 154, 161, 162
sefirah (third), 154, 162, 169
sefirah (fourth), 13, 76, 162, 169–170, 192
sefirah (fifth), 76, 162, 170–171, 192
sefirah (sixth): earth, 189; as face of God (potentially), 72–73; as the "glory" *(kavod)*, 163; heaven, 190; maleness and, 162, 191; mercy, 78, 186; and upper waters, 116
sefirah (ninth), 77, 143–144, 147–148, 186
sefirah (tenth): bride as, 163; as "cause" *(sibbah)* of rains, 116; corona of the penis, 147; as the "divine presence" *(shekhinah)*, 163; and earth, 185–187, 189; as female, 191; and holy of holies, 231n50; *khol* ("all"), 181; *kodesh*, 131; and the lower waters, 116; and Metatron, 70, 71–72; the queen, 148; Rachel as, 13; references to, 71; and Sanctus prayer, 77, 200; as the sea, 12–13; secrecy of, 3; in visions, 186–187
sefirot, 3–4, 159, 161; Abraham/Isaac/Jacob, 76; alternative terminology, 169–171; ben David, Asher on, 187–188; in Azriel of Gerona, 169–171; and created world, 92; as discrete, 184, 188, 197–198, 206; and divine unity, 81–82; as gendered, 186; human being as microcosm of, 150; and Israel, 77–78; lower, 4; and Sanctus Prayer, 76–78; and sexual union, 8, 73, 199–200; three holies as, 76; and *vav* (letter), 181, 256n16; and waters, 115; in the Zohar, 44–45
self-defense, 14

Seth (biblical figure), 145–146
sexual organs, 147, 154
sexual relationships, 95
sexual union: in Abraham ben David, 87; Asher ben David on, 174, 184–185; and divine union, 8, 15, 77–78, 86–87, 92–93, 180, 184–85, 194, 199, 204, 213; of mercy and judgment, 87, 193, 199
Sha'arei kedushah (Vital), 32, 33
Sha'arei orah (Gikatilla), 12–13, 25, 29, 159
Sha'ar ha-razim (Todros Abulafia), 38–39
Sha'ar ha-sho'el (Azriel of Gerona), 166–168, 178, 211
Sharabi, Shalom, 33, 40–41, 43
Shatzmiller, Joseph, 101, 203
ShDY, 53
Shekel ha-kodesh (Moses de León), 25, 159
shekhinah (God's presence): and glory, 78–82, 163; and Jerusalem, 80; Maimonides on, 83; and Rachel (biblical figure), 13. *See also* sefirah (tenth)
Shem (Noah's son), 144–145
Shema' (prayer), 121, 197, 200
shemittot (kabbalistic doctrine), 251n69
Shemoneh 'Esreh (prayer), 107
shetei rashuyyot (two powers), 87, 101, 202
Shimon bar Yohai, 43, 47
Shi'ur komah (pseudepigraphic text), 69
Shmueli, Leore Sachs, 51
Shneur Zalman of Liadi, 53
Shorshei ha-shemot (Zacuto), 33
Sifra (halakhic midrash), 111
Simmel, Georg, 9, 21–22, 227n106
social capital, 21, 201, 210
Sodom and Gomorrah, 87, 193
Song Commentary. See Commentary on the Song of Songs (Ezra of Gerona)
Song of Songs, 78, 162, 164, 200–201. *See also* Commentary on the Song of Songs (Ezra of Gerona)
"The Song of Unity" (anonymous), 39
spiritual entities *(ha-devarim ha-ruḥaniyyim)*, 150
Strauss, Leo: critiques of, 61; and esoteric writing, 3; on Maimonides, 2, 3, 41, 43, 180; oral esotericism *versus* written esotericism, 48; *Persecution and the Art of Writing*, 14, 103; and protective esotericism, 17–18; scholarly reception of, 61
Straussianism, 2–3, 60, 219n5
Stroumsa, Guy, 233n99

sublunar realm, 50
symbolic capital, 9, 10, 22, 209
symbolism, 44–45, 154, 161, 171–172

tabernacle, 163, 194, 198–199
techniques. *See* allusive writing; dispersion of knowledge; intentional contradictions
tefillin, 67–68, 69, 161–162, 171
temple, 79–83, 136
temple sacrifice, 108
Tetragrammaton, 53, 145–146, 181. *See also* YHVH
theurgy, 23, 76–78, 111, 131, 164, 200, 206
"a time of favor/will" *('et ratson)*, 90, 188, 189
"time of unity and will," 132
Tiryakian, Edward A., 20
Tishby, Isaiah, 124, 143, 156–158, 248n47, 251n65
Togarmi, Barukh, 38
Toldot Ya'akov Yosef (Jacob Joseph of Polnoye), 53
Torat emet (Heshel), 53–54
Tree of Life (commentary on), 134
Trinity, 8, 100, 202–203
tserufei otiyyot. *See* letter combination
Tsvi Elimelekh Shapira of Dinov, 54–55
Twersky, Isadore, 74, 79, 80, 91, 98, 99
two-faced, 88–89, 231n63. *See also* Adam and Eve
two powers *(shetei rashuyyot)*, 101, 202

understanding (third sefirah), 162
unity. *See* divine unity
Urban, Hugh, 9–10; on Blavatsky, 11; descriptions of secrecy, 14; double bind, 15–16; Urban's model, 20–21, 26, 209

Vajda, Georges, 135, 158
Valabregue-Perry, Sandra, 183, 196
veha-mevin yavin ("the understanding will understand"), 48
ve-haven zeh ("understand this"), 48
Vermeir, Koen, 12
Visual Cultures of Secrecy in Early Modern Europe (collection), 17
Vital, Hayyim, 19, 31–32, 47
von Stuckrad, Kocku, 14

Weiss, Tzahi, 222n26, 243n96, 254n7
well/expound *(be'er)*, 35

will, 89–90, 115–116, 185–188, 189, 190, 259n43
wine, 154
wisdom: "essences of wisdom," 132; and Ezra ben Solomon of Gerona, 139, 161–162, 171, 251n72; kabbalistic, 46, 54, 136–137. *See also* sefirah (second)
Wolfson, Elliot: on Abraham Abulafia, 50; on allusive writing, 49; on circumcision, 143–147, 147; on elusiveness of Kabbalah, 4; on Ezra ben Solomon of Gerona, 155; on homoeroticism, 154; on oral transmission, 113; on sefirot, 184, 257n29; on Schneerson, Menachem Mendel, 55; on Maimonidean language, 155; on significance of secrecy, 1; on two-faced first human, 205; on writing of secrets, 23; on the Zohar, 44, 225n62
wordplay, 144–145, 163

"world to come," 151–152, 154, 158
writing: act of, 1; brevity of, 40–41, 115, 139; lengthy, 129; repetition in, 176; and secrecy, 2. *See also* allusive writing

Yagel, Abraham, 36
YHVH: and judgment, 232n66; and mercy, 86, 88, 89, 187, 193; and sefirot, 181, 188, 190, 197. *See also* Tetragrammaton
Yisraeli, Oded, 96, 245n19
Yosher levav (Hai Ricchi), 32–33
"you already know," 76, 143, 157
"you must know," 157

Zacuto, Moses, 33
the Zohar (text): allusive writing in, 44–45; comprehensibility of, 45–46; decoding, 57; esoteric writing in, 43–47; sefirot in the, 44–45; symbolism in, 6, 27, 44–45, 10

Lightning Source UK Ltd.
Milton Keynes UK
UKHW010341070722
405476UK00002B/105